D0884993

The Social Organization
of Industrial Conflict

Warwick Studies in Industrial Relations

General Editors: G. S. Bain, W. A. Brown and H. A. Clegg

The Social Organization of Industrial Conflict

Control and Resistance in the Workplace

P. K. Edwards
Hugh Scullion

BASIL BLACKWELL · OXFORD

© Social Science Research Council 1982

First published in 1982 by
Basil Blackwell Publisher
108 Cowley Road
Oxford OX4 1JF
England

British Library Cataloguing in Publication Data

Edwards, P. K.
    The social organisation of industrial conflict.—
    (Warwick studies in industrial relations)
    1. Industrial relations—Great Britain
    I. Title   II. Scullion, Hugh   III. Series
    331'.0941   HD8391

    ISBN 0—631—13127—2

Typesetting by System 4 Associates Limited, Gerrards Cross
Printed in Great Britain by T J Press Ltd, Padstow.

Contents

List of Tables

Editors' Foreword

The University of Warwick is the major centre in the United Kingdom for the study of industrial relations. Its first undergraduates were admitted in 1965. The teaching of industrial relations began a year later, and it now has one of the country's largest graduate programmes in this subject. Warwick became a national centre for research in industrial relations in 1970 when the Social Science Research Council located its Industrial Relations Research Unit at the University. The Unit has a full-time staff of about twenty and undertakes research into many aspects of industrial relations.

The series of Warwick Studies in Industrial Relations was launched in 1972 as the main vehicle for the publication of the results of the Unit's projects. It is also intended to disseminate the research carried out by staff teaching industrial relations in the University, and the work of graduate students. The first six titles of the series were published by Heinemann Educational Books of London, and subsequent books have been published by Basil Blackwell of Oxford.

This book reports the findings of a study of industrial conflict in seven British factories. The types of behaviour which are generally seen as expressions of conflict were examined in detail in each of these factories in order to test a theory of industrial conflict. The central argument is that differences in patterns of conflict can be explained by the way in which the process of production is controlled in each factory. Absenteeism, for example, is often interpreted as a means of escape from the monotony of work; but this study shows that rates of absence, and, what is more important, the ways in which managers and workers see absenteeism, can be related to different patterns of control. Where workers have considerable control over the timing and pace of work, going absent is not needed as a form of escape; whereas tight managerial control over the way the job is done tends to increase absenteeism. Variations in a number of other forms of workplace behaviour which are commonly taken to indicate conflict, both individual behaviour such as quitting and collective behaviour such as go-slows, can also be explained by differences in the way work is organized. By correcting many common assumptions about industrial conflict, this study will assist practitioners and policy-makers as well as students of industrial relations and industrial sociology.

G. S. Bain
W. Brown
H. A. Clegg

Preface

This book is about the working lives of people in seven British factories. Everything in it depends ultimately on the assistance and co-operation that we were given by countless individuals in those factories. The extent of the willingness to help a couple of researchers, whose interests must have seemed pointless, esoteric, or downright odd, was remarkable. A general acknowledgement of the assistance that we have received is inadequate, but we hope that it goes some way towards repaying our debts. Apart from the impossibility of listing everyone who helped us, guarantees of confidentiality prevent us from naming even those whose help went far beyond the call of duty. And to select particular individuals would, in general, be invidious. But, as many field researchers have acknowledged, the conduct of research often depends on the development of a personal rapport between the researcher and the researched and on a small number of 'key informants'. We therefore wish to record two special words of thanks: first, to managers and to the whole of the shop steward body in what we have called the Small Metals Factory, for the remarkably open way in which they took us into their confidence, often at times when industrial relations were delicately balanced; and, second, to two individuals in particular, whose sympathy for what we were doing was considerable and whose willingness to give us positive help and encouragement went far beyond the role of 'respondent' or 'informant', and whom we must thank as simply R. C. and R. S.

Our academic debts may be acknowledged more openly. Most generally, the project depended on the existence of the Industrial Relations Research Unit. Apart from the presence at Warwick of a group of experienced researchers to whom we could turn for advice, an established unit was important in two main ways. First, by being able to work full-time on the project we were able to concentrate our energies on it. Paul Edwards started the project in September 1977 and was joined by Hugh Scullion in October 1978. The case studies were carried out during 1978, 1979 and 1980, with the final draft of the manuscript being completed at the end of 1981. The possibility of carrying out and writing up the research in a reasonably short period of time has enabled us to provide a more up to date picture than would have been possible had we been reporting material gathered in the different climate of the mid-1970s. Second, we have been able to carry out the research freely, following the needs of the project instead of being committed to a rigid programme laid down in advance and without being bothered with progress reports, applications for extensions of funding, or other distractions. Specifically, had the project been defined in advance we doubt whether it would have gone beyond the four of our seven factories that are located in the engineering industry; our freedom to develop the project in a less restricted way has, we feel, made a major contribution to the value of the study as a whole.

We have received a great deal of assistance from past and present colleagues in the IRRU and elsewhere at Warwick. For crucial help in gaining access to our plants, we are grateful to George Bain, William Brown, Hugh Clegg, Joe England, and Keith Sisson. Several people have read and commented on the manuscript, of whom we would particularly like to thank Eric Batstone, William Brown, Hugh Clegg, David Deaton, Stephen Frenkel, and Richard Hyman. But a special acknowledgement is due to Anthony Ferner and Peter Nolan, whose help and encouragement in formulating our ideas and in removing obscurities, inconsistencies, and absurdities have been invaluable. The pulling together of a mass of research material into a continuous argument requires a great deal of drafting and re-drafting. We are very grateful to Connie Bussman for the way in which she has, with the assistance at times of Norma Griffiths, typed successive drafts with efficiency and good humour.

None of these people should be held responsible for the final product, for we have not always taken the advice that we have been given and we have, no doubt, failed to appreciate some of the points made to us. We take joint responsibility for what follows: apart from some initial preparation and planning and the carrying out of one of the case studies, we have worked closely together on the fieldwork and on the writing up of the results. While the drafting of particular sections began with one or the other of us, the manuscript has gone through so many changes that individual responsibilities can no longer be disentangled.

Paul Edwards
Hugh Scullion

Introduction

Industrial conflict is an enormously broad topic of investigation, for conflict is often seen as one of the mainsprings of social life. In this study our concern is not with conflict in the generic sense indicated by statements that 'work relations (within capitalism) are an inevitable source of dispute' (Hyman, 1975: 186) or that conflict is 'inevitable in industrial relations as in other aspects of social life' (Clegg, 1979: 452). Instead we focus on the ways in which conflict may be expressed in practice, asking why some forms of behaviour that are often seen as indices of conflict occur in some settings and not in others, and considering their significance for the social structures of which they are part. We do not provide any general definition of conflict, but consider how workplace behaviour gains a particular significance and how it can then be related to a notion of conflict.[1] Specifically, we examine industrial relations in seven British factories to assess how and why 'conflict' takes a particular form in particular environments.

The Problem

It has long been recognized that industrial conflict can be expressed in a wide variety of ways. Typical lists of the forms of conflict include such apparently diverse phenomena as absenteeism, labour turnover, accidents, pilferage, sabotage, and restriction of effort as well as strikes and other collective actions (C. Kerr, 1954: 232; Knowles, 1952: 210). Yet despite the widespread recognition that a study of conflict requires attention to a wide range of behaviour,

1. There have been several determined attempts to define and categorize conflict (see Fink, 1968; Mack and Snyder, 1971). Yet they have failed to produce a definition which is broad enough to subsume all the aspects of the social world which might be seen as forms or expressions of conflict while being precise enough to provide analytical leverage. The way forward is not to become enmeshed in sterile definitional debates but to provide a framework which can encompass a discussion of the complex phenomenon of conflict even though it cannot provide a simple definition of the term.

there have been remarkably few attempts to look systematically at different forms of conflict. An initial need is thus to remedy this deficiency. But a further problem is immediately apparent, namely what it is about the various activities listed which enables them to be treated as forms of the same thing: what is it about accidents and restriction of effort, for example, which qualifies them as types of conflict? We do not, therefore, assume that the forms of conflict can be unambiguously listed. It is undoubtedly true that conflict may be expressed in many ways, but this leaves open the related questions of how in fact it is expressed and of how the investigator is to discover this expression. It is obvious, for example, that 'individual' actions such as going absent or quitting may be alternatives to more collective actions, and a considerable literature has grown up around this point (Paterson, 1960; Scott et al., 1963; Bean 1975; P. Edwards, 1979a). Yet absence rates plainly reflect many things apart from 'conflict', and it remains to be demonstrated how far absenteeism in a particular setting can be related to a notion of conflict.

Our aim, then, is to take the debate about the alternative forms of conflict back a stage. Instead of asking whether absenteeism is an alternative to strikes we ask how absenteeism gains its significance in particular settings, how far it can be seen as a form of conflict in one situation and not in another, and why this is so. By 'social organization' we mean the processes whereby specific practices gain significance within workplace relationships. Investigation of the processes of organization thus involves analysis of the social meanings which are given to various actions by those engaged in them. The role of absenteeism, for example, as an 'expression' of conflict cannot be understood without considering what workers themselves think about going absent. This may seem obvious but the predominant tradition in studies of such things as quitting and absenteeism has been to look at rates of behaviour or at the link between absence behaviour and indices of 'job satisfaction' (e.g. W. Kerr et al., 1951; Waters and Roach, 1971), with the wider question of what going absent actually means to workers in terms of their needs and expectations tending to be forgotten (see Hyman, 1976; Nicholson, 1977).[2] In studying these 'individual' actions it is, moreover, easy to concentrate on the dispositions of individual workers, ignoring the perceptions of management. Yet how far an action can be seen in terms of conflict will be influenced by managerial responses to it. The implications of a high rate of casual absence will plainly differ according to the nature of the managerial response. The social meanings given to a form of behaviour will depend in part on managerial definitions, and these are thus important in their own right; in addition, what managers actually do, as distinct from what they think, will influence the nature of behaviour.

2. For specific criticisms of studies relating absenteeism to job satisfaction see Nicholson et al. (1976).

This point about the difference between actions and perceptions is central. Perhaps the dominant tradition of industrial sociology is marked by a reliance on questionnaire surveys of workers in which perceptions are given central attention. Baldamus (1976: 71) is among the most stringent critics of this, arguing in the case of the work of Beynon and Blackburn (1972) for instance that examination of perceptions alone not only ignores such crucial behavioural indications of workers' attitudes as turnover and absence but also tends to trivialize the discussion by dealing with perceptions as if they are unrelated to practice. In addition, perceptions as reported in the context of questionnaires will not necessarily give an accurate reflection of the complex, shifting, and possibly contradictory social meanings which workers develop out of their work experience (R. Brown, 1973). A concern with the social organization of conflict requires an attempt to relate meanings to their context. As Eldridge (1973: 176, 182) says in discussing various approaches to conflict which concentrate on perceptions and subjective interpretations, 'at some point a term denoting social structure has to be introduced.... The sociological problem then becomes to identify particular forms and expressions of industrial conflict and to tease out their significance for the social order in which they take place'. While there are problems with the details of Eldridge's formulation (P. Edwards, 1979b: 209–11), this statement of the need to link meanings to their context, or to consider both the 'subjective' and the 'objective' aspects of conflict, admirably summarizes our starting point.

This approach places our study in the midst of several debates. In addition to disputes relating to specific forms of behaviour, of which the most active currently is that concerning sabotage, perhaps the key debate is that over the labour process and worker resistance which has emerged as part of the revival of Marxist scholarship. At the most general level writers such as Mandel (1978) and Castells (1980) have placed struggle within the workplace at the centre of their analyses of capitalist development. Thus Mandel (1978: 40) criticizes attempts to explain one of the key elements in the Marxist system, namely the rate of surplus value, in terms of 'a mechanical function of the rate of accumulation'; instead, says Mandel, the 'degree of resistance displayed by the working class' plays a crucial role. Since resistance is likely to take the form of 'restriction of effort' and other types of conflict the overlap with our current concerns is obvious. More specifically, studies such as those of Friedman (1977) and Richard Edwards (1979) have given renewed attention to the twin notions of resistance and control:

> Conflict exists because the interests of workers and those of employers collide, and what is good for one is frequently costly for the other. Control is rendered problematic because, unlike the other commodities involved in production, labor power is always embodied in people, who

have their own interests and needs and retain their power to resist being treated like a commodity (R. Edwards, 1979: 12).

Both writers consider the different strategies which employers use to achieve and maintain control of the workplace, together with the possibility of different types of worker resistance.

The general parallel with our current concerns is again obvious, but it is also necessary to make clear why the debate about control and resistance is important and what analysis in these terms can say that the older discussion in terms of the forms of industrial conflict cannot say. It is, of course, possible to argue that there is nothing specifically Marxist in the points being made, but we are not concerned here with demarcating Marxist from non-Marxist social science. For present purposes all we need to argue is that Marxist discussions of control and resistance have asked questions which have been ignored in other approaches and have re-oriented the analysis of those areas which have been tackled. Four aspects of these discussions are relevant here.

First, in terms of broad historical developments, trends such as 'de-skilling' have been explained not in terms of technological imperatives but as the product of deliberate strategies of control by employers (Braverman, 1974) or as the outcome of strenuous battles between employers and workers (Clawson, 1980: 31–3). As both Edwards and Friedman stress, employers adopt different strategies to secure control; Edwards (1979: 18–21) for example distinguishes between simple, technical, and bureaucratic types of control and argues that each suits particular circumstances. There are many ways of securing control and pursuing profit apart from the close supervision, rate-cutting, and the speed-up of work which are typical of direct control strategies. For our purposes, however, broad managerial strategies are not of central importance: we are concerned with specific patterns of behaviour at workplace level and not directly with management's reasons for introducing various control strategies. We do not, for example, discuss in detail the reasons for introducing new forms of technology, although we do consider at various points the social relations which have emerged around them. We were not in a position to look systematically at managerial motivations, particularly since detailed historical analysis of particular instances would have been required and this would have deflected attention from our comparative focus. We do not, however, ignore these wider matters. In particular, when we come, in the final chapter, to speculate on the implications of our findings we consider the impact of changing economic circumstances on shopfloor relations.

Second, and more directly related to present concerns, Marxists argue that conflict is structured into the labour process, that is the process in which labour power is translated into effort. As mentioned earlier writers from many different traditions argue that conflict is inevitable because interests clash. But this does not pinpoint the basis of the conflict. It is perfectly possible, for example, to argue that, once a wage rate has been agreed, workers and employers have an interest in co-operating to maximize output and that there is no essential conflict between them. What is needed is a means of moving from the truism that conflict is inevitable to a way of identifying the material basis of that conflict. This is done within Marxism by noting that what the employer buys is the labour power of the worker. This labour power is bought at its exchange value, and the exchange may be perfectly fair in that the established market wage rate is paid. But labour power creates value for the employer only in use: the employer's aim is to maximize the difference between the exchange value and the use value of labour power. Hence, quite apart from any conflict over exchange values, conflict is built into the process by which use value is created: the process of production involves continuous conflict over the terms on which employers extract effort from workers.

An obvious objection to this is that employers may not follow a simple maximizing strategy and that conflict is neither ubiquitous nor continuous. We return to these points later. All we claim here is that a crucial starting point in the analysis of conflict lies in the recognition that the terms on which labour power is expended constitute a basic conflict of interest between employers and workers. There are two alternatives to this. First, attention may be restricted to what participants see as conflict, with the result that any conflict which does not reach the 'bargaining arena' is neglected. Second, and this is the more common situation, objective factors are taken into account but the attempt is either partial, as we now go on to argue is the case with the concept of the effort bargain, or simply idealist in that a general conflict of interest is asserted without any means of establishing the material grounds of the conflict. An acceptance that there is a continuous struggle for control, which need not in itself involve a commitment to Marxist concepts such as surplus value, avoids these problems.

The third benefit of a Marxist approach is that it helps to place in context the widely-used concept of the effort bargain. The notion that workers and employers bargain not only over the wage rate but also over the amount of effort to be expended has been used in a variety of ways, and we cannot go into them all here. The most important insight of users of the concept is that it cannot be assumed that bargaining is limited to the fixing of the wage rate: no contract can specify precisely how much effort shall be expended in return for a wage, and there is a continuing bargain within the process of production (Baldamus, 1961). In terms of the present argument this is equivalent to saying that production involves a conflict of interest over the way that labour power is translated into effort. But the concept of the effort bargain is insufficient in itself since it does not explain the origin of that conflict. It merely recognizes that the relationship between wages and effort has to be worked out in practice and does not address itself to the question of why this system exists (Burawoy,

1979: 11–12). By taking account of the employer's interest in translating labour power into labour the Marxist approach can explain why the effort bargain is so important: it is not simply the difficulty of specifying how much effort shall be expended but also the employer's interest in making the level of effort as great as possible which is the source of conflict within the process of production.

Apart from this general point, a particular problem with the concept of the effort bargain concerns the claim by Baldamus (1961: 105, 108) that the notion of a disparity between wages and effort serves to locate 'the very centre of industrial conflict' and that it is 'applicable to all manifestations of conflict, even if the participants themselves are not aware of their conflicting interests in terms of changing effort values'. Baldamus claims, in other words, to have found a way of integrating the subjective and the objective aspects of conflict, for participants' perceptions will influence merely the 'overt manifestations of conflict', with the objective substance being provided by a change in effort values. Yet, despite explicit claims that actions such as absenteeism and quitting can be explained in these terms, the notion of a wage disparity provides no independent insights into these phenomena. The fact of a worker's going absent, for instance, can be re-described in terms of a need to correct a 'wage disparity' but such re-description is no more than formal: it does not help to explain anything about the phenomenon. The position is even more difficult with matters such as factory discipline, for managerial attempts to establish discipline are inexplicable in terms of a strictly-defined effort bargain. Consider for example a pure piecework system where so much is paid per piece. Provided some minimum level of output is maintained the employer apparently has no interest in controlling when and how workers do their work. Yet the establishment of factory discipline has long been a problem for employers concerned with creating a regular supply of labour (Pollard, 1965). The problem disappears once it is recognized that employers have an interest in controlling all aspects of the labour process: they wish to secure the conditions for extracting effort and for preventing the growth of challenges to their own control (Marglin, 1976). The effort bargain provides, then, neither a broad enough view of the origins of conflict nor a touchstone for the analysis of the observable manifestations of conflict. Despite these and other weaknesses,[3] the concept is a useful tool in the analysis of certain aspects of workplace behaviour. We use it, for example, in considering the operation of piecework systems, and in

---

3. A central difficulty in the presentation of Baldamus, and also of other writers (Behrend, 1957 and 1961; Eldridge, 1971: 58–61), concerns the assumption that imbalances in the effort bargain lead to behaviour which re-establishes an equilibrium. While it is important to recognize that workers can try to control the effort bargain, the notion of an adjustment of a 'wage disparity' tends to imply that there is an automatic response by the worker. This neglects the pattern of organization of the labour process and its impact on different types of response. The notion of a balance in the bargain, moreover, goes against the view, which is certainly not a uniquely Marxist one, that industry is characterized by great inequalities

examining changes in the patterns of bargaining associated with changing payment systems. Seen as a means of linking abstract categories to actual events it can provide a useful organizing focus.

The fourth, and final, point about Marxist analyses is that they allow workers' behaviour to be viewed in a more rational light than is often the case. Instead of seeing absenteeism as the result of individuals' inability to come to terms with their environment, or instead of viewing restriction of effort as a purely negative (albeit understandable) response to uncertainties, these and other forms of behaviour can be seen in terms of an overall strategy of resistance. While writers such as Roy (1952) and Lupton (1963) have certainly revealed the rational bases of output restriction it is possible to go further by relating such practices to control over the labour process. With the notion of control as the starting point these practices can be analysed more adequately.

This is not to claim, however, that there are no difficulties with the Marxist writings which we have mentioned. One central problem is the exact opposite of the difficulty, discussed earlier, of studying attitudes without reference to structural conditions: it is easy to assume that specific actions are a direct form of resistance to an existing control system but more difficult to show that this is so. For example, the increasing absenteeism and sabotage which occurred during the late 1960s in the United States and elsewhere have been widely seen by radical writers as reflections of workers' increasing discontents with assembly-line work, the intensification of work resulting from the 'speed up' of operations, and so on (Aglietta, 1979; Bosquet, 1972: 26; Green, 1980: 221). Not only is the evidence for a widespread growth in casual absenteeism far from convincing but such evidence is also, in itself, insufficient to show that workers were indeed using absence as a form of protest against managerial control. Now we must not go to the opposite extreme of denying a phenomenon significance as a form of conflict simply because workers themselves do not specifically relate taking a day off to an attempt to challenge managerial rules and authority. But there is a danger of assuming some less articulated link without exploring the situation in detail. Much of the discussion is, moreover, couched in very general terms, as if all manual work involved assembly lines and as if all workers responded in the same fashion. The question has to be asked of why workers respond in different ways, and this requires attention to the highly particular circumstances

---

between employers and workers. An individual effort bargain may be 'fair' in so far as it is consistent with traditionally accepted standards of effort, but it may still be part of a wider structure of inequality. Hyman and Brough (1975) discuss these points at length, but, in view of the use by economists of notions of effort changes and fairness in their models of wage determination (e.g. Addison and Burton, 1978), we need to make clear our own position. We do not see the effort bargain in terms of equilibrating mechanisms but as part of a continuing struggle which is marked by an absence of 'balance' or 'fair exchange'.

to which they are subject. Consider the following for example: 'people who find themselves in subordinate positions... do what they can to mitigate, resist, and transform the conditions of their subordination' by means of sabotage, strikes and restriction of effort (Miliband, 1978: 402). While this may be true at a very general level, the question remains of why resistance takes different forms in different settings. Yet most of the studies we have mentioned have a very broad focus. Friedman (1977: 51–2) for example, recognizes that the 'forms of resistance' used by workers can be very varied but, given his general historical treatment, he is unable to say anything about changing patterns of absenteeism or sabotage. As one reviewer of R. Edwards's book (Van Houten, 1980: 587) has noted, 'a much closer examination of everyday realities of the labor process' is required. Such an examination is precisely our concern here.

A recent Marxist account which has close parallels with the present concerns is the study by Burawoy (1979) of an American engineering factory. Burawoy argues at length that close attention is required to the details of labour processes. He recognizes that discussion cannot proceed on the assumption that resistance is universal: 'conflict and consent are not primordial conditions but products of the particular organization of work... it is necessary to explain not only why workers do not act according to an imputed set of interests but also why they attempt to realize a different set of interests. The labor process, therefore, must be understood in terms of the specific combinations of force and consent that elicit cooperation in the pursuit of profit' (Burawoy, 1979: 12, 30). In other words it is a misconception to see sabotage, say, simply as a form of conflict; we must examine it in terms of the organization of work in a particular setting, asking what particular interests it seems to serve. At the same time, however, Burawoy can ask why certain interests are not followed and why workers co-operate in what he sees as their own exploitation. In other words he does not adopt what is essentially an elaborate evasion of the issue proposed in a recent British study (P. Armstrong et al., 1981: 15), namely that we should examine only the interests which workers and managers in fact follow and not those which might ultimately be to their own advantage. Such an evasion is intuitively appealing, in that it avoids muddy waters concerning the determination of a group's real interests, but it prevents analysis of any form of latent conflict, that is conflict which is not recognized by the parties. It is also unnecessary if analysis is conducted not in terms of the admittedly difficult concept of real interests but in terms of the struggle for control and the structures of domination which prevent certain presumed interests from emerging.[4]

4. It will be clear from this that we do not follow Lukes (1974: 24–5) in trying to assess latent conflict in terms of the real interests of the parties. The difficulties with Lukes's position are now well-known (see Bradshaw, 1976; McEachern, 1980; Benton, 1981). In particular, analysis in terms of the real interests of subordinate groups provides too narrow

Burawoy's study is limited, however, by its focus on the creation of consent. Such individual forms of 'resistance' as quitting, absenteeism, and indiscipline are given no attention. And the focus on one factory allows changes in the labour process to be discussed but differences between very different forms of labour process cannot be analysed. Our seven factories, by contrast, provide a wide range of situations which allow us to relate various forms of behaviour to the organization of the labour process.

We have suggested, then, that the notion of control over the labour process provides us with a crucial starting point in the analysis of conflict. This is not to say that abstract concepts can be related unproblematically to our research material. We have indicated, for example, that any labour process involves elements of co-operation, and we do not expect to find unrestrained hostility. It is often taken as a criticism of Marxism that workers do not follow imputed sets of real interests, but the strength of studies such as Burawoy's lies in their ability to go beyond crude notions of false consciousness to explore why particular patterns of conflict and co-operation exist. We begin with the concept of control since it provides the only adequate means of analysing latent conflict, but it needs to be supplemented with a framework which can bring together the various levels at which conflict can be expressed.

Levels of Conflict

We have argued that the conflictual nature of various forms of workplace behaviour is a topic for investigation and not something which can be assumed. We have also suggested that actions must be related to the context in which they occur and that a broad conflict of interest can be identified in the area of control over the labour process. The one term 'conflict' cannot cope with these various propositions, and we have therefore developed a model of conflict to guide the analysis. The model needs to be discussed in fairly formal terms so as to indicate its main features and how it differs from other attempts to categorize conflict. It is intimately connected to the earlier analysis, however, since it is an attempt to bring together a consideration of concrete behaviour with a concern for structural factors. Just as writers such as Lukes (1974) have identified

---

a focus since it ignores the possibility that different interests may be contradictory. Workers may be presumed to have interests in high wages as against low ones and in secure jobs. Moderation in a wage claim need not mean that their real interests in high wages are being prevented from realization by the exercise of power; it may simply be that other interests are involved. Although put forward as a radical view, Lukes's argument is in fact not radical enough because it is based on an unwillingness to assert on the basis of sociological argument that there is a structural contradiction between the interests of particular groups. It leaves real interests free-floating and ungrounded.

different 'faces' of power, so we need to identify different 'levels' of conflict
and to show how they are related. The model, which is outlined in Table 1.1
has three levels of conflict, one of these being subdivided so that there are
four categories in all.

TABLE 1.1

CATEGORIZATION OF CONFLICT

Level of Conflict	Categories of Conflict
Behavioural	Overt Non-directed
Institutional	Institutionalized
Structural	Implicit

Before discussing each of our four categories in detail we must indicate how
we use the metaphor of levels. As argued elsewhere (P. Edwards, 1979b), a
model of levels of conflict is inadequate if it implies that there is a simple
causal chain running from the most fundamental level to the level nearest the
'surface'. It is unsatisfactory to discuss strikes, for example, as though they
necessarily 'reflect' or 'express' the deepest contradictions of capitalism. As an
example of the tendency against which we are arguing consider the study by
Nichols and Beynon of the 'Riverside' plant of 'ChemCo'. At the end of their
study Nichols and Beynon (1977: 204) cite the decision of one of the workers,
'Jacko', to leave the plant, and go on:

> to categorise Jacko's leaving Riverside as just another case of 'natural
> wastage' is a travesty: a travesty because so much of Jacko's life has been
> *unnatural* wastage…whatever the management 'style', and whether
> particular managers are good blokes 'personally' or not, relations between
> people who are workers and managers are class relations. Grasp these
> central facts and a lot of things begin to fall in place — why men waste the
> product, why their lives are wasted…

Here labour turnover and sabotage are presented as the direct product of class
relationships. While accepting, as argued above, that capitalism contains contradictions between the interests of workers and managers, we do not wish to
explain sabotage in terms of the existence of such contradictions. Instead, we
ask why sabotage occurs in some situations and not others and what significance
the behaviour has within a particular labour process. We use the model of levels
of conflict to explore how particular 'manifestations' of conflict are related
to their social setting. It is, in other words, a device to ask how in practice

underlying contradictions are 'expressed' in action, not a statement that any relationship will necessarily exist.

Our usage will also be clarified if we contrast it with one of the most widely-used distinctions in the analysis of conflict, namely that between manifest and latent conflict. In a closely related discussion Dahrendorf (1959: 178), for example, defines the latent interests of an individual as 'undercurrents of his behavior which are predetermined for him for the duration of his incumbency of a role, and which are independent of his conscious orientations'; under specifiable conditions, such latent interests may become manifest. This distinction is, however, insufficient. On the manifest side, it fails to distinguish between behaviour which is expressly aimed at securing a recognized interest and behaviour which, while possibly a 'reflection' of an interest, is not directly seen by participants as a means of securing it. Absenteeism, for example, may be seen as an expression of workers' desires for autonomy, or of a desire to escape the boredom of work, or whatever. Yet, as we indicated earlier, it is easy to slip from this 'objective' analysis to the assumption that workers themselves see absenteeism in this way. At the behavioural level we therefore distinguish between 'overt' and 'non-directed' conflict according to the extent to which an action is expressly used by participants to manifest conflict. The category of latent conflict is also unsatisfactory in that it conflates two different situations: conflict may not emerge in action if the power of one side is so great that all forms of protest are suppressed or if there are institutional means of handling the conflict so that it does not reach the behavioural 'level'. The two situations are plainly very different. Indeed, it is not clear whether institutionalized conflict is to be treated as latent, on the grounds that there is no specific action such as a strike which expresses the conflict, or as manifest, in that an institution is an observable entity. We deal with this ambiguity by treating institutionalized conflict as a distinct type, and therefore have three levels of conflict, and not the two implied by the distinction between manifest and latent conflict. The characteristics of our categories may now be outlined.

Overt Conflict

Overt conflict is the most straightforward category: it refers to cases where a conflict is recognized by participants and where action is taken to express it. This does not mean that the action must be deliberately used as a sanction in a dispute on a specific matter such as a wage demand. As Clegg (1979: 269) says of strikes, 'the two main motives for striking are: to exert pressure ... in order to achieve a collective bargaining objective; and to express frustration over some aspect of the work situation'. Expressing frustration will be treated as a form of overt conflict as long as participants explicitly connect their actions to the source of the frustration. Absenteeism, for example, could qualify for this category if workers were using absence expressly to indicate their discontent with management or a specific aspect of their work. The overt recognition of conflict is plainly a matter of degree, and this category therefore merges with the second category, to which we have given the clumsy but accurate label of non-directed conflict.

Non-directed Conflict

By non-directed conflict we mean cases where there is concrete behaviour but where the behaviour is not overtly conflictual. We have seen that it is too easy to see absenteeism as a form of worker resistance, but we do not want to go to the opposite extreme of arguing that the behaviour has no implications as a form of struggle simply because workers do not connect their actions with their objective conditions. As Gramsci (1971: 327) argued, we must draw a distinction 'between thought and action': a social group may 'have its own conception of the world, even if only embryonic; a conception which manifests itself in action, but occasionally and in flashes'. The thought of the group may be based on different conceptions and may imply an acceptance of the existing order which is belied by the group's actions.[5] We use the notion of non-directed conflict to explore the significance of actions which are not overtly conflictual, asking for example why workers take a particular view of absenteeism and what implications this has for the stability of their relations with management. Increasing absenteeism during the 'heroic period' of the late 1960s may imply a breakdown of traditional forms of authority, but it is also possible for high rates of absenteeism to exist for long periods with no particular implications for social structure. Absenteeism here may be an expression of conflict which is insulated from other workplace concerns. This raises the question of what institutions exist to control and regulate conflict.

Institutionalized Conflict

The institutionalization of industrial conflict is a theme running through much of the literature (Dubin, 1954; Lester, 1958). Our use of the concept has some parallels with broad historical and comparative usages, but is more specific: conflict is institutionalized to the extent that it receives some institutional recognition through a formal agreement, a customary rule, or even a traditionally-accepted practice which has not attained the status of a rule. Consider for example a rule governing the movement of workers between jobs which states that workers can be moved only if production difficulties make it 'reasonable'

---

5. As argued above (p. 3), assessments of workers' approaches to conflict cannot be limited to perceptions, for workers' actions may say more about their 'attitudes' to work than any number of replies to questionnaires. See Benton (1981: 172) for a discussion of this passage from Gramsci and in particular for the argument that Gramsci offers not a definition of objective interests in Lukes's sense but simply a way of increasing the range of evidence available to the observer in assessing the aims and aspirations of a social group.

for management to request a move and only on condition that earnings will not be adversely affected. Such a rule recognizes that management's interest in the free movement of labour clashes with workers' interests in not being moved around arbitrarily and is an institutional means of dealing with this clash of interests. The rule, together with understandings as to what constitutes a 'reasonable' managerial request, will control that aspect of the labour process concerned with the allocation of labour and will, other things being equal, tend to prevent the outbreak of such things as spontaneous strikes over allegedly unfair managerial demands. In other words, the manner and extent of the institutionalization of conflict will affect the pattern of conflict at the behavioural level.

Three riders must be attached to this definition. First, institutional controls will have varying degrees of force: a formal rule is, other things being equal, more likely to contain behavioural conflict than is a weak series of vague understandings. Second, rules are not absolute guides to conduct: as the whole tradition of studies of the 'negotiation of order' (Strauss et al., 1971) stresses, rules have to be interpreted in practice. This implies that institutionalized conflict does more than simply provide the 'framework' for action, for institutional arrangements are involved in day-to-day practices and such practices may alter the way that the arrangements are understood. In other words, the 'structure' of the situation affects actions, and actions reflect back onto and may change existing structures (see Giddens, 1979: 91). Third, and closely related to this, what is treated as institutional will change according to the aims of the parties and the resources available to them. To continue the example of mobility rules, management may feel that pressures on profit levels require the more flexible use of labour and may begin to call into question past understandings on the terms on which workers may be moved.

Implicit Conflict

What of situations where managerial domination is so complete that not even informal rules exist to institutionalize conflict? To avoid the ambiguities of the term latent conflict, we refer to cases where conflict is not expressed, at either the behavioural or the institutional level, as situations of implicit conflict. If this is taken to mean that, if there is no observable conflict then the conflict is implicit within the nature of the employment relationship, then the category is plainly useless. We mean something more specific. Conflict is implicit in the structure of the situation if there is a recognizable clash of interests and if specific reasons can be adduced to explain why this clash does not lead to an observable expression. We use the category of implicit conflict not to analyse the contradictions built into the employment relationship but to ask why these contradictions obtain some expression in some situations and not in others. In particular we rely on the comparative method to provide some empirical content for the category of implicit conflict. Perhaps the closest parallel is Crenson's study (1971) of air pollution in American cities: by comparing the political processes of a range of cities Crenson was able to show how people's interests in unpolluted air were furthered in some cities but were systematically suppressed in others. Similarly, starting from the premise that workers have an interest in controlling the labour process, we ask why this interest is more fully realized in some factories than in others. For example, why do workers accept relatively harsh discipline in one factory and not in another, and does this acceptance reflect a commitment to broad managerial legitimatory arguments or merely a 'pragmatic' accommodation (Mann, 1970) to an existing structure?

The category of implicit conflict, like our other three categories, is not designed as a box into which our findings can be dropped; we do not, for example, end up with a picture in which conflict over job allocation is implicit in one factory but institutionalized in another. The category is a means of understanding the differing significance of matters such as job allocation and of relating specific practices to the structure of control in which they are embedded. With this broad framework, we may now outline how we applied the framework through our research strategy.

Research Strategy

General Considerations

Given our general view of the centrality of control over the labour process and our concern to relate behaviour to its context, our argument may be summarized as follows. Patterns of conflict at the behavioural and institutional levels can be related to the pattern of control over the labour process; in other words, there are identifiable links between the three levels of conflict which we have distinguished. For example, in Chapters 3 and 4 we argue that patterns of turnover and absenteeism reflected the intensity of managerial control: in two of our factories where management had considerable control over all aspects of effort levels and the allocation of work quitting or going absent was a common response by workers. In factories where such control was less intense workers could obtain leisure on the job and going absent was a less important strategy. Here, we use a simple 'more or less' measure of control. Yet the frontier of control is multi-dimensional (Goodrich, 1975) and firms use very different means of controlling their workers (R. Edwards, 1979). We also distinguish among types of control. For example, under a policy of what we call sophisiticated managerialism management is able to legitimize its own position. One consequence was that workers in our factory where this policy was pursued most thoroughly internalized a duty to the firm and felt that going absent was irresponsible. As compared with firms with other broad approaches the potentially conflictual aspects of absenteeism were reduced. In later chapters we go on to examine the 'effort bargain' in detail, again relating the presence or absence of bargaining on particular matters to the wider structure of control.

In exploring these matters we try to give as much attention to management as to the workers. The importance of management in shaping the character of industrial relations in general has, of course, been recognized for some time (e.g. Clegg, 1976: 10). Yet the amount of attention which has been given directly to management has been limited. In this study we try to bring management to the centre of the stage, for management's importance may be indicated at a number of levels. First, it is plainly impossible to examine tactics within particular disputes without attention to both sides; hence when we are dealing with specific examples of strikes or whatever, and particularly in the detailed analysis of a dispute in Chapter 9, we try to unravel managerial strategies. Second, in assessing participants' perceptions of behaviour such as quitting we try to discover managerial views of the behaviour. This is important in its own right as far as the analysis of 'subjective' elements of conflict is concerned, but it also leads to a third aspect of management's role: managers are charged with the responsibility for controlling such things as casual absenteeism and breaches of discipline, and how they exert this control will throw a great deal of light on the significance of the behaviour. Fourth, management operates on the wage-effort bargain in much the same way that workers do; an attempt to alter the bargain by cutting piece rates or tightening work study standards is as much a form of struggle as is action by workers with the opposite aim (Burawoy, 1979: 162). Finally, management can affect the wider structure of the situation in terms of the broad strategy of control which is followed. We have indicated how different control policies have different effects on absence behaviour, and the nature of these general policies requires investigation.

The precise meaning of the term 'management' plainly varies between these various areas of interest. On perceptions of absence, for example, we are referring to the attitudes of specific managers whereas on managerial interests in control over the labour process the reference is not to any particular manager. In most cases, however, the meaning of the term will be evident from the context, and we do not need to enter the debate as to how 'management' is defined. We simply point out here that we do not operate with a monolithic model of management. In particular we distinguish, in discussing such things as policy on absence control, between foremen and low-level line managers on the one hand, and more senior managers on the other; marked differences were observed between these groups. We also discuss where relevant particular differences between personnel managers and others over labour relations policies and other matters.

Research Procedures

We wished to compare labour processes while at the same time giving detailed attention to patterns of concrete behaviour. This ruled out both a wide-ranging historical treatment, which could not deal with patterns of absenteeism or sabotage, and a highly detailed observational study, which would provide an insufficient range of situations. We thus decided to conduct a study falling between these two extremes, looking in some detail at a number of factories where patterns of control differed. It would plainly have been impossible to have obtained a sample of plants in which the extent and nature of control was known in advance. Control is, as we have pointed out, complex and multi-dimensional, and we found important variations even within individual factories. We simply used such obvious variables as plant size and industrial location, together with general knowledge of the firms concerned, to find plants where we were fairly sure that the pattern of control differed. The degree of variation was sufficient to investigate different linkages between the nature of control and forms of conflict, although we are certainly not in a position to make statistical generalizations to the effect that the amount of behaviour X varies according to the degree of managerial control on dimension Y. It is worth recalling that the widely-quoted study by Scott et al. (1963) on the relationship between 'organized' and 'unorganized' conflict was based on two collieries within one region of the coal industry and that other studies have had even smaller empirical bases. Our seven plants came from three industries and were of very different sizes. They give us a reasonably secure basis for generalization.

Given our interest in concrete behaviour, and in particular in making comparisons between plants in forms of behaviour, the obvious starting point in each case was the organization's files on labour turnover, absenteeism, and any other relevant aspect of industrial relations. Details of our procedures for recording information on a comparable basis are given in the relevant chapters, while the more important technical details are summarized in Appendix A.

While providing essential quantifiable comparisons between plants, this kind of information was plainly no more than a starting point for the analysis of patterns of social organization. For this wider task we relied heavily on unstructured interviewing together with some observation. It would have been possible to have used more formal methods, and we indicate below how we used a questionnaire of shopfloor workers to tackle a particular problem. Yet for many of our purposes such formal methods would have been inappropriate. In discovering foremen's views of absenteeism, for example, a formal one-off interview would not have provided the depth of insight which we required. We therefore attempted to speak to people over a fairly long period of time, returning to a particular topic on several occasions. So far as we can judge, some degree of trust was built up, and we were certainly able to obtain a better understanding of perceptions of an issue than would have been possible on the basis of one generalized interview. Research in each of the first four plants which we studied, which were all in the engineering industry, was spread over a period of about four months. By the time we studied the other three factories our methods for assembling statistical data were more refined and the nature of the problem which we were addressing was more precisely articulated. This, together with the fact that two of these final three plants were much smaller than our other plants, enabled us to accumulate information relatively rapidly. Although our research in these plants was less detailed than that in the engineering plants, lasting about a month in each case, we feel that our understanding of them was sufficient for our purposes.

An unstructured approach obviously has the danger of tapping only vague and general attitudes to a particular issue. We attempted to deal with this problem by asking for specific examples of general points and, as we became better informed of the context of a workplace, by going back to discuss individual incidents on a day-to-day basis. Apparently trivial events and casual comments can often give a better picture of the situation than a general and ungrounded analysis of 'attitudes'. This approach naturally involved considerable overlap between 'interviewing' and 'observation'. We might, for example, discover or be told about some event such as a disciplinary case or a dispute about overtime payments and use it as a concrete basis for a more general discussion.

For most purposes casual observation was sufficient. In the chapter on absenteeism, for example, we discuss absenteeism in the context of such opportunities for 'leisure in work' as extensions to break times and starting work late and finishing early. Information on these matters was obtained simply by being in the factories for long enough to discover the normal pattern of working. More systematic observation, either in the sense of minute-by-minute recording of the activities of shop stewards (Batstone et al., 1977) or in terms of access to meetings between managers and stewards, was never a central part of the research design. We did, however, attempt to observe events which seemed to be important enough to warrant special study; for example, we were present in one factory during the negotiations on manning levels for the introduction of a new product, and observation of these negotiations provided important insights into the nature of control over manning and the 'balance of power' on the shopfloor. More generally, of course, simply by being present in the factory we came across numerous conversations between managers, stewards, and workers which often provided useful insights into the conduct of shopfloor relationships.

There were four main ways in which we tried to control our methods of data collection so as to provide a reasonably precise picture of a range of practices, as distinct from a hotch-potch of unrelated bits of information. First, and most generally, the research interest was not 'life on the shopfloor' or a general appreciation of work relations under capitalism but fairly specific forms of behaviour. Such things as absenteeism and forms of control over effort provided an initial focus. From general discussions of these matters it was possible to follow up specific aspects of them and, as always happens in this kind of research, activities which had not been thought of in advance. An example of matters to which we had not given much prior attention is the whole area of factory discipline; this assumed considerable importance in several plants even though, as we shall see in Chapter 5, it rarely figures in listings of the forms of industrial conflict. Yet in following up unexpected aspects of workplace behaviour there was always a fairly clear end in view, namely the examination of the frontier of control and its relationship to specific practices. This, we claim, provides a crucial focus for the analysis of our data as well as for the conduct of the fieldwork.

A second way of structuring our data collection was obviously our use of managerial records of turnover and absenteeism. Such data were supplemented, where appropriate, with analysis of other records on strikes and disputes, piecework earnings, accidents, and disciplinary actions. Wherever possible we tried to produce information on a comparative basis. This was not always possible; only one plant, for example, kept detailed strike records. But even if we could not obtain data from all seven factories we tried to make some key contrasts. For example, we argue in Chapter 7 that the pattern of machine breakdown in one factory was consistent with the deliberate reporting of false breakdowns so that workers could control the amount and timing of their own efforts; this argument is strengthened since we are able to show that a very different pattern of breakdowns occurred in a factory where workers' control over effort was much weaker.

Third, with two researchers engaged in fieldwork, it was possible to moderate some of the personal biases which inevitably develop in this kind of work. One means of avoiding idiosyncrasies was for both of us to work in each factory instead of dividing the factories between us. This may have led to some duplication of effort but this was more than outweighed by our ability to discuss matters from the different perspectives provided by our different ranges of contacts.

Fourth, we used our questionnaire of shopfloor workers as a source of comparative data. Our informal interviews, often with groups of workers, provided a great deal of useful information on general attitudes to a firm, workers' reasons for joining and perceptions of the likelihood of their leaving, attitudes to taking time off, and a whole range of matters of obvious relevance to a discussion of quitting and absenteeism. Yet some 'harder' data from a questionnaire sample would supplement this information by having some claim to representativeness and by allowing variations in responses to a specific question to be indicated. We are able, for example, to show that variations in replies to questions about casual absenteeism reflected differing patterns of workplace control. This plainly helps us to link the 'subjective' and the 'objective' elements of the analysis. The questionnaire results must not, however, be treated in isolation. As we point out in discussing the details of the questionnaire (see below, pp. 73–4), we used a limited battery of questions, and the results are insufficient to stand on their own.

We thus used documentary material, managerial statistics, structured and unstructured interviewing, and observation in an attempt to provide what Cicourel (1973: 124) calls a means of 'triangulation' on the phenomenon in question. Yet this geographical metaphor is not entirely appropriate. It implies, on the analogy of the height of a hill, that, by looking at conflict from different positions, we can measure its true extent. It is essential, however, to distinguish between the use of different research tools to look at different aspects of a phenomenon and the theoretical claim that there is a true amount of conflict which can be measured. There is, in other words, a difference between triangulation as a research method and triangulation as an epistemological claim that, given sufficient independent measurements, reality can be unambiguously discovered.[6] For our purposes here this difference is crucial: we can talk sensibly about the amount of absenteeism or the number of strikes (although even here social meanings are important in the definition of what is to be counted as an instance of absenteeism or as a strike) but not about the amount of conflict. The nature and significance of potentially conflictual actions has to be investigated in terms of the way that specific practices are organized in specific settings.

Plan of the Book

Part of our argument is that previous studies have been partial in so far as they have looked at only a narrow range of the phenomena listed as forms of conflict. We are therefore obliged to try to examine as wide a range of behaviour as our factories permit. At the same time, however, we do not simply look at a list of unconnected activities but attempt to analyse apparently disparate phenomena in terms of the structure of control. We therefore begin by outlining, in Chapter 2, the broad differences between our plants in terms of the frontier of control, together with such relevant details of their industrial relations as their payment systems and forms of union organization. We then proceed in three main phases.

First, we use very general differences in the extent of control as a central

6. It is this difference which explains how Cicourel can advocate triangulation when in his more methodological work (e.g. Cicourel, 1964) he is, of course, at pains to demolish the notion that social facts have an independent existence and to establish a phenomenological theory of knowledge in its place.

focus in the analysis of 'individual' expressions of conflict, with separate chapters being devoted to labour turnover and absenteeism. The other main phenomenon which appears in lists of the individual forms of conflict is industrial accidents. Our material permits us to assess the debate on accidents and to suggest that certain common arguments and assumptions are mistaken. Yet, while certainly related to the notion of control, the material on accidents does not directly advance our more general argument and it is therefore discussed elsewhere (P. Edwards and Scullion, 1982a). Our argument about control is developed in the chapter on absence in relation to the point that the significance of many forms of behaviour is negotiated in terms of a web of rules. While broad differences in patterns of behaviour can be related to equally broad differences in the nature of control, more detailed activities such as managerial means of monitoring and responding to the 'absence problem' require closer attention. These activities may be related to control, however; we argue, for example, that variations in managerial perceptions of absence as a problem owe a great deal to differences in the extent of management's own control over workplace operations. Analysis of the 'negotiation of order' naturally leads into the discussion of factory discipline in Chapter 5, for a central argument of the chapter is that formally illicit breaches of discipline attain their significance according to customary understandings which cross-cut formal organizational rules.

A related argument of Chapter 5 is that discipline, although often treated as an individual matter, has important collective elements. This leads into the second phase of our analysis in Chapters 6, 7 and 8. The central focus here is the frontier of control: previous chapters have been based on broad differences in control patterns, and the concern is now to investigate those patterns in their own right. Sabotage, for example, is discussed in terms of workers' needs: in several settings apparently conducive to sabotage, for example, the presence of other means of controlling effort levels made sabotage unnecessary. Similarly such things as shopfloor controls over the mobility of labour are discussed, in Chapter 8, in relation to the concept of institutionalized conflict.

Up to this point the discussion is largely in terms of structures of control and their effects on behaviour. A study of the organization of conflict also involves, however, a more direct concern with social processes. In Chapter 9 we therefore look at patterns of strikes and sanctions in terms of the processes involved in them. One crucial aspect of the analysis is the study of managerial strategy: as noted above, such strategy is often seen as a central aspect of industrial relations but there have been few detailed studies of its operation. Our concern is not with managerial strategy as such, however, but with the link between the strategy and the struggle for control. Hence we argue that management strategy in disputes can be related to a wider policy of regaining control over the work process.

Finally, in Chapter 10 we turn to the wider significance of our findings.

Having explored the significance of a large number of workplace activities we can return to the debate about alternative forms of conflict by considering how far it is useful to talk in terms of individual and collective actions. In addition to putting this debate in a wider context we also address other debates about the nature of action at the point of production and its significance for broader notions of conflict and resistance.

2
Research Settings

Introduction

In choosing factories for study our general aim was to obtain a range of plants according to their patterns of shopfloor control, but we also had some more specific needs. One of these was that we should have some means of making more precise comparisons than those which would be possible had we simply picked half a dozen plants from a wide variety of companies and industries. In other words, in addition to assessing broad differences in control patterns we wanted to make more detailed comparisons in which a number of influences could be held constant and in which the detailed operation of differences in types of control would be revealed. We therefore started by looking at one industry, the engineering industry, taking two plants from each of two companies (which we have called Company A and Company B). We could compare, for example, situations in which company industrial relations policies and pay structures were held constant and in which particular aspects of plant traditions varied. Moreover, since the two Company B plants were of very different sizes we could make some assessment of the much-discussed 'size effect' (see George et al., 1977) in a setting in which technology and pay systems were virtually identical.

In very crude summary terms the frontier of control had been shifted more in the shopfloor's favour in the two Company B plants than in any of our other factories. Shop stewards played a crucial role in all aspects of the wage-effort bargain, having a substantial role in the planning of work, being able to prevent if they so wished the movement of workers between jobs, and controlling rotas for overtime themselves. This degree of control was exerted by stewards of craft and of production areas alike. In Company A craft stewards had established somewhat similar forms of control, although these were of rather more recent origin than those in Company B. In production areas, however, there was substantially less control by the shopfloor over day-to-day matter of mobility, manning levels, overtime, and the like. This did not mean that stewards had no role to play. Indeed the formal recognition of stewards and their involvement in company pay bargaining had gone further in Company A than in Company B. Neither did extensive shopfloor control mean that workers in Company B were better off in terms of wages and security of employment than those elsewhere. The reverse was the case, with the firm's decline in the local wages league and the increasing threat of plant closures being central sources of complaint. This control did mean, however, that workers had ways of expressing their discontents which were not available to production workers in Company A.

From the extremes of shopfloor control in Company B we moved to the opposite situation of the clothing industry, studying two plants in which managerial control over all aspects of workplace relations was considerable. Though this contrast was very great we must stress that the clothing plants did not represent the extremes of managerial domination. They were far from being sweatshops, the relevant trade union was recognized, and managers were genuinely concerned for the welfare of their workers. We have not, in other words, covered the whole range of managerial control, a limitation which we take explicitly into account at various points. But we have covered a sufficient part of the range to reveal important variations, and this is our main concern.

Our final plant, which we have called the Process Factory, fell somewhere between these two extremes, but it is less important as an intermediate case than as an illustration of a particular form of organization of the labour process. Both our engineering companies recognized that there was likely to be a division of interest between management and the shopfloor over a wide range of issues and attempted to deal with any difficulties by negotiating with shop stewards. Management of the firm of which the Process Factory was part certainly recognized the importance of straight negotiation on wages and conditions. But on shopfloor matters the firm had a long tradition of arguing that the interests of workers and managers were broadly similar, in that both sides wanted to produce as efficiently as possible so that they could then share out the largest possible 'cake'. Stewards were certainly involved in local bargaining but, to use Burawoy's terms introduced in Chapter 1, the organization of consent was based less on explicit negotiation than on consultation as to the best way to manage the joint enterprise of production. The result of this system was that workers had more control over some aspects of their work than did even those in Company B. Work groups were largely autonomous, for example, and they themselves planned the allocation of work among group members. Yet such control had not been wrested from management, and it was part of a system in which workers could generate little direct challenge to managerial decision on such things as effort levels. The implications of the control system as a whole are thus of most interest for the light they throw on behaviour such as absenteeism in an environment in which management had made conscious efforts to moderate challenges to its own authority and in which consent and trust were

TABLE 2.1

SUMMARY OF COMPANY AND FACTORY CHARACTERISTICS

	COMPANY A		COMPANY B	
Total company employment	20,000		80,000	
Main pay bargaining level	Company		Company[a]	
Main payment system for production workers	Complex PBR with high full-back rate		MDW	
Management style	Sophisticated Negotiatory		Traditional Negotiatory	
	Electrical	*Components*	*Large Metals*	*Small Metals*
Number manual employees	1200	700	6300	650
Per cent women	65	10	2	Nil
Per cent coloured	15	25	2	1
Type of product	Standardized electrical component	Mouldings and castings	Pressings, metal assembly	Pressings, metal assembly
Main technology	Assembly line	Machine op.	Assembly line, machine op.	Assembly line, machine op.
Shift system	*Women:* F—T, 0600—1400; P—T, 1400— 1800 or 1800—2200. *Men:* Double Day, Perm. night	*Women:* Day *Men:* Day and night, 3 shift	Day and night	Day and night
Number personnel/IR managers dealing with manual workers[b]	2	2 to 3	5 to 6	2
Number recognized manual TUs	2	3	8	3
Number recognized full-time shop stewards	2	2 to 4[d]	14[c]	6

a. Elements of plant bargaining remained in the Large Metals Factory.
b. Refers to number of plant-level officers, excluding clerical staff, dealing with personnel matters. Where two figures are given, some officers spent only part of their time on such matters.

Table 2.1. Summary of company and factory characteristics *continued*

	COMPANY C	COMPANY D	COMPANY E
Total company employment	600	350	70,000
Main pay bargaining level	Industry	Industry	Company
Main payment system for production workers	Piecework	Piecework	Time Rate
Management style	Paternalist/ Autocratic	Paternalist/ Consultative	Sophisticated Consultative
	Hosiery	*Underwear*	*Process*
Number manual employees	200	350	1,500
Per cent women	60	90	Nil
Per cent coloured	2	5	Negligible
Type of product	Stockings, tights	Underwear, leisure wear	Man-made fibre
Main technology	Machine minding, machine op.	Machine op.	Machine minding
Shift system	*Women:* Day *Men:* 3-shift	*Women:* Day *Men:* 3-shift	Continuous shifts, 7 days a week
Number personnel/IR managers dealing with manual workers[b]	Nil	Nil	2 to 3
Number recognized manual TUs	1	1	3
Number recognized full-time shop stewards	Nil	Nil	1 to 2[d]

c. Number recognized at plant level; there were many stewards who were *de facto* full-time at shop level.
d. The lower figures show numbers formally recognized; the higher figures include stewards who were *de facto* full-time and who operated largely at plant level.

articulated principles for gaining the co-operation of the work force.

Although we thus have several different forms of control system within our seven factories it might be objected that control is not the key distinguishing feature. In particular it might be argued that the small size of our clothing plants, as compared to the size of our other plants, prevents any proper comparison: differences attributed to control differences may in fact be due to differences in size. Size differences were indeed, substantial: one clothing plant employed about 350 workers and the other employed only 200 workers, while our other plants ranged in size from 650 to over 6000 manual employees. Yet we doubt whether these differences were central. First, although size has been correlated with rates of turnover, absenteeism and other things, the strength of the observed relationship has varied considerably between different studies (Acton Society Trust, 1953; Revans, 1956; Ingham, 1970). Observed differences cannot be written off to a size effect, since it is unclear whether such an effect necessarily exists. Second, as George et al. (1977) point out, there are few adequate explanations as to why the size of a plant has specific effects on workers' morale. There are large numbers of hypotheses about, for example, the alienating effects of working in large and anonymous units, but few specific mechanisms have been adduced to explain how the physical size of a plant affects the attitudes of workers within it. Thus Ingham (1970: 65) argues that it is not size itself which is important but the extent of bureaucratization of operations: since size and bureaucratization are correlated, the former may act as a proxy for the latter but is not itself the key variable. Ingham suggests that the degree of bureaucracy will rise rapidly as plant size increases to 100 workers and that the rate of growth will be slower among larger plants. Since all our plants were substantially above the threshold of 100 workers it is unlikely that there would be such dramatic differences in organizational structure that behavioural differences could be written off to a size effect. More generally, Ingham's argument suggests that there may well be differences between plants of similar size; we did indeed observe such differences, which suggests in turn that explanation must be sought in terms of variables other than size. Finally, one of our clothing plants, which we have called the Hosiery Factory, was owned by a company which operated another plant a mile or so away. The two plants, employing in all about 600 workers, were operated as a unit; there was, for example, no works manager for the Hosiery Factory as such, and the various shop managers came directly under the control of the firm's production director. In many respects the Hosiery Factory can be treated as a department of a 600-strong organization.

For all these reasons we doubt whether the differences which we observed can be written off to a size effect. It may well be that size is correlated with patterns of control, although with a sample of seven plants we are not in a position directly to confirm or deny such an association. In any event, control is, as we try to demonstrate, a truly explanatory variable whereas plant size merely sets certain constraints on behaviour, which then has to be explained in terms of additional variables such as 'alienation'.

A summary of some of the key features of our five companies and seven plants is given in Table 2.1. This is no more than a rough guide; technologies, for example, are hard to describe in a few words, and there were important differences between plants. But, since we adopt a thoroughgoing comparative approach in our substantive chapters, the reader may find the table useful as an *aide memoire*. In the remainder of this chapter we provide a fuller summary of the plants' characteristics. This also serves as a preliminary account of their patterns of control.

The Engineering Industry

Company A

Both plants studied were part of the same operating company, a subsidiary of a larger group of companies employing in all several tens of thousands of workers in Britain, Europe, and further afield. Company A, defined as the one operating company, had over a dozen plants in Britain producing a wide range of general engineering and electrical goods. Many of its products were small, standardized items, mass-produced in very long runs and varying little from year to year. These characteristics encouraged the company to employ large numbers of women on routine assembly work.

The company's personnel policy seems to have been closely connected with these technological and labour force factors: the company had a tradition of being a 'responsible' employer, providing welfare and other benefits and operating a relaxed management style which was based on gaining the co-operation of the work force. Workers were expected to be loyal and company-minded. In the past the firm had provided a secure place to work, with a friendly and cosy atmosphere but with a level of wages that was low by engineering industry standards.[1] The growing strength of unions in the company meant, however, that this last aspect had been changing: by the late 1970s the company was offering wages which were at least as good as those available elsewhere in the local engineering industry. In addition, the company had come to terms with unions by recognizing them for bargaining purposes and by giving stewards an important role within the plant. There was now a sophisticated approach to industrial relations, with plant-level and company-level matters being carefully co-ordinated. But the tradition of being a responsible employer and of expecting

---

1. We derive this description from our own interviews and also from several published accounts of the company which we are, for obvious reasons, unable to cite.

loyalty to the firm remained important since it set the context for the general climate of shopfloor relations.

The company had grown from its early base in one plant through a process of growth rather than merger or take-over, and it retained a distinct image. In line with this, it had always had a centralized bargaining structure, with basic rates, shift premia and the like being uniform across all plants, and with the structure of the piecework system also being established centrally (although details of its application and rates of piecework earnings varied between plants). There was an influential industrial relations department which carried out annual wage negotiations centrally and which carefully monitored all plant-level agreements. Each plant had one or more personnel specialists, who kept in close touch with the central department and who were careful to avoid making agreements that might set precedents which could then be exploited by workers in other plants.

Despite this centralization, collective bargaining was highly fragmented between bargaining groups. This was the outcome of the way in which unions had developed in the company. Until the 1950s union organization had generally been weak, and shopfloor organization began among skilled workers, particularly toolmakers. The toolmakers formed their own organization, which covered all toolrooms in the company and which was eventually granted bargaining rights by the company. The toolmakers were followed by groups such as electricians, machine tool fitters, and tool setters in establishing separate bargaining units. Production workers were the last to be constituted into a distinct group. The result of this system was that membership of a particular union was less important than allegiance to a group. Production workers who belonged to the union representing all the toolmakers, the Amalgamated Union of Engineering Workers (AUEW), had more in common with their fellow production workers in a different union than with union colleagues in the toolmakers' group. Similarly, at plant level, the bargaining group was the main organizational focus. A matter affecting electricians, for example, would be handled by the electricians' steward and then referred, if necessary, to the electricians' central bargaining group; there was no call for the whole body of stewards in a plant to have anything to do with the issue.

In view of this, it was not possible to talk of a single domestic shop steward organization in the plant (compare Batstone et al., 1977). For each bargaining group, organization at company as well as plant level was crucial; and, within each plant, differences between groups militated against the formation of a plant-wide identity. The importance of the company level of bargaining had a further consequence for plant level industrial relations. Key changes in management policy were made at company level, and the results were then generalized to all plants. For example the decisions to recognize full-time conveners (or senior stewards as the company insisted on calling them) and to introduce the check-off of union dues were made centrally and spread to all plants without the need for workers in those plants to act together to achieve these benefits. This does not imply a complete organization 'from the top down': many gains were made only as a result of pressure from particular plants. But it does mean that organization in many plants was not the result of conscious struggles by workers in those plants. Indeed, the growth of shop steward organization in Company A seems typical of general developments in engineering: the recognition of full-time conveners, the check-off, and a *de facto* closed shop reflected managerial attempts to formalize industrial relations and to strengthen bargaining relationships.

The company's approach to industrial relations meant that the two plants we studied had many features in common. Each had an industrial relations officer who dealt with day-to-day negotiations and the application of company-level agreements; but a crucial part of his role was to assist central personnel managers to keep in touch with the shopfloor. And each had a personnel officer who dealt exclusively with individual employment matters and welfare. More generally, the company's management style meant that the atmosphere on the shopfloor was similar. Foremen were expected to gain the co-operation of the work force through persuasion and not force. The company retained control of the planning and allocation of work, the distribution of workers to particular jobs, and overall manning levels. But within this framework it attempted to treat its workers 'fairly'. So long as they did their work adequately workers were free to talk to each other and to move around their sections. They were not tied to the machine and it was accepted, for example, that they could make tea outside the official break times. There was thus a relaxed and friendly atmosphere on the shopfloor; many foremen had worked for the company for long periods and said that knowing the workers personally meant that they obtained a high level of co-operation. All this was, however, within the context of managerial control of many aspects of the situation.

The Electrical Factory. The Electrical Factory was in many ways typical of the company. Two-thirds of its workers were women and it had a reputation for being an extremely harmonious plant. It had been in operation for about ten years, having been established to expand the company's output of a standardized electrical product. Many of the component parts of the product came from other plants within the company, but the plant also did some of its own sub-assembly and machining operations. The plant was dominated, however, by assembly-line operations; the product was small enough for workers to sit at their work stations, with the semi-assembled part being moved along a small conveyor belt. These assembly operations were carried out during the day by women, most of whom worked an eight-hour morning shift or a four-hour afternoon or evening shift. There was a small permanent night shift, staffed largely by Pakistani men. Apart from these night shift workers, the men in the factory were employed in indirect jobs as labourers, inspectors, or maintenance fitters. They worked a double-day shift, doing mornings one week and afternoons the next. There was also a small toolroom doing repair and maintenance work for the rest of the factory.

Production workers were paid on a piecework basis, but the relationship between individual effort and earnings was remote. Over the years the guaranteed rates for waiting time (that is, time spent doing no work, as when there was a machine breakdown) and day work (work for which there was no piece rate) had risen as a proportion of average earnings. This meant that earnings on waiting time were about 95 per cent of average piecework earnings. Moreover, workers on assembly lines were paid according to the output of the line and not individual effort. At the time of the research there was, however, a productivity scheme in operation which had restored some of the incentive element. With the complexities of piecework and productivity schemes and the varieties of shift systems, it is difficult to estimate average earnings levels. However, a semi-skilled assembler working a 40-hour day shift could expect to earn about £67 in early 1979; with the addition of shift premia a worker on the same grade doing a 37½-hour double day shift would earn £72. These rates were considered to be quite good for the district, and were certainly much higher than those available to women elsewhere. Even for skilled men the wages were now comparatively good; the rate for a toolmaker on a 40-hour day shift was £90, and stewards said that, apart from those in contract toolrooms which were dismissed as 'sweatshops', there were no toolmakers in the area on a higher basic rate.[2]

In view of the recent establishment of the factory and the large number of women employed one might expect union organization to be weak. In terms of such conventional criteria as union density and the presence of full-time shop stewards this was not the case. There was a *de facto* post-entry closed shop for production workers and, in line with company policy, full-time senior stewards were recognized and provided with office facilities and the like. But it is true that the union organization was not aggressive. Stewards stressed

2. The Department of Employment (1979: 977–8, 982) gives the following figures for the average earnings (in pounds), excluding overtime, of full-time adult workers:

	Men	Women
Mechanical engineering	82.6	61.6
Electrical engineering	79.7	59.5
Clothing and footwear	73.0	50.0
Man-made fibres	84.9	n.a.

Since these figures are broad industry averages, and since they cover all grades of labour and include bonus payments, they cannot be compared directly with the information for each plant which we give here and subsequently. It is clear, however, that the pay rates for women in Company A were comparatively good. For men, industry averages reveal little, except that toolmakers were certainly well above the average.

co-operation with management and the inadvisability of conflict. One indicator of this was the low level of 'piecework drift' compared to other plants. The establishment of an influential steward movement had been a recent event in the plant; in the early years it had been difficult to persuade women workers, particularly the part-timers, of the need for union membership. The growth during the 1970s of the company's policy of recognizing senior stewards, granting the check-off of union dues, and so on was a crucial influence.

Production workers were divided approximately equally between the AUEW and the TGWU. The stewards of the two unions worked very closely together, sharing a union office and dealing jointly with matters affecting production workers. There were two conveners, one from each union. While the AUEW convener was elected by all AUEW stewards the skilled groups such as fitters and toolmakers conducted their business through their own trade group organization. As a result the joint stewards' committee, comprising stewards from both unions, had little real influence.

The conveners spent a considerable amount of their time away from the plant at company-level meetings; in particular they represented the plant in the pay negotiations for production workers. Each therefore had a recognized deputy on the morning and afternoon shifts; in the absence of the convener the deputy could spend a good deal of his or her time on union business. This arrangement, together with the facilities for handling union matters which were given to all stewards, reflected the extent to which the company had gone to give the unions a significant role in the plant. The steward movement was now well-established but was far from militant.

The Components Factory. In the Components Factory there was a more aggressive tradition. The plant had been in operation for many years, which had given the shopfloor organization more of a chance to develop its own traditions. Toolmakers, of whom there were about 100, constituted a particularly militant and solidaristic body, seeing themselves as being in the forefront of union organization in the company. They felt that they were one of the main parts, if not the main part, of the toolmakers' group, which was itself seen as the leading union body in the company: toolmakers attributed many of the gains which production workers had made in recent years to the militancy of the toolmakers' group, whose successes had then been generalized to other groups. This tradition, together with the fact that production workers in the factory belonged to a different union, meant that toolmakers were far more distant from production workers than they were in the Electrical Factory. They had their own senior steward, who operated from his own office and who had very little contact with the production workers' stewards.

In view of their tradition of solidarity it is not surprising that toolmakers had established a greater degree of shopfloor control than other groups in either of our Company A plants. For example, the rule of 'one man, one machine' meant that management were not free to allocate labour as they chose. Tool-makers saw themselves as autonomous craftsmen who were prepared to sell their services to the company but who were unwilling to accept detailed managerial control over their work. This lead had been followed by the fitters and the electricians, who had also established a considerable degree of control over such things as the allocation of work and the distribution of overtime. They too operated entirely independently of the production workers' organization. At the time of the research there was no joint shop stewards' committee, one or two attempts to set up such a body having foundered on the considerable suspicions which lingered between the various groups.

The work of production operatives was very different from that in the Electrical Factory. The Components Factory produced a wide range of metal castings and plastic mouldings for use in a large number of the company's products. These components were produced on individual machines so that, apart from inspection and finishing operations, there was no sequence of jobs within the factory. All the machine operators were men, who generally worked a 40-hour week, alternating between five days and four nights. In the whole of the metals shop and one section of the plastics shop each man operated one or two machines, going through a separate series of operations each machine cycle. Although routine, this work required the operator to be sensitive to the condition of the machine, the nature of the raw material, and the temperature of the process, all of which were critical in the production of a good component. The men were therefore classed as skilled. In one part of the plastics shop automatic machines had replaced machines operated by hand. In this section the machines worked twenty-four hours a day with male operators being employed on the trimming work on a three-shift system for five days a week. In the other areas finishing operations were done by women, of whom there were about seventy in the two shops.

Systems of payment varied considerably within the factory. At one time all production workers had been on individual piecework, but it had become apparent that this was inappropriate for workers on the automatic machines, where output was not related to individual effort, and a fixed bonus was there-fore introduced on this section. Managers had also become dissatisfied with the amount of work involved in administering the system, for example the accurate booking of the time spent on each piecework job. This led to the establishment of a group-based scheme in the metals shop: an average efficiency level was calculated for each group of machines, with a fixed payment being made for production at or below the average and with an additional sum for production in excess of the average. Individual piecework remained only on the non-automatic plastics machines and on some associated trim operations.

Earnings levels were somewhat higher than in the Electrical Factory. A worker on the same grade as a semi-skilled assembler in the Electrical Factory could expect about £71 for a 40-hour week. This difference was due to the higher levels of bonus in the Components Factory, which can in turn be attributed to shopfloor pressure on the piecework system. Pressure was exerted in three main areas: the negotiated times for jobs, which affected the amount of 'bonus time' earned; the 'calculator' which was applied to translate this time into money; and the level of fall-back payments for day work and waiting time. At the time of the research, however, there was little day-to-day pressure on rates, since most jobs were long-established. Moreover, although the company felt that some rates were too loose, there was no overt rate-cutting, and covert cuts, by for example making minor modifications in a component and introducing it as a new job with a new time, seem to have been rare. There was little direct conflict over piece rates. Most workers, indeed, earned substantially more than £71 a week. Very few were on the same grade as semi-skilled workers in the Electrical Factory, and in a good week a high earner could gross up to £100, although average earnings were lower than this. Part of workers' higher grading reflected their higher skill, and part reflected bargaining pressure in that it seems likely that the monetary reward for certain 'skills' depended on definitions of skill that were created by social pressures.

Although the payment system was more under challenge than it was in the Electrical Factory, managerial control over the allocation of labour and the detailed planning of operations was considerable. Although union density had been high for many years, it was not until the 1960s that the union began to develop a significant shopfloor presence.[3] Pressure began to be put on wages and there was a long strike over one of the company's annual pay offers. This strike had been a critical experience for the stewards. It was the first serious strike by production workers in the company and it stopped not only the Components Factory but also several of its customer plants. It resulted in the largest wage increase ever won by production workers and, in the stewards' view, it made the company treat these workers much more seriously than it had done in the past, not just in the Components Factory but throughout its plants. The stewards felt that the company could never again ignore the claims of production workers, which meant that, in day-to-day negotiations too, the balance of power had shifted in favour of the shopfloor: they could now obtain fair wages through negotiation. They thus felt that the key battle had been won, that a framework for negotiation had been established, and that there was no longer any need for strong pressure on piecework times or similar issues. Management had a similar perspective: the stewards had achieved a strong position, but they used their power responsibly.

3. All production workers belonged to one union. Because management treated the two shops as distinct for production purposes (although they shared personnel and work study functions) there were two senior stewards, one for each shop.

Union organization thus owed more to shopfloor action and less to managerial sponsorship than was the case in the Electrical Factory. As a result stewards
took a more critical approach towards management, accusing them of an inability to take decisions and an unwillingness to invest in the plant. But all this
must be seen in the context of the company as a whole. Only in the toolroom
and maintenance areas was there a persistent and organized campaign to wrest
control of shopfloor decisions from management. Elsewhere stewards and
workers were content to co-operate with management, and both sides stressed
the good working relationships which existed and the degree of trust which
had been built up. In both factories management retained significant control
over manning and effort levels. But this control was not exerted in any direct
or obvious way, and management placed considerable weight on negotiations
with unions and on the creation of trust on the shopfloor. On the other hand
it did not go in for consultation schemes or job enlargement. It is for this reason
that we have labelled its style as 'sophisticated negotiatory'. The unions generally
accepted this broad approach and did not actively attempt to shift the frontier
of control in their own favour. Relations on the shopfloor were thus friendly
and relaxed and workers were not subject to harsh discipline or to the arbitrary
exercise of power.

Company B
Company B, like Company A, was a large multi-plant concern operating in a
broadly similar market and with similar traditions derived from the engineering
industry as a whole. Its style of operation and the general atmosphere on the
shopfloor were, however, very different. It is difficult to summarize the key
differences, but the label of 'traditional negotiatory' management brings out
some of the contrasts. Collective bargaining had a long history, but the bargain
did not extend beyond establishing a package of wages and conditions. There
was little attempt actively to attract the co-operation and loyalty of workers
through such things as merit payments and extra holidays for long service, both
of which were used in Company A, or through welfare schemes. Foremen in
Company A stressed the trust which they built up with their workers, and cited
the fact that workers would discuss the whole range of personal problems with
them as evidence for this. In Company B a 'good working relationship' was
restricted to the practicalities of the work task.

This is not to suggest that management retained a high degree of control of
operations. Indeed, the reverse is the case. In both plants which we studied the
unions had established a strong shopfloor presence for many years and had
challenged many aspects of managerial control which were taken for granted
in Company A. For example, manning levels were subject to negotiation, the
allocation of workers to particular jobs was jointly determined, and shop
stewards controlled rotas for overtime. In most respects the frontier of control

had been moved more in the workers' favour, and effort levels were less subject to determination by management than they were in Company A.

Both plants had, then, traditions of strong autonomous union organizations, although their histories were very different. They were concerned with the production of similar goods, and their technologies were correspondingly similar. The main operations in both were the machining of metal components and their assembly into standardized units which were then taken to other plants of the company for final assembly. And, although measured day work systems were in operation in both plants, they had both been on piecework until recently and workers retained a 'piecework mentality' in many respects. In addition to other sources of interest the two plants thus provide an opportunity for examining the 'size effect': given that differences between them cannot be explained in terms of payment systems or technology, were there any differences in such things as absenteeism which can be explained by the marked difference in size between them?

The Large Metals Factory. This factory had five main production shops, each entirely self-contained and employing several hundred workers, together with a large toolroom which had about 400 toolmakers and a separate administrative block. Women were employed on some of the lighter jobs in the machine shop and on one or two trim operations, but the great majority of manual workers were men. In the machine shop production jobs were highly repetitive requiring the worker to place a component in the machine, wait for the machine to operate, and then take it out and replace it with another. There were none of the variations of cycle time and temperature which made machine operation in the Components Factory a skilled job. Many of the other jobs in the factory also fell within the semi-skilled category. In the assembly shops large numbers of workers were employed in putting together sub-assemblies; this was routine work which was performed individually or in teams and it was possible for workers to control their speed of working. The final stage of assembly took place on moving lines. Since the lines moved at a set pace it might be expected that workers would be very firmly 'tied to the track'. Workers were employed in teams which performed a series of operations on each unit, moving down the track as they worked. At the end of each cycle, which could last half an hour on the more complex operations, the team would return to the beginning of its section and pick up another unit. Working in teams and doing a whole series of operations, workers did not in the least fit the common picture of the alienated assembly line worker doing a fragmented task. Jobs on the track were, moreover, the most skilled production jobs in the factory in that they required workers to produce a high quality finished article with precise clearances between moving parts. Although improved machining techniques had taken some of the skill out of the job, a considerable degree of ability still had to be exercised.

Within the factory several distinct grades of skill were identified. For example, jobs on the assembly line were divided into two quite distinct categories, with the workers being organized by different unions. In the Small Metals Factory this distinction was not made, with workers moving between the two types of jobs quite freely. Moreover the precise dividing line between them owed as much to custom as to skill level. For example a job had been transferred from the less skilled to the more skilled trade in the 1950s because, on one particular product, the job required the shaping of metal, which was recognized as the prerogative of one union. Similar jobs had been retained by that union ever since, even though the particular operations requiring its exclusive skills were no longer needed. In other words the division between one occupation and another owed as much to social definitions, in this case those generated by inter-union differences, as to 'genuine' differences in skill. Moreover these social definitions cannot be explained solely as a result of 'demarcations' between unions: in several instances divisions within a union were as strongly enforced as those between unions. For example both the unions organizing the assembly lines also had members in the semi-skilled grades; but skilled and semi-skilled workers belonged to entirely different sections with their own shop steward organizations, and it was not possible for a worker to move from one grade to the other.

The plant's union organization was, then, highly complex. Of the eight manual trade unions, five organized semi-skilled assembly shop workers. Some unions represented a wide range of trades; the AUEW, for example, organized all the toolmakers and fitters in the plant as well as covering the semi-skilled and unskilled grades in the assembly shops and a small proportion of the semi-skilled jobs in the machine shop. Other unions had a more limited constituency; for example, the majority of workers in the machine shop belonged to one union which had only a few members elsewhere in the factory. Each union had a convener and a deputy-convener who had their own offices and who were recognized as full-time.[4] In addition, many of the leading stewards in the individual shops spent all or most of their time on union business; it is difficult to give precise numbers here, but in each of the main assembly shops the five semi-skilled stewards and a steward from each of the skilled production unions spent most of their time on union business. A simple indicator of the extent and complexity of union organization is the presence of almost exactly twice as many recognized stewards as there were in the similarly-sized plant studied by Batstone et al. (1977: 18), a plant which was itself highly organized.

---

4. There was a partial exception to this in the case of one small craft union whose convener and deputy-convener worked at their trades, although still attending all meetings with management and thus spending a considerable amount of their time on union business. Hence Table 2.1 shows 14 and not 16 full-time shop stewards.

There were several unifying forces. First, in the semi-skilled assembly grades the five stewards acted together as a group, and frequently met to consider action on various matters. However, even this unity was limited. Joint action related only to matters within a particular shop, so that there was no distinct semi-skilled organization across the whole factory. And there was no question of a whole section electing one steward to represent it, on the lines of the practice in some other factories (Dore, 1973: 131; Batstone et al., 1977: 17): a steward represented only members of his own union. The second unifying influence was the Conveners' Committee. This body, comprising the eight conveners and their deputies, was the major means of bringing the unions together. It was recognized by management as the main representative body, and negotiated on all plant-level matters. As its constitution implies, however, it was not a full negotiating body in the sense of being able to bind all unions to its decisions. Since the largest general unions each had over a thousand members, and the smallest craft union only fifty, the principle of majority vote did not operate. Instead, each union insisted on its right to act independently if it chose; on several crucial occasions, this certainly happened. The committee could be a powerful body if it could agree on a common course of action, for the conveners generally had considerable influence within their own unions. And it provided a forum for the discussion of matters of common interest and thus performed some of the functions which would be carried out by a joint stewards' committee elsewhere. A third source of unity was simply that each union had established a firm position within the factory and that there were few sources of direct conflict with other unions. Demarcation disputes were unusual, and the rights of each union were generally recognized. For example one reason for the lack of conflict between unions organizing the semi-skilled assembly grade was that recruitment was based on the proportions represented by each union: if 100 men were to be recruited, so many would come from the AUEW, so many from the TGWU, and so on. This practice, which eliminated fears of aggrandizement by one union, obviously owed a great deal to management's policy of containing inter-union conflict and of accommodating to the pattern of organization which had grown up: the practice rested not only on management's willingness to recruit on a proportional basis but also on the long-standing arrangement that all recruitment would take place through union offices.

As might be expected from this outline of union organization, the unions had established much greater control over the factory's operations than was the case in either of the Company A plants. The recruitment system, for example, meant that management could not hire workers as it chose. As mentioned above, many features of day-to-day operations were controlled by the stewards or were under joint control by stewards and management. Most importantly, manning levels and track speeds were subject to negotiation; for example, when a new product was introduced there were lengthy discussions about manning with all production worker stewards, which meant that the 'effort bargain' was, at least in part, under shop steward control. More generally the stewards had established a high degree of 'institutional centrality' within the plant: they had a say in many matters, and it was taken for granted that they controlled, for example, overtime rotas, a practice which would be unthinkable in many of our other factories. This did not necessarily mean that there was a high level of overt conflict. In the terms introduced in Chapter 1, the unions had established themselves at the level of structure, and many of the areas in which they had pushed the frontier of control in their own favour were not areas of active struggle. Management had acquiesced in many practices, to such an extent, indeed, that many arrangements which would be strongly challenged by management elsewhere were taken for granted as entirely normal.

This does not imply, however, that 'union power' was absolute. The weakness of the unions despite their success in many areas appeared most strikingly in discontents about wage levels. In the past the factory had the reputation of being one of the best-paying in the area, and workers recounted stories of men queuing up outside trying to obtain a job in the plant. During the 1970s, however, the plant had slipped rapidly down the earnings league: as workers put it, 'even dustmen' earned more than they themselves did. Such claims had a substantial degree of truth. We were not in a position to investigate previous wage levels in detail, but current rates were certainly far from the top of the league. In early 1979 a semi-skilled worker earned a gross wage of about £75 for 40 hours on day shift. As we have seen, men in the Components Factory, which had until recently been a poor payer, could earn considerably more. Skilled production workers in the Large Factory, who considered themselves to be among the elite of the engineering industry, earned less than £80 for 40 hours, and complained that other plants were paying over £100 for the same hours.

This fall in the earnings league was the dominant issue throughout the factory: workers displayed a high degree of resentment against management and they revealed little pride in their control of the factory despite the strength of their shopfloor organization. There was, rather, an atmosphere of apathy and generalized discontent. This situation exerted such a strong influence on such a wide range of workplace relations that we must outline how it had come about. The company was facing a severe crisis of profitability, which can be related to a failure to invest in new products and new capital equipment. It was losing its share of the market and had entered what has been called a 'regressive spiral' whereby an organization fails to adapt to external pressures and a progressively worsening situation develops (Legge, 1970: 3). As a result the firm attempted to control its labour costs by severely limiting the annual rises which it was willing to grant. In addition a company-level decision was taken some years before our research to end piecework. According to shopfloor workers this decision was the heart of the problem: under piecework, earnings could be increased by raising the level of effort whereas the new system of measured day work (MDW) provided no incentive to work harder. This argument was extremely widespread, and many of its precise details were reproduced in identical form by different workers. For example, a figure of £120 a week was often mentioned as the amount a semi-skilled man could have been earning had piecework been continued.

Much of the condemnation of MDW can be attributed to a more general decline in relative wages which would, given the firm's economic problems, probably have occurred even if piecework had continued. The firm was trying to recover from a long-term collapse of its market position, and it is not surprising that wages suffered in the process. The reform of bargaining arrangements, of which the introduction of MDW was part, had some specific effects, however. First, it involved a shift in the level of bargaining away from the shopfloor to plant level and then to the level of the whole company. This meant that specific shopfloor concerns received little attention and that shop stewards felt that they had lost control over important aspects of wages, for negotiations now took place at a level which was, they felt, very distant from the plant. Similarly, managers and foremen within the plant perceived a loss of their own control; many of them shared the shopfloor view that piecework had been a successful system. This is closely tied to the second effect of MDW, namely a shift in the pattern of shopfloor bargaining. Although stewards could still negotiate about manning levels, line speeds, and the like, they could no longer negotiate directly over earnings. The change was particularly significant in the assembly shops where there had been a well-developed gang system, with the production of a particular sub-assembly being assigned to a distinct gang. The gang leader had been responsible for negotiating piecework prices with management and for the detailed planning and allocation of work within the gang. The introduction of MDW destroyed a gang's control over its own earnings. It did not, however, affect the gang system, or shop steward control more generally, as a key part of the production process. Management did not succeed in sweeping aside patterns of control which had grown up under piecework: gang autonomy and the lack of direct control by foremen over the allocation and performance of work tasks were little affected. Indeed, precisely because of strenuous opposition to MDW by the stewards, no final agreement had been made at the time of our research on the terms of the 'piecework buy-out'. The plant operated according to interim arrangements which preserved many of the existing aspects of control, although the impact of those aspects on earnings had been removed.

The factory was, then, undergoing considerable change. As we shall see, its decline in the wages league had a dramatic impact on several aspects of workplace relations. Yet, in comparative terms, its most notable feature was the extent of shop steward control over all aspects of the work process. Although this shopfloor control could not prevent external changes from affecting earnings levels, it did lead to a pattern of response which was very different from that in our Company A plants. Put simply, instead of pressure on earnings there was pressure on effort levels. Foremen felt relatively powerless, for, unlike their counterparts in Company A, they had little direct involvement in the planning of work or in related matters such as monitoring workers' attendance or generally being responsible for the operation of their own sections. The whole pattern of shopfloor relations was very different, with the shop steward in the Large Metals Factory playing a central part in the production process.

The Small Metals Factory. Many aspects of relations in the Small Metals Factory were similar to those in the Large Metals Factory, and require no detailed discussion. The plant's decline in the pay league and the attribution of blame for this to the measured day work payment system closely paralleled events in the Large Metals Factory. More generally, there was a strong and well-established steward organization which had developed a pattern of control which was at least as firm as that in the Large Metal Factory; in one or two areas, indeed, the control was stronger. The main difference lay in the overall climate of relations. In the Large Metals Factory management criticized union demarcations and what were seen as excessive manning levels, and there was a marked distance from the shopfloor. In the Small Metals Factory relationships were closer and there was more of a feeling among management that they were able to co-operate effectively with the shopfloor; for example, there was considerable pride in the plant's ability consistently to meet production targets. Among more senior managers there was certainly disquiet about the plant's efficiency, but junior managers and foremen had a relaxed and easy-going relationship with the shopfloor. There was more of a feeling of trust and 'give and take' than there was in the Large Metals Factory.

The plant's union organization was relatively straightforward. Apart from a few electricians all workers belonged to one of two unions. Historically the plant had been organized by an ex-craft union which had established control over all direct metal-working operations. But its craft traditions meant that it had been unwilling to organize unskilled workers, with the result that a general union began to establish a presence among these groups during the late 1950s. By the time of the research, this pattern of organization was well-established, although there were still disputes between the unions on the boundaries of their respective spheres of influence.

The ex-craft union contained apparently contradictory elements of elitism and democracy. Skilled and semi-skilled men were rigidly distinguished, and the union had not been prepared to have labourers among its membership at all. In terms of union organization the main effect of this distinction lay in the rule that only a skilled man could hold the position of chief steward in a particular shop. Other groups such as machine operators and semi-skilled workers elected stewards, as did the skilled men. But the chief steward had to be a skilled man and it was he who formally represented the shop. There were three chief stewards, one for each of the main sections of the factory. These three stewards together with representatives from each of the main trades formed a central committee. The chairman of the committee was elected directly by the membership, and was the closest equivalent in the union to a convener, although that title was not used. For several years the position had been held by a semi-skilled man who was not, therefore, even the chief steward in his own shop.

The democratic element in the union was expressed in very frequent elections for the key posts[5] and the tradition of holding regular shop meetings. Every week each chief steward held a mass meeting of his shop in which any matters affecting the shop could be discussed; the meetings were always well-attended. Unlike other factories, where conveners and leading stewards tended to form an elite which was distant from the shopfloor, the stewards thus remained in close contact with the membership. One expression of this was the refusal of the convener to have a union office; he preferred to remain on the shopfloor, working at his trade when his union duties permitted, so that he would not become separated from his members. Similarly, the chief stewards, although in practice spending all their time on union business, remained in their own shops and were always accessible to the membership.[6]

The general union had a more conventional structure, with stewards being elected from each shop and with these stewards choosing one of their number to be the convener. The convener and his deputy effectively spent all their time on union business. These two men, together with two other stewards, comprised what was known as the union's negotiating committee.

The central committee of the ex-craft union, the general union's negotiating committee, and the two electricians' stewards formed the Joint Union Committee (JUC) of the plant. This was not a joint shop steward's committee in the usual sense since not all stewards were members of it and since it had little by way of formal machinery. Indeed each union retained the right to act on its own initiative and could not be bound by the decisions of the JUC. In the context of deep suspicions between the two main unions, the JUC was a significant development, but it was nonetheless a far from united body.

Both unions were, then, well-established in the plant. The ex-craft union in particular was a good example of a strong, autonomous workplace organization

5. The convener was elected every six months and shop committees were elected every three months. In practice there was little turnover of key personnel.
6. A further indication of the style of the stewards was the practice of dressing in working clothes, whereas very few of the conveners in the other three engineering plants made any such claim to be actively working at their trades.

which owed little to managerial sponsorship. Under piecework the union had, as part of its democratic tradition, established the unusual principle of wage equality: from the few toolmakers and fitters in the factory to the semi-skilled operative, rates were identical. Control over the piecework system had been so strong that stewards could ensure that earnings, as well as rates, were equalized across the factory. The union had imposed a strict earnings ceiling, and had even gone to the lengths of carrying out periodic checks on pay slips and fining anyone found to be earning above the ceiling. Every so often, the stewards would announce that they had decided to raise the ceiling to increase earnings, and output would be increased accordingly. This implied, of course, even greater shopfloor control of piecework than that in the Large Metals Factory. The control was, moreover, centralized: there was no gang system, and the operation of the details of the system depended on each shop committee and ultimately on the central committee.

The introduction of measured day work did not disrupt traditional patterns. The unions already operated a centralized scheme for controlling output which had obvious parallels with daywork. In the Large Metals Factory individual stewards saw daywork as a potential threat to their own power, but the centralized system in the Small Metals Factory meant that the individual steward had less to fear. There were also fewer inter-union rivalries, and agreement was reached relatively quickly.

In both factories, however, piecework traditions ran deep. Daywork did not destroy these traditions; foremen did not suddenly begin to assert control over the planning of work, and workers continued to work as they had done under piecework. In particular the idea of working at a planned rate throughout the day was not accepted. Daywork quotas were in most cases simply translated piecework times and workers operated in the traditional way of working hard in the morning and of finishing as soon as possible. Given that there was now no incentive to produce more than the agreed quota, workers simply did the quota as quickly as possible so that they could enjoy some leisure at the end of the shift. With the control over manning levels which the shopfloor had achieved, the leisure period was often considerable.

Summary

Although there were important differences between the two Company B plants, they shared a broad pattern of control which was very different from that in the Company A Factories. Despite the introduction of measured day work, much day-to-day control of operations remained in the hands of the shopfloor. Workers were subject to very little direct control by foremen, and manning levels were such that work tasks could generally be accomplished relatively easily. In Company A management retained a greater degree of control, one aspect of which was a generally higher level of effort from the workers. Managerial control was, however, exercised in a relaxed way: there was little overt pressure on workers and management tried to develop a friendly spirit. Although both engineering companies shared several important features, notably the recognition by management of the position of shop steward organization, differences in shopfloor practice were considerable.

The Clothing Industry

The differences between our engineering companies pale into insignificance when the companies are compared with the clothing plants. The clothing industry is characterized by small plants, low entry barriers, and a high degree of product market competition, influences which have been seen as impediments to the growth of autonomous shop steward organizations (Boraston et al., 1975: 182). In the two plants which we studied steward organization was rudimentary and the full-time official retained a central role.

As might be expected in this environment, managerial control of the labour process was considerable: manning levels, working arrangements, and the allocation of overtime were not even seen as negotiable. The most obvious contrast with engineering, however, lay in the climate of the factories and in particular in the level of effort which was expected from workers. Starting and finishing times were strictly enforced. As one supervisor put it, workers might stop work a minute or two before the official finishing time, but this was never stretched to as much as five minutes: stopping work even five minutes early was defined as a major problem, whereas in our engineering factories it was taken for granted that workers would stop work at least a quarter of an hour before the end of the shift. Times for tea breaks were kept down to the official periods of ten minutes in the morning and afternoon, whereas it was possible for engineering workers to stretch break times, often by substantial amounts. More generally, workers were expected to be at their machines all day: moving around the section and talking to work mates were fairly actively discouraged. And the general pace of work was much more intense than it was in the engineering plants.

It should not be thought, however, that the factories were sweatshops or that managers practised direct repression of the workers. Two characteristics of the firms' operations are crucial to understanding their industrial relations. First, the instability of product demand which is typical of industries such as clothing was less severe than might be expected. Both firms were long-established, and they had developed strong links with retail chains which took the bulk of their output. Not only were jobs more secure than they were in the many small firms in the area but wage rates were also relatively stable; there was none of the rate-cutting which characterized much of the industry. Second, both managements avoided an authoritarian approach; while there were differences between them, which we discuss later, both adopted a broadly paternalist policy. There are, of course, many strands to the concept of paternalism (Newby, 1977b: 63–70) and we can deal here only with the most important. Both managements stressed the strength of their personal ties with their workers. Thus the production director of the Hosiery Factory said that he toured the plant every day and that any worker could approach him with problems; and work schedules in the Underwear Factory were varied to meet the personal needs of individual workers. This approach was explicitly anti-bureaucratic and was related by managers to another feature of the situation which is often associated with paternalism, namely a small one-industry town in which everyone knows everyone else. Both plants were located in an area dominated by the clothing industry, and the strength of personal ties was felt to be significant not only by managers but also by shop stewards.

Traditions of paternalist concern for the work force, together with the benefits of fairly high and secure wages, meant that workers did not necessarily find their work dissatisfying. Although managerial control was, to the outside observer, more intense than that elsewhere, workers were absorbed into the industry's traditions. Many aspects of managerial control were thus likely to be taken for granted. The importance of the two factories for our wider concerns may thus be expressed in two questions. What effects did managerial control over the labour process have on patterns of worker behaviour? And how was a paternalistic system of control experienced, that is, how far were workers aware of the control system and what was their interpretation of it?

A subsidiary question is: are there differences within the broad type of control which we have called paternalist, and do they have identifiable effects? There were certainly differences between our two firms in their general philosophies of management, and some of these differences had an effect on the conduct of workplace relations. Yet the overall impression was one of similarity. We suggest in Chapter 3, for example, that the introduction of a self-consciously consultative style in the Underwear Factory had few effects on workers' attitudes to management. The main line of cleavage was not between management styles but between the forms of control exerted over the work of men and women; this contrast was present in both factories, but was most marked in the Hosiery Factory.

The Hosiery Factory

We have called the management style in the Hosiery Factory paternalist/ autocratic to indicate certain features of the factory's operations which seemed typical of the industry. Management expected to take decisions with little or no consultation with the shopfloor and to be able to deal with workers as individuals and not necessarily through union representatives. For example when some new machinery was to be introduced management discussed the matter with the workers who would be directly affected and not with the shop steward. Although redundancies were involved management did not see the issue as a collective matter: management took it for granted that it was reasonable to ask individual workers whether they were prepared to work on the new machines or whether they wanted to go redundant and, if agreement could be reached (as indeed it was), that was the end of the matter.

This is not to suggest that managers were simply anti-union. On the contrary, management not only recognized the union but actively encouraged workers to be members. And managers were generally enthusiastic about the good working relationship which existed with union officials. Yet this acceptance of the union's role largely referred to the union outside the plant. In addition to the union's role in standardizing wage rates, which is of course a well-known reason why managements in competitive industries accept unions, managers laid particular emphasis on the role of the district official in resolving shopfloor problems. Whenever a dispute arose management's first step was to call in the district official, with whom a close bargaining relationship was felt to exist. In other words managers did not see the union as an active participant in shopfloor relations; they expected to take most day-to-day decisions themselves. There were only two shop stewards in the Hosiery Factory, one representing the men in the 'knitting rooms' and one representing all the women in the plant, and their involvement in bargaining with management was slight.

A more important feature of the plant for our purposes lay in the different ways that the labour processes of male and female workers were organized. The contrast was, so far as we could judge, general throughout the industry but, given the small number of men employed in the Underwear Factory, we consider it in relation to the Hosiery Factory. There were about eighty male employees of whom the majority worked in the knitting rooms. Each knitter ran a bank of machines numbering up to thirty. He was responsible for setting up the machines, ensuring that they were running smoothly, and carrying out routine maintenance. If all his machines were running properly there was nothing for a knitter to do and he was therefore free to chat to his mates, have a cup of tea, or whatever. Since knitters could cover for each other for limited periods they could extend break times and otherwise exert some control over the way they did their work. This autonomy was strengthened by their employment on shifts: knitting was carried out round the clock for five days a week, with the shifts rotating weekly so that a man was on afternoons one week, mornings the next, and nights the third. For a considerable part of their working week they were therefore in the factory with no member of management present apart from the shop foreman.[7] But perhaps more important than

7. Out of 120 hours worked on a three-week cycle, 75 were outside the period from 8 a.m. to 5 p.m. when managers were normally in the plant.

these technological factors was the attitude of management: knitters were treated as responsible workers who had developed a considerable skill at their tasks and who were difficult to replace at short notice. They were therefore permitted more freedom than were women workers. Yet even this must be seen in context: knitters had substantially less ability to develop 'leisure in work' than did many of our engineering workers, and their freedom rested more on managerial tolerance than on any collective rights over mobility between jobs or overtime rotas.

There were about 120 women in the factory, employed on two main operations. The first was the preliminary sewing up of the garment; each operator worked as an individual performing tasks which, while requiring speed and dexterity, did not demand a high level of skill in terms of the time taken to learn the job. The standard training period was four weeks. The second operation was the preparation of garments prior to their completion in the firm's other factory. Some preparation work was done by hand and some involved machines but in both cases the work was extremely routine and monotonous with virtually no variation and the need for the exercise of very little skill. As noted earlier managerial control was considerable, covering not only starting and finishing times but also details of the way that the work was carried out. Women here and in the Underwear Factory were subject to far more direct and detailed control than any other group.

Although the clothing industry has a reputation for low wages, earnings levels, for women as well as men, were higher than might be expected. Knitters were paid a flat time rate, which stood at £76 a week in late 1979; a bonus related to production levels could bring in a further £4.[8] This rate was comparable with that in our engineering plants, although the shift premium was much lower: the maximum premium, for a week spent on nights, was only £6. The size of the shift allowance was certainly a source of complaint among workers, but the general level of wages was generally felt to be quite good; in particular, workers contrasted the stability of their earnings with the frequent lay-offs and periods of short time working in other industries. Women were on straight piecework so that, apart from small fall-back rates for machine breakdowns and the like, earnings varied directly with output. There was a wide range of earnings, with workers averaging, over a one-year period, as much as £85 or as little as £50 a week; the general range, however, was between £60 and £65 a week. Again these figures belie the industry's reputation for low wages, and, as we shall see, satisfaction with wages was an important reason for workers' lack of protest. Yet two qualifications must be made. First, women had to work extraordinarily hard to earn as much as £80 a week, and there

8. Note however that labourers and ancillary workers earned considerably less than this. Compare the figures given in note 2 above.

was no certainty that this figure could be maintained consistently. Second, a point which applies to men as much as to women, the firm offered none of the benefits available in our engineering plants such as guaranteed lay-off pay, sick benefit at average earnings, pensions, or generous redundancy entitlements. The value of these benefits is hard to quantify, but their presence makes the total 'earnings package' in the clothing industry less favourable than might at first appear.

The Underwear Factory

Company D which operated the Underwear Factory was, like Company C, a privately-owned business. It was even more directly 'owner controlled' in that members of the owning family were closely involved in the day-to-day running of the factory whereas in Company C the main owners concentrated on the financial and sales aspects of the business. Company D's managerial style had undergone a revolution a few years previously. Under its previous managers it had had an even more autocratic approach than the Hosiery Factory, as illustrated by management's traditional hostility to unionization. A younger generation of the owning family had taken over, however, and set out to create a more self-consciously 'modern' style. In the past there had been very few supervisors and all production problems had gone straight to the managing director. The present managing director recounted how he had spent all his time, as he himself put it, marching up and down berating the workers. He felt that this was inefficient and outdated and therefore appointed a production manager to take charge of day-to-day problems and greatly increased the number of supervisors. He was still to be seen on the shopfloor, however, and was certainly closely involved with the running of the factory.

The handling of industrial relations went through an equally dramatic change. The industrial union's weakness in the plant had led several workers to join the TGWU, an event which management, not surprisingly, regarded with concern. Management's response reveals a great deal about the role of the industrial union: notwithstanding his firm's tradition of hostility to the union, the managing director had been able to contact directly the general secretary to point out the danger which the incursion of the TGWU posed to the union's established position in the industry. The general secretary had persuaded the TGWU that it was in breach of the Bridlington Rules concerning the poaching of members, and the workers agreed to leave the TGWU as long as the industrial union was granted a closed shop. Management readily agreed to this and reported no difficulties with the arrangement.[9] This remarkable change, which led to the

---

9. Granting a closed shop to a favoured union is an obvious managerial tactic. During the course of our research we came across an engineering firm which had given the GMWU a closed shop, also to keep out the TGWU. But the precise chain of events in the Underwear

union's only closed shop in the district, was followed by a reform of domestic arrangements. More shop representatives were to be elected and a joint consultation committee was established. This committee had managerial and shopfloor representatives and met regularly to discuss any matters concerned with the running of the factory. For example, plans to re-organize and extend operations were thoroughly discussed in the committee and were also made widely available to all workers. This new openness and willingness to involve the shopfloor in decisions was in marked contrast to the Hosiery Factory.

Many aspects of managerial control remained unaffected, however. Management stressed that, despite the firm's relatively secure market position, competition always remained a threat and that it was essential to remain efficient. The general description of the intensity of work given earlier applied as much to the Underwear Factory as to the Hosiery Factory. Moreover the consultation committee was explicitly prevented from discussing anything to do with wages or piece rates. Piecework prices were still settled in the traditional way of management proposing a rate for a specific job to the workers who would perform the work; any dispute about the rate would go to the district official. The general wage level remained that set by the industry's national agreement.

Payment systems and wage levels were thus similar to those in the Hosiery Factory. The production system was rather different, however. There was only a small knitting room, employing in all about fifteen men. The material produced here was sewn up into garments by women in what was known as the traditional shop. An increasing part of the firm's business was carried out, however, by the 'modern shop': material was bought in from outside and used to produce a wide range of underwear and leisure wear. Unlike the Hosiery Factory, where each worker was performing the same operation as her neighbour, there was a whole sequence of operations from the basic fabric to the finished product. There was, however, no assembly line in the accepted sense, for workers were given batches of work which were then moved as a whole to the next operation; workers thus worked as individuals and not as members of teams. Jobs were generally more skilled than those in the Hosiery Factory, as indicated by the length of the formal training period: ten weeks as against four. Moreover, since there was a wide variety of operations and of styles of garment it could take a worker much longer than ten weeks to become fully skilled on the whole range of jobs.

Summary
These two clothing factories provide a wealth of contrasts with engineering. They were, for example, the only plants operating systems of straight piecework.

Factory is probably unusual and illustrates the variety of phenomena falling under the rubric of the closed shop. For the general benefits which management derive from the closed shop see Hart (1979).

Yet the key difference lay in patterns of control, for they were marked by intense managerial control over all aspects of work and by a limited union presence on the shopfloor. At the same time, however, there were differences within the broad pattern of paternalism; in particular the forms of control exerted over men and women were very different.

Process Production

As noted earlier the main significance of our final plant, which we have called the Process Factory, lies in the way in which management sought the compliance of its workers. Managerial philosophy revolved around the idea of avoiding the 'them and us' attitude which was felt to bedevil much of industry. Consultation and discussion were its hallmark. There was a complex hierarchy of joint consultation committees, ranging from meetings at foreman level through plant-level committees to meetings at the highest company level to inform stewards of investment plants and the like. As noted above, part of this philosophy involved treating workers as responsible people. Work groups were allowed, and indeed encouraged, to plan their own work, and foremen were seen more as advisers than as people who would give direct orders to subordinates. Associated reforms included the abolition of time clocks and generous schemes to protect earnings. Thus workers were paid a basic annual salary which was not affected by lay-offs, and they were entitled to sick pay at full earnings for an absence of any length.

In terms of the detailed planning of work, and of such formal rights as the recognition of a full-time shop steward and the check-off of union dues, workers faced a situation which was similar to that of workers in our engineering plants; indeed, some aspects of work group autonomy and, in particular, the scheme to guarantee earnings were well in advance of engineering practice. Yet these advances were restricted to the two areas of the allocation of specific work tasks as between workers and of the broad package of wages and fringe benefits. As Goodrich (1975: 54) acutely pointed out in his classic study of the frontier of control, there are crucial aspects of the wage bargain which fall outside these areas. Specific examples include manning levels, the mobility of labour between one work group and another, the amount and distribution of overtime, and the operation of factory discipline. On these matters shop stewards had established few rights, either formally or at the level of custom and practice. Indeed, management's stress on consultation included the principle of consulting all workers or at least representatives chosen for the purpose. Trade union matters were limited to the wage rate and similar issues, and shop stewards were not used as the sole means of communication with the work force. In Company A, by contrast, a 'sophisticicated negotiatory', as against a 'sophisticated consultative', managerial style was based on use of stewards as the main, and generally the only, means of discussing proposals with the shopfloor. In many respects, then, the frontier of control remained within managerial control. The company can be seen as a prime example of the dictum that management 'can only regain control by sharing it' (Flanders, 1970: 172): particular aspects of control were given to, and not won by, workers with the aim of strengthening management's position.

The Process Factory was known throughout the company as one in which the consultation system was well-established and in which shopfloor workers accepted the need for change. Managers were proud of a record of continuously increasing productivity and of amicable industrial relations. The plant had been established about twenty years before our research began to meet a rapidly growing demand for man-made fibres. There were about 1500 manual workers of whom the great majority were production operatives; they all belonged to one union which had a full-time convener. There were several craft unions, although the great majority of craftsmen were in the AUEW. These unions constituted an informal craft group with its own convener, but there was no joint shop stewards' committee comprising craft and production stewards.

The plant's production was turned out in a continuous stream, and it was therefore necessary to operate round the clock for seven days a week. Workers were employed on the 'Continental' shift system: there were four separate shifts, with the shift pattern of each rotating in a complex cycle lasting four weeks. The system was identical to that described by Nichols and Armstrong (1976: 28–9) and we do not need to go into its details, except to note that workers worked for seven consecutive days between rest periods and that each spell of seven days included days on mornings, afternoon and nights. The disruption to normal routines was considerable; for example a worker would have one week-end off in four. This was quite unlike the experience of workers in any of our other factories.

Although operating a continuous process technology, the plant did not fit the common picture of such a technology in which workers watch dials and push buttons. The great majority of production operatives were employed on routine manual tasks which were carried out in conditions of considerable heat or extreme noise. The first set of tasks involved the setting up and minding of machines which produced the basic material. In the second set the material was spun onto bobbins, the workers' task being to connect up each bobbin at the start of a machine run and to remove and pack the bobbins when they were full. Since the machines ran untended once they had been set up workers could create leisure for themselves by doing their operations on one machine as quickly as possible, thus earning a break before the next machine had to be dealt with. Workers were divided into teams, each of which was responsible for a bank of machines. How and when they did their work was up to them, as long as they attained the standard times which had been established for each series of operations.

The basic wage rate, of £79 a week for a semi-skilled worker in late 1979, was similar to that in our other factories. It was supplemented in several ways, however. The premium for Continental shifts raised the wage to £102, and there was a bonus related to company sales, which was guaranteed between certain limits and which brought in, on average, a further £7 a week. A profit-sharing scheme for long-serving workers could add to this, and there were other fringe benefits such as subsidized transport. And, as we have seen, the guaranteed wage and the sick pay scheme gave workers a considerably greater degree of income security than that enjoyed by workers in our other plants. The plant was, moreover, located in a traditionally low-paying area and had always been near the top of the local earnings league, although there was some feeling that it had slipped back somewhat in recent years.

Workers were, then, rewarded quite well for performing mundane tasks in a hot or noisy environment and subject to the substantial dislocation of continuous shift work. Management recognized that there were potential sources of friction, and indeed explicitly saw its consultative style, together of course with the material benefits that were provided, as a means of minimizing conflict. Yet such a style is not without dangers for management, for if joint consultation comes to be interpreted as giving the shopfloor the right to veto proposed changes then it may involve a shift of the frontier of control in the shopfloor's favour. As we will see in later chapters, there were areas where this had begun to happen. Craft workers for example were seen as a particular problem for management. Yet the absence of a strong shop steward organization among production workers, together with the effectiveness of management's policy of by-passing union organization, limited the extent of any widespread challenge to managerial control.

Conclusion

We have described a range of ways in which the labour process is organized. At one extreme there was the fairly intense managerial control over all aspects of work which was associated with the paternalist approach of the two clothing plants. At the other extreme there was the negotiatory approach of the four engineering plants, although within this approach there were substantial differences between the considerable control which stewards had attained in both Company B plants and the rather lower level of shopfloor involvement achieved by their counterparts in Company A. Finally the Process Factory exemplifies a different means of obtaining compliance, based on consultation and participation.

This is to present, however, a very static picture whereas we stressed in Chapter 1 the possibility that the frontier of control can shift. Throughout the following discussion we therefore try to take account of the origin of the practices which we describe and of changes which were taking place. The following chapter, for example, discusses the changing significance of labour turnover in the Large Metals Factory as a response to the plant's decline in the local earnings league. Similarly, in discussing managerial control in the Process Factory we argue that relatively favourable market circumstances during the 1960s and early 1970s helped to create an amicable atmosphere in which management made few direct demands and in which shop stewards could appear powerful. By the end of the 1970s, however, pressures on costs forced management to take a much more aggressive stance, and several changes in working practices were made with very little organized opposition. We thus try to take account of changes over time where these were particularly significant, and we discuss the general question of changes in 'shopfloor power' in the final chapter. Our main task, however, is to compare different factories to explore the ways in which workplace behaviour is constituted into various 'forms of conflict' under various types of control system.

3

Labour Turnover

The expression of discontent is not limited to direct, vocalized protest: quietly to leave a situation can be an important way of expressing dissatisfaction with it (Hirschman, 1970). In this chapter we examine patterns of quitting before considering, in later chapters, the various forms of conflict within the workplace.

Turnover has, of course, been studied from a large number of perspectives. Bowey (1976: 188) for example lists eleven ways in which 'labour wastage' can occur. These different ways tend to be the concern of different disciplines, with quitting to increase wages being the preserve of the economist, leaving as a result of 'interpersonal conflict' being the concern of the social psychologist, and so on. One result of this disciplinary fragmentation has been that the significance of quitting as such has been lost; it has been seen as one element in a model of 'wage adjustment processes' for example (Addison and Burton, 1978) and not as an important phenomenon in its own right. In claiming to present a more adequate view we do not suggest that we can bring together the (at least) eleven different aspects. Indeed our aim is to move away from rather arid lists of types of turnover. We look at quitting in the context of workplace relations, asking how different patterns of turnover reflected the organization of the labour process. This requires us to do two things. First, we examine turnover statistics to provide a picture of the pattern of quitting. The metaphor of a pattern must be taken seriously, for there is no simple index which can reveal all the relevant aspects of turnover and a proper picture has to be built up using several indices. Second, we turn to workers' perceptions of their jobs, in particular their views of the desirability and possibility of quitting. Such attitudinal data do not, of course, tell us directly about the motivations of leavers for they are derived from interviews with workers who have not left. Our aim, however, was not to discover what aspects of work were felt to be dissatisfying by those who left but to relate patterns of quitting to patterns of shopfloor relations. Our data allow us to make a general assessment of the sources of attachment to work, and this is more central to our overall concerns than the attitudes of leavers for it obviously helps us to discover how far and in what ways relationships were felt to be conflictual.

We do not expect an intimate connection between the organization of the labour process and quit rates. As noted above quitting reflects a variety of forces and we do not, therefore, expect a neat pattern of low quit rates where the frontier of control was most in the workers' favour and higher rates where managerial control was greater. We argue that a broader pattern of association was present and in particular that the nature of managerial control over women's work in the clothing industry explains the distinctive patterns of turnover and of worker attitudes which we observed. The labour force displayed a remarkable rate of turnover, and current employees' attitudes to work reflected some discontent with the way in which they were controlled. We therefore give particular attention to the situation here, arguing that certain conventional expectations about the nature of attachment to work in small paternalistic firms are mistaken and that our own argument is correspondingly strengthened.

In analysing patterns of turnover we adopt a thorough-going comparative approach: we move through various aspects of those patterns, giving comparative data for each plant. We do not, however, need to describe in detail every aspect of turnover in each factory. The contrast between the clothing plants and the others comes through consistently, and analysing more specific variations would serve little purpose. There are, however, three other themes which appear in the course of the discussion and which need highlighting in advance. First, turnover rates in the Large Metals Factory were increasing rapidly as a result of widespread discontent over wage levels. This unprecedented quitting was an expression of a collective sense of grievance but also a reflection of the weakness of plant-level collective controls in the face of external pressures on wages. Second, in this plant, and more particularly in the Small Metals Factory, there were substantial numbers of workers who, while highly dissatisfied with their wages, did not leave. It is an obvious but neglected point that low quit rates do not necessarily imply 'satisfaction'; we provide documentation of this. It is also obvious that there are constraints on a strategy of exit, and we indicate the power of those constraints: workers felt that they could not afford to take the risks of leaving and hence felt trapped in a situation which gave them no satisfaction. Third, and in direct contrast to this, we relate turnover patterns in the Process Factory to management's sophisticated control strategy. This strategy enabled managers to do two things: to keep the volume of turnover within narrow bounds, and to persuade workers that quitting could be seen in terms of individuals' inability to come to terms with the shift system, with the result that possible collective challenges were prevented.

We begin by examining turnover figures. This is followed by a consideration of workers' attitudes, while the concluding section of the chapter outlines the implications of turnover as an aspect of conflict.

Turnover and Stability

The argument about how best to measure turnover has a long and largely inconclusive history. The central points are summarized in Appendix A, which also contains an indication of the nature of our own data. In our view there is no one best way to measure the phenomenon, and we deploy a range of indices moving from simple rates of turnover to data on the survival rates of cohorts of workers entering our factories at different times. Our concern with turnover is thus not limited to quitting on its own. We need to consider the stability of the work force, most obviously since it has long been recognized that a factory characterized by instability is less likely to develop a strong shopfloor organization than is one where the majority of workers have been present for many years: this has obvious implications for the discussion of collective action in later chapters.

Crude Turnover Rates

The crude turnover rate simply gives the number of leavers during a period as a proportion of the total number of employees at the start of the period. As is well-known, it is likely to be influenced by patterns of recruitment: leaving tends to be concentrated among short-service workers, and heavy recruitment will therefore be followed by increased quit rates. But this does not prevent use of the index. If the observer is aware of the problem, proper account can be taken of it. For example, the fluctuations in turnover rates in the Process Factory shown in Table 3.1 can be largely attributed to recruitment patterns; thus we do not infer that the expression of conflict through quitting fluctuated as the bald figures might seem to suggest. More generally, if trends in crude turnover rates cannot be explained away in terms of recruitment patterns some 'genuine' effect can be inferred.

For a study of quitting as a form of conflict, leaving of one's own accord is plainly more important than leaving through retirement or ill health. We have therefore calculated indices of 'voluntary' turnover wherever possible, by excluding the categories of death and ill health, retirement, dismissal, and redundancy from overall rates. Neither clothing plant, however, had records which enabled voluntary and involuntary quitting to be distinguished, and we therefore give the overall rates for our other plants for comparative purposes. The dividing line between voluntary and involuntary separations, in any event, is far from clear, as is most obvious in the case of 'voluntary redundancy', and overall rates thus deserve attention in their own right.

As Table 3.1 shows, turnover rates varied dramatically. Among women in the clothing plants quit rates were generally over 25 per cent whereas rates elsewhere were usually around 10 per cent. This simple contrast is apparently

TABLE 3.1

TRENDS IN CRUDE LABOUR TURNOVER RATES

| | Electrical | | | | Components | | Large Metals | | Small Metals[a] | | Hosiery | | Underwear | Process | |
| | Men | | Women | | Men | | Men | | | | Men | Women | All[b] | Men | |
	All	Vol.	All	Vol.	All	Vol.	All	Vol.	All	Vol.	All	All	All	All	Vol.
1970	59.9	49.6	42.8	36.8	11.4	6.5	7.7	0.6						4.9	3.0
1971	35.2	27.2	26.3	22.4	9.1	5.9	3.6	0.6						4.8	2.0
1972	18.8	16.0	16.2	13.9	13.6	7.7	6.2	1.9			72.6c	30.0		6.0	3.1
1973	25.9	21.0	20.9	17.2	12.5	8.6	6.5	1.8	12.0	5.6	63.6c	39.4		12.5	9.0
1974	23.0	18.4	24.6	21.7	20.6	4.2	13.0	1.4	6.1	2.9	71.4c	41.9	25.4	14.1	9.5
1975	34.6	11.6	25.8	9.4	6.1	2.9	3.9	2.0	10.1	1.0	44.7	37.0	36.4	7.8	3.5
1976	10.8	8.7	6.8	5.7	9.9	6.0	8.6	4.5	3.9	0.8	22.3	23.2	27.3	6.9	1.9
1977	15.7	13.1	9.1	7.9	9.8	4.1	6.7	4.0	6.7	4.0	16.0	31.0	34.7	7.2	2.4
1978									7.4	2.4	22.7	27.6	33.3	10.6	4.7
1979							23.6	9.8			19.5	20.9	28.0	11.6	4.9

NOTES

a. No women employed in this factory.

b. The small numbers of men in this plant mean that the figures can be taken as an approximation of women's turnover rates.

c. The accuracy of these figures is hard to establish, given difficulties with obtaining estimates of labour force size.

contradicted by two things: the high rates among men in the clothing industry, and the high rates for both men and women in the Electrical Factory during the early 1970s. The second point is the more easily dealt with: the Electrical Factory was newly-established in 1970, which meant that the vast majority of its workers were new recruits. There was no established core of long-serving workers, and early quit rates cannot be taken as typical.[1] On the first point, quit rates among men were certainly high. This reflects two separate patterns: relatively low rates among the core group, the knitters, and higher rates among ancillary workers. Difficulties with labour force statistics prevent us from making any precise comparison of these patterns, but inspection of the data, together with evidence which we present below on such things as the length of service characteristics of current employees, suggests that they diverged significantly. Ancillary workers formed the majority of the male labour force, and their high quit rate can be explained in terms of the fairly direct managerial control which was exercised over them and their low level of wages as compared to the wages available for similar work in other industries. Even this statement is complicated, however, by differences between those ancillary workers who worked in the knitting rooms and who were under little direct control and those who worked as labourers elsewhere and who were much more immediately subject to managerial authority. Exploring these differences would take us too far away from our main concerns. In some respects patterns of turnover among men reflected forces similar to those operating among women, but the contrasts between groups of men make it simplest to concentrate on the relatively straightforward picture for women.

In view of this pattern it might be expected that managers in the clothing plants would see quitting by women and ancillary workers as a great problem. Yet managers did not feel that they had a 'turnover problem' despite an annual loss of between a fifth and a quarter of their workers. Still less did they see quitting as a reflection of workers' discontents or as a protest action.[2] This can

---

1. In addition to the Electrical and Components Factories we were able to examine turnover rates in two Company A plants which employed between them about 900 women. Turnover rates in both were about 12 per cent, and the contrast with the clothing industry is thus strengthened.

2. Here and elsewhere we summarize what 'managers' or 'workers' thought on a particular issue, and it may be helpful for us to spell out our approach to the presentation of this material. We try to bring out the key point, in this case that managers did not perceive a problem of turnover, perhaps using an illustrative comment or two. But our central concern is not with attitudes, and it would add little to our argument to give lengthy quotations from what managers told us. We might create an image of 'telling it like it is' but it is doubtful what else might be achieved; indeed, the reader would have no way of knowing whether our selected quotes were in any way typical or even of whether we had made them up. The use of chunks of quotation has been much in vogue recently. Yet quotes plainly do not speak for themselves: it is their selection and interpretation which is important. Partly in an attempt to avoid this style of reporting we have preferred to give our interpretation direct, backing it up where appropriate with comments which appear to be particularly revealing.

be explained by two factors. First, turnover presents itself as a problem to management if it is difficult to recruit new workers or expensive to train them. Managers had few problems of labour supply since, in an area dominated by the clothing industry, there were plenty of workers with some experience in the industry and no other industries which could offer comparable wages for 'women's work'.[3] Second, if they were forced to think about turnover, managers had a ready explanation in terms of the composition of the labour force: women could be expected to leave because of family or domestic commitments. As one manager in the Hosiery Factory put it, few of his 'girls' left unless it was for such understandable reasons as marriage or pregnancy. Turnover was, he felt, highest among young girls who would try the work for a while and leave if they were not suited to a factory environment. This view that there is an 'induction crisis', whereby workers either leave quickly or survive the crisis and then stay for long spells, is of course a central feature of the literature on turnover; we assess it later. Apart from the intriguing but secondary point that a notion of induction crisis was part of 'everyday' as well as academic theorizing about quitting, its present significance is that it gave managers a means of explaining away turnover. Quitting was not the result of any failings on their own part but was the result of some workers' finding that they were not suited to work in a factory. More generally, a certain amount of turnover could be expected when the workers were women; again quitting was explained in 'natural' and not conflictual terms.

The argument that women 'naturally' have a high quit rate requires further consideration: if turnover can be written off as a reflection of labour force composition our argument that it was, on the contrary, an outcome of the pattern of control of the labour process is compromised. At the most general level it is plainly unsatisfactory to take it for granted that women behave in a certain way because they are women. More specifically, it may be true as a matter of fact that women tend to leave for domestic reasons but this explains neither the difference between women in the clothing and engineering industries nor the high quit rate of men in the former industry. On the question of labour force composition, the situation is complicated by differences in the age structures of the work forces. Many of the women in the clothing industry were young and were thus more likely to leave for family reasons than were their counterparts in engineering. But we doubt whether this can account for more than part of the difference in quit rates; and in any event our view of the

3. Managers in the Underwear Factory modified this argument in view of problems they had experienced in recruiting to meet increased production schedules. But their problem was the lack of skilled workers, not a general inability to recruit in the desired numbers. The problem was not related by managers to the 'problem' of high quit rates; and, in any event, turnover was high before the recruitment drive and cannot be attributed solely to the recent increase in the number of recruits.

clothing industry relies on several other indices which we discuss below. And the high quit rate among men is plainly consistent with the view that there was a 'genuine' difference between industries. Or, more precisely, men in the clothing industry fell into two groups: the knitters, who were treated as responsible workers by management and who formed the stable core of the workforce, and ancillary workers whose wages were relatively low and who were subject to more intense control. The high quit rate for men as a whole reflects the behaviour of the latter group.

The contrast with the Large Metals Factory could hardly be greater. As noted in Chapter 2, this was a traditionally well-paying plant, and there had been little reason for workers to want to leave once they had been lucky enough to obtain jobs there. There had been a dramatic change in the situation, however. The plant's rapid decline in the local earnings league had created an extraordinary amount of discontent. The universal response of workers was that low wages were their main grievance. Men complained, for example, that the basic rate in a nearby factory was £25 a week higher than their own, and many said that the only way to earn a 'living wage' was to rely on overtime. Associated with this was a general complaint that measured day work had removed all incentives to work harder, a point which we assess in more detail in later chapters. 'Apathy' was a word commonly used to describe workers' opinions; one group of semi-skilled workers said that their own morale was at 'rock bottom', while a skilled supervisor said that the morale of his workers had reached 'zero'. Workers were, moreover, aware of increasing quit rates: several pointed out that it used to be a very rare event for someone to leave voluntarily but that this was now a common occurrence. The reason was, in their view, obvious: better wages were available elsewhere. In our other factories workers (and managers) advanced particular reasons why people might quit: perhaps they did not like shift work, or maybe they had domestic responsibilities. By contrast in both the Large Metals and Small Metals Factories workers produced an explanation of turnover as a reflection of more general, and indeed collective, discontents.

This raises three questions. First, what was the reason for the collapse of morale which lay behind increasing quit rates? We have suggested that the answer lies in the company's worsening economic performance and in the change in the payment system. Since we are concerned here with the effects and not the causes of the collapse of morale this is sufficient for present purposes; we go into the origins of the problem, and the enormous range of its effects, in later chapters. A supplementary question takes the issue further back: why did the firm allow such a dramatic slide down the wages league? We suggested in Chapter 2 that the slide could be seen as part of a 'regressive spiral' in which the firm tried to tackle its production and profitability problems. The logic of the company management's situation (Jarvie, 1972) required an attempt to control costs so as to re-establish profitability, the unintended consequence being a severe fall in relative earnings. The collapse of morale was, in turn, unforeseen but, given the firm's overriding aims and the situation in which it found itself, there was little that could be done to correct the situation.[4]

The second question is: if workers were so discontented why was the quit rate not even higher? And, third, since workers in the Small Metals and Large Metals Factories were very similar in terms of their dissatisfaction with their wages, why were quit rates so much lower in the former plant than in the latter? The answer to both these questions depends on an argument about the relationship between quitting and an individual's needs. Quitting has been seen as the product of two forces: the individual's desire to maximize the net balance of benefits over costs in any employment, and the opportunities of finding another job (Price, 1975: 66-7). As we will see when we consider workers' attitudes in detail, those in the Small Metals Factory felt that their jobs retained important benefits, particularly redundancy and related rights, which helped to outweigh the 'cost' of unsatisfactory wages. And there were not always opportunities of moving to new jobs. There were few skilled crafts-men in the Small Metals Factory and, since it was generally easier for these workers to find other jobs than for semi-skilled workers to do so, part of the difference between the factories may be due to differences in labour force composition.

In the Large Metals Factory crude turnover rates were certainly differed between occupational groups, as Table 3.2 shows. There was a rapid increase in the quit rate among toolmakers and skilled production workers. The growth of voluntary quitting was particularly marked after 1977: during 1979 over one-sixth of craft workers left of their own accord. Rates for semi-skilled

---

4. This case throws an interesting light on the concept of the regressive spiral. Legge (1970) uses the notion to explain behaviour in a garment factory: the firm tried to operate in an intensely competitive market by controlling costs and meeting delivery dates. This led to pressure on wages and short production runs as production was switched between lines to meet changing orders. The resulting job changing reduced workers' earnings and led to a perceived imbalance in the effort bargain, which in turn led to quitting. Legge suggests that market-oriented firms, using labour-intensive technologies and operating in competi-tive product markets and tight labour markets, tend to enter regressive spirals when labour costs are seen as decisive in costing. Our results from the Large Metals Factory suggest that this result is not limited to the intensely competitive markets characteristic of the clothing industry: even large firms with considerable market power can enter profitability crises, and pressure on labour costs is the likely result. Our clothing firms seem to have avoided regressive spirals for two reasons: there was a ready supply of labour, and their established positions with major customers meant that they did not enter a cycle of cost-cutting and short production runs. There are varieties of 'competitive' conditions which have to be distinguished before their implications for workplace relations can be understood: the particular constraints faced by firms, and the precise character of their response in terms of labour costs, cannot be read off from features of the external market such as the number of firms in an industry or similar indices of competitive conditions.

workers were considerably lower.[5] A dramatic illustration of the quitting
of craftsmen, many of whom had lengthy periods of employment and who
were thus giving up substantial redundancy rights, was provided by one of
the craft conveners who, in addition to the rights associated with his thirty
years' service, gave up his influential position on the Conveners' Committee
to take semi-skilled work paying considerably more than his craft job.

TABLE 3.2

**LARGE METALS FACTORY: RATES OF VOLUNTARY TURNOVER
IN SELECTED OCCUPATIONS**

(Per Cent)

	1971	1973	1976	1977	1978	1979
Toolmakers	0.2	0.5	1.8	3.3	4.1	18.2
Other crafts	0.3	0.8	2.3	4.2	6.0	17.4
Skilled production	1.2	4.4	3.7	9.1	7.7	12.6
Semi-skilled assembly	0.1	1.0	3.2	3.8	2.8	3.5
Semi-skilled machine op.	0.9	6.2	4.5	12.7	10.0	11.5

This remarkable loss of valuable skilled workers is only partially attributable
to the relatively favourable labour market position of these workers. Indeed,
one aspect of the phenomenon which was widely discussed was that workers
were taking jobs outside their own trades; one young toolmaker was leaving to
become a policeman, and several similar cases were widely mentioned. The key
factor in the growth of quit rates was that the collapse of morale was even
greater than it was among less skilled workers. Skilled men, and particularly
toolmakers, felt that they had been totally let down by the company, which
made noises about the importance of skills but did nothing to recognize them.
Our fieldwork notes of interviews in the toolroom record universal condemnation of the company. One toolmaker, for example, said that in the past it had
been very hard to obtain a job in the Large Metals Factory since hiring standards
had been very strict, but it had been worth it because it was a 'good shop' with a
good atmosphere. Yet in the space of a few years he had seen morale 'plummet'
to an 'all time low'. Like those of many other workers his criticisms extended
from wage levels to conditions of employment more generally: he described
aspects of employment such as clocking in and sick pay arrangements as 'dis-
gusting' and felt that the company treated its manual workers 'like second class
citizens'. This wider criticism was rare among less skilled workers, and it reflects

5. The increase for machine operators can be attributed to heavy recruitment of these
workers during 1977 and 1978.

toolmakers' expectations that they would be treated as responsible craftsmen. The intensity of discontent also owed a great deal to the failure of various attempts by toolmakers within the Large Metals Factory to resist what they saw as the company's attempt to impose new bargaining arrangements on them: in the past toolmakers had bargained separately from the rest of the plant but this had been replaced by a system in which toolmakers felt swamped by the great mass of semi-skilled workers, and there had been several disputes about this. Toolmakers thus felt defeated and angry.

Apart from the increasing quit rate, two other aspects of this situation are important. First, quitting was merely part of a set of responses. Many toolmakers said that their main way of expressing their grievances was to chat to their mates instead of working, to work without enthusiasm, and generally to reduce their level of effort; as a standard saying had it, 'part time wages deserve part time work'. As we show in more detail in Chapter 7, this reduction of effort was widespread and was, toolmakers felt, the result of such great discontent that it was impossible to motivate oneself to work properly. Second, toolroom managers shared the workers' perspective. They were well aware of the reduction of effort but felt that it was an entirely understandable response by men whose skills they respected. They made few attempts to control the behaviour, for they were painfully aware that any clamp-down would merely result in more men leaving. Indeed, they actively encouraged workers to do as much overtime as they wanted in the hope of tempting them to stay. In other words, managers' response to their undoubted turnover problem was to acquiesce in shopfloor practices which would not otherwise have been tolerated.

The growth of quitting was particularly notable since it was occurring at a time of rising unemployment. It is widely assumed that turnover rates will vary inversely with the unemployment rate since high unemployment means that there are few alternative jobs (see Hyman, 1970: 160–3). To assess this, we calculated crude turnover rates on a quarterly basis and compared them, over a nine-year period, with the local unemployment rate.[6] There was, contrary to the usual assumption, a positive correlation ($r = +0.37$) between the voluntary quit rate and the unemployment rate. Moreover, in the Electrical Factory and in one of our other Company A plants, negative correlations, albeit small ones, were obtained. This test is certainly far from conclusive: we were unable to compare occupation-specific quit rates with relevant unemployment rates, and thus the positive correlation between unemployment and quitting in the aggregate may have obscured a different relationship in the case of, say, toolmaking jobs. But at least some skilled men left for semi-skilled jobs, which suggests that the availability of jobs in general and not of jobs in a specific occupation may after all be the best indicator of labour market conditions.

6. We are grateful to the local Department of Employment office for unemployment data.

And the wider significance of unemployment must not be forgotten: plant closures and increasing insecurity were being widely discussed, and anyone who left for another job was not only giving up an established position but was also risking unemployment in the future with no cushion of redundancy rights. The rapid increase in quit rates plainly reflected such intense discontent that workers saw leaving as their only option despite a worsening economic climate.

Here, then, quitting undoubtedly reflected 'conflict': in the terms introduced in Chapter 1 such conflict was overt in that workers were leaving because they were extremely dissatisfied with their wages and because they blamed the company for the position in which they found themselves. Leaving was, moreover, an expression of collective discontents: workers still with the firm shared the dissatisfaction of the leavers, quitting was seen as a rational response to shared problems and not as an individual's inability to come to terms with the work environment, and the behaviour was a focus of concern for workers and managers alike. This great shared sense of grievance was in part the product, we suggest, of previous shared pride in collective controls. Hence toolmakers said that in the past their toolroom had been the best in the area: high paid, well disciplined, and turning out good products to schedule. Yet managers and workers now felt that all this had been lost. In terms of our wider argument this implies two things. First, collective controls over the labour process may be a precondition for the emergence of turnover as a genuinely collective expression of conflict. But, second, such expression is required only because those controls are no longer able to yield acceptable outcomes. As we argued in Chapter 1, the frontier of control is neither static nor unidimensional. In this case the frontier had shifted away from the shopfloor on the dimension of wages. As we shall see in later chapters this certainly did not mean that collective controls were seen as being less effective than they were in the past.

Although workers were now leaving in increasing numbers, until very recently the Large Metals Factory had been marked by the great stability of its work force, which was plainly one factor in the development of collective attitudes. We now consider this further by examining the stability of the labour force in our factories.

Labour Force Stability

The simplest indicator of the stability of the labour force is the distribution of the current employees by length of service: this is given in Table 3.3. Not too much should be read into the detailed figures, for they represent a snap-shot view and, like the crude turnover rate, are obviously affected by patterns of recruitment. But the general picture is clear. Thus the 'traditionalist' Small Metals Factory had a highly stable work force, with over 60 per cent of the workers having been in the plant for over ten years. Long-serving employees

TABLE 3.3

LENGTH OF SERVICE CHARACTERISTICS OF CURRENT EMPLOYEES

	Electrical		Components	Large Metals	Small Metals	Hosiery		Underwear		Process
	Men	Women	All	Men	All	Men[a]	Women	Men	Women	Men
Under 3 months	2.1	2.2	0.3	1.1	0.6	5.4	9.0	11.9	4.7	2.9
3–12 months	8.9	2.3	3.1	4.4	1.2	7.2	18.1	19.1	25.6	8.6
1–2 years	21.5	18.3	7.2	10.6	7.3	12.6	10.7	2.4	13.8	1.1
2–3 years	3.7	0.7	9.5	12.4	15.1	3.6	1.6	4.8	9.4	0.6
3–5 years	13.5	26.1	10.8	6.9	4.2	3.6	9.8	11.9	11.3	5.8
5–7 years	9.8	19.3	9.3	6.3	4.2	17.1	23.8			9.5
7–10 years	28.0	23.7	14.6	7.9	7.6	17.1	19.7			6.9
10–20 years	12.4	7.3	30.2	17.1	43.8	18.9	4.1	33.3[b]	25.6[b]	64.7
Over 20 years			15.0	33.1	15.7	13.5	0.8	16.7	9.7	0
D.K.	0	0	0	0.2	0.3	0	2.5			0
Number in sample	428	809	697	894[c]	332[d]	111	122	42	320	380[e]
Number employees	428	809	697	6300	664	111	122	42	320	1525

NOTES
a. Includes all labourers in Company C, not just those in the Hosiery Factory.
b. More detailed breakdown not available.
c. Random samples among grades of workers at all skill levels, weighted to be representative of these grades as a whole.
d. Random 50 per cent sample of all workers.
e. Random 25 per cent sample of all workers.

were also predominant in the Large Metals, Components, and Process Factories. Such stability was an important pre-requisite, although not, as we shall see, a sufficient condition, for the emergence of collective controls over the labour process.

In the clothing factories this condition was absent: 30 per cent of female workers had been present for less than a year.[7] Short periods of service were also more common among men than was the case in engineering, but this overall picture contained two different elements. Knitters generally had long periods of service: 48 per cent of the group comprising knitters and knitting room inspectors in the Hosiery Factory had been with the firm for ten years or more. By contrast, only 12 per cent of ancillary workers and labourers had been in the plant for ten years or more, while 22 per cent of them had been with the firm for less than a year. This pattern helps to explain not only why managers did not see turnover as a problem but also argued, perhaps surprisingly, that their work force tended to be stable. Knitters were the key group and were given a significance out of proportion to their numbers. Moreover, and this is a point which is easily neglected, workers who stay in a plant a short time are not very visible. While workers staying six months or a year will obviously become known to their immediate work mates, managers are unlikely to know them on personal terms. Hence when managers think of their workers they are more likely to recall only the familiar faces, forgetting the changing background of unfamiliar ones.

While data on the current labour force say something about workers remaining with a firm, they give no direct indication of the characteristics of leavers: is leaving limited to those with little experience in a plant or is it a more widespread phenomenon? The argument that leaving tends to be concentrated among short-service workers has been given the clearest theoretical rationale by Hill (1951; 1972, and 1975). Hill sees quitting as one aspect of a person's relationship with a firm: coming to terms with a job is a lengthy process, and workers who do not complete the 'induction crisis' successfully will leave, while those who survive the crisis will settle down for long periods. While this may be true in general, our factories displayed substantial variations in the extent of the induction crisis, as Table 3.4 shows. For example, in the clothing plants over 40 per cent of leavers had stayed for less than six months, while the comparable figure in the Process Factory was 12 per cent.

Thus the clothing industry again had a distinctive pattern marked by a high degree of volatility. Now it might appear that we are exaggerating this: the overall differences from the Company A plants shown in Table 3.4 were small

---

7. No information was available for several workers in the Underwear Factory. This reflected incomplete record-keeping in the past, and most of the 'don't know' category can be presumed to have had five or more years' service.

TABLE 3.4

LENGTH OF SERVICE OF LEAVERS

(Per Cent)

	Electrical Men	Electrical Women	Components Men	Large Metals[a] Men	Small Metals[a] Men	Hosiery Men	Hosiery Women	Underwear Women	Process Men
Coverage of sample	8 years	8 years	9 years	1 year	4 years	1 year	1 year	1 year	4 years
Number of sample	757	1113	1049	180	90	63	185	184	474
Under 1 month	11.2	4.4	11.4	3.2	4.5	17.5	17.8	19.0	2.1
1–3 months	13.5	11.2	9.5	2.1	6.8	11.1	16.2	9.2	4.6
3–6 months	12.9	12.4	10.3	10.6	9.1	14.3	12.4	15.8	4.9
6–12 months	14.1	15.2	11.5	18.1	21.6	12.7	11.4	18.5	5.5
1–2 years	16.1	19.6	12.1	16.0	15.9	15.9	14.1	13.0	3.0
2–3 years	8.9	11.6	6.1	8.5	2.3	4.8	4.9	9.8	2.1
3–5 years	12.0	16.2	10.1	18.1	5.7	7.9	8.1	7.1	4.4
5–7 years	7.8		6.5	2.1	3.4	6.3	7.0		3.8
7–10 years	2.4	9.4	6.1	12.8	9.1	3.2	1.1	7.6	2.7
Over 10 years	1.1		16.2	8.5	21.6	6.4	7.0		66.9

NOTE
a. Voluntary leavers only.

and, since figures for these latter plants include substantial numbers of long-serving workers who were made redundant, the picture for voluntary leavers might in fact be similar to that in the clothing plants. However, our data on Company A span a period of years over which the characteristics of leavers changed considerably. This is illustrated in the case of the Electrical Factory by Table 3.5, which shows that in the early years of the plant three-quarters of women leavers were employed for less than six months, a figure which had fallen to under 20 per cent by the end of the period. Part of this trend may be attributed to the recent establishment of the plant, but this is unlikely to be the whole explanation: in the long-established Components Factory a similar process was at work, with the proportion of voluntary leavers with under six months' service falling from 68 per cent to 10 per cent. A comparison of voluntary leavers during 1979 with leavers from the clothing plants during the same year would reveal marked contrasts.[8]

TABLE 3.5

**CHANGES IN LENGTH OF SERVICE DISTRIBUTION
OF WOMEN LEAVERS FROM THE ELECTRICAL FACTORY**

(Per Cent)

Period N	1968–9 530	1970–1 350	1972–4 445	1975[a] 194	1976–7 124	All[b] 1643
Under 1 month	16.7	5.4	6.1	0	2.4	8.3
1–3 months	22.2	18.6	11.9	0	5.6	14.7
3–6 months	26.9	16.0	14.8	1.0	11.3	17.1
6–12 months	19.9	18.3	13.9	12.9	14.5	16.7
1–2 years	11.0	22.0	16.0	25.8	16.1	16.8
2–3 years	3.0	9.4	11.2	15.5	12.9	8.8
3–5 years	0.4	9.1	19.6	18.6	20.2	11.1
Over 5 years	0	1.1	6.5	26.3	16.9	6.4
All	100	100	100	100	100	100

NOTES
a. Redundancy year: 56 percent of leavers were made voluntarily redundant.
b. Figures differ from those in Table 3.4 because the present table includes the 1968–9 period.

The trends within Company A are, moreover, important in themselves for they add weight to the argument that the decline in crude turnover rates was not

8. We do not make this comparison directly since, apart from the absence of data on voluntary quits from the clothing factories, the number of voluntary leavers from the Company A plants had become very small.

an indication of a decline in the degree of 'conflict'. We have suggested that external factors, and not increasing satisfaction with the job, may explain the fall in the turnover rate, but this was not simply a matter of workers' decisions to cling more closely to their jobs. The company's actions in setting the context for these decisions was crucial. In particular the company reduced its labour force requirements as economic conditions worsened. This meant that employment in the Components Factory, for example, was cut by about one third between 1971 and 1979 and that during much of our fieldwork there was a total ban on all recruitment. This reduced the proportion of short-service workers in the total, and thus the labour force was progressively stabilized. Although we have no direct comparative data for the clothing plants, it is unlikely that a similar process was under way here; we have certainly seen that crude turnover rates did not fall. In this industry there seems to have been a self-perpetuating system in which there was a constant flow of labour between factories so that, in each individual factory, quits and replacements were kept in a rough balance. Jobs remained available despite a generally worsening economic climate, and the constraints on leaving were correspondingly weak. The wider significance of this is taken up further below.

As against the volatility of the clothing industry work force, two-thirds of leavers from the Process Factory had worked there for ten years or more. This, together with the low crude turnover rate, may suggest that quitting was a minor problem here. It is certainly true that there is little evidence of an induction crisis during the first year of employment, despite the plant's continuous shift system which might be expected to create such a crisis in a particularly acute form. This can be attributed to management's recruitment policy: considerable effort was made to recruit only those who were likely to tolerate shifts, with previous experience of shifts and the financial commitments of a young family being points in an applicant's favour.[9] As one personnel manager put it, 'we try to weed out those who can't take to shifts', with unmarried men and particularly those aged under 25 being seen as least likely to tolerate the restrictions on social life imposed by shift work. 'Every effort' was made to warn recruits of the problems of shift work, and a lengthy induction programme helped to ease new workers into the system. Managers felt that this policy, together with the relatively high wages and job security offered by the plant, helped to minimize wastage rates.

Most managers recognized, however, that, as one put it, the 'main cause' of voluntary quitting was dislike of shifts. We found that, over a four-year period, 30 per cent of voluntary leavers gave shifts as their reason for leaving;

---

9. Compare Blackburn and Mann (1979: 102–8): when recruiting non-skilled labour, employers generally seek workers who will be co-operative and fit into the system and not those who demonstrate particular technical abilities.

and a further 14 per cent cited personal, domestic, or health problems, which can reasonably be seen as concomitants of the shift system. Moreover, 36 per cent of 'involuntary' leavers left under the firm's early retirement scheme; as the scheme's earlier name of the 'chronic sick plan' implies, this arrangement was a means of allowing workers who were no longer capable of working shifts to leave with some retirement benefits and without the stigma of having been sacked. In all, 39 per cent of leavers left for reasons which can be connected with the shift system. It appears that, although workers were often prepared to tolerate shifts for some years, the strain became too great for many. There was a gradual movement away during the first years of employment, combined with substantial quitting by long-serving workers. For example, 35 per cent of voluntary leavers had been in the plant for more than ten years, a proportion higher than that in other plants: for these workers the strains of shift work could be tolerated for some time but not avoided altogether.

Despite the existence, in shift work, of a common source of problems for workers, management's success lay in individualizing the response through quitting. The need to work shifts was presented as natural and inevitable, with managers seeing the matter in terms of the degree of fit between shift work and an individual's needs. As we shall see, part of management's success lay in the adoption by workers of a very similar perspective. We may call this policy one of sophisticated managerialism: the 'problem' of shift work was recognized and considerable attempts were made to moderate it by careful recruitment and training, by providing a generous package of wage and related benefits, and by enabling workers for whom the problem was still too great to leave for 'health' reasons. It was difficult for workers to develop a conscious critique of this system, for did not management do everything possible to help those who could no longer cope with its demands? And managers were genuinely compassionate about individual cases. The pattern of turnover can thus be related to the nature of control over the labour process: there was in the shift system an obvious source of discontent which management recognized and which was contained by a careful policy of sophisticated control. There were hints in the pattern of turnover of the impact of shift work, but managers were successful in restricting the size of their problem to very small proportions.

Before turning to workers' perceptions of this problem we may consider our final measure of labour force stability, namely the survival rate of cohorts of entrants to a plant. This index allows us to control for differential patterns of recruitment and it thus shows more clearly than previous measures the rate of 'wastage' from each plant. Our earlier picture of patterns of stability is generally confirmed, with high levels of stability in the Large and Small Metals Factories and lower levels in the Electrical, Components, and Process Factories. For example, as Table 3.6 shows, 58 per cent of men entering the Large Metals Factory between seven and ten years before the research period were still there,

TABLE 3.6

SURVIVAL RATES: PER CENT OF ENTRANTS STARTING AT GIVEN TIME STILL IN FACTORY

	Electrical		Components	Large Metals	Small Metals	Hosiery	Process
	Men	*Women*					
Under 6 months	97	91		87	79	74	86
6–12 months	72	80	82	70	74	44	74
1–2 years	68	72	73	65		18	65
2–3 years	69	85	70			22	
3–4 years	34	46	51			29	
4–5 years	23	46	39	68	84		
5–7 years	18	39	30	59	67	21	48
7–10 years	12	24		58		n.a.	32[a]

NOTE

a. Relates to cohort beginning 10 to 11 years previously.

A blank indicates that there were no entrants in a given period, or that numbers were insufficient for significant calculations to be made. No suitable data were available for the Underwear Factory.

while the comparable figure for the Electrical Factory was only 12 per cent.[10]
Apart from showing that differential recruitment patterns do not destroy our
earlier contrasts, the main feature of the table is the dramatic picture it gives
of the volatility of the labour force in the Hosiery Factory. There was a very
rapid depletion during the early years of service so that under half those joining
the plant between one and two years before our study were still there, whereas
in other factories the proportion was 70 per cent or more. This was followed,
however, by stabilization after two years' service: those original entrants (comprising one-fifth of the total) who survived the first two years were likely to
remain for considerably longer.

An even more detailed analysis is provided by considering each cohort of
entrants and calculating the length of service distributions of leavers from it.
This exercise requires quite large numbers, and was not possible for all plants.
And in most cases it would add little to the picture which we have already
built up. The contrast between two plants, the Components and the Large
Metals Factories, is, however, instructive. Thus, Table 3.7 confirms the argument
that there was increasing stability in the Components Factory: among the
'oldest' cohort 30 per cent of workers had left during their first six months,
while this figure had fallen to 10 per cent for the most recent cohort. By contrast, as Table 3.8 shows, there was an increase in the tendency to leave during
the first six months of service with the Large Metals Factory. Indeed, reading
across each row of the table from right to left shows an increase in the proportions of leavers in virtually every length of service category. Although the
overall level of depletion remained lower, with 40 per cent of the oldest cohort
having left as against 70 per cent in the Components Factory, the trend was
upwards whereas in the Components Factory it was downward.

Conclusions

These data on survival rates add weight to the argument that quitting was most
significant as a conscious 'expression' of conflict in the Large Metals Factory
even though absolute rates of turnover remained lower than those in other
plants. This has two implications for general discussions of quitting. First, as
we have seen, the extent of the 'problem' is not necessarily reflected in the rate
of turnover: high quit rates in the clothing factories for example were not in

10. The low survival rates for men in the Electrical Factory owe a great deal to the composition of the work force: 53 per cent of leavers, compared with 29 per cent of current
employees, were Pakistanis, and many of those who left did so to return to their home
country (P. Edwards, 1979c: 1068, 1078). This particular pattern, which was most dramatic
when the plant was being set up, was absent elsewhere. The contrast between the clothing
and the other plants made in the text is not vitiated by this: compare for example the survival rates of the newest cohorts.

TABLE 3.7

**COMPONENTS FACTORY: PER CENT OF COHORTS
OF ENTRANTS LEAVING AFTER VARIOUS
PERIODS OF SERVICE**

	Cohort Entering Given Number of Years Previously					
	Less than 1	*1—2*	*2—3*	*3—4*	*4—5*	*5—7*
Less than 1 month	3.8	7.6	4.7	7.6	10.4	12.1
1—3 months	2.6	5.3	0	2.9	7.6	10.9
3—6 months	3.8	3.8	4.7	8.6	7.2	10.4
6—12 months	7.7	9.1	8.1	17.1	10.4	8.5
1—2 years		1.5	10.5	7.6	15.3	8.7
2—3 years			0	3.8	4.8	5.3
3—4 years				1.0	2.4	5.1
4—5 years					0.8	4.7
5—7 years						4.9
All left	17.9	27.3	28.0	48.6	58.9	70.6
Present	82.1	72.7	72.0	51.4	41.1	29.4

TABLE 3.8

**LARGE METALS FACTORY: PER CENT OF COHORTS OF ENTRANTS
TO SELECTED OCCUPATIONS LEAVING AFTER VARIOUS PERIODS
OF SERVICE**

	Cohort Entering Given Number of Years Previously					
	Less than ½	*1—2*	*2—3*	*3—4*	*4—5*	*7*
Less than 1 month	1.0	2.3	1.9	0.7	2.2	0
1—3 months	2.0	2.3	4.7	4.1	3.8	2.0
3—6 months	9.9	8.3	2.8	1.4	2.2	0
6—12 months		4.5	4.7	2.7	4.9	2.0
1—2 years		12.9	9.3	5.5	6.5	4.0
2—3 years			11.2	10.3	4.3	6.0
3—4 years				7.5	7.1	6.0
4—5 years					9.8	6.0
5—7 years						16.0
All left	12.9	30.3	34.6	32.2	40.8	42.0
Present	87.1	69.7	65.4	67.8	59.2	58.0

the least a cause for alarm. Second, and more importantly, while there may be a general 'induction crisis' when workers join a firm, the nature of the crisis, as measured by the length of service of leavers and by survival rates, varies between plants and over time within plants. On changes over time, two influences seem to have been important. In the Large Metals Factory, widespread and intense discontent about earnings levels contributed to an increase in quit rates to unprecedented levels. In the Electrical and Components Factories an influence tending in the opposite direction, namely the economic climate, seems to have had a profound effect on the quit rate by influencing management's recruitment policy as well as workers' freedom to move to other jobs. At the same time the improvement of the plants' position in the local earnings league which we noted in Chapter 2 may have helped to take the edge off the discontent of those who would have preferred a move. Compared with the situation in the early 1970s rates of turnover seemed low and management had no general recruitment problems; it is not surprising that quitting was not seen as a problem here.

At first sight it is surprising that turnover in the clothing industry was not given more attention. But, as we have seen, it raised few problems for managers. Women would come in, try a job for a while, and then move on to be replaced by others. This does not mean, however, that the behaviour was unimportant as a 'reflection' of conflict. We need to know why workers behaved in this fashion by looking at their own motivations.

Attitudes to Work

It is obvious that a high rate of turnover does not necessarily mean that workers are 'dissatisfied' with their employers in the sense of feeling a clear sense of grievance; quitting may well mean that opportunities are felt to be better elsewhere without there being any particular feeling of antagonism to the current employer. The most direct means of examining whether it is indeed the most 'discontented' workers who quit is to compare groups of leavers and current employees on measures of job satisfaction and so forth (Hulin, 1966; Ley, 1966; Waters and Roach, 1979). This approach would not have served our purposes. We did not want to know whether leavers were in some sense more dissatisfied than stayers but whether there were more general sources of discontent which could be related to patterns of quitting. We have asserted on the basis of our own observation that work in the clothing factories was more likely to be 'dissatisfying' than that elsewhere because of the way in which control was exerted over it. We now need to know whether workers themselves were attuned to this and, if so, what implications this has for quitting as a means of escape.

In this section we draw heavily on our questionnaire of shopfloor workers, the general rationale for which has been given earlier.[11] The questionnaire was designed to meet a particular problem which we had not fully anticipated in advance. We were unable to use it in the first two plants which we studied, the Electrical and Large Metals Factories, even had it been feasible to do so.[12] And we had already gone some way in our study of the Small Metals Factory, which explains why our sample here was rather small. Yet the results which we obtained gave a gratifyingly similar picture to that which we were building up through more informal methods, and we feel that the results can be treated with considerable confidence. The questionnaire was a brief document, and in some cases it took us as little as a quarter of an hour to complete. The results cannot, therefore, be compared to those derived from more extensive interviews in terms of their detail. But many of our questions have been used in previous research and if they are valid in longer interviews they are valid here; in addition we restricted ourselves to general attitudes to work and did not attempt to go outside this framework by asking about, say, political attitudes. In any event, we do not see our results in isolation from our more informal interviews. If the limitations of the instrument are understood, its results can be treated with reasonable confidence.

The numbers of workers interviewed in each of the five factories where we used the questionnaire are given in Table 3.9. In the Components Factory[13] and the clothing factories substantial proportions of the work force were interviewed. In the Small Metals Factory the proportion was lower, but was still around 7 per cent of the work force. In these four factories we selected workers across all grades and sections. In the Process Factory we were interested in the effects of shift work and therefore interviewed only semi-skilled process workers. For convenience we also limited ourselves to one of the two main shops, so that our results are strictly applicable only to workers in that shop (of whom we interviewed between 20 and 25 per cent). But most of our results are generalizable to process workers in the rest of the factory in that work relationships were, in relevant respects, broadly similar. Because of the small number of men in the Underwear Factory we have combined results for them with those for men in the Hosiery Factory; of the 56 men from the clothing factories in the sample, 13 were from the former factory and 43 from the latter.

We will argue that there were strongly-felt discontents within the clothing factories which can be related to the pattern of turnover discussed above but

11. See above p. 19.
12. We doubt whether a questionnaire would have met with much enthusiasm in either plant. An attempt to use a formal questionnaire with foremen and shop stewards in the Electrical Factory had met with a polite refusal. The Large Metals Factory had been the subject of a questionnaire survey a short while before our own study, and the investigator told us that it had taken a great deal of effort to have even a modest survey accepted.
13. Given the small number of women employed, we limited the questionnaire to men.

TABLE 3.9

PREVIOUS JOB EXPERIENCE

	Components Men	Small Metals Men	All Clothing Men	Hosiery Women	Underwear Women	Process Men
Number in sample	123	43	56	41	86	98
Number with previous job experience	118	40	46	25	35	98
Of those with previous experience, number of reasons given for leaving previous job	134	49	48	27	35	110
Reason as per cent of all reasons given						
Pay	29	43	33	44	23	47
Insecurity	13	10	10	0	0	18
Nature of work	16	14	8	22	20	8
Unfriendly shop	1	0	0	0	3	0
Bad management	3	2	4	0	3	1
Redundant	23	27	25	11	20	12
Family needs, travel problems, etc	7	0	6	11	17	1
Other	5	4	10	7	9	13
D.K.	3	0	2	4	6	0

SOURCE
Shopfloor questionnaire.

NOTE
Here, and in subsequent tables, figures for reasons given relate to the total number of replies, not the number of respondents. We coded up to three responses to each open-ended question but most people gave only one reply so that the percentages approximate to the percentages of respondents: in the present table there was an average of 1.1 replies per respondent.

that there were also powerful forces operating which prevented the emergence of any truly collective approach to using quitting as a form of protest. Of these forces the limited labour market experience of many workers was the most obvious.

Labour Market Experience

As Table 3.9 shows, previous job experience of any sort was much less common among the women in the clothing industry than among the men in the same industry or elsewhere. This may appear to conflict with the argument that workers moved rapidly between plants, but such conflict is removed when the nature of our two sorts of data is made clear. Rates of turnover measure the 'flow' of workers in and out of the factories, whereas our questionnaire sample constitutes a 'stock' of workers at one moment. The flow may be rapid but the stock represents a variety of workers with differing experiences. In particular it includes large numbers of workers who had been recruited straight from school who might be expected to move on in the future but who had as yet no other work experience. It also includes older women who worked for a firm in the past, left to have a family, and then returned because it was convenient. The presence of such groups is crucial for understanding the absence of strong collective organization in these factories. Less than half the factories' female employees had ever worked for another firm and they thus had no standard of comparison when assessing, for example, the fairness of managerial controls of piece rates. This situation was actively fostered by management. A senior manager in the Underwear Factory said that he preferred to recruit school-leavers and workers without experience in other firms. This was not simply because young workers were cheaper than older ones but also because they could be trained into the discipline and quality standards which the firm required. Another manager referred to the 'bad habits' which workers picked up elsewhere, meaning shoddy or slap-dash work and a generally unacceptable attitude to effort; a high-level of effort and good quality work was essential if the firm was to retain its customers.

Of those women who had worked elsewhere just over half had previously worked in other clothing firms, generally firms in the one major town in the district or in the immediately surrounding area. Thus in all three-quarters of the workers had experience which was limited to the one firm or to other firms which were very much like it. Several workers in the Underwear Factory sample, for example, had previously worked in the Hosiery Factory or in the other plant owned by the same firm. The reasons these workers gave for leaving the Hosiery Factory illustrate the nature of turnover in the industry: an autocratic shop manager and the general tedium of work were the main factors mentioned. Workers might try a job for a while but move if they found that some aspect of it such as the attitude of supervision was unsatisfactory. But their moves were within a narrow range of plants and jobs: it was a matter of finding a job which was tolerable, not one of moving away from the industry completely.

In our other factories work experience was much more diverse. The position in the Process Factory is particularly revealing, for although previous work experience was universal among our sample, the nature of this experience meant that, like the clothing factories, collective identities were retarded. Only about 40 per cent of our sample had experience of factory work, with the remainder having done semi-skilled non-factory jobs (25 per cent), having worked as butchers or painters and decorators or the like (15 per cent), or having held some form of non-manual job (20 per cent). Most of the remainder had come straight out of the armed services, and it was widely said that the company preferred men with military experience because they were accustomed to authority and were unlikely to be aggressive. The very wide range of previous employment experience, particularly that of a non-industrial kind, meant that workers tended to take managerial perspectives for granted and to lack a comparative perspective.

There was, by contrast, a much greater fund of knowledge about other jobs among shopfloor workers in the Small Metals Factory. Although we do not have any precise quantitative information on this the general impression of the plant was that workers kept a close eye on wages in nearby firms. Since the factory was located in the centre of a metal-working area workers could fairly readily obtain some knowledge of the local labour market. We were told by several workers that in the past they had 'moved around where the money was'. This had brought them to the factory when it was a high payer and they had settled down in it for a considerable time. When they found that they were no longer among the best-paid workers in the area they considered moving. But they were constrained by their assessments of the marketability of their skills and by the dangers of leaving the known for the unknown. We now examine these constraints by considering workers' views on leaving their present jobs.

Leaving the Present Job

We asked workers whether they had thought of leaving their present jobs 'say, within the last year', going on to ask about reasons for thinking of leaving and about reasons for staying. There was a remarkable similarity between plants in the proportion of workers who had thought of leaving: as Table 3.10 shows, between 46 and 62 per cent had done so. But the reasons given for this varied markedly. Although the total number of replies from the Hosiery Factory was small the pattern was so different from that in other plants as to warrant special attention. The great majority of replies related to the nature of the work, with tedium and boredom being specifically mentioned. In other factories this general

TABLE 3.10

OPINIONS ON LEAVING PRESENT JOB

	Components	Small Metals	All Clothing Men	Hosiery Women	Underwear Women	Process
Per cent who had:						
Not thought of leaving	62	53	55	46	60	59
Thought of leaving and:						
Had not done anything	20	30	20	32	20	27
Had done something about it[a]	19	16	23	20	20	14
DK/Other	0	0	2	2	0	0
Number who had thought of leaving	48	20	24	21	34	40
Number of reasons given for having thought of leaving	55	29	30	19	36	43
Reason as per cent all reasons given						
Level of pay	5	31	17	0	17	5
Insecurity	2	7	0	0	0	0
Nature of work	45	34	57	74	31	12
Bad management	15	10	10	0	33	0
General need for change	9	7	10	21	6	0
Independence/freedom	9	0	0	0	0	0
Shift work	na	na	na	na	na	58
DK/Other	15	10	7	5	14	26

NOTE
a. For example, had applied for another job or had taken some steps to find out about other jobs.

category was less important, and replies tended to refer to some specific aspect such as having to do night shifts and not to the nature of the work tasks.

This question of 'boredom' needs to be considered carefully. It does not imply that there was widespread 'job dissatisfaction'. We asked our sample how satisfied they were with the specific tasks which they performed and, in line with many previous surveys using this sort of question (Blauner, 1967), found quite high levels of satisfaction in all our factories: about two-thirds of workers said that they were 'completely' or 'quite' satisfied with the job itself, the proportion among women in the Underwear Factory being as high as 79 per cent. Yet, as is becoming widely recognized, a worker who says that he or she is 'satisfied' does not necessarily find the job inherently stimulating. Workers in all our factories often said that mundane and routine jobs were all that they could expect and that, viewed in that light, their present jobs were not too bad. What distinguished workers in the clothing factories was not boredom with work tasks but a more general frustration with the way in which tasks were carried out. Now we would not necessarily expect workers to articulate such frustration directly since, as we have seen, standards of comparison were limited. Hence workers in the Hosiery Factory who said that their work was 'boring' did not always ask why this was so. Some, however, did begin to make a connection between boredom and authority relations. A group of machinists said that 'you put up with the boredom and the foreman standing over you'. And a few women reported that work had become more boring recently because of changed working practices which management had introduced. As one put it, they were having to check work more carefully and, although management had the right to demand that work be done 'properly', this did create difficulties since it was hard to build up a rhythm of work and since, of course, more careful checking involved a reduction of earnings. In other words, the legitimacy of the managerial request was accepted, but one consequence was boring or frustrating work. Other workers, as we shall see, criticized management's approach to discipline without directly linking this to the boredom which they experienced.

The patterns of replies in the Hosiery and Underwear Factories reflected, then, broadly similar conditions. In the former plant the contingencies of work made 'boredom' a particularly salient feature of the job whereas, in the latter plant, managerial authority was experienced more directly. In our other plants reasons for thinking of leaving related less closely to the organization of work. In the Process Factory shift work was, not surprisingly, the major factor mentioned. In the Small Metals Factory the level of pay was, again unsurprisingly, more important than it was elsewhere. In the Components Factory the overall range of replies was very wide, reflecting particular sets of individual circumstances, and there appeared to be no central focus of discontent.

Why, then, did workers not leave? In particular, to return to a question which

we raised earlier, why did workers in the Small Metals Factory stay in the plant
when they were thoroughly dissatisfied with their wages and with their work as
a whole. Our questionnaire results certainly indicated widespread dissatisfaction
with wages: 42 per cent of workers here said that they were 'very dissatisfied'
with their wages, with a further 33 per cent saying that they were 'a little dissatisfied', proportions which were much higher than those in our other factories.
Yet, as we have seen, over half the Small Metals Factory sample had not thought
of leaving and only one-sixth of the total sample had made any attempt to look
for another job. We therefore asked those who had thought of leaving why they
were still in the plant, with a similar question being posed to those who had
not thought of leaving in terms of what appealed to them about their jobs.
The results are set out in Table 3.11.

Workers faced several constraints on their ability to move, the most obvious
being the lack of suitable jobs. In all plants apart from the Small Metals Factory
about 20 per cent of reasons for not leaving involved this problem. In this
plant, however, workers claimed that several nearby plants not only offered
higher wages but were also actively recruiting. Their reasons for not leaving
reflected the presence of many constraints other than simply the availability
of jobs. There were, first, the non-wage benefits of their present jobs. These
included such well-known factors as the companionship of workmates and
a feeling that one is too old to move or has become too settled into the ways
of the factory. One long-serving worker, for example, said that he was simply
used to the routine of the plant: he knew everyone in it, was well acquainted
with all the jobs he might have to do, and could go to work in a settled frame
of mind. In addition, however, one factor which loomed much larger here than
elsewhere was the possible loss of redundancy rights: several workers said that
they were simply waiting for the chance of taking their redundancy pay. One
man, indeed, resented the redundancy legislation: in the past 'you could just
tell the boss to fuck off, and go where the money was', but now workers felt
tied to jobs they did not like because redundancy compensation was too important to lose. We obtained similar replies in our informal interviews in the Large
Metals Factory, the relevance of which was reflected some months after our
main research period when a large redundancy was announced and when large
numbers of volunteers came forward. The attention paid to redundancy rights
in these two plants obviously reflected the particular circumstances of the
factories, for rumours of partial or total closure had circulated for some time.
Such rights were an important constraint on workers' moving. Yet a second
set of constraints concerned with the costs of moving was also important.
Anyone who left was exchanging the certainties of the present job for a situation whose details could not be known in advance. In particular, as several
workers stressed, the nearby factory which was recruiting most heavily relied
on contract work, and, although work was plentiful at present, the factory

TABLE 3.11

REASON FOR STAYING IN PRESENT JOB

	Components		Small Metals		Clothing Men		Hosiery Women		Underwear Women		Process	
	Yes	No	Yes	No	Yes	No	Yes	No	Yes	No	Yes	No
Whether had thought of leaving present job												
Number of workers	48	75	20	23	24	32	21	20	34	52	40	58
Number of reasons for staying	67	121	33	30	27	41	20	25	40	58	58	78
Reason as per cent of all reasons												
Level of pay	28	14	6	20	7	10	60	44	23	19	34	28
Security	6	12	6	10	15	10	0	0	0	0	17	28
Nature of work	4	30	0	13	4	15	5	16	0	26	0	19[a]
Lives near plant	3	3	6	7	15	7	0	4	8	7	0	6
Too old to move	24	7	18	13	11	12	0	0	0	0	10	6
Good workmates	3	8	15	23	0	17	0	8	23	24	2	5
Loss of redundancy rights	4	9	30	0	0	0	10	0	0	0	3	1
No jobs available	18	0	6	0	19	0	20	0	25	0	22	1
Nothing appeals	0	0	0	3	4	10	0	20	0	12	2	1
Other	9	16	12	10	26	20	5	8	23	12	9	9

NOTE
a. Includes benefits of shift work, ability to spend time with family, etc.

was known for the fluctuations in the demand for its products. Anyone going there could well find himself without a job and without a cushion of redundancy money. As several workers said, they might have risked moving when they were younger but they were now too old for it to be worth their while. In summary, workers felt discontented but trapped.

The other main feature of Table 3.11 concerns the clothing factories. One might expect on the basis of much of the existing literature about such small, paternalistic, family-owned businesses that workers would cite close relations with management and the friendliness of supervisors as reasons for liking their work (e.g. Indik, 1963 and 1965, Talacchi, 1960). We had, indeed, included in our classification of replies to the question about reasons for leaving the previous job (Table 3.9) a category labelled 'unfriendly shop' in the expectation that workers would report having moved for this kind of intrinsic reason (compare Ingham, 1970: 91). We found, however, that our clothing industry workers did not seem to have chosen their jobs for such non-pecuniary reasons. Similarly, Table 3.11 shows that replies citing good management as a reason for remaining in the present job were conspicuous by their absence. Among workers in the Hosiery Factory the level of pay was the predominant reason for staying in the job, while, in the Underwear Factory, the nature of work tasks and 'good workmates' were, along with money, important reasons for staying. This pattern of replies, together with our previous assertion that the intensity of managerial control lay behind the factories' high quit rates, led us to explore workers' perceptions of management in more detail.

Loyalty and Bureaucracy

We asked a standard question about how workers 'got on with' their foreman or immediate supervisor. In every factory between 80 and 90 per cent of workers said that their relationships with foremen were good or very good. When asked why this was so most workers said that foremen did not bother them, were reasonable in their demands, or were otherwise understanding. These similarities might seem surprising in view of marked differences in managerial styles as well as in the general pattern of control. For example, the co-operative style in the Process Factory might be expected to call forth a favourable response, while intense managerial control in the clothing factories would be expected to produce an unfavourable one. Similarly, traditions of strong shopfloor autonomy in the Small Metals Factory might be expected to be associated with resentment against foremen as the immediate agents of managerial attempts to limit such autonomy. We certainly came across complaints about individual foremen in most of our factories, but these tended to be criticisms of specific personal characteristics. Relationships with foremen are generally limited to day-to-day matters and, so long as supervisors carry out their tasks reasonably competently, it is unlikely that workers will report that they get on badly with them. Even in the Small Metals Factory, where there was certainly a feeling that foremen were unnecessary and that workers could handle the job themselves, workers reported that they 'got on with' foremen at the interpersonal level. Several workers said that they got on well with everyone; they seemed to be considering the question in terms of purely personal relationships. It is thus far from surprising that replies in all our factories tended to be similar. What is surprising is the weight which has been placed on this type of question in the past, as if 'getting on with' the immediate supervisor were the only test of a worker's view of management in general.

We therefore went on to ask a broader question about management, expecting that workers in the Small Metals Factory would be very critical of managerial failings (particularly those concerned with wage rates). From the argument that workers in small firms will display feelings of loyalty towards management, workers in the clothing factories would be expected to have the most favourable view. The results (Table 3.12) confirm the first part of this hypothesis but not the second: workers in the Small Metals Factory were the most critical group, but they were followed by women in the Underwear Factory, with unfavourable comments about management being more common among all groups in the clothing industry than among men in the Components or Process Factories. Now the large number of 'don't know' replies in the Hosiery Factory might suggest that the results should be treated with scepticism, and it is certainly true that the question was very simple. Yet one might reasonably expect that workers in small factories will have a very clear view of management based on frequent personal contact. The absence of such an image is significant in itself in suggesting that there was no fund of loyalty towards management.

To assess this issue in more detail we went on to ask workers their reasons for a particular view of management. The results, given in Table 3.13, differ from those in the previous table because a person could say that management was 'average' and go on to give a thoroughly critical appraisal. One result of this is to accentuate the differences between plants; for example 68 per cent of Small Metals Factory workers produced unfavourable comments as against 15 per cent of Process Factory workers. A second result was the enlargement of the 'don't know' category': it was possible for workers to give a positive reply to the fixed-choice question without their being able to supply a reason for the reply. This was particularly true in the clothing factories where about a fifth of workers could not rationalize an opinion about management.

The outcome of all this was to render any notion that clothing industry workers would be uniquely attached to their firms even more questionable. Over half the women in the Underwear Factory produced unfavourable comments on management, with a further third being unable to articulate any view. In the Hosiery Factory there were fewer unfavourable responses, but a very large number of 'don't know' replies. Now we have already seen that workers

TABLE 3.12

WORKERS' VIEWS OF MANAGEMENT IN GENERAL

(Per Cent)

	Components	Small Metals	Clothing Men	Hosiery Women	Underwear Women	Process
Much better than most	10	2	2	2	0	7
A bit better than most	38	14	18	10	8	29
Average	32	26	41	34	35	22
A bit worse than average	12	19	7	5	29	7
A lot worse than average	2	28	13	10	17	2
Other	0	1	4	7	0	1
Don't know	7	9	16	32	10	31

TABLE 3.13

WORKERS' COMMENTS ON MANAGEMENT

(Per Cent)

	Components	Small Metals	Clothing Men	Hosiery Women	Underwear Women	Process
Number of comments	*138*	*45*	*57*	*41*	*87*	*99*
Favourable comments						
Understand shopfloor problems	12	4	2	2	0	2
Friendly/helpful	14	9	11	10	2	11
Other	2	4	2	0	5	11
Neutral comments						
Don't bother you/see little of them	25	7	19	20	8	17
Adverse comments						
Distant from shopfloor	12	20	7	2	0	5
Strict/unfriendly/ inconsistent	1	9	7	7	44	2
Don't know job	11	24	5	2	0	1
Other	9	15	11	5	8	7
No opinion on management[a]	7	8	16	32	10	31
Opinion, no reason[b]	6	0	21	19	23	12
All favourable	28	17	15	12	7	24
All neutral	25	7	19	20	8	17
All adverse	33	68	30	16	52	15
All don't know	13	8	37	51	33	43

NOTES
a. i.e. gave a 'don't know' reply to question on whether management were better or worse than average: see Table 3.12.
b. i.e. gave a positive reply to above question but offered no reason for choosing a particular option.

in the latter factory were the more likely to find their work 'boring'. That is, their discontents were expressed in terms directly related to the work task, with management being no more than a background influence. In the Underwear Factory the presence of management on the shopfloor was more apparent in many ways. Senior members of management were frequently to be seen on the shopfloor, and they took a direct interest in the *minutiae* of workers' behaviour. As they said to us, they did not like having to be strict, and the new system of management based on more supervisors had been introduced to reduce the direct disciplinary role of senior managers. Yet a high level of effort was the only way for the firm to stay competitive, and tight control of discipline was essential in maintaining a suitable level of effort. This was, they said, in everyone's interests, for otherwise there would be no jobs. Yet, as Table 3.13 shows, workers did not entirely share this perspective: comments about managerial strictness and inconsistency were widespread.

The depth of feeling among women in both our clothing plants was considerable, and quite unlike anything in our other factories. Large numbers of women produced spontaneous comments like 'it's worse than school', 'it's like a prison', and 'it's worse than Colditz'. Managers in the Underwear Factory were variously described as 'moody' and 'nasty', while one shop manager in the Hosiery Factory was singled out for special comment: he stood over people while they worked, tried to stop workers talking to each other, and even timed visits to the lavatory. To cite just one example from the Underwear Factory, a worker said that management were far too strict: 'they book you for the slightest thing' (that is, workers were given disciplinary warnings which were entered in the 'book'). She could occasionally leave her machine for a few minutes, but 'they jump on you. They don't like us talking on the shopfloor. They watch over you all the time'.

Such feelings can be explained by the nature of relations on the shopfloor. Eating while at work, for example, was forbidden on the grounds that food stains could damage the garments. A manager might see a worker taking an illicit bite of food and reprimand her, proceeding on his way without giving further thought to the matter. This might be the worker's only contact with the manager, whose behaviour was easily seen as unfriendly or downright unpleasant. This was particularly so when the 'offence' in question was a common practice and when other workers were not reprimanded.[14]

This is not to suggest that discontent was universal. We have noted the large

---

14. As noted earlier (p. 47) management were now adopting a self-consciously 'co-operative' style. One apparently plausible argument is that workers who had been recruited recently, and who had not been exposed to the more overtly autocratic approach of the past, would be less critical of management than were longer-serving workers. But we found that the extent of the criticism was not related to length of service. Workers' perceptions reflected the way in which control was exercised regardless of surface differences in managerial style.

number of 'don't know' replies in the Hosiery Factory to our general question about management; as one worker put it, 'I wouldn't know management if I saw them'. For these workers managers were an irrelevance. And other workers accepted the position, saying for example that they knew what the work would be like when they came and that they did not let the occasional row with managers bother them. And other workers were positively pleased to have a reasonably well-paid job near home. Although such workers might be generally aware of managerial action on discipline, if they themselves were not directly subject to it they were not too concerned about it. Yet the dominant impression was of workers who felt discipline to be too tight and who resented managers' domineering approach; and even those workers who paid little attention to managers can hardly be said to have held great feelings of loyalty.

This evidence, together of course with that of high quit rates, seems to contradict other writers' findings about the loyalty and deference of workers in small firms. We must tackle this possibility for two reasons. Most obviously, if our findings are outside the mainstream of the research literature it may be that they can be written off to idiosyncrasies in our method or the factories studied. And, more importantly, a common expectation is that differences in attitude can be explained by differences in the degree of bureaucratization of a factory; if we can show that this is mistaken then our own account in terms of control over the labour process is strengthened.

Ingham (1970) suggested that the relatively strong feelings of loyalty which he observed among workers in small factories could be explained not by the size of these firms but by the fact that small firms are less bureaucratic than large ones, with an absence of bureaucracy encouraging strong ties between workers and managers. Similarly, Newby (1977a: 301–17) in his study of agricultural workers found that farms with 'bureaucratic' modes of control had less face-to-face interaction between farmers and workers than less bureaucratic ones. Now our clothing factories were undoubtedly less bureaucratic than the other plants on any criteria which might be suggested. For example, on what Bendix (1974: 211) sees as the single most useful index of bureaucratization, namely the proportion of salaried workers in the total number of employees, the ratio of staff to manual workers was about one in ten; in the other factories it was between one in five and one in seven. More generally, relationships were conspicuously less governed by rules and formal procedures, and the whole atmosphere of the plants was one of personal ties and informality. Yet, as we have seen, workers were in general more critical of managers than were those in more bureaucratic settings. The difference from Ingham's and Newby's findings may well be due to differences in the kind of organization studied. Ingham's small factories were very small, employing between nine and 63 workers, and farms are of course even smaller. In such very small organizations it is possible that the absence of bureaucracy may lead to a highly particularistic relationship between workers and managers. When the comparison is between larger units it is doubtful whether a direct link between bureaucratization and workers attitudes can be expected. Once a certain size of establishment has been reached, and the very close relationships of small units have thus been removed, there is no reason to expect that low levels of bureaucracy should lead to worker satisfaction.[15] Indeed, the problem for workers in the Underwear Factory was precisely that relations with managers were too immediate and were based on managers' arbitrary reactions to a situation and not on established procedures.

Our results do not, then, contradict those of Newby or Ingham. Indeed, they are consistent with the very detailed work of Curran and Stanworth (1979a; 1979b; and 1981) on the supposed 'small firm effect'. Curran and Stanworth demonstrate that in many respects workers in small and large firms are alike: they are subject to the same sorts of authority relationships, and attitudes towards management are correspondingly similar. And many differences can be attributed not to some prior orientation whereby workers deliberately seek out small firms for their intrinsic rewards but to 'objective' differences in hiring practices and the like. In view of all this we can treat our own more limited findings with some confidence. Workers in the clothing factories displayed considerable feelings of discontent which belied management's image of these factories as harmonious workplaces. Such feelings owed more to the way in which control was exercised over the workers than to the degree of bureaucratization of the plants.

Conclusions

This evidence on workers' attitudes strengthens our argument about quit rates in the clothing industry. We have seen that women workers lacked the positive ties of attachment to their employers which might be expected in such small firms. In the Underwear Factory there was, on the contrary, a very critical view of management, while the Hosiery Factory workers tended to feel that management were too distant for them to be able to form any opinion about them. This is consistent with the previous finding that reasons for thinking of leaving concentrated, in the former plant, on 'bad management' and, in the latter, on 'boredom'. In the Underwear Factory managers were only too conspicuous, and complaints focused on them directly, whereas in the Hosiery Factory it was the less direct result of managerial control, namely an authority system which prevented workers from talking to each other and which thus rendered the work 'boring', which was the focus of complaints. There was thus a marked similarity of attitudes, as well as of behaviour in the form of quitting, which belied the apparent differences between our plants in terms of managerial 'style'.

15. As noted in Chapter 2, Ingham (1970: 65) himself places the threshold at the level of 100 employees.

The new consultative approach in the Underwear Factory had not succeeded in breaking down critical views of management, for it was based on a system in which, regardless of their personal preferences, managers felt constrained to demand a high level of effort and very tight work discipline. Management's control system provides the key to understanding workers' attitudes as well as quit rates.

Our material on attitudes has also confirmed that workers in the Small Metals Factory not only felt that their wages were thoroughly unsatisfactory but also held strongly critical views of management; this picture also applies, we argue, to the Large Metals Factory. Yet there was also a strong feeling that the constraints on quitting were very powerful: these two plants give a sharp illustration of the point that deep frustrations are not necessarily 'expressed' in quitting. What, then, is the significance of quitting as a form of conflict?

Turnover and Conflict

That turnover can express conflict is not in doubt. Yet detailed discussion of the way in which it actually does so, and of how turnover patterns can be shown to reveal conflict, is far from common. We have tried here to provide statistical evidence that turnover patterns varied according to the form of control over the labour process in our various factories and to back this up with evidence on workers' perceptions. We have concentrated on those situations where the link between turnover and conflict was most important, and we therefore consider the question of the significance of turnover in relation to them before bringing together our findings from our other plants.

As we have argued throughout, turnover in the clothing factories can certainly be related to a notion of conflict. Managerial control of work was considerable, and workers experienced this in a negative way. Quitting can be readily understood in the light of the comment of one woman that she had found the work hard at first and had wanted to leave but that she had eventually learnt to live with it: anyone who could not accept the situation on its own terms, and in particular anyone who was unwilling to put in the considerable effort required to earn a satisfactory wage, found quitting to be the only option open to her. Yet there were several influences which moderated the significance of the behaviour. We have seen that management did not feel that they faced a turnover problem; no manager related quitting to workers' grievances about the disciplinary system for instance. And we are not suggesting that managers were misreading the situation, either wilfully or through ignorance. Management's overriding concern was to maintain discipline and hence, they argued, efficiency. They might admit that workers did not like close discipline but there was, in their view, no alternative. Hence workers' complaints were largely irrelevant in that nothing could be done about them. They were also irrelevant in another sense, namely that they created few challenges within the workplace. Workers continued to co-operate with the system and managers were not forced to alter it.

There was, then, a gap between workers' critical attitudes and their compliant behaviour. This is not to suggest that workers were failing to realize their own interests in terms of challenging the system. The point, rather, is that they were faced with a situation which gave them little choice. The dominant impression which we received from replies to our questionnaire was that workers saw few positive attractions in their work apart from the money and that they knew that they could not expect the same level of wages elsewhere. Given this situation, and given their own lack of experience outside the clothing industry, it is not surprising that resigned acceptance was a common response. Another response, of course, was to quit. Yet the two responses remained isolated: workers still in the factories did not identify with leavers in the way that workers in the Large Metals Factory did. We discovered no feeling that leavers were expressing collective grievances; indeed, leavers seemed rarely to be discussed at all. Although turnover reflected the pattern of control, and although workers showed an awareness of control in their views on discipline, workers themselves did not articulate a connection between the two things. There was awareness of certain aspects of the system but this was not generalized. Indeed, we doubt whether those who quit necessarily saw their leaving in terms of the control system as a whole; certainly those workers in the Underwear Factory who had previously worked in the Hosiery Factory concentrated on specific aspects of their work there and not on the control system as such.

This suggests that the system of quits and replacements which operated in the industry was self-reinforcing: an individual who disliked some aspect of the system would leave to be replaced by someone who might tolerate the work for a while before, in her turn, trying her luck elsewhere. There was thus a constant flow of labour, and quitting was not a major break with the employer in the same way that it was in plants marked by a greater stability of employment. Quitting was probably not a very significant act for the workers involved; hence we cite examples in later chapters of workers who had not particularly thought of leaving but who would suddenly decide to quit after a row with a manager or a series of warnings for bad work. The behaviour was certainly not very significant for workplace relations in that it did not disturb the established pattern. Indeed, it strengthened that pattern by helping to prevent the development of a collective identity on the shopfloor. In particular, and most immediately, it meant that potential leaders of collective organizations left. Again, we cite examples later of workers who were, in effect, forced to leave when nascent collective actions collapsed. This quitting was plainly in management's interests, for the removal of 'troublemakers' meant that managerial domination was secured. Indeed, management's success went deeper than this, for situations did not reach the point where there were identifiable leaders who appeared to be victimized. Matters were less overt, and it was more a matter of potential and not actual leaders, and of 'voluntary' quitting and not dismissal.

Here, then, quitting lay on the borders of what we have called non-directed conflict and implicit conflict. We have defined the former as concrete behaviour which 'expresses' a conflict of interest without being overtly conflictual. Now quitting may be felt to fall into this category more or less by definition, in that a worker who leaves can be said to be expressing discontent with some aspect of the employment relationship. But we have seen that moving around between jobs was taken for granted and that it was not invested with particular significance. And quitting was far from being an unambiguous way of acting against managerial interests; as we have just argued, it was in some respects in line with those interests. Hence quitting was a non-directed form of conflict in that it was concrete behaviour which could be related to the pattern of control, but its more general significance for the 'social order' of which it was part was very limited. Hence it also had elements of implicit conflict: we can identify a conflict of interest not only in terms of our own view of the nature of managerial domination but also in the presence among the workers of some criticism of that domination. Yet there were various forces, notably the absence of collective organization and the lack of any perceived alternative, which kept this conflict of interest implicit within the structure of the situation. Acts of quitting did not bring this into the open: on the contrary, they helped to prevent collective awareness from developing.

We have argued that these aspects of turnover among women reflected the nature of their labour process and not such things as managerial style or levels of bureaucratization. We have also suggested that the differential quit rates of men and women reflected the different modes of control to which they were subjected. It is widely argued that the quit rates of men and women differ not because of inherent differences in the 'propensity' to quit of the two sexes but because men and women occupy different places in the division of labour. Conversely, where labour market situations and other factors are similar quit rates may be similar. Purcell (1979: 128) for example makes the point explicitly in relation to the clothing industry that, where collective organization is weak, men and women 'are similarly characterised by high job turnover'. The clothing factories which we studied seem to contradict this, for patterns of turnover as well as just crude turnover rates differed as between men and women. There is, however, no contradiction unless Purcell's argument is read as implying that the positions of all workers in an industry are identical. We found substantial differences between men, and particularly knitters, and women in the intensity

Labour Turnover

of control which was exerted over them. These differences help to explain differences in patterns of turnover.

The other factories where quitting could be directly related to a notion of conflict were the two Company B plants. It was a direct and obvious reflection of workers' discontents over wages; and it was not individualized as it was elsewhere, for workers felt a strong sense of identity with those who had left. Quitting can thus be described as a conscious strategy of protest involving important collective elements. Yet, particularly in the Small Metals Factory, it was limited by powerful constraints on leaving, notably the loss of redundancy and other rights and the risks associated with moving to a new firm. These two plants illustrate a point which, although obvious, has tended to lack detailed empirical support: actual quit rates hold no necessary relation to the extent of felt discontents. More importantly, they indicate the limitations of a strategy of quitting. The clothing plants show that a high quit rate need not reflect back onto the structure of the situation. Similarly, the rapidly increasing quit rate in the Large Metals Factory brought little pressure directly to bear on management to remove the source of the discontent. The main impact was on managerial action in the workplace, notably toolroom management's acquiescence in declining effort levels and their willingness to allow unlimited overtime. The impact on higher management was much less apparent. Indeed, workers recognized the limitations of the strategy when they complained that their previous pride in their work itself and in belonging to a high-paying and successful plant had been dissipated. Quitting was seen as an undesirable option but as the only realistic one for a large number of workers. It was a reflection of a shift of the frontier of control against the shopfloor in the sense that collective controls no longer yielded satisfactory outcomes.

This might seem to imply that 'individual' forms of conflict such as quitting emerge when collective controls become weaker. We tackle this issue more fully in the final chapter, but we can already note that the distinction between individual and collective actions is not in fact the most appropriate here. We have argued that quitting was unable to resolve collective grievances and that it was, therefore, not necessarily a strategy that furthered workers' interests as a whole, although it did of course permit individual workers to escape to a preferred job. Other forms of individual action, however, can further collective interests: as we shall see in Chapter 4, absenteeism in the Large Metals Factory increased the amount of leisure available to workers and gave them some control over when their efforts were to be exerted. It is not the contrast between individual and collective actions which is important but that between actions which advance specific interests and those which do not.

What, then, of our other three factories, namely the Process Factory and the two Company A plants? We have analysed quitting in the Process Factory in terms of a policy of sophisticated managerialism, and there is little to add to this except to note how workers' attitudes to their jobs reflected aspects of this control system. Two sets of attitudes are important. First, as would be expected in a firm offering high wages and good fringe benefits, wages and security were the dominant reason for staying in the job. This is not to suggest that wages were felt to be adequate: 51 per cent of workers said that they were a 'little dissatisfied'. Discontents reflected, however, the expectation that workers on continuous shifts should be very well paid and a widespread feeling that other workers had moved up to, or surpassed, the earnings levels possible in the factory. Yet some workers stressed that the benefits of security and guaranteed wages outweighed apparent disparities in wage rates, while others argued that, while their wages certainly did not meet their expectations, they could not do much better elsewhere. There was thus compliance with, if not acceptance of, this part of the system. Similarly, and this is our second set of attitudes, though perceptions of management were far from hostile neither were they very favourable: as Table 3.13 shows, the largest category of responses to the question about management was 'don't know'. The system did not succeed in creating strong ties of loyalty and positive views of management, such as might be expected given the firm's stress on participation and consultation. But neither did it create strong feelings of hostility, and this generally non-committal approach of workers permitted sophisticated managerialism to attain its ends in terms of low quit rates even if one claimed concomitant, namely moral commitment among workers, appeared to be lacking.

Finally, in the Company A plants turnover reflected a diffuse set of influences. There was no overwhelming factor such as intense managerial control, declining relative wages, or continuous shifts which dominated the scene. The only general influence was the presence of a large number of Pakistanis among the work force; this affected the quit rate since it was common for these workers to move to and from Britain, but it was plainly not a 'conflictual' element in the situation. In the past turnover had been quite high, presumably because of the availability of better-paid jobs elsewhere and, in the case of the Electrical Factory, because of the recent opening of the plant and the consequent length of service distribution of the work force. As labour market conditions changed and as the firm's relative wage position improved reasons for leaving became less significant. It is not surprising that turnover was rarely seen as a problem by the time of our research. As we have said, it is possible to see quitting as a form of conflict because it necessarily reflects workers' discontents. Such a perspective is particularly unhelpful here, however. Workers obviously have a range of needs such as a job which is near home and one where the shift arrangements fit their domestic situations. As these needs change, or as workers' willingness to tolerate contradictions between their work and their other needs changes, a certain amount of quitting can be expected. For example we spoke to a worker in the Large Metals Factory who had previously worked as a fitter in the Components

Factory; he said that he had left the latter plant because he disliked night shifts but that he had otherwise been quite content there. In the Company A plants it was these mundane and proximate influences which seem to have been most important, and ascribing any particularly conflictual role to quitting would be unhelpful.

This example bears out our initial statement that we should not expect an intimate relationship between patterns of control and quit rates. Yet attention to control questions helps us to explain a great deal about turnover in the clothing industry which would otherwise be inexplicable. It directs attention to certain aspects of relations in the Process Factory which would otherwise be obscure. And it helps to explain trends in quit rates in the Large Metals Factory. We can suggest that, if we take control in simple more or less terms, quitting is likely to be an important form of escape in situations where managerial control is relatively intense. Where such control is less intense other forces also come into the reckoning; as we have just seen, quit rates in the Company A plants reflect a range of influences. In addition, however, managerial control cannot be reduced to the intensity with which managers exert pressure to extract effort from workers. We have seen that sophisticated managerialism can have identifiable effects on the extent and significance of quitting (as in the Process Factory) and that patterns of shopfloor control can affect managerial responses (as in management's toleration of effort reductions in the Large Metal Factory as a way of trying to reduce the quit rate).

Our general argument about the effects of different patterns of control on worker behaviour would plainly be strengthened if it could be applied to the other main form of 'unorganized conflict', absenteeism. An assessment of this is the task of the following chapter.

4
Absenteeism

Absenteeism is, perhaps to a greater extent than even labour turnover, an endlessly popular topic. Measures of absence often feature in studies of the correlates of job satisfaction, for example, while, more generally, excessive absenteeism is widely seen as a problem which must be controlled (see for example Crawford and Volard, 1981). Our aim is not so much directly to criticize the existing tradition of absence studies as to shift the focus of the analysis. Instead of seeing absenteeism as a self-evident problem which must be controlled or as a component, index, or correlate of morale, we concentrate on the social conditions which lead to particular patterns of absence and which define whether, and in what ways, absence is seen as a 'problem' by those involved with it. The dominant approach to absenteeism, which goes back to the early studies by Hill and Trist (1953 and 1955), sees it in terms of the adjustments which individual workers make to their work environment. Apart from the undue emphasis on individual psychology in this early work (R. Brown, 1967: 39) there are two main problems here. First, the environment is taken for granted, and the question is not raised as to whether dissatisfactions stem from the physical environment or the boredom induced by particular technologies or, as we would argue, from the social organization of work. Second, worker responses are seen as attempts to 'adjust' and not as conscious actions which meet specific needs (Hyman, 1976).

We attempt to escape from the constraints of this approach by following a strategy similar to that used in relation to turnover: we begin with absence patterns, arguing that they reflect variations in the organization of work, before moving on to workers' views of absenteeism as a strategy of 'conflict'. In addition we give detailed attention to the role of management. Existing studies of absenteeism have been criticized for being managerialist (Nicholson, 1977: 237–8) in that they treat the phenomenon largely in terms of the problems which it creates for management and of ways in which these problems can be minimized. Yet, ironically, management itself has been largely neglected: few studies have examined how managers perceive their absence problem or how they try to control it. Managerial perceptions are important in themselves for the light they throw on the 'subjective' aspects of absenteeism as a form of conflict. They also affect the significance of the behaviour, for different managerial control systems can be expected to have different implications for worker strategies.

Our argument is similar in form to that of the previous chapter. Women in the clothing factories again stand out: their rates of absence, particularly of one-day absences, were higher than those elsewhere. And they were more likely than were workers elsewhere to argue that taking days off was reasonable and indeed necessary. Yet the lack of a wider critical awareness of managerial control, which we discussed in Chapter 3, again meant that the significance of absenteeism as an 'expression' of conflict was muted. The opposite extreme was provided by the Company B plants, but not because absenteeism was increasing: although the rising quit rate reflected increasing discontent over wages the notable thing about absenteeism was the low level of absence rates. This reflected two aspects of workplace control which, unlike wage levels, remained largely unaffected by recent developments. These were the opportunity for 'leisure in work' provided by collective controls over effort and (a closely related aspect) the availability of time off which was not open to managerial sanction. The 'individual' actions of quitting and absenteeism reflected different aspects of the frontier of control.

Absence Rates

For a study of absence as a form of voluntary withdrawal or conflict, an index which excludes such unavoidable reasons for absence as sickness might seem to be 'the ideal measure. However, there is, in addition to severe practical problems with the construction of such an index, an important objection to this. Excluding all absence which can be attributed to sickness assumes that 'sickness' is a fixed category whereas the decision as to how sick one has to be to stay away from work, and how long a period of recovery is needed, is to some extent within the worker's control. In managerialist terms, there may be abuse of sick leave; in terms of the debate on forms of worker resistance, staying away from work while claiming to be ill may be a significant way of turning the system in one's own favour.

We have therefore calculated an overall rate of days lost through absence, excluding certain types of absence as explained in Appendix A and calculating the remaining figures as a percentage of the number of shifts due to be worked. In view of differences in shift systems between factories this is a more useful comparative measure than the number of days lost per worker per year (compare Behrend and Pocock, 1976). Rates of days lost are, however, heavily influenced by a few long spells of absence, and they say nothing about the number of workers who go absent. Two measures of the frequency of absence were therefore used. The first is the frequency of absences lasting one day or less, an index which has been widely used as a proxy for voluntary withdrawal from work since it is less likely than other measures to be affected by sickness and other involuntary reasons for absence (Behrend, 1959: 110–15). The second measure is simply the number of separate periods of absence lasting more than one day or shift.

Overall Absence Rates
Figures on overall rates of absence are given in Table 4.1[1] In addition to the three measures mentioned above, the table shows the proportion of workers who were present throughout a one-year period who did not have one spell of absence; this gives an indication of how widespread absenteeism was among workers staying in the plant for some time. The table confirms the well-known point that the rate of days lost, which is the most easily-available and hence the most widely-quoted absence measure, is in many ways the least useful. It is very heavily affected by a few long spells of absence, as may be illustrated by the case of the Small Metals Factory. For absences lasting one day the frequency rate is identical to the rate of days lost due to such absences. Thus of the total days lost rate of 9.8 per cent, 0.6 per cent was attributable to one-day absences with the remaining 9.2 per cent being due to longer absences. A frequency rate of 0.5 per cent for these longer absences implies that their average length was 18.4 days. This high figure is due to the presence in the sample of workers who were absent for six months or a year at a time. Variations in the frequency of absence give a closer indication of absence as a form of withdrawal.

Our main concern is the link between patterns of absence and patterns of organization: why, for example, was the rate of one-day absences among women in the Hosiery Factory four times that of workers in the Small Metals Factory? But before we can deal with such questions we must consider briefly the possibility that the differences shown in Table 4.1 can be explained by various specific factors such as the age, skill, and sex of the workers (see Department of Employment, 1971, for a list of factors used to explain variations in absence rates). The effects of many of these factors do not seem to have been clear-cut in the present case. For example, in the case of skill, differences between skill groups were often slight and in some cases were contrary to the usual assumption that absenteeism tends to be lower the higher the skill level. We also carried out more detailed analyses according to the age and length of service of workers

1. For reasons explained in Appendix A the figures should not be compared directly with those reported in other studies.

TABLE 4.1

OVERALL ABSENCE RATES

	Rate as % Shifts Scheduled			Workers Present Throughout a One-Year Period: Per Cent with no Spell of Absence
	Frequency		Days Lost	
	One-day	Other		
Electrical				
Men skilled[a]	0.70	0.57	4.8	19.9
semi-skilled[a]	0.93	0.68	7.1	14.5
Women[a]	1.9	0.79	7.7	5.2
Components				
Men skilled[b]	0.96	0.90	8.2	10.7
production workers[a]	1.3	0.78	7.8	12.8
Women[a]	1.8	1.1	8.3	3.8
Large Metals				
Men skilled indirect[b]	0.72	0.41	4.4	17.4
Men skilled direct shop X[b]	1.3	0.71	7.2	25.5
shop Y[b]	1.0	0.36	6.3	25.2
Men semi-skilled shop X[b]	0.75	0.41	3.8	33.0
shop Y[b]	0.52	0.24	3.1	41.0
Men machine operators[a]	1.1	0.48	7.9	25.8
Women machine operators[a]	1.6	0.62	8.6	6.7
Small Metals[b]	0.60	0.51	9.8	23.3
Hosiery				
Men[a]	0.44	0.30	3.6	38.9
Women[a]	2.4	0.90	7.1	6.2
Underwear				
Women[a]	2.0	0.76	11.4	2.7
Process				
Men[b]	0.43	0.54	5.5	18.6

NOTES
a. Figures based on census of all workers in relevant group.
b. Figures based on random samples of the group; sampling fractions vary but are not less than 25 per cent.

and found few marked or consistent differences.[2] The one pronounced contrast was that between men and women: as many other studies have shown, women tended to have higher absence rates, in terms of frequency and days lost, than men. The contrast was particularly marked in the extent of one-day absences. Moreover, the difference remained in one of the few cases, namely machine operators in the Large Metals Factory, where men and women did similar work so that any occupation-specific effects could be controlled.

Now, the observation that the 'sex variable' had an effect can easily be seen as the end of inquiry whereas in fact it is the beginning since it is necessary to explain why the effect was present. For example women are often assumed to lack 'commitment' to their work or to need to take time off to deal with family responsibilities, and their absence patterns are taken as confirmation of such assumptions. But actually to demonstrate a relationship would require, for example, a study of women with differing family responsibilities and an assessment of the effects of these on the need to take time off work.[3] We cannot pursue such matters here, and will simply stress that we are not arguing that the pattern of control explains everything about absence rates: differences between men and women in the Electrical Factory were too great to be explained by differences in control structures.

Attention to control patterns does, however, illuminate other differences which would otherwise remain, to say the least, obscure. Thus it is already apparent from Table 4.1 that there were differences between women in the engineering and clothing industries which cannot be explained by a 'sex effect'. These differences are brought out more sharply when the averages given in that table are expanded into frequency distributions showing how many workers had no spell of absence, how many had one spell, and so on. As Table 4.2 shows, in the Underwear Factory 22 per cent of women had more than ten separate spells of one-day absence in the course of a year while the comparable figure in the Electrical Factory was 5 per cent. In the former factory the median person in the distribution had twice as many one-day absences as her counterpart in the

2. Some results for men in the Electrical Factory are reported elsewhere (P. Edwards, 1979c). Similar exercises were carried out for women in the same factory and for men in the Components Factory, the most interesting result being that in the latter plant there were no differences between ethnic groups despite the prevalence of the view that black workers lack commitment to work.
3. Family responsibilities are plainly only one set of factors to be taken into consideration. Thus unmarried women may be expected to have few such responsibilities but other factors may encourage them to take time off. For example several of the younger women in the clothing plants operated under the 'giving in' system (Millward, 1968) whereby they paid their wages to their parents and received a fixed amount of spending money. For them, a day's absence was a largely costless activity. Interestingly, in the Underwear Factory, where young workers were almost entirely limited to certain departments and older women to other departments, those departments dominated by young women had rates of absence frequency almost twice those of the other departments.

TABLE 4.2

WORKERS EMPLOYED THROUGHOUT A ONE-YEAR PERIOD:
DISTRIBUTION OF FREQUENCY OF ABSENCES (SELECTED GROUPS)

(Per Cent)

	Electrical: Women			Underwear: Women			Components: Male Production Workers			Large Metals: Semi-skilled, Shop Y		
	One-day	Other	All	One-day	Other	All	One-day	Other	All	One-day	Other	All
0	10.6	26.9	5.2	8.2	24.5	2.7	29.7	31.1	12.8	54.3	70.2	41.7
1	15.0	29.5	7.0	5.4	17.7	4.8	23.7	28.9	18.3	15.9	15.9	15.2
2	19.2	22.7	14.8	9.5	17.0	8.2	13.9	18.3	16.9	12.6	6.6	19.9
3	12.5	9.9	11.8	8.2	13.6	9.5	10.1	10.9	11.2	6.0	3.3	7.3
4	10.9	5.2	12.7	8.8	12.2	5.4	4.4	5.7	7.4	4.6	2.0	2.6
5	8.6	2.9	9.5	9.5	2.7	5.4	6.3	2.2	10.1	2.6	0.7	4.6
6–10	18.1	2.6	27.8	28.6	12.3	25.2	9.5	2.7	16.7	2.0	1.4	7.3
11–15	4.5	0.1	8.3	12.9	0	20.3	1.6	0.3	4.4	2.0	0	0.7
16 and over	0.6	0	2.9	9.0	0	18.4	0.8	0	2.4	0	0	0.7
Mean	3.8	1.6	5.4	7.1	2.4	9.5	2.3	1.6	3.9	1.2	0.6	1.8
Median[a]	3	1	4	6	2	8	1	1	3	0	0	1
Third quartile[b]	5	2	7	10	4	13	3	2	5	2	1	2

NOTES

a. i.e. number of absences of middle person in distribution.
b. i.e. number of absences of person for whom three-quarters of the distribution had fewer absences and one-quarter had more absences.

latter factory. Going absent was thus a more widespread and frequent activity for women in the clothing industry than it was for their counterparts in engineering. This can in turn be related, albeit in a preliminary fashion, to differences in control patterns: intense control of work within the factory made absence an attractive form of escape in the clothing plants whereas a much more relaxed managerial style in the Electrical Factory made such escape much less necessary.

Apart from the 'sex effect' the other main feature of Table 4.2 is the considerable contrast between men in the Components Factory and men in the Large Metals Factory. The group of semi-skilled workers from the latter factory for whom data are given are in fact typical not only of that factory but also of the Small Metals Factory. Over half the group did not have a single one-day absence and very few had more than three one-day spells. The reason for this contrast with the Components Factory can be found in the degree of control over manning and effort levels which shopfloor organizations in both Company B plants had built up. One result of this was that workers were able to finish their work well before the end of the shift so that there was relatively little need to take time off to escape the pressures of work. This point is the more notable given that the jobs of semi-skilled workers in the Large Factory were the epitome of the picture of 'alienated' work, with workers doing repetitive jobs in large and noisy shops. Yet few workers said that they found their jobs boring. Just as the 'boredom' of clothing factory workers which we discussed in Chapter 3 can be related to the social context of specific job tasks, so that lack of boredom and of any substantial amount of absenteeism in Company B reflects the fact that workers had sufficient leisure on the job to compensate for the frustrations of the immediate work task.[4]

This point may be rendered even more specific by comparing two shops in one factory. In the Large Metals Factory a new assembly shop, Shop X, had recently been opened. It differed from older shops in having an advanced conveyor belt system for the assembly of components whereas in other shops such sub-assembly was carried out by gangs which were not machine-paced. This had two consequences: workers in Shop X were more closely tied to individual work stations than were workers elsewhere; and, since the track ran at a pre-determined speed, it was not possible to finish work early by working hard in the morning. This might be expected to lead to a high rate of absenteeism. Yet, as Table 4.1 shows, the absence patterns of semi-skilled workers, who were those most affected by the new technology, differed little from those of their counterparts in the similarly-sized Shop Y. The extent of collective control over manning may help to explain this. Manning levels which were

4. The general similarity between the Small and Large Metals Factories despite their marked difference in size suggests that no simple 'size effect' was at work: absence patterns reflected patterns of control.

negotiated when Shop X was established were more generous than management's work study calculations suggested they should be. The result was that break times could be considerably extended and groups of workers could cover a series of work stations so that it was possible to take turns at having an additional break. Pressures of work were thus not very different from those elsewhere in the factory. It was not the technology as such which was important but the degree of control which was established over its operation.

A further factor which moderated the pressure of work was the presence of informal rotas for periods of time off lasting up to half a day. These were well-established in the main assembly shops and resembled the well-known practice in the docks whereby members of a gang take it in turn to take time off (Mellish, 1972: 71–4: Wilson, 1972: 215). Such practices are probably less common in manufacturing. Certainly one worker told us of his surprise, after joining the plant from another firm, at being told by his new work mates that it was his turn for an afternoon off; he had discovered that this was a regular practice and, while retaining his sense of disbelief that management could tolerate it, he found it a very useful perk. The established nature of the rotas can be illustrated by the existence in one shop of written lists for time off which were openly displayed at work stations. Their origins will be examined in more detail in the following chapter, but their present significance for what we may call unrecorded absenteeism is two-fold.

First, if workers can take up to half a day off work without being counted as absent then the figures given in Table 4.1 will obviously underestimate the extent of absenteeism. This may in turn seem to vitiate the contrast between the two Company B plants and the other factories. However, while there certainly was some under-recording, we doubt whether it was so great as to destroy the contrasts in Table 4.1. Periods of unauthorized absence were obviously very short and may not even have fallen within our definition of absenteeism.[5] And the system of rotas was far from universal; it seems to have been absent in the toolroom, for example, and, for reasons which we explore in Chapter 5, it was not used at all in the Small Metals Factory. Moreover, unrecorded absence was, by definition, not counted as absenteeism by management; Table 4.1 indicates the amount of absenteeism which was formally recorded and which was thus open to sanction, and for many purposes this is the most important measure. The system of rotas was simply one aspect of the shopfloor control over effort levels which existed throughout Company B: workers in some areas of the Large Metals Factory extended their control by consolidating the leisure they had created into separate periods of time off.

5. Our definition of absence excludes absences lasting less than half a shift (see Appendix A, p. 293) and hence a proportion of unrecorded absences would not fall within it. In any event, such absences will not affect figures for the frequency of absences lasting a day or more or for total days lost.

This leads into the second aspect of unrecorded absence, namely its implications for managerial control. Although it was unrecorded, managers were plainly aware of it; indeed workers who were caught leaving the factory at unauthorized times were 'recorded' in files of disciplinary action and not absenteeism. There were also several attempts to control the behaviour. But it was a failure of managerial control which led to the growth of the practice in the first place. We have mentioned loose manning standards but there was also a more specific influence at work since even the most generous manning levels do not in themselves mean that workers can leave the plant without being disciplined. This influence was the inability of foremen closely to monitor who was working on a particular section, which was in turn the result of the lack of control by foremen over many matters where such control was taken for granted in other factories. These included the allocation of work and the movement of workers between jobs. The result was that a worker could slip away without his absence necessarily being noticed; and if a foreman did remark on it there was little that he could do since he could not prove that the workers was absent as distinct from being somewhere else in the plant. We go into control over man allocation and related matters in later chapters. Its present significance is to show how very specific aspects of the control structure of a factory affected apparently unrelated phenomena such as patterns of absence.

Without relating absenteeism to the nature of the control structure of the plant it would be impossible to understand the patterns of behaviour summarized in Tables 4.1 and 4.2. These tables describe, however, only broad differences between plants, and we must ask whether there were any other variations in absence patterns which can be explained in terms of patterns of control. Apart from fluctuations due to epidemics of illness and the like, absence resulting from 'genuine' causes can be expected to run at a more or less steady level. Any deviations from this might then indicate that workers were using absence as a conscious strategy to further their own interests. Two types of patterning, variations by day of the week and trends over time, are of particular interest.

The Blue Monday Syndrome
Behrend (1951: 46, 104–6) introduced the 'blue Monday' index to measure absence as a form of conscious withdrawal: it was hard to distinguish absence which was strictly voluntary from the remainder but, since genuine sickness could be assumed to vary randomly across days of the week, an index of the variation of absence over the week would provide an indirect indication of the extent of voluntary withdrawal. Behrend calculated the index as the difference between absence rates on the best and worst days for attendance and, since Friday was consistently the best day and Monday the worst, she called the index the blue Monday syndrome. Although there are technical difficulties with the

index (Chadwick-Jones et al., 1971) and although it should not be assumed that the blue Monday syndrome is universal, the index is useful here less as a proxy for voluntary withdrawal than as a means of assessing whether there were differences between our factories which can be related to the more general picture presented above.

We allocated the total number of days of absence in two of our engineering factories to the day of the week on which they fell. As Table 4.3 shows, there was no pronounced blue Monday effect; indeed, in the Electrical Factory Friday was the most, and not the least, popular day for absence. There was no blue Monday effect here nor, as far as we can judge, in our other engineering plants; certainly no manager mentioned absence on a particular day of the week as a significant problem.[6]

TABLE 4.3

ABSENCE BY DAY OF THE WEEK IN TWO ENGINEERING FACTORIES

| | *Per cent of Days of Absence Falling on* | | | | |
	Mon.	*Tues.*	*Wed.*	*Thurs.*	*Fri.*
Electrical:					
Men	19.3	20.1	19.7	19.6	21.4
Women	20.1	19.1	19.6	20.2	21.0
Large Metals	21.5	19.9	19.6	19.4	19.7

The situation was very different in the clothing plants. Managers in the Hosiery Factory had become so concerned about absenteeism on Fridays that they had moved pay day from Thursday to Friday; they claimed that this had helped to solve the problem, although the change was too recent to make a proper assessment of its effects. In the Underwear Factory the problem was tackled differently: under a long-standing arrangement work on Friday ended at 1.00 p.m., with the time being made up on other days. This seems to have reduced the problem of Friday absenteeism to insignificance, as the distribution of absences by day of the week in Table 4.4 shows. But there was a substantial blue Monday effect, with over a third of one-day absences falling on Mondays and over half of longer absences starting on that day. A proper assessment of this effect requires further consideration, however, for a strict model based on the random distribution of 'genuine' sickness should include week-ends in the

6. The complex seven-day shift system in the Process Factory made the notion of a blue Monday syndrome irrelevant here. The question of whether workers tended to go absent at week-ends and other prime times is considered below.

analysis. Hence one-day absences recorded as falling on Monday will include a proportion of longer absences starting at the week-end and finishing on Monday; and longer absences recorded as starting on Monday will in fact have started earlier. It is possible to try to make some allowance for this, but precise estimates cannot be made from our data. In any event, a random model begs several questions about illness: it implies that there is a fixed level of sickness such that illnesses can be said to have started at week-ends, whereas equally important is the social process by which people decide that they are too ill to go to work. Certainly the extent to which absences fell on Mondays cannot be explained in terms of a random effects model. And we saw earlier that one-day absences in the clothing plants seem to have reflected the pressures of work induced by tight managerial control: in this context it is reasonable to infer from Table 4.4 that workers were planning their escapes and were not acting 'spontaneously'. Since Friday was less than a full working day, Monday was the obvious day to go absent since the week-end break was extended. But the blue Monday syndrome was not universal: its presence depended on the use which workers made of casual absence as a response to the type of control that they experienced.

TABLE 4.4

UNDERWEAR FACTORY: ABSENCE AMONG WOMEN WORKERS BY DAY OF THE WEEK

| | *Per Cent of Absences Falling on* | | | | |
	Mon.	*Tues.*	*Wed.*	*Thurs.*	*Fri.*
One-day absences	36.1	21.1	17.9	17.6	7.3
Other absences:					
Starting	54.8	20.5	16.3	6.7	1.7
Finishing	3.5	24.0	15.7	10.5	46.3
Total starting	41.3	21.0	17.4	14.5	5.7

Fluctuations over Time

This is not to suggest that workers in the clothing factories were the only ones to use absenteeism strategically. Thus, in the Electrical and Large Metals Factories we found marked peaks of absence during the summer months. The obvious explanation of this is that a day off during the summer is more attractive than one during the winter. In addition, the main factory holidays came in the summer and the dramatic peak of absence just before the holiday can be explained in terms of a desire to extend this break.

A revealing example of the strategic use of absence occurred in the Components Factory during the national engineering dispute of 1979.[7] It will be recalled that the dispute developed from an overtime ban into a series of one- and two-day strikes which were spread over eight weeks in this factory. One might well expect all three indices of absence rates to decline during the strike. If casual one-day absences are a response to the boredom of work, a period during which workers were taking a break (admittedly an enforced one) of one or two days a week might be expected to lead to very little spontaneous withdrawal. Similarly, the loss of earnings caused by the strike might be expected to have led workers to cut back on longer absences. As Table 4.5 shows, however, neither expectation was met: the rate of one-day absences fell only slightly, while the frequency of absences lasting more than a day was twice the usual rate.

TABLE 4.5

ABSENCE RATES IN THE COMPONENTS FACTORY
DURING THE NATIONAL ENGINEERING STRIKE

(Per Cent)

	Strike Period[a]	*12-month Period*[b]
Total shifts lost	12.1	7.8
Frequency: one-day absences	0.9	1.3
other absences	1.5	0.8

NOTES
a. Figures cover an eight-week period for two departments, one from each shop, male production workers only.
b. All production workers (male).

Part of the latter increase is plainly a statistical artefact: a worker who was absent for a whole year would count as having one spell of absence but, expressed as a percentage of the number of shifts due to be worked, this one spell would give a higher rate the shorter the period of measurement. But since the rate of days lost was also substantially higher than usual there seems to have been a genuine effect at work. Workers seem to have taken a strategic view, feeling perhaps, in the case of short absences, that if they were on strike for a day or two another day would make little difference. A more important strategy may have been to go sick for a long period, thus qualifying for sick pay and avoiding any loss of earnings. Foremen certainly reported that they had had

7. We discuss the detailed impact of the strike at factory level elsewhere: see P. Edwards and Scullion, 1982b.

workers doing this but it is impossible to say how common the practice was. Some workers may have been constrained by doubts as to whether those off sick would receive sick pay for every day they were away or only for the non-strike days. And we question in a later section how widespread abuse was in 'normal' times. During the strike, however, there was a strong incentive to report sick: even if the strike days did not qualify for benefit a worker could gain a lengthy break without losing any more money than if he or she reported for work. It seems likely, therefore, that there was a degree of 'abuse' of the sick pay scheme during the strike. Or, to put it less emotively, workers were using the system of sick benefits strategically even though they did not necessarily do so at other times.

Conclusions

As with labour turnover, our absence data show a great range of situations, with the clothing plants (or, more strictly, the women in those plants) at one extreme and the Large Metals Factory at the other. Intense managerial control in the clothing factories was associated with the widespread use of one-day absences. These absences were not distributed randomly but seem to have been timed strategically to suit workers' interests. In the Large Metals Factory, and also in the Small Metals Factory, workers' ability to exert control over manning standards and effort levels meant that there were considerable opportunities for leisure at work, with the result that going absent was rare. In addition workers in the Large Metals Factory had developed their own informal system to extend leisure in work into leisure outside work. Their rotas for time off had become part of custom and practice, with the result that 'unrecorded absence' had a very different role from that of normal casual absenteeism. In particular it was collective and it challenged management's right to demand that workers be present when management wanted them. As such it was far removed from the image of absenteeism as spontaneous, individual, withdrawal.

There is a danger, however, of implying that all workers were consciously using absence to 'exploit' the system wherever possible. Most workers attend work for most of the time, and the strategic use of absence needs to be related to the constraints on the behaviour which were imposed by managerial controls and by workers' perceptions of the possibility and legitimacy of using absence as a form of escape. To continue our account of absence patterns we begin with shopfloor views before turning to managerial control systems.

Shopfloor Views on Absence

General Images of Absence

Despite the widespread tendency to assert that absenteeism is a form of withdrawal from work, there have been few direct investigations of workers' perceptions of the issue. For example, it has become widely accepted that Hill and Trist (1953) in their study of an iron and steel works demonstrated that there was a cultural norm of absence. This implies that evidence on workers' attitudes to absence was collected and that informal rules on when it was proper to take time off were discovered and explained. In fact, the idea of a norm on absence was developed from inspection of a table of the frequency distribution of absences similar to Table 4.2 above. The table showed 'a pronounced mode with considerable positive skewness. *This suggests* the existence of *some kind of a norm* as regards absence behaviour' (Hill and Trist, 1953: 364, emphasis added). In this section we analyse norms on absence more directly.

Ingham (1970) attempted to deal with this issue by asking his Bradford engineering workers to select one of two statements about absence from work, and to explain their choice. The two statements were: 'a man should not stay away from work in any event, except when it is really necessary, as in the case of genuine sickness'; and 'it's a free society and a man has the right to take a day off work once in a while if he wants to'. Ingham (1970: 119–21) found that workers in his small plants were somewhat more likely than those in large plants to choose the first option. But what really stood out were the reasons for this: two-thirds of workers in the small plants who chose the first option cited their duty and responsibility to the firm as the reason for the choice. These were the responses of 'morally involved workers'. Workers in large plants took a calculative approach, stressing the loss of earnings involved in casual absence. In his study of agricultural workers Newby (1977a: 313) found that two-thirds of his sample chose the first option, a proportion somewhat lower than that of Ingham's small-plant workers.

We put the same question, shorn of its sexist language, to our questionnaire sample. As Table 4.6 shows, the most pronounced contrast in replies was between men and women in the clothing industry: only 22 per cent of the former chose the 'free society' option as against 69 per cent of the latter. This result might come as something of a surprise taken on its own but it is completely consistent with the argument of Chapter 3: women in the clothing factories were the group most subject to managerial control and, despite expectations that they would display a high degree of loyalty and deference, they were also the most likely to express an anti-managerial view on absenteeism. Men in the same industry experienced less direct control and were also more responsive to managerial paternalism, and they selected the 'genuine sickness' option in large numbers. Even they, however, did not follow Ingham's morally committed workers by giving duty to the firm as the reason for choosing this option. For them, as for most other groups, loss of money was the main reason for not taking days off.

The Process Factory had the greatest proportion of replies stressing duty to the firm. As one man put it in justifying his choice, 'I don't want to sound a

TABLE 4.6

GENERAL ATTITUDES TO ABSENCE FROM WORK

	Components (N=123)	*Small Metals* (N=43)	*All Clothing* Men (N=56)	Women (N=127)	*Process* (N=98)
Per cent of workers choosing 'genuine sickness' option[a]	58	49	78	31	60
Number of reasons for choice	92	30	62	44	77
Reason as per cent of all reasons given					
Duty to firm	23	17	18	20	36
Duty to workmates	11	17	13	2	9
Loss of money	38	47	40	36	10
General[b]	18	10	23	32	27
Other/don't know	10	10	6	9	17
Per cent of workers choosing 'free society' option[c]	42	51	22	69	40
Number of reasons for choice	53	26	13	94	45
Reason as per cent of all reasons given					
Boredom	23	12		23	18
Outside commitments	15	12		7	13
General[b]	53	50		54	58
Other	10	27		15	11

NOTES
a. Per cent agreeing with statement 'a person should not stay away from work in any event, except when it is really necessary, as in the case of genuine sickness'.
b. i.e. reasons that were little more than rephrasings of the option given: see text for fuller explanation.
c. Per cent agreeing with statement 'it's a free society and people have the right to take a day off once in a while if they want to'.

company man, but anyone who works owes loyalty to the employer'. This is again consistent with our earlier argument that workers' attitudes in this factory were shaped by the lack of the collective identity which characterized the engineering plants and by the success of management in creating an atmosphere of co-operation and trust. We also suggested, however, that aspects of quitting reflected a muted response to the problems induced by shift work, and we will argue later that there was a similar situation in the case of absence: the atmosphere of co-operation was not totally dominant.

Even in the Process Factory moral commitment in Ingham's sense was rare: those mentioning duty to the firm comprised only 22 per cent of the whole sample in this factory. Such commitment may be stronger in very small units but, again as indicated in Chapter 3, in plants employing more than, say, 100 workers strong feelings of loyalty based on interpersonal contact are unlikely, and the degree of bureaucracy cannot explain variations in workers' attitudes. Now it may be suggested that our figures underestimate the importance of duty to the firm because of the inclusion of the category of replies labelled 'general'. In fact we probed to see what lay behind a worker's reply and if, say, duty to the firm was mentioned we coded it accordingly. Only those replies which were so vague as to constitute little more than a rephrasing of one of the options which we offered were categorized as 'general'. The number of such replies, particularly in the case of the 'free society' option, suggests that many workers did not have a thought-out view on absence or, at least, that they took the matter as being so obvious as to require no further elucidation.

From many points of view this is far from surprising: if workers agree with the statement that it is reasonable to take a day off once in a while they need not be expected to provide detailed justifications for this. The finding is sur- prising, however, if the issue is approached with the expectation that workers' main reasons for taking days off will reflect boredom, 'alienation', or whatever. Indeed, we gave workers every opportunity to argue that it was the boredom of their work which led them to want to take days off. However, not only were replies mentioning boredom rare among all groups but several workers explicitly denied that boredom was involved. Instead, replies focused on what we may call the routine frustrations of going to work such as the problem of getting up in the morning. One woman worker in the Hosiery Factory for example said, 'It's not really boredom with the job. It's just that things get too much for you and you need a rest; you feel generally fed up.' One or two others said that they would be just as bored at home as at work, a view echoed by a Components Factory worker who felt that taking time off was pointless since he would not know what to do 'wandering round the streets all day'. More generally, workers in all our factories said that work became boring at times but that it was simply necessary to overcome boredom: 'you just get used to it', 'it's mind over matter'. Others argued that taking a day off did not achieve anything since the job was still there the next day; and some said that they feared that knocking days off could become a habit if they started doing it every time they felt a little dis- gruntled.

Now this is not to deny that these statements reflected negative views of work. The drudgery and petty frustrations of routine manual work were plainly evident. Yet workers' discontents were much more diffuse than an account based on the boredom of specific tasks would suggest. Going absent was not a direct failure of the worker to adjust to work tasks but a more general response to the continuous demands of factory work. And neither was it a universal response. We argued earlier that workers' needs to take time off varied according to the degree of control which they could exercise over their work. We have now seen that workers took for granted the need to work regularly, even to the extent that no alternative could be envisaged: comments about the boredom of being at home reflect the dominating effect of working regularly and the lack of positive alternatives.

Self-Reported Absence

Our question about absenteeism was, however, couched in very general terms. On a question more directly related to their own experience workers might talk about boredom or other task-related matters. We therefore went on to ask, 'How about you, have you ever felt like taking a day off when you have been able to get into work?' Those who had felt like a day off were also asked whether they had acted on the feeling and, if not, what had prevented them from doing so. The results are shown in Table 4.7.

The great majority of women in the clothing industry not only reported feeling like having a day off but also said that they had acted on the feeling: two-thirds of them said that they had taken a day off when they had been able to get into work, and their reasons for feeling like a day off concentrated on the frustrations of work itself: women reported that they 'got fed up' or 'needed a change', and, as we have already seen, several talked explicitly about the pressures of work. Absence appears clearly, then, as a conscious form of escape rather than time off to attend to outside commitments.

The greatest contrast was again with men in the same industry: only 14 per cent of men had taken a day off work voluntarily. As argued earlier, this reflects differences in patterns of control: as one ancillary worker said, there was a very relaxed atmosphere on night shift with workers being able to move around as they pleased. A large proportion of these workers felt that there was little need to take time off. Those who had felt like taking a day off, however, did not exhibit any marked feeling of duty to the firm, with the loss of earnings being the main reason for not taking time off.

There was one group which approached women in the clothing industry in terms of the extent of self-reported absence: skilled men in the Components Factory. This similarity must be seen in context, however: the frequency of absence among these men was, as Table 4.1 shows, low. Although many men said that they had taken time off, it did not follow that they did this very often. Moreover, their reasons for wanting time off differed greatly from those given by the women in the clothing industry. The main category of replies was 'outside commitments'. This reflected not just family commitments but a more general feeling that there were legitimate concerns outside the workplace which workers had the right to pursue. This was most clearly expressed by a toolmaker who said, when asked whether he took days off, 'I suit myself. If I feel like a day off with the wife that's my business'. He went on to argue that if he

TABLE 4.7

FEELINGS ON HAVING A DAY OFF WORK

	Components Skilled	Semi- skilled	Small Metals	All Clothing Men	Women	Process
	(N=48)	(N=75)				
Per cent who had:						
Not felt like day off	6	27	21	43	6	21
Felt like day off and:						
Acted on feeling	52	29	42	14	68	33
Not acted on feeling	42	44	37	43	26	46
Number of reasons for						
feeling like a day off	62	71	41	47	150	109
Reason as per cent of all reasons						
Boredom	8	21	27	11	31	16
Outside commitments	53	34	24	24	18	45
Routine frustrations of						
going to work	34	38	24	40	41	34
Other	5	6	20	8	5	4
Don't know	0	0	5	17	4	0
Number of reasons for not						
having acted on desire						
for day off	25	43	17	41	34	54
Reason as per cent of all reasons						
Duty to firm	20	9		12	3	28
Duty to workmates	10	21		17	6	6
Loss of money	68	51		61	53	19
General	0	2		0	0	24
Other	0	5		5	26	22
Don't know	4	12		5	12	2

could afford to lose a day's pay then he had the right to do as he liked with his time: 'after all, we are only hourly paid'. More generally, several skilled men said that they should be treated as responsible people; as one electrician put it, discipline should be enforced not by chasing everyone but by dealing with the few people who broke the rules. These skilled men were saying that they had independent skills and should not be tied too closely to the firm. As we show in later chapters this claim to autonomy was expressed in such things as resentment at close supervision as well as in attitudes to time off.

These attitudes are the more notable in that they conflict with a common image of the craft worker. Thus Davis (1979: 103) says in his discussion of maintenance fitters that 'as a general rule, "pride in the work", and hence personal satisfaction and self-esteem for the self-styled craftsman, is incompatible with "restrictive" practices, withdrawal and mild forms of sabotage which are expressions of conflict in other work situations.' But we have seen that, while withdrawal was certainly not common, craft workers were very different from other workers in asserting the right to take time off. More generally, Davis seems to ignore the whole range of 'restrictive practices' such as controls on entry to the trade and collective restrictions of effort which are widely seen as the distinguishing characteristics of the craft form of organization in Britain. In later chapters we describe a wide range of such practices employed by craft workers in the Components Factory and elsewhere. 'Self-esteem' involved autonomy, and such autonomy was not in contradiction with restrictive practices or withdrawal; indeed, it was central to them. Davis's confusion seems to arise from using attitudinal data to make inferences about behaviour: he actually presents no information on the absence behaviour of his workers or on their collective 'restrictive practices'.

The limitations of Davis's approach would be of no more than passing interest were it not for their ability to illustrate a more general problem, namely that of making inferences about behaviour from more-or-less sophisticated attitude surveys. The problem is most obvious in the literature which examines unionization in terms of the expressed attitudes of individuals and not the organizational context in which those individuals are placed (see Bain et al., 1973). For example white-collar workers are said to possess sets of attitudes which militate against their joining unions. Yet there may be no contradiction between holding those attitudes and being in a union. Similarly, Davis infers from craftsmen's pride in their work that these workers will not be prone to conflictual action, whereas pride and self-esteem are in fact consistent with, and may indeed encourage, conflict with those who challenge that self-esteem. It is often said that attitudes do not predict behaviour; here is a prime illustration of the dangers of failing to take such statements seriously.

Craft workers in the Components Factory had, then, a high rate of self-reported absence even though their general views on absence did not differ from those of semi-skilled workers in that plant and even though their rate of absence frequency was not particularly high. The explanation of these apparently contradictory findings is that, while craftsmen were prepared to take days off, they did not need to do so more than occasionally. Like workers in the Company B plants they had considerable control over the timing and character of their labour. A toolmaker, for example, was assigned to a particular machine and could not be moved to another job without his steward's agreement; and maintenance fitters worked through a list of repair jobs made out by the foreman so that if there was no job listed they could legitimately do nothing. Such leisure plainly reduced the need for a day off. Craftsmen were prepared to take time off when they wanted but did not often need to do so. This raises the question of whether craft workers in the Large Metals Factory, who not only shared a tradition of craft autonomy but who were, as we saw in Chapter 3, thoroughly disenchanted with management, took a similar view of absenteeism. While we have no quantifiable information on this, our interviews suggested that absenteeism was not an important means of escape, for the obvious reason that workers who were dissatisfied with their wages did not want to lose money by taking days off. There was, instead, a withdrawal of effort within the workplace.

Our argument about craft workers in the Components Factory raises the obvious issue of whether there was a link between self-reported absence and replies to the general question about the legitimacy of taking time off. We use the craft workers as the most important substantive example.[8] A simple cross-classification of replies indicated that there was a statistically significant association: there was a tendency for workers saying that people had the right to take a day off to report having taken a day off themselves. But the degree of association was not strong, and the nature of 'significance' needs to be carefully assessed (see Morrison and Henkel, 1970). The relationship was significant in that there was only a small likelihood that the observed pattern differed from an expected pattern by chance. But the expected pattern here was simply that there was no association at all between the two variables. An equally plausible, and more interesting, null hypothesis is that replies on the general question were sufficient to predict replies on the self-report question. When we tested this hypothesis we also found a 'significant' deviation from expectations: we could not predict replies about an individual's own behaviour from the general question. In addition to strengthening the point that attitudes do not predict behaviour, for here answers to a general attitude question did not accurately predict workers' reports of their own behaviour let alone their actual behaviour, this has a substantive importance. Craftsmen, and indeed other workers, held general views about the legitimacy of taking time off for the sake of it. But they found that they themselves needed time off to meet outside interests and they had little compunction about meeting the need. There was no contradiction between general views and specific practices.

Despite the willingness of craftsmen, and of women in the clothing plants, to take a day off when they felt like it, substantial numbers of workers in all factories said that, although they had at times felt like a day off, they had never acted on the feeling. As Table 4.7 shows, loss of earnings was, except in the Process Factory, the dominant reason for not taking time off. In many ways this is obvious, but it is still important evidence against the view that workers internalize a sense of duty to attend regularly: the overwhelming fact was that a day's absence costs money.

In the Process Factory feelings of duty were fairly widespread: duty to the

---

8. We carried out the analysis for several other groups, with similar results in all cases.

firm was explicitly mentioned by 28 per cent of those who wanted a day off but had never taken one, while a further 24 per cent gave more general arguments, such as that the desire for time off was natural but should be resisted, which can plainly be related to a notion of duty. Some men had an articulated view of duty: one used the word 'loyalty' and said that he tried to be a model worker, while another had no time for 'malingerers' and felt that holidays and rest days provided plenty of time off.[9] These workers formed a significant group of 'morally committed' employees. Other workers, however, felt the constraints of shift work to be more severe: a common argument was that the only way to meet the normal commitments of family life was to take a day off from time to time. We assess this in more detail in relation to management's disciplinary system in the following section. Its present significance is that even those who did not talk in terms of duty to the firm saw absence in terms of outside needs and not of the frustrations of mundane work. Here, as in our other factories, attitudes to absence reflected differing needs for time off and differing perceptions of constraints on meeting these needs.

Conclusions

The attitudes to absence described here cannot be understood in isolation. The very similar patterns of self-reported absence among women in the clothing industry and skilled men in the Components Factory, for example, stemmed from very different circumstances. This sharply illustrates the dangers of divorcing attitudes from behaviour which we mentioned in Chapter 1: the significance of attitudes to absence has to be understood in the context of workplace relations. Seen in this light, the attitudes of women in the clothing industry can be seen as a response to managerial control over the labour process: not only were rates of one-day absence high but women themselves reported that they felt a need to escape and were willing to act on it. This evidence, together with that on the much less widespread use of absence as a means of escape from our other factories, complements our earlier findings on rates of absenteeism.

We began this section by pointing to the inadequate evidence on which existing arguments about cultural norms on absence are based. Since we have now discovered the presence of distinct sets of attitudes to absence the question arises as to whether these attitudes stemmed from distinct work group norms on absence. If such norms are taken to mean distinct expectations as to the conduct of members of the group, which may be enforced by sanctions against nonconformists, then no clear norms existed. Workers might complain about 'skivers'

9. In view of our argument in Chapter 3 that the diversity of work experience in this plant reduced workers' awareness of collective interests as against management it is notable that these men were, respectively, a man with over thirty years' service in the armed services and an ex-railwayman.

but in most of our factories there were few sanctions which work groups as such could deploy. The main exception was the Large Metals Factory where, as we have seen, control of attendance was part of a wider set of controls over effort and where absence could thus be seen as part of collective custom and practice. Even here, however, social norms, like other aspects of custom and practice, depended on interpretations of formal managerial rules (William Brown, 1972). As argued in the following section and in Chapter 5, managerial interests have to be taken into account, and such interests can change. Work group norms do not exist in a void.

We have pointed to the similarities between the Large Metals Factory and industries such as the docks in terms of informal control of attendance. The factory also exemplifies the more general lesson which Mellish and Collis-Squires (1976) draw from studies of customary controls, namely that matters of absenteeism and discipline cannot be treated as purely individual affairs and that collective norms are crucial. Yet, in contrasting formal, individualistic legal norms with informal social norms, these writers exaggerate the importance of social norms. They contrast legal norms with what actually happens in well-organized industries such as printing, the docks, and those parts of engineering where custom and practice is well-established. Our evidence on the clothing plants, together with that of Armstrong et al. (1981) on similarly weakly-organized workplaces, points to the lack of anything like customary control over absence (and, as we shall see in later chapters, over many other aspects of work) in situations of intense managerial domination. And even in the Company A plants and the Process Factory, where shop stewards had accepted roles in shopfloor relations, collective workers' control over attendance did not exist. Norms, moreover, have a positive as well as a negative character: they involve workers in punishing those who do not perform adequately as well as permitting the bending of managerial rules. Thus we were often told by workers and foremen in the Large Metals Factory that, under piecework, gangs of workers would insist that anyone who did not pull his weight must be removed from the gang. With the end of piecework workers' incentives to engage in such positive sanctions became less important.

Mellish and Collis-Squires (1976: 170–1) argue that 'the union – or fellow workers – may be a greater disciplinary force upon the individual worker than the employer'. We would suggest that this possibility becomes realized in fact only when workers have developed considerable autonomous control over the labour process and where management has abdicated an important part of its control function. This was certainly the case in the Large Metals Factory. The relative weakness of collective controls over attendance in the Small Metals Factory suggests that this is not, however, a sufficient condition. We explore the differences between these two factories in Chapter 5, but may indicate here that part of the difference lay in the practice of working in autonomous gangs in the Large Metals Factory, which encouraged the development of highly specific norms. Finally, a pay system relating earnings to effort encouraged positive sanctions on members of gangs.

The obvious source of discipline is not the work group but management. Yet the fear of punishment did not feature at all strongly in workers' statements about why they did not take time off work. This must be investigated by looking more closely at management's role in the control of absence.

Management and Absence

Two aspects of management's role will be given particular attention. First, perceptions of absence held by managers and foremen are important indicators of how far absenteeism is seen as a 'problem' by participants. Second, as we have just seen, organizational rules are only part of the negotiation of order: management's role in the interpretation of rules is plainly central. These two aspects are obviously closely related, for management's general perception of the problem will affect how it is tackled. We therefore consider our factories in three groups: the two clothing plants, the four engineering plants, and the Process Factory as a distinct case on its own.

The Clothing Factories: Absence as a Non-Problem
As with perceptions of labour turnover, perceptions of absence were not closely related to the 'facts' of the behaviour as measured by rates of absenteeism. For example, there was relatively little concern about absence in the clothing plants despite the very high frequency of absences here. Again as with turnover, mangers in this industry explained the situation in terms of the characteristics of the workforce: women had family responsibilities, they were more prone to illness than men, and so on. We have already seen that such accounts are inadequate as complete explanations of the position in the industry, but it is not difficult to see why managers employed them: there was no external basis of comparison and, given the 'obvious' 'fact' that women are inherently more absence-prone than men, managers had an account which was sufficient for their own purposes. We must go further than this, however, for the crucial point about absenteeism was not so much the rate of the behaviour but its use as a means of escape from management's own control system. Managers might be expected to respond to this by, for example, complaining about the 'irresponsibility' of young women. In fact, they took the opposite view, stressing that workers were responsible and that they did not take time off unless they needed it. They were thus denying what in our view was a central feature of their factories namely that absence was an expression of conflict. How can this be explained?

It might be argued that the answer lies in the self-consciously anti-bureaucratic approach which these firms took to record-keeping: perhaps supervisors had no reliable system for recording absenteeism. In fact, supervisors kept detailed records, and were at least as knowledgeable about the behaviour of individual workers as foremen elsewhere. Indeed, both firms had tighter controls than others in that workers were required, and not just expected, to inform their supervisors if they were unable to attend work. This requirement was incorporated in the works rules of the Underwear Factory: 'If for any reason you are unable to attend work you should telephone your section Supervisor at once giving your reason for being absent and when you expect to return .... Time off is definitely not encouraged, but if you have a special reason for leaving work you must ask your Supervisor and produce appointment cards etc.' But women were still able to evade the demands of the system. Thus, foremen's claims to the contrary notwithstanding, they were able to go absent without informing their supervisors of the reason. We obtained a rough check on this by examining the foremen's record book in one section of the Hosiery Factory where absence control was said to be particularly strict. As Table 4.8 shows, almost 20 per cent of one-day absences were recorded by supervision as being for no reason. Moreover, of course, an unknown proportion of those saying that they were ill were in fact using this as the most obvious excuse for absence. Certainly, several of the workers whom we interviewed said that when they took a day off they just told their supervisor that they had been ill; as they stressed it was very hard for management directly to challenge such statements.

TABLE 4.8

HOSIERY FACTORY: STATED REASONS FOR ABSENCE AMONG WOMEN IN ONE DEPARTMENT

	Per Cent of Absences	
	One-Day (N=344)	Other (N=115)
Ill, with doctor's note	—	41.7
Ill, no note	58.4	31.3
Family responsibilities	16.3	8.7
Travel problems	2.9	0
No reason given	19.5	10.4
Other	3.0	7.8

Ignorance about absenteeism cannot, then, explain managerial actions. The key to the situation lies in the nature of management's control within the workplace. At the most general level managers did not feel that their authority was under challenge from the shopfloor and they did not need to develop arguments about the irresponsibility of the modern worker; as we shall see, such arguments were common in Company A even though absenteeism was 'objectively' less of a problem here. Managerial control also had specific consequences. For example, in the clothing plants managers had a very great deal of freedom to move workers between jobs; they could ask a worker to move at a moment's notice and clearly took it for granted that such 'requests' would be obeyed. Absenteeism on one section could thus be covered easily and quickly, whereas in our engineering plants, where there were more shopfloor constraints on managerial control over labour mobility, absenteeism could create substantial problems for foremen. Moreover, machinery was not expensive so that a day's absence did not impose large costs in terms of idle capital equipment; in the Components Factory, by contrast, having a machine idle was a major concern. A day's absence did not, then, create any severe problems for managers in the clothing industry. In addition, of course, it would have been difficult for managers, with their view of their plants as peaceful and co-operative places, to admit that absenteeism was an expression of worker resentment against the system of control within the factory. They therefore gave absenteeism little attention, and there were, for example, no widespread attempts to control it through the disciplinary procedures or otherwise.

A final aspect of absenteeism in these plants was the lack of any company-financed sick pay scheme. Absenteeism thus imposed no direct financial penalty on the firms, whereas in our other factories sick pay schemes were in operation and any 'abuse' cost management the value of benefits paid out as well as the value of production lost. This might be expected to affect the patterns of absenteeism described earlier. It is certainly possible that aspects of those patterns, notably the importance of one-day absence in the clothing plants, were influenced by differences in sick pay arrangements: since sick pay is typically paid only for absences lasting three days or more, firms with schemes would be expected to have longer but fewer absences than firms without schemes. Yet the main effect of such expected differences is simply to strengthen the contrasts already made. Even without sick pay schemes the clothing plants had rates of days lost, and frequency rates of absences lasting over a day, which were similar to those elsewhere. Rates would be expected to be even higher if sick pay was introduced.

The Engineering Factories: The Abuse of Sickness Benefit and the Role of the Foreman
Our main concern with sick pay schemes is the effect they had on managerial perceptions of absence. Criticism was most acute in the two Company A plants,

with virtually all foremen and shop managers[10] seeing absence, and particularly that which could be related to the firm's sick pay scheme, as an important problem. This can be explained, we argue, not in terms of any 'abuse' of the scheme but as a reflection of foremen's more general concerns with their own position in the managerial hierarchy. They felt that face-to-face relations on the shopfloor remained good, and hence did not see casual absenteeism as a significant problem. But they were concerned about an erosion of the foreman's ability to deal with all aspects of workers' behaviour: formal procedures for giving warnings about attendance and time-keeping were operated by personnel departments at a distance from shopfloor realities. As a result, foremen felt, their own skill in generating good relationships with the shopfloor was unable to counteract tendencies set in train by senior managers, one of which was the exploitation by workers of sick pay arrangements. Benefits were provided by managers who, while well-intentioned, lacked the insight into shopfloor affairs to realize that workers would make the most of any benefits given to them.[11]

Hence very few foremen engaged in blanket condemnations of absenteeism. Two foremen in the Components Factory, for example, said that workers occasionally went missing on Mondays but that there was no general problem of one-day absenteeism: for a shift-working factory, absenteeism was 'not too bad'. Similarly, foremen did not subscribe to various common views about the nature of the 'absence problem'. A foreman in one of the dirtier and noisier sections of the Electrical Factory, for example, argued that, despite these unpleasant conditions, absence rates on his section were no different from those elsewhere. Absenteeism was not seen as the result of poor working conditions or boredom. Foremen saw workers' motivations in more rational terms. To summarize a view which was often presented diffusely, they felt that workers naturally sought to avoid work but that, by the development of 'good human relations' or by judicious use of 'the carrot and the stick', they could be persuaded to be responsible.

10. Throughout our discussion we use the term shop manager to refer to any member of line management above the level of foreman and below that of factory manager. This includes departmental or section managers, shift managers, and shift supervisors. Since terminologies differed between factories we cannot make a hard-and-fast distinction between managers and foremen. People called managers in the clothing factories for example controlled fewer workers than 'shift supervisors' and 'senior foremen' in parts of our engineering factories. We use the term shop manager simply to give a rough idea of a person's place in the managerial hierarchy.

11. It is possible to demonstrate that foremen's perceptions did not stem directly from their own experience. As Table 4.2 shows over a quarter of women in the Electrical Factory and nearly a third of male production workers in the Components Factory went through a year without an absence lasting over a day. These workers, together with those whose absences lasted less than three days, would not even come within the boundaries of the sick pay scheme. We have discussed sick pay schemes more generally, using data from the Large Metals Factory and a Company A plant, elsewhere (P. Edwards and Scullion, 1979). Doherty (1979) has analysed trends at national level, showing that state, as distinct from company, sickness benefit has had an impact on absence rates.

At shopfloor level the careful exercise of supervisory skills created an atmosphere of trust and responsibility.

Abuse of the sick pay scheme was the result, foremen argued, of a wider social malaise. As several argued at length, there was a general decline in people's willingness to work, which was part of a broad social trend and not specific to their own plant or company. The sick pay scheme merely exacerbated this trend. The intensity of these feelings, which contrasted not only with more sanguine views in other factories but also with the general argument of Company A foremen that industrial relations were generally good, reflects foremen's changing position in the firm. Like supervisors more generally (Child, 1975; Clegg, 1979: 157–60) foremen felt that their status and authority were declining. The growth of trade unionism meant that differentials over manual workers were being eroded and that influential senior stewards were being treated with more respect by the company than were supervisors. Thus one of the early activists in foremen's unionism in the company said that, while shopfloor relations remained good, there was an increasing gap between foremen and higher management. Other supervisors argued in similar vein. That such arguments were more than idle complaints may be seen from a long-running dispute with the company over differentials and a wage structure for foremen. Throughout our research in the Electrical Factory foremen banned covering for absent colleagues in pursuit of their claim, and antipathy towards senior management was considerable. At one point the dispute developed into a three-day strike, during which foremen complained bitterly about the lack of recognition they were given by the company and, a particularly important aspect here, about the failure of senior management to support first-line supervisors in the handling of discipline.

Foremen's views on absenteeism stemmed directly from this context: control of attendance had passed to personnel departments which relied on formal rules and not detailed knowledge of the shopfloor. As one foreman put it, he could deal with a poor attender sympathetically by using his knowledge of the particular case, whereas the personnel department applied rules which cut across personal understandings. The 'abuse' of sick pay arrangements was not universal: foremen argued that, while many workers were still responsible, a minority would think up excuses to go sick and would not be disciplined by management because the formal rules were inadequately applied. Workers could 'get away with things' with little fear of reprisals.

Foremen's views on absence were, then, less important as reflections of the 'absence problem' itself than as indices of important divisions within management. 'Management' is not a homogeneous entity, and the response of management as a whole to a particular issue will depend on the balance of groups within it. We assess particular cases where divisions within management were significant influences on patterns of conflict in the following chapter and in Chapter 10. But we may indicate in a preliminary way here the range of situations in our factories. In the clothing plants there was insufficient hierarchy for distinct groupings to emerge. In our other three companies foremen were seen as the first level of management. At one extreme, supervisors in the Process Factory were well integrated in the hierarchy, as we illustrate below in the case of responses to absenteeism. In the Company A plants foremen felt that they retained control of shopfloor relations but resented the imposition of control systems on top of this. Foremen in Company B felt that even control of day-to-day shopfloor matters had slipped from their grasp. The contrast with Company A in the way that absence was controlled provides a useful illustration of this.

In Company A the day-to-day monitoring of absence, and the initiation of any disciplinary action, lay in the foreman's hands. Any bending of formal rules rested on personal interpretations of the characteristics of workers and not on any articulated customary rules. Each foreman kept an attendance book and was able to discuss the behaviour of each worker in his section in some detail. In Company B, as we have seen, shopfloor controls over the effort bargain had created a series of informal rules around the practice of unrecorded absenteeism. The foreman's role in dealing with absence was correspondingly muted. The Small Metals Factory had until recently had no system at all for monitoring absenteeism, while in the Large Metals Factory absences had always been carefully recorded by the wages department but foremen had no direct role in the process. The contrast is remarkable: in Company A foremen had their own absence records on which they expected to act when necessary, whereas their counterparts in Company B would have to obtain information from the wages department. And if a problem became apparent the authority of foremen in Company B to act on it was limited. As one foreman explained, if he was worried about a particular worker his first action would be to 'have a word' with the shop steward. As the foreman went on to argue, however, this did not necessarily mean that problems were acute: if a worker was known to be acting improperly the steward would generally help management by pointing out to him the error of his ways.

This reflects two aspects of the situation. First, foremen could in many ways be seen as part of the shopfloor culture and not as part of 'management'. They shared the shopfloor view that the end of piecework had destroyed incentives and stressed the need to proceed by negotiation and by retaining the good will of the shopfloor, contrasting this with what they saw as a heavy-handed approach by senior management. This did not mean that foremen took a sanguine view of workplace relations, for many were highly critical of excessive shopfloor power as well as of higher management. But they took for granted many customary ways of doing things, one of which was the reliance on informal rules and negotiation with the steward to control absence. The second aspect of the situation was the stewards' acceptance of the same rules: only certain forms of behaviour were legitimate, and stewards were as keen as foremen to prevent 'excesses'. This did not, of course, imply that stewards would refuse to defend workers accused of poor time-keeping or excessive absenteeism. Such accusations were based on formal managerial rules, and these rules were often dismissed as being unrealistic and inconsistent. It was the informal rules which stewards were more concerned to enforce.

This is, of course, consistent with previous studies of custom and practice and the contrast between formal and informal rules (William Brown, 1973; Terry, 1977), and we do not need to develop the argument further. Our present concern has been to demonstrate that custom and practice takes a variety of forms: in Company A foremen retained considerable control over day-to-day matters, and collective custom and practice on absenteeism was weak. We have also shown how the perceptions of absence held by foremen stemmed from their own role within the managerial hierarchy. In both companies foremen were somewhat estranged from the formal control system, though the extent of this differed. The contrast with the Process Factory, where there was a systematic policy for the control of absence, is instructive.

The Process Factory: Sophisticated Control
Sickness benefits in the Process Factory were more generous than elsewhere since workers were paid their full earnings for a spell of illness of any duration; that is, there was no need for absences to last three days or more to qualify for benefit. And the full benefit was paid for shorter absences even if they were not covered by a doctor's note. This, together with the attraction of taking time off in a continuous shift environment, might be expected to lead to widespread managerial complaints of abuse. Yet managers felt that workers were generally responsible and that abuse was minimal. Now we have seen that this assessment was largely accurate: absence frequency was low and workers' attitudes revealed a greater sense of duty to firm than was apparent elsewhere. Managerial satisfaction with the system can be attributed to these facts and to the lack of sources of concern which marked the engineering factories. But the important question is how this situation had come about.

At the most general level management consciously articulated an ideology of responsibility: the firm provided considerable material benefits and tried to be a responsible employer, and workers were expected to respond in a like spirit. More specifically, as we saw in Chapter 3, management's strategy was to recruit workers who would be likely to accept, or at least to acquiesce in, the view that workers had obligations to the firm. More specifically still, the system of absence monitoring and control was carefully designed to minimize the problems caused by shift working. This had two aspects, the control of casual absence and the programme for the 'retirement' of the long-term sick.

On the former, supervisors were expected to keep a close eye on their absence records and to step in whenever they felt that action was needed. They described, for example, how they looked for a 'pattern' in which a worker started going absent whenever he had to work, say, a Saturday afternoon shift. They also kept a special watch for absences on certain shifts, such as those prior to rest periods, when time off was particularly desirable. Anyone building up a 'pattern' of two or three absences on a particular shift would find his foreman having a 'quiet word' about it. As would be expected from the firm's sophisticated style, every effort was made to handle matters in a relaxed and personal fashion, with the aim being to persuade the individual to improve his attendance record and not simply to punish him. The formal disciplinary procedure of written warnings was used reluctantly.

Without needing to use formal procedures managers were thus able to make clear to workers what level of attendance was required and where improvement was needed. This careful approach tended to limit workers' complaints about absence control: managers went out of their way to be fair and understanding, and hence it was difficult for workers to criticize the system as a whole. There was, however, a surprising amount of more specific discontent with the operation of the system. Workers complained at length and in detail about the allocation of holidays and rest days in particular. The plant ran with cover for these days equivalent to 10 per cent of the manpower of each shift and the general rule was that, once this level was reached, no other absences would be allowed. If a worker discovered that he urgently needed a particular day off but the holiday book was full he had three options: to forego his outside interests, to try to persuade his foreman to exceed the limit, or to take the day off. As several workers put it, the company was 'encouraging us to be dishonest': a man who was refused time off could not go absent that day without serious repercussions, whereas if he took the day off without notice and said he was ill there was little the company could do. Some workers reported that they had done just this. Indeed, the practice had acquired a name of its own ('taking a ringer') which suggests that it was seen as a distinct activity.

The implications of this must be treated carefully. We have seen that absence rates were low; and, as even those who complained most bitterly about the availability of days off argued, men did not take time off just because they felt like it but because they had a particular outside need which clashed with the demands of shift work. It was the company's inflexible attitude, and not the shift system itself, which was the source of complaint. 'Taking a ringer' was thus far from widespread, and was used for particular reasons.

Workers' responses were, moreover, highly individualized. There were complaints about the way that foremen looked for 'patterns' of absence and about the tightness of the monitoring system more generally. But these were far from universal, and they did not form part of a wider criticism of management. Part of the reason for this lay, we have suggested, in the sophistication of the managerial control system, but part of it may also lie in the lack of collective awareness on the shopfloor. If the collective organization of some of our engineering plants were to be transported into an environment of continuous shift work, we would expect custom and practice rules to emerge over the allocation of rest days. There would be pressure on foremen to allow time off in excess of the 10 per cent limit, particularly when production schedules were slack; workers might demand that they should operate the rotas for time off; and there would be the implicit threat that, unless foremen were reasonable in their approach to time off, co-operation on the shopfloor would be lacking. And there is one specific aspect of absence control in the Process Factory which had been removed from our engineering plants as a result of union pressure: Process Factory management kept the whole of a worker's personal file, including any disciplinary warnings, so that they would have a 'complete picture' of his past. In all our engineering plants warnings remained 'live' for only a set period, and we came across several instances where a steward had successfully insisted that a warning be deleted from a worker's record. In all of this, then, managers in the Process Factory were able to treat absence control in terms of the behaviour of individuals and to advise someone who was straying from managerial definitions of acceptable attendance to mend his ways.

There was a very similar situation with the second aspect of managerial control, namely control over long-term sickness. Management felt that, while shift work might impose strains on workers which must be treated sympathetically, the firm could not afford to carry people who were unable to tolerate the strains. There were some day jobs to which workers might be moved if necessary, but if none of these was available management would make it clear to a worker that he would be sensible to look for work elsewhere. While this was done as fairly as possible, the pressures on workers were obvious.

There was some feeling on the shopfloor that managers were prone to 'lean on' people who were felt to be unable to cope. One man, for example, said that he had been off sick twice in the space of a year. Although covered by doctors' notes he had also been seen by the works doctor, who had admitted that it was general policy for him to see anyone who had been absent for six weeks or more. The personnel department had also been involved, issuing an informal warning about absence and suggesting that a job on days might be the answer. The man's foreman later told him that it seemed to be generally understood that he had been told to be a 'good boy' for a year. As the man put it, 'they just lean on you a bit, though it's hard to actually sack you'.

The stewards presented a similar picture: the company had been tightening up on absence over the previous year or two, particularly by putting pressure on the long-term sick to leave and by being less willing than formerly to make use of the chronic sick scheme, hoping instead that workers would leave 'voluntarily'. This perspective was far from common on the shopfloor, however. Some workers accepted the managerial position, saying, for example, that people knew what they were taking on when they did continuous shift work and that if they could not cope they should leave. Others felt that they themselves had always been treated fairly either when they were off sick or when they had a special need for time off.

These differences reveal a great deal about the subtlety of management's approach. There was certainly no overall strategy of taking a hard line on absenteeism, although personnel managers admitted that they were attempting to tighten up somewhat by making foremen aware who the 'bad attenders' were and by encouraging foremen and shop managers to take action where necessary. It is not surprising that many workers, possibly even the majority, were not aware of any particular policy of the control of long-term absence, for only the few 'problem cases' would experience the policy directly. Even if they were aware of it, many accepted at least the basis of management's argument on the need for control. This exercise of managerial control was experienced not as a direct threat of the sack but as an attempt to help. If anyone left 'voluntarily' as a result of such help, few workers still in the factory would be any the wiser. Finally, this kind of approach made it very difficult for the stewards to develop a consistent policy of resistance. Informal pressures, rather than formal disciplinary hearings, made action difficult, particularly when there was little shopfloor feeling on the matter. This can again be related to the nature of collective organization in the factory, for management successfully asserted its rights to deal with workers on an individual basis if it saw fit. The union was not the sole vehicle for communication with the shopfloor, and this made it relatively easy for management to put its message across.[13]

On both casual and long-term sickness, then, management made it clear that the main concern was the efficient use of manpower. While they would try to meet this concern in as humane a way as possible, they could not afford to carry 'passengers'. Now we do not wish to suggest that managers in the Process Factory were unique in their desire to remove passengers or in their wish to do so fairly. Company A, for example, made considerable use of welfare visitors whose job was to visit the long-term sick at home and, in addition to offering help, to assess whether they were likely to return to work. Visitors' reports formed the basis of cases of dismissal. But the concern in the Process Factory was more explicit and was more central to a distinct managerial policy. This reflects, we would suggest, management's awareness of the particular problems of control posed by shift work.

Conclusions

The question of how management controls absenteeism can too readily be seen in terms of the success of formal disciplinary procedures, the legality and

13. In contrast to the engineering plants, the disciplinary procedure was not formally agreed with the trade unions.

fairness with which dismissals are handled, and so on. But such matters may be little more than the tip of the iceberg: a successful policy of control will prevent conflict reaching this overt level. The Process Factory provides the clearest example of the subtle and covert control of absence such that management could successfully claim that they did not have a problem. Similarly, a problem with attendance will not necessarily be reflected in a high rate of disciplinary action. Managers in the clothing industry did not even feel that they had a problem, while in the very different environment of the Large Metals Factory managers were only too aware of the difficulties of keeping workers in the plant but rightly saw these as part of a wider, collective, issue of control over effort levels and not as a matter for individual discipline. Managerial responses cannot be seen positivistically as reactions to certain facts but must be interpreted in terms of managers' situations. Where managers felt that they had control over the labour process, or where problems were collective and not individual, absenteeism received little attention. Only in Company A, where foremen's immediate control over their own sections was felt to be contradicted and threatened by a wider breakdown of responsibility, did complaints about absence emerge as an attempt to rationalize the situation.

Absence, Withdrawal and Conflict

The central theme of this chapter has been that the phenomenon of absence, understood to mean not just rates of behaviour but the perceptions and strategies of workers and managers, must be explained in terms of the organization of the labour process. Viewing absence as a withdrawal from boring tasks or as the result of inadequate adjustments to the work environment is unhelpful: equally 'boring' jobs had different absence rates, and workers do not necessarily see going absent as a response to boredom. By taking account of patterns of control we have tried to provide a different perspective. Hence, the high rates of one-day absence of women in the clothing industry, the view of these workers that taking time off was a legitimate means of escape from the pressures of work, and managers' surprisingly sanguine view of the 'problem' can all be related to the nature of managerial control: absence was a form of escape but, because it did not challenge managerial authority in the workplace, it was not seen as a central problem by management. The contrast with men in the same industry is perhaps the most revealing, for men were on the whole subjected to much less direct control and their patterns of absence were strikingly difference from those of women workers.

The implications of this need to be considered carefully. Although the absence behaviour of the women can be related to a notion of conflict, in that, 'objectively', it reflected patterns of control to which they were subject and, 'subjectively', it involved a conscious strategy, such conflict did not imply direct resistance to managerial control. As mentioned in Chapter 1 (p. 7) several radical writers see the apparently rising trend of absenteeism as an expression of resistance to managerial control, with workers increasingly questioning management's right to determine how many hours they will work.[14] One possibility is that workers will deliberately use absence as a means of exerting some counter-control against management and that they will articulate a clear strategy: what we call a state of overt conflict. Such direct and open resistance was plainly not in evidence in the clothing factories: we suggested to workers on several occasions that taking a day off might be a way of 'getting back' at management but were invariably told that this would be a pointless and, as one worker put it, a rather childish response. A more subtle argument is that, while staying away from work may not be part of a deliberate policy of resistance, the behaviour still indicates a refusal to accept managerial logic and an assertion by the worker of control over when his or her labour power shall be expended. At one level it is obvious that absenteeism challenges managerial interests, which are, to put it crudely, the minimization of labour costs and, perhaps crucially, the retention of control over the labour force. But it is the extent of this challenge which is important. Rising absence trends during the 1960s and the 1970s were important because they seemed to be one index of a general problem of motivation and managerial control. In the clothing factories there was no such general problem: as we show in detail in later chapters control over such things as effort levels remained intact. And, since capital equipment was not expensive and since absenteeism imposed no direct costs on sick pay schemes, the implications of high rates of absenteeism for labour costs were also slight.

Thus in the clothing factories absenteeism, like quitting, did not directly challenge managerial control: it certainly reflected a conflict of interest but did not bring that conflict into the open. The behaviour also had a very limited role as a form of direct resistance in most of our other factories, a point which can best be understood if we examine some of the wider implications of our findings. Burawoy (1979: xi–xii) has posed the question of why workers work as hard as they do once they are in the factory. He argues that direct coercion is only part of the answer and that the reasons for workers' co-operation in the system of their own exploitation have to be examined. A similar argument

14. This is, of course, an inversion of 'liberal' concerns with the decline of the work ethic. The well-known *Work in America* study (Special Task Force, 1973: 11) for example saw 'malignant signs' of this decline in 'reduced productivity and in the doubling of man-days per year lost from work through strikes. In some industries there is apparently a rise in absenteeism, sabotage, and turnover rates'. The radical argument is based on these same 'facts' but sees them in terms of workers' and managers' strategies in the struggle for control and not as the result of a decline in moral values.

can be advanced as to why workers attend work as regularly as they do. There was little direct coercion in any of our factories, as was most clearly evident in the rarity of workers' comments that the fear of punishment was a reason for not taking days off. Yet neither was there any simple internationalization of a duty to the firm: attendance at work was not the result of direct ideological control by 'capital' of workers' consciousness. A more subtle process was involved whereby workers took for granted the norms of regular attendance.[15] The main drift of the comments of those who had taken time off was that the routine frustrations of going to work became unacceptable from time to time and that a break from routine was necessary. Some even said that they felt better after a day off and that they worked harder; one or two argued explicitly that an occasional day off was in management's interests because it kept up their morale. In other words, the need to work regularly was accepted, with an occasional day off not being seen as any fundamental challenge to this need. Workers who said that they did not take days off argued that absenteeism could become a dangerous habit or that it achieved nothing. Work was a dominating reality which was largely taken for granted. Workers were embedded in a system in which the need to work for a living was so obvious and all-embracing that they did not seriously question its rationale.

At this general level, then, workers in all our factories accepted the need to work. This need is so central to modern societies, and it is inculcated through such a variety of institutions, notably the schools (Bowles and Gintis, 1976: 126–48), that it would be surprising to find open questioning of it. Our main concern, however, has been to demonstrate how, within this broad unreflective acceptance of regular attendance at work, various patterns of absence emerged. In the Process Factory, for example, a relatively important influence was what may reasonably be called the dominant managerial ideology: managers explicitly tried to create a sense of loyalty to the firm and, as we have seen, they were quite successful in this. Yet even here more 'coercive' elements must not be ignored, for there was a sophisticated system for the monitoring and control of absenteeism. Moreover, the financial inducements to work shifts were considerable. Indeed, the factory provides a neat example of the way in which

15. Abercrombie et al. (1980: 1–2) have stridently attacked 'the dominant ideology thesis': the notion that there is a dominant class which creates a coherent set of beliefs, that these beliefs affect the consciousness of subordinates, and that such ideological control incorporates the subordinates in a system which operates against their own interests. Our argument that workers did not internalize a duty to the firm is similar to the more general argument advanced by Abercrombie et al. Yet, as Rootes (1981: 440) points out, these writers attack a very strong version of the dominant ideology thesis. Ideologies need not be systematic or coherent. Rootes identifies 'a level of ideology directly relevant to practice, directly influenced by experience, and unreflectively uttered as "commonsense".' It is this level which is most important here: while workers did not internalize dominant values their views on absence reflected a less immediate, but nonetheless important, acceptance of the norms of attendance at work.

various ways of attaining compliance can be combined. Etzioni (1961: 5) for example has distinguished between normative, coercive, and remunerative sources of power, suggesting that each tends to characterize a different kind of involvement of subordinates in an organization; normative power implies moral involvement, coercive power leads to alienative involvement, and remunerative power creates calculative involvement. Yet all three sources of power were used, the success of management being the covert nature of its coercive powers. This meant that most workers were unaware for most of the time of any distinctive managerial policy of control.

In our other factories management had a less self-conscious policy of attaining compliance. Hence managers in our clothing factories did not recognize a contradiction between high absence (and quit) rates and their claim that harmony and industrial peace prevailed. The organization of work was crucial, for within the workplace there was compliance with managerial directives and absenteeism occurred on the boundaries of this system. This does not imply, however, a linear relationship between absence frequency and the extent of managerial control, with frequency rising with the intensity of control. Despite the relatively intense control in the clothing factories these plants were not sweatshops and managers did not attempt to force workers into the factory by questioning every spell of absence. By contrast, from accounts of firms such as Grunwick's (Rogaly, 1977; Dromey and Taylor, 1978) one would expect that extremely autocratic managements would vigorously punish absenteeism. If this is true absence frequency would be related to the intensity of managerial control in the form of an inverted U: low in highly autocratic systems, rising to a peak where control was quite intense but where managers were less concerned to dominate every aspect of workers' lives, and then declining as managerial control is challenged on the shopfloor. Whether this is in fact the case is for future investigations to discover. What is crucial here is that absenteeism owes much to the social context in which it occurs: in some cases, as in the Large Metals Factory, it may even reflect collective custom and practice, while in others it is an 'individual' expression of social forces. It is not useful, therefore, to see it as simply 'unorganized' action, for it is a reflection of the social organization of production. Moreover, in the Large Metals Factory absence in the sense of being away from work for a whole shift merged into other forms of 'indiscipline' which can be related even more directly to social organization. These activities are the subject of the following chapter.

5

Factory Discipline

Breaches of factory discipline are rarely included in lists of the forms of industrial conflict but they are potentially as important as absenteeism or strikes. The creation of a work force which was willing to obey the routines of the time clock was a substantial problem for early capitalists (Pollard, 1965; Thompson, 1967), and the maintenance of discipline remains a problem for modern management: if workers are unwilling to obey rules about attendance at work and behaviour within the workplace then management's ability to control the labour process is considerably weakened. Our concern here is not, however, with discipline in the most general sense of 'the co-ordination of activities in the labour process' (Lea, 1979: 82), for this very broad definition of discipline could plainly be applied to the concerns of our study as a whole. Neither do we attempt to cover all aspects of rule-breaking; we do not, for example, consider theft of company property or aspects of indiscipline such as fighting or drunkenness.[1] In this chapter we continue the discussion of rules concerning attendance at work which we began in Chapter 4 by looking at rules governing

1. These phenomena may well be important in some situations. Theft, for example, is a well-established practice in hotels (Mars, 1973) and the docks (Mars, 1974). But it did not appear to have any particular significance for industrial relations in our factories, and we doubt whether detailed attention to it would have allowed us to add to existing studies of 'crime in the factory' (e.g. Horning, 1970). Similarly, to have looked in detail at such things as fighting and arguments among workers would have deflected us from our main concern, namely the frontier of control between management and workers. Relations among workers would, however, repay further study. Burawoy (1979: 65–71) is one of the few writers to appreciate their importance, arguing that conflict between management and workers had been replaced in his factory by conflict among workers. If workers fight among themselves their collective solidarity against management will be weakened. We take some account of this where relevant; for example we suggest later (p. 193) that one reason why workers in the Process Factory were unable to resist managerial pressures on effort levels was their fragmentation into separate work groups and shifts. But, in general, evidence on the extent of inter-worker disputes in, say, the clothing plants would merely add further documentation to our argument that control over the labour process had identifiable consequences for worker behaviour. Our main concern is with the impact of patterns of control on worker-management relations and not with the personal consequences of work, important as these may be.

such things as being away from the place of work without permission, arriving late, and leaving early. In subsequent chapters we go on to look at other forms of rules and rule-breaking which are more directly related to behaviour within the workplace.

We begin by examining workers' attitudes to discipline. Like perceptions of absenteeism as a strategy of withdrawal, perceptions of discipline are a surprisingly neglected aspect of workers' 'attitudes to work'. Yet they are important in general terms for the light they throw on workers' reactions to particular aspects of their work, as distinct from the unspecific aspects of work which are tapped by questions about job satisfaction and the like. Their present importance is that they demonstrate that women in our clothing factories were again marked by hostile attitudes towards management. This helps to strengthen the argument of the previous two chapters that these women were aware of the deprivations of their work situation but that they were unable to transform attitudinal hostility into action. We then turn to actual infringements of discipline, giving particular attention to a problem which exercised management in the Large Metals Factory and which had obvious parallels with the unrecorded absenteeism discussed in Chapter 4, namely workers leaving before the official finishing time. By comparing this situation with that in the Small Metals Factory and with the similar, although less widespread, practice of early leaving in the Components Factory we can indicate the specific features of the control system which permitted it to occur. And, by looking at a dispute which arose over managerial attempts to prevent early leaving, we show how the behaviour which had hitherto been accepted by management as part of the structure of the situation entered the arena of overt conflict. Here we have a useful example of the way in which the existing frontier of control, as represented by customary and informal rules about leaving early, can be questioned.

Attitudes to Discipline

As their general lack of concern with matters of discipline implies, previous studies based on shopfloor surveys have not asked questions about attitudes to factory discipline. The questionnaire used here attempted to fill this gap, and it will be useful to begin by considering the results. In the absence of any guide from previous research we decided to follow the pattern of the question on absence, namely a forced choice between two statements, followed by a request to say why one option rather than the other had been chosen.[2] The two statements were presented as follows:

2. It was decided that the question should be as specific as possible, referring to particular practices and not to discipline in general. This did lead to some difficulties, with one or two

Here are two views about the way management should handle such things as people coming in late, going early, and clocking each other in. Which one comes nearer to your own view?

1. Management must be firm about these things, because if they are not firm a few people can get away with things at everyone else's expense.

2. There should be a bit of give and take, because everyone needs to bend the rules from time to time, and no real harm is done.

The results are set out in Table 5.1. Not surprisingly in view of the phrasing of the question most respondents chose the second option. But there were significant variations in the replies. As with general attitudes to management (see above, pp. 83–7), the men in the Small Metals Factory and the women in the clothing industry were similar in being most likely to take an anti-management position. By contrast, men in the clothing industry were most likely to agree that there was a need for firmness. The reasons given by workers choosing the latter option do not suggest, however, that there was any strong acceptance of management's right to exert control over discipline. Very few workers replied in this vein, the over-whelming tendency being simply to assert that there was a general need for firmness or consistency. As we found with replies to the question about absenteeism, selection of the 'responsible' option did not imply any deep commitment to the goals of management. In the present case workers generally said that there had to be some rules to govern behaviour; this did not imply that they accepted management's definition of those rules.

For workers saying that there must be some give and take, the most popular reason for the choice was again a general one: it was better to have some freedom than to be firmly bound by rules. To some extent this is a weakness of the question since many replies were in effect re-statements of the second option. Many workers felt that the need for some give and take was so obvious as to require no specific justification. But this is of considerable interest in itself. Workers did not have a well-articulated view on discipline or on why firmness was not a good policy. It was rare for them to argue that management were inconsistent in applying the rules to workers. This did not, however, mean that managers were felt to be consistent: as will be seen below, inconsistency in the application of rules was a major complaint where specific aspects of

workers considering only the issue of clocking offences and not the other matters mentioned. Moreover, the questionnaire was developed in the Small Metals Factory where the issues mentioned were particularly salient. Elsewhere different matters were important: in the clothing industry discipline within the workplace was central, and in the Process Factory the absence of clocking made part of the question irrelevant. But we decided to retain the question as it stood to retain comparability. Most people did not seem to experience any difficulty in understanding what it was about; within the limitations of any fixed-choice question the results can be analysed with reasonable confidence.

TABLE 5.1

ATTITUDES ON DISCIPLINE

	Components (N=123)	Small Metals (N=43)	All Clothing		Process (N=98)
			Men (N=56)	Women (N=127)	
Per cent saying:					
Management must be firm	42	25	50	21	30
Give and take	54	72	43	78	67
D.K.	4	3	7	1	3
Number of reasons for choosing 'firmness' option	57	12	30	27	30
Reason as per cent of all reasons					
Management has right of control	7		7	7	0
Need to punish offenders	9		7	7	20
General need for firmness	68		80	85	77
Other	12		7	0	3
D.K.	4		0	0	0
Number of reasons for choosing 'give and take' option	75	35	26	104	66
Reason as per cent of all reasons					
Management are inconsistent	16	14	0	10	8
Workers are responsible	37	26	38	20	12
Legitimate outside needs	1	6	0	2	2
General	39	37	58	49	73
Other	5	14	4	11	3
D.K.	1	3	0	9	3

rule-breaking were concerned. It simply meant that there was no need to cite managerial inconsistency when general questions of discipline were being considered.

We went on to ask workers about perceptions of discipline in their own factories, presenting them with a series of choices running from 'firm and inflexible' through 'fair' to 'very weak'. The results are shown in Table 5.2.

TABLE 5.2

**ASSESSMENTS OF DISCIPLINE IN WORKERS'
OWN FACTORIES**

(Per Cent)

	Components	Small Metals	Clothing Men	Women	Process
Firm	4	5	29	43	8
Flexible/fair	62	76	54	51	86
Weak/very weak	32	19	4	2	5
Other/D.K.	2	0	14	3	1

Among all groups a majority felt that management were flexible or fair, but there were substantial variations. In the Components Factory a significant proportion felt that management were weak; this reflects a feeling, which will be analysed in detail below, that workers in other departments were treated more leniently than respondents themselves. The clothing industry was the only area where a substantial number of workers felt that management were firm or strict. In view of the general intensity of managerial control, particularly over women, this is not surprising. Indeed, it is perhaps more surprising that a majority of women said that discipline was generally fair. There are several reasons for this. First, as noted in Chapter 3, most of the women either had no work experience outside their present job or had worked only within the clothing industry. They therefore took for granted many aspects of managerial control which would not be accepted elsewhere. For example, it was not necessary for management directly to order workers back to work at the end of a tea break; workers returned at the end of the ten minute period with little apparent complaint. Second, workers who obeyed the rules did not themselves experience the application of discipline; the rules appeared to be fair to these workers because they were not directly confronted by them. Third, in many respects management were fair. We have stressed that these factories were not sweatshops, and there were important strands of paternalism. As well as taking a 'responsible' attitude to their workers in general terms, managers were responsive to individual needs, as when workers were allowed to leave to attend to outside emergencies or were taken home when they were ill.

All this occurred, however, only within the context of managerial control. As Table 5.2 shows, this control was not universally internalized: discipline was perceived as being firm to a much greater extent than was the case elsewhere. Moreover, differences between men and women which we have already noted in relation to attitudes to management and to absence from work were again important. Although nearly a third of men experienced discipline as firm, there was not the depth of feeling about the issue that there was among women. There were also differences between male knitters, who were largely left on their own, and labourers and other auxiliary workers who were treated more strictly. For example, in the Underwear Factory in particular we came across several instances of labourers being reprimanded in severe tones for not working properly. Attitudes to discipline reflected the differential intensity of managerial control fairly closely.

There are several reasons why concerted attempts to challenge the disciplinary system did not occur. We have mentioned some specific reasons why the system was taken for granted, and these clearly reflect the nature of the control system as a whole: there was no simple pattern of repression, and as long as people accepted the rules they would be treated with fairness and consideration. The availability, in quitting and absenteeism, of 'alternative means' of expressing discontents must also be considered. Lateness and early leaving were consequently rare. Their significance is indicated by the supervisor's comment noted in Chapter 2 that workers might leave a minute or two early but never as much as five minutes. If workers in any of our engineering factories could be persuaded to work until even fifteen minutes before finishing time management would be delighted. There were one or two spontaneous protests over the enforcement of rules. A good example occurred in the Hosiery Factory shortly before Christmas, when workers began to decorate their work areas with cards and balloons. Management insisted that the decorations be removed because they were a fire risk: they would be tolerated for only a short period. Several workers protested at this by ripping the decorations down and bursting their balloons. They spent the rest of the day complaining about management's 'unreasonable' and 'dictatorial' attitude. The example is typical in that the protest was small-scale and negative: no direct challenge was made to management, and there was no attempt to put pressure on the company to change the rule.

As in other areas, strong hostility to managerial control was not matched by action in the clothing industry. In other factories there was less hostility, but it is possible that workers find disciplinary rules acceptable not because they agree with their general spirit but because they have negotiated arrangements whereby their application is moderated by custom. As we saw with absenteeism, formal rules about the treatment of casual absence were relatively unimportant, and it was the interpretation of rules by foremen which was significant. Rules concerning attendance at the factory were similarly subject to negotiation. In two of our plants, the Large Metals and the Components Factories, they were the subject of overt disputes; examination of these disputes can throw considerable light on the status of the rules.

Early Leaving

The Large Metals Factory: Effort Levels and Early Leaving

As pointed out in Chapter 4, some absenteeism in the Large Metals Factory went unrecorded because workers had devised means of taking time off without losing pay. Much of this went unnoticed, but the problem forced itself on management's attention at two main times. First, workers were often able to do work allocated to overtime during their regular 40 hours so that many either did not turn up at all for Saturday morning overtime or clocked in and went straight home. Second, during the week there was generally a mass exodus between a quarter and half an hour before the official shift finishing time. Management attempted to control this by stationing supervisors at the main exits from each shop and in the routes to the factory gateways. The whole process often took on the air of farce, with groups of workers assembling at strategic points ready to dash past the foreman on guard if the opportunity presented itself. Foremen attempted to hold back the tide for a while, but at some point those in one shop would give way, which was the signal for workers elsewhere to leave.

It would be easy to present these practices as indicating worker irresponsibility or managerial failures of control, or both. But their significance is considerably more complex than this. Consider first the reasons for the behaviour. Two facilitating factors stand out. Clocking out at the end of the shift had been eliminated for at least twenty years, which meant that it was possible for a worker to leave the plant early without having to rely on someone else to clock him out. Clocking in was still required, so that for longer absences collusion with others was required. Yet the Process Factory, for example, had abolished all clocking without experiencing any problems of this sort. The second, and crucial, factor was the level of effort required from each worker. Put crudely, a shift to day work had removed any incentive to work harder, and workers now sought increased leisure instead.

Yet this provides no more than a first approximation to an explanation of early leaving. It certainly shows why the two Company B plants stood out from the others, for in these two plants shopfloor controls over the effort bargain countered managerial control in several areas. But this does not explain why the particular problem of leaving the factory early developed, or why it was restricted to the Large Metals Factory.

Part of the answer is that the Small Metals Factory retained clocking out; this tended to prevent early leaving from becoming a widespread activity. But more important is the pattern of managerial control in the two factories. As Brown says of the experiment to end clocking in and out at Glacier Metal, 'at the time of abolishing clocking, we were giving some serious attention to the subject of authority of those in command of the shop floor. *I do not think we should have been able successfully to do without clocks had this not been so'* (Wilfred Brown, 1962: 87, emphasis in the original). In other words the successful abolition of clocking depends on established managerial control over discipline. In the Large Metals Factory this condition was absent, for reasons which we go on to explore. In the Small Metals Factory a different shopfloor atmosphere meant that identical problems of 'effort drift' did not lead to the practice of early leaving.

In the assembly shops of the Large Metals Factory in particular the gang system, described in Chapter 2, meant that foremen did not have any direct involvement in the details of production. Under piecework the gang contracted to do work at an agreed price per piece, with the foreman's role being limited to ensuring a supply of raw materials and dealing with any problems encountered by the gang. Thus it was for the gang to decide how and when to work. A consequence of this system was a widespread feeling among workers that it was they who ran the job and that foremen were mere 'progress chasers'. Foremen thus had no position of authority or respect on the shopfloor. The problem of ensuring regular attendance at work was probably already apparent under piecework, but the move to day work made the difficulties far more acute. Workers still expected to operate autonomously, but since they now had no incentive to increase output they sought increased leisure instead. The tradition of working in gangs made it natural for gangs to decide when to expend their effort. It also appeared natural for workers to leave the plant when they had achieved their quotas for the day: as several pointed out, they had done their work and management had no reason to keep them in the plant. In the Small Metals Factory shopfloor controls over effort levels and the growth of leisure at the end of the shift were equally well-developed. But the absence of the gang system meant that foremen were less explicitly distanced from control functions. In addition the size of the plant was here, and perhaps only here, an important factor. In the Large Metals Factory some shops employed as many workers as the whole of the Small Metals Factory. A worker might legitimately be anywhere within his own shop or could be transferred to one of several other shops. While foremen formally retained a role in the allocation of labour, in practice they had no means of knowing whether an absentee had left the plant or had merely gone somewhere else. In the Small Metals Factory it was much easier to know where a particular worker was supposed to be and whether he was indeed there. A related factor was the preservation of moderately good face-to-face relations between foremen and workers. While it is hard to analyse precisely the atmosphere of shopfloor relations, we can suggest that in this factory some degree of interpersonal trust remained. As we saw in Chapter 4 foremen felt that they could talk to stewards about a problem: there was an easy-going relationship based on long knowledge of each other and an acceptance by foremen of the traditional way of doing things. For example stewards in one area were warned that management were unhappy about people leaving early on the night shift and that there would be a check on one particular night to see who was present. One man ignored the warning and was disciplined; so far as the steward was concerned, this was the man's own fault and he could expect no sympathy. In contrast to this relaxed approach, foremen in the Large Metals Factory were felt to be far more distant and there was very little feeling of trust.

This 'low trust symdrome' (Fox, 1974) was not free-floating; it can be located in the growth of loose production standards and in the weakness of foremen's authority. The nature of management's problems which this created may be illustrated by an event which occurred in one of the assembly shops. A foreman discovered that, out of a group of four welders who were supposed to be doing overtime, only two were present. He threatened to stop the pay of the two who were not present, at which the rest of the welders walked out for the remainder of the overtime period. The next day, there were rumours that the welders would ban overtime until the matter was resolved. Eventually their convener was brought in by management, and he agreed that in future the stewards would formally submit a list of names of those doing overtime. In some ways this was a victory for management: as one of the foremen most closely involved in the issue explicitly argued, management in the past had tried to buy co-operation by acquiescing in early leaving and related practices, but it was now necessary to 'pull back' control. He felt that the welders had been made to 'come to heel'. Yet the case also reveals the limitations of management's position. The stewards argued that management had no right to stop pay because they did not know that the missing men had indeed gone home: they could quite properly have been elsewhere in the factory. As one steward put it, workers should 'pay their respects' to the foreman before leaving the section but they were under no obligation to do so. It was, in other words, taken for granted that foremen had no right to know whether or not a particular worker was present on their sections. Indeed, the dispute was significant precisely because it was so unusual. Stewards explained it in terms of the unreasonable behaviour of an individual foreman: it was a provocative action which had gained management nothing, for there had been no question of any loss of production. There was a substantial degree of truth in this, since for most of the time foremen did not attack practices of which the welders' case was but an isolated example.

The question of production requires close consideration, for stewards and managers alike found support for their arguments in the overriding need for production. According to the stewards, the acknowledged failure of the plant to produce the required level of output was the result of managerial failings: production depended on the good will of the work force, and arbitrary managerial attempts to assert control, such as the incident discussed above, merely upset working relationships. Stewards often argued that 'we run the factory', a claim which had a good deal of truth, as we see in subsequent chapters. This view stemmed fairly clearly from the type of control over the labour process which had been achieved: detailed involvement of stewards in the control of work encouraged pride in shopfloor abilities and contempt for managers' inability to make use of this potential. Stewards did not reject managerial arguments about the need for production; indeed, as we show at more length in Chapter 7, they were committed to a general ideology of production. But they turned specific arguments about particular cases back against management: if managers wanted production the best way to get it was to try to co-operate with the shopfloor on the basis of customary understandings. The unspoken but acknowledged threat was that co-operation would not be forthcoming if these understandings were broken. How this worked in practice is indicated in the following section in relation to a significant dispute which arose over early leaving.

What, then, lay behind management's actions? We argued in Chapter 1 that management has a general interest not simply in production but in controlling the labour process so as to secure the conditions for extracting effort from workers. Managerial actions such as the incident discussed above can be seen as a recognition of this point. It was recognized that attempts to control discipline would adversely affect production in the short run but it was argued that in the long-term preventing early leaving and other practices was a prerequisite for re-establishing the efficient use of labour. Or, as one manager put it more bluntly, the first need was to get the work force in the plant on a regular basis: if this was done it would then be possible to try to improve effort levels. This perception was, however, not shared by all members of management. As we saw in Chapter 4 foremen tended to share the shopfloor view that production was to be obtained through co-operation and that managerial attempts to regain control merely upset an already delicate balance. This contrast between senior management's strategic concern to regain control and foremen's scepticism about this was one feature of the factory-wide dispute about early leaving which we now discuss.

The Large Metals Factory: Attempts to Control Early Leaving

The most prominent example of management's attempt to regain control over discipline in the Large Metals Factory occurred in a dispute about overtime.

Workers were not required to clock out at the end of the normal period of Saturday morning overtime, but management claimed that this period of over-time was being so abused that it would be necessary to demand clocking out. This was seen by the conveners as an attack on long-established customary rights. They argued that there was already a procedure for disciplining people caught leaving early or engaging in clocking offences and that management's failure to operate the system properly was to blame. Despite the deep divisions between them on other matters, all conveners saw this issue in the same light; they therefore acted jointly to ban all overtime, not just on Saturday but also during the week.

Management did not expect the ban to last long: the shopfloor relied on overtime and would begin to put pressure on stewards to have the ban lifted. This expectation was, however, based on a serious misunderstanding of shop-floor attitudes. First, although workers often criticized conveners in general terms for their distance from the shopfloor, on an issue such as this conveners could mobilize considerable support for their position. They argued that manage-ment were acting in breach of established agreements and that failure to resist such encroachments would lead to further attacks on shopfloor rights. Mana-gerial bad faith is a powerful and commonly-used argument (Batstone et al., 1978: 47–8), and management here found it very difficult to counter.[3] Second, none of the shopfloor workers we questioned during the overtime ban saw the conveners as responsible for the loss of their overtime: it was management's fault that overtime had been cut, a decision which was felt to reflect manage-ment's general lack of concern for the workers. This again reveals the depth of the mistrust of management on the shopfloor. There was thus little imme-diate pressure on the conveners to withdraw the ban. Indeed, even if workers had wanted to do overtime, it is hard to see how they could have exerted direct pressure on the conveners. They could certainly have complained to their stewards, but most stewards took the view that the ban had been agreed by all unions at the highest level in the plant and could not be ended other than by a joint decision of the conveners. Moreover, the conveners' very distance from the shopfloor meant that most workers felt that matters of policy were up to the union hierarchy and that there was nothing they could do to influence this.

Lengthy discussions took place in an attempt to resolve the deadlock, with both sides arguing for a return to the *status quo* so that negotiations could pro-ceed. The problem, however, was what this meant. For the unions the *status quo*

3. Management argued that workers had effectively broken agreements first by abusing the 'privilege' of not having to clock out. The conveners met this by pointing to the disciplinary procedure and by questioning whether the practice of not clocking out was a privilege which could be withdrawn unilaterally. The management argument, although plausible, did not possess any telling logic which would persuade the shopfloor of the error of their ways.

involved a full return to the position before management demanded clocking out: overtime to be available as usual, with no clocking out on Saturdays. Management rejected this interpretation, realizing that, if they accepted it, they would be in a worse position than they were before the dispute started: they would have accepted that existing practice was the norm and would have found it hard to employ a sanction like insisting on clocking out if early leaving persisted.

These arguments about the various meanings which could be placed on the concept of the *status quo* reflected a shift in the terms of the dispute. As managers ruefully admitted, and as the conveners continually stressed, the initial question of early leaving had become obscured, with the issue now being clocking out and management's alleged breach of long-standing agreements on this. As one convener said, he would be in favour of clocking as a general principle, but management had broken an agreement: when he made an agreement he stuck to it, and he expected others to do the same.

Apart from tactical mistakes which allowed the conveners to shift the terms of the dispute by putting management in the wrong, management's position was weakened by the need to reach production targets. In addition to losses due to the overtime ban programmes for the basic week were not being achieved. It was accepted as a fact of life, at least by foremen and shop managers, that managerial action on discipline would have an impact on the apparently unrelated area of production levels during the week. As argued in Chapter 1, the employment contract is necessarily indeterminate, and workers were able to exploit this indeterminacy by withdrawing their 'normal' amounts of co-operation. We give several examples of this in later chapters. One method which was used during the dispute was to refuse to work with equipment which was normally considered to be satisfactory. Hence on one section workers insisted that welding guns be spotlessly clean before they would work with them, whereas in the normal way they were far less fussy. But examples like this imply that there was a carefully planned strategy of hitting back at management. The general response was more diffuse: workers had long-standing grievances about wages and what they saw as general managerial incompetence, and the current situation merely increased these feelings. Workers felt disgruntled and plodded through their work tasks, looking for reasons to stop work whereas normally they were eager to finish as quickly as possible.

This response can best be described as semi-organized in that it was neither spontaneous and unplanned nor systematically orchestrated by stewards or gang leaders. Management found such action difficult to counter, for they could only complain to the stewards who could easily show that they were not directing any overt campaign. Stewards laid the blame on management and saw the shop-floor response as so obvious as to require no special organization. As one said, 'you get superintendents saying "the [section] seems to have gone off the boil"' when they've just stopped the men £20 a week each. It's pathetic'.

Foremen shared this critical view of management. As one complained, he had been given instructions about keeping workers on his section until the official finishing time but there was no indication of how he was to achieve this or of what support he would receive if he tried to discipline anyone for leaving early. Foremen spent a considerable amount of time complaining among themselves about senior management's failure to back them up in disciplinary cases. In addition they felt that their authority was being called into question since they were having to keep workers in the plant against their will.

In view of all this it is not surprising that the outcome of the dispute came closer to the unions' than to management's aims. The unions had offered to agree to an increase in the penalties for those caught leaving early on Saturdays. Management had initially rejected this, arguing that they wanted to stop the abuse and not to punish the few workers who were caught, but they eventually accepted the suggestion. In the terms introduced in Chapter 1, management had moved the matter of early leaving to the level of overt conflict from its previous position as a form of non-directed conflict whereby managers complained about the problem but did not do anything about it. The outcome of the dispute was affected by structural factors, notably management's inability to maintain production levels, and it meant that the issue was returned largely unaltered to the non-directed level. The interests of the parties were also clear. Managers wanted to control early leaving as part of a wider policy, of which we give further examples in later chapters, of regaining control. They did not want simply an agreed level of production within the existing pattern of control but a system in which labour could be used more efficiently on management's own terms. In their tactics, however, they attacked, in early leaving, merely a symptom of a deeper problem namely the establishment of effort levels which were unacceptably low. Stewards were therefore able to resist this and to preserve their own interests in the existing structure of control.

Monitoring Discipline in the Large Metals Factory

One immediate outcome of the dispute was the creation of a new system for monitoring disciplinary cases: the aim was to replace the *ad hoc* use of discipline with a consistent body of 'case law' so that apparent concessions in one shop could not be used as precedents elsewhere. The records of this system are of considerable interest, for they reveal the extent to which early leaving and related practices dominated the disciplinary procedure and they also point to significant differences between areas of the factory which can be related to differences in the detailed application of management's control strategy.

The records do not, of course, indicate the true extent of rule-breaking since they count only those who were caught and punished. Even variations between shops may not reflect genuine differences in rates of indiscipline because of differences in the intensity of managerial attempts to catch offenders. These problems are, of course, identical to those faced by users of criminal statistics (Rock, 1973: 193–4; Box, 1971). They may, however, be evaded here since the interest is not in a 'true' rate of rule-breaking but in precisely those areas which are problems for conventional uses of criminal statistics, namely the extent to which rule-enforcement agencies act to punish deviance. In other words, a high level of disciplinary action need not reflect a high level of rule-breaking, but it certainly indicates a high rate of activity by the rule-enforcers. This in turn is likely to have implications for the way that the rules are perceived by those subject to them.

With these points in mind, figures on disciplinary action may be examined. In a seven-month period, there were over 100 formally-recorded incidents of discipline. These ranged from sackings and suspensions, through the application of the early-leaving discipline procedure (enforced clocking out and loss of overtime entitlement), to formal written and verbal warnings. Over half (52 per cent) of the incidents involved early leaving or time-keeping, while a further 13 per cent were concerned with clocking offences which, as has been seen, were often the concomitant of informal rotas for time off. Another 14 per cent were for absences from the place of work without permission; these plainly reflect attempts to leave the plant during working hours. The great majority of instances of discipline therefore concerned early leaving and related practices.

More importantly, there was a very marked variation between departments. Two areas, the machine shop and the highly mechanized assembly shop (Shop X), had a high incidence of discipline: each had a rate of 10 incidents per 100 workers. The other large assembly shop, Shop Y, had a rate of 2.5 actions per hundred workers, while the other assembly shops and the toolroom and maintenance areas had negligible rates.

These differences cannot be attributed to any inherent differences in the proneness of workers in various areas to break disciplinary rules. The explanation lies in managerial strategy and the nature of workers' response to discipline, although technology is also important in the case of Shop X. As we saw in Chapter 4, the system of working at a set pace throughout the day in Shop X was moderated by generous manning levels which meant that an apparently 'alienating' technology did not lead to high absence rates. But the working of the system still meant that it was not possible for workers to make leisure for themselves at the end of the shift. This in turn made absence towards the end of the day more obvious to management than it was elsewhere. These technologically-induced facts were given added significance by management's approach to discipline. Even before the plant-wide monitoring system was introduced, shop managers operated their own system: in an eighteen-month period over 200 cases of disciplinary action were listed, with the great majority being for early leaving or an 'unreasonable finishing time'. This approach to discipline seems to have been one part of a managerial strategy of establishing control of operations in an environment where there was a distinct break from the plant's tradition of autonomous gangs. The contrast with other assembly shops is dramatic: here workers did their day's quota as they saw fit and management adopted a less formal approach to discipline.

In the machine shop, the other area of high disciplinary rates, management operated with a strict approach to discipline, although the basis of this seems to have been different. Managers themselves explained their approach by saying that the assembly shops had given up all attempts to control their workers, whereas they themselves tried to be firm but fair. In particular, they complained that laxity in other areas was making it hard for them to discipline their own workers. The high rate of discipline can thus be seen as a managerial attempt to maintain control: workers saw those from other shops leaving early and sought the same benefits, and management responded with disciplinary action. Workers and stewards agreed about the laxity of the assembly shops but, significantly, did little to resist their own management's use of discipline. The shop generally operated entirely separately from the assembly areas; it was organized by a different union, and there seemed to be insufficient direct links with the rest of the factory for comparisons with it to be a live issue. The shop's tradition of firm discipline was thus crucial. The reasons behind this tradition are hard to establish, but the effects of the production system may have been important. In the assembly shops, finished products were being turned out for sale to customers. The production manager of the plant kept a close eye on output, and was concerned about fluctuations, even those from hour to hour. In this environment, where the number of products turned out per day was of central significance, the power of stewards to 'stop the track' was considerable. In the machine shop, on the other hand, a stoppage had no immediate effect on the output of finished products; management could therefore afford to adopt a firmer approach and, short of a major confrontation, there was relatively little that the stewards could do.

In the machine shop, then, workers generally had to accept discipline. A precisely opposite response occurred in the toolroom. Here, workers were proud of their own self-discipline, which they contrasted with the 'irresponsibility' of production workers. The first reason for the low level of disciplinary action in the toolroom is thus simply that workers retained a collective ethic of craft responsibility. But this ethic was coming under strain: workers felt an increasing resentment when they saw other workers using the toolroom as an escape route out of the factory. Toolmakers began to follow suit, and were disciplined. But here a further aspect of their collective response became significant: when toolmakers were disciplined, it was much more likely than elsewhere that there would be an organized response against management. Toolmakers already felt that they were being treated dishonourably by management, and the imposition of discipline was the final insult. For example, when six toolmakers were caught leaving early, the stewards took up their case and were able to have the discipline suspended.[4] The intensity of feeling is even more dramatically illustrated by the case of a man who had had to accept discipline: as a protest against management, he paraded around the shop carrying a polystyrene crucifix and a placard bearing the words 'forgive them, they know not what they do', to the accompaniment of cheering and applause from other toolmakers. Such collective responses, together with their other problems of retaining labour, encouraged management to take a soft line on discipline. They were unwilling to inflame the situation further. On the other hand, it must be said, the toolmakers had decided that, in general, they would accept discipline, while referring the matter through the official disputes procedure. Although a collective response was stronger than in other areas, it was weaker than it would have been in the past; as several workers put it, morale was so low that there was little will for a strenuous campaign against management in the area.

These variations between the assembly shops, machine shop, and toolroom show that the 'problem' of discipline was not what the monitoring system might suggest. Assembly Shop X and the machine shop were not particularly lacking in discipline, but were, for various reasons, more likely than other areas to have a positive managerial strategy on discipline. The case of the toolroom illustrates a collective response to discipline. These various situations reflect the central problem for management: restoring a degree of control where trust had broken down and where the shopfloor felt that management's actions were neither consistent nor relevant to the main concern of the plant, namely production.

The Components Factory
The problem of early leaving in the Components Factory originated, according to management, in the organization of the site as a whole. The factory shared a site and some facilities with another of the firm's plants, whose workers finished work earlier than those in the Components Factory, and the example of these workers was said to arouse the jealousy of Components Factory workers. But, as in the Large Factory, internal comparisons were also important. Production workers, for example, felt that management were weak in their treatment of toolmakers in allowing them to leave early. The problem for management was not, however, nearly as great as that in the Large Metals Factory. The most obvious difference between the two factories was that levels of manning and effort in the Components Factory did not permit workers to finish particularly early. There was certainly no chance that systematic rotas of free time could

4. Interestingly, this event sparked off a brief demonstration by ancillary workers employed in the toolroom, who demanded that they should have the same treatment as the toolmakers. The problems of consistency and fairness are vividly illustrated here. See below, p. 233.

be employed. In addition, even though workers could finish somewhat early, there were constraints on actually leaving the plant. As in the Small Metals Factory the small size of most shops made it fairly easy for foremen to check whether a particular worker was present. And, as we saw in Chapter 4, foremen retained a much more central role in the allocation of labour and in planning the production process. There was no tradition of work group autonomy which could exploit any looseness in effort levels to create a substantial amount of early leaving.

In the production areas the 'problem' was thus restricted to workers' leaving about twenty minutes before the official finishing time, and even this practice was far from universal. The problem was rather greater, however, in the maintenance areas. For example, until recently systematic overtime had been 'abused' with the result that some workers had been paid for overtime when they were not in the plant. There was also a range of more limited attempts to 'beat the system'. For example, one semi-skilled mate said that he was prepared to cover for his fitter by doing jobs which he was not supposed to do. Towards the end of a night shift, for instance, a job had come in but the fitter had not been found, presumably because he had gone home; the mate did the job, thus protecting the fitter while keeping the foreman happy. The foreman concerned would plainly have been aware of what was going on, but it was not in his interests to challenge the arrangement. Other managers expressly adopted a policy of give and take. For example, a production manager cited a case of a man who had reported for the night shift 'the worse for wear' for drink. Instead of sending the man home and disciplining him, he had told him to go away to sober up for a couple of hours. This had the desired effect of keeping the situation under control without making a great issue out of a minor incident.

This policy of understanding, 'treating workers as people', and so forth had obvious advantages for line management. But, as has been seen in the case of the Large Metals Factory, it created problems for personnel managers seeking a consistent policy on discipline. The 'problem' of early leaving grew up slowly and largely unrecognized, possibly as the result of some stimulus such as workers from other factories leaving early. Once it had achieved momentum and management had had to respond through threats of discipline and so on, workers naturally began to compare themselves with others who were, it was felt, being treated more leniently. The problem for management was not to stamp out early leaving completely, but to restrain it within limits. In other words, management was not concerned about people leaving a few minutes early, but about the danger that the situation would 'get out of control', with a few minutes stretching into half an hour.

The pattern of replies to the questionnaire, shown in Tables 5.1 and 5.2 can now be understood. Workers were not demanding a return to strict control, but felt that existing rules must be enforced fairly. Some workers within, say, the maintenance department felt that some of their mates were abusing the system and should be brought under control. But, as has been said, the major focus of comparisons was between departments. As stewards in production areas explicitly put it, they would keep their members in the factory for as long as toolmakers were required to stay. At one point, women in one shop operated the very effective tactic of saying they would stay until they saw the first toolmaker go out with his coat on. Maintenance supervisors, too, claimed that they retained a fair degree of control over their workers whereas toolmakers were allowed to come and go as they pleased. It would be difficult, if not impossible, to assess how far these accusations were true. Their present significance is twofold. First, they reveal the importance of consistency and fairness when discipline over early leaving was concerned. Second, it is not surprising that the toolroom was singled out for criticism; this was only one part of the more general jealousy and mistrust which existed between the toolroom and other areas.

Plant management shared workers' critical view of the toolroom in so far as they felt that toolroom supervision was less willing to take a firm line on discipline than was management elsewhere. It was certainly true that toolroom foremen, in the Large Metals Factory as well as in the Components Factory, saw themselves as members of the trade and as co-ordinators of production rather than as supervisors in the sense of standing over workers and ensuring that they put in adequate levels of effort. This is not to say that they denied the importance of discipline. They stressed, as did toolmakers themselves, that toolmaking was a skilled and responsible job and that an important element of self-motivation and self-discipline was involved. They disagreed with other managers over the possibility and desirability of imposing discipline from above.

As in the Large Metals Factory, then, disputes between management and workers over the application of discipline cannot be separated from disagreements within management. These problems made the creation of an accepted framework of discipline more difficult, but they were counter-balanced, to some extent, by trade union willingness to co-operate in the control of the work force. This was not simply a matter of straightforward collaboration or incorporation, but depended on the behaviour involved and the circumstances of any discipline imposed. As noted in Chapter 4, a man who was sacked for persistent lateness and absenteeism was not defended, other than formally, by his steward, and the general view in the shop was that he deserved what was coming to him. Even the toolroom stewards, who were the most strongly anti-management in their general approach, were prepared to co-operate in disciplining persistent offenders. Such cases depended, however, on the feeling that general norms on correct behaviour had been violated. In other cases, however, stewards felt that certain behaviour was reasonable and should be defended. A particularly clear case occurred during one of management's purges on discipline. From previous purges, it had been established that anyone leaving the shop ten minutes or more before the official finishing time would be liable to discipline. In practice, this rule had been bent, and management warned the senior steward that it would be rigidly enforced again. When workers left before the ten minute limit, the whole shop was stopped a quarter of an hour's pay. The stewards soon forced management to rescind this punishment. First, they pointed out that, although they had been informed of the coming crack-down, this information had not been given direct to the shopfloor. It was not the stewards' job to carry messages for management. More importantly, it was taken for granted that management should give warning of a crack-down, even when the current rules were clear. In other words, it was current practice and not the formal rules which stewards saw as important. The second argument was simply that it was not within management's rights to stop the whole shop money when management admitted that some workers had been present until the ten-minutes limit. As one foreman admitted, the purge had not been carried out properly, because no precautions had been taken to establish who had left and who was still in the factory.

Stewards' views on the application of discipline were thus that the matter was negotiable; hard and fast rules drawn up in the personnel department were not directly relevant to shopfloor practice. It was unreasonable to penalize some workers and not others, and crack-downs should not take place without warning. In all this there were pronounced similarities with the Large Metals Factory, but the overall discipline problem was much smaller. Some degree of trust remained, and management's main concern was to retain a degree of control, not to re-establish it.

Discipline and Control

We have argued that, like absenteeism, discipline and breaches of discipline have to be understood in terms of specific aspects of factories' control systems. Hence, at the most general level, discipline is not something which management can write into the employment contract and then take for granted: it has to be actively sustained. Yet challenges to managerial expectations are far from inevitable. We have tried to show why such challenges developed to a substantial degree only in the Large Metals Factory, and to a lesser degree in the Components Factory, and why they took a particular form. Hence we have indicated in some detail the differing control problems faced by management in different sections of the Large Metals Factory and related them to the nature of disciplinary practices. The peculiarities of that factory, particularly the combination of loose effort standards, a strong piecework tradition, and an established gang system, led to the emergence of early leaving as a substantial problem for management. Elsewhere managerial control was, indeed, largely unquestioned.

Sometimes there were specific reasons for this. For example in the Electrical and Process Factories many shift workers travelled to work on contract bus services, so the quickest and cheapest way to go home was to wait for the bus at the end of the shift. Leaving early was thus an irrelevance.

While such mundane factors are important a more general influence must also be taken into account. As with absenteeism, breaches of disciplinary rules cut across working-class norms of doing one's bit, not being a shirker, and so on. Hence, even in the factories where the 'problem' of discipline was most acute, workers did not directly challenge management's right to set the times at which work would take place. The apparently unchangeable demands of a system of production based on bringing together large numbers of workers in one place, and the broad disciplinary system which resulted, went unquestioned. Similarly, criticisms of white-collar workers' freedom to come and go with few questions asked tended to be generalized complaints and not a call for the granting of similar privileges for all. Even toolmakers in the Large Metals Factory, who were more aware than most workers of the inequality of treatment between themselves and white-collar workers, did not make their complaint that they should be given staff status an explicit demand. But this is not to deny the significance of early leaving in the Large Metals and Components Factories. Although workers were not consciously resisting managerial control in its widest sense, they were engaging in practices which served to bring some aspects of this control into question. Indeed, management in both plants had felt obliged to take overt action to control breaches of discipline. Workers were responding, in other words, to particular aspects of the control system and were turning them to their own advantage. While not an articulated strategy of resistance, breaches of discipline certainly involved a less conscious questioning of control. This point is developed further at the end of Chapter 7 in relation to the wider question of managerial control over effort levels.

In the clothing factories workers' complaints about managerial handling of discipline can obviously be described in terms of our category of non-directed conflict. Yet, despite the intensity of feelings among large numbers of workers, discontent was, for reasons which we have indicated, far from total. This, together with the absence of attempts to challenge the disciplinary system, indicates an important sense in which conflict remained implicit. In so far as workers had an interest in a less strict managerial style (an interest which was at least partially articulated by the workers themselves) and in so far as this interest was not being realized, there was a conflict of interest at the structural level. The picture of these plants which we have developed here and in the two previous chapters gives a consistent view of intense control over the labour process, some recognition by workers of the nature of this, and few direct expressions of conflict. All this makes it possible to argue that there was a 'real' conflict of interests but that it was, for identifiable reasons, kept largely implicit.

In our other three plants, namely the Electrical, Process, and Small Metals Factories, open disputes on discipline were, as in the clothing plants, rare. Yet it would be unhelpful to argue that there was implicit conflict over discipline in any of them. If it is assumed that workers' interests lie in the absence of all discipline or in the creation of an ideal state without compulsion then it would be possible to argue that there was a state of conflict. But this argument does not get us very far. The liberal style of management practised in the Electrical and Process Factories, with paid time off for medical visits and with bureaucratic procedures for dealing with breaches of the rules, is more in workers' interests than an autocratic style based on arbitrary power. And the relaxed style of the Small Metals Factory, with its basis in established custom and practice and traditional ways of operating, could be said to be even more in workers' interests. Certainly by comparison with the clothing plants there was no basis for asserting that there was implicit conflict over discipline. Now this is not to suggest that conflict had been eradicated from the system, for we have stressed the contingent nature of managerial control and the possibility of challenge. But, in attacking the cosy assumption that harmony can prevail, or at least that conflict can be channelled into harmless directions, there is a danger of moving too far in the opposite direction. Managerial control certainly has to be created and sustained, but there are instances where this process need not be active and where, in comparative terms and in particular spheres of control over the labour process, conflict is, for the time being, not present.

In this and the previous two chapters we have considered means whereby workers can challenge managerial attempts to secure a ready supply of labour power. In the next three chapters we turn to matters 'at the point of production': once workers are present in the factory, how are they persuaded to release their labour power?

6
Sabotage

Introduction: Sabotage And All That

Sabotage was, until a few years ago, given little serious attention as a form of industrial conflict. It received a mention in ritual listings of the forms of conflict, but this would be little more than a passing comment about Luddism. It was easy to assume that sabotage was an immediate and unplanned response by unorganized workers and that its significance declined with the growth of more 'modern' forms of protest. This image has recently been challenged in two ways. First, it has been argued that sabotage, defined as 'that rule-breaking which takes the form of conscious action or inaction directed towards the mutilation or destruction of the work environment' (L. Taylor and Walton, 1971: 219), remains a widespread phenomenon. Second, the concept of sabotage has been widened beyond destruction. For Brown it involves any action which clogs the 'machinery of capitalism' by direct action at the point of production (G. Brown, 1977: xi). For Dubois (1976: 10) it goes wider still to include all 'intentional acts' which result in a reduction in the quantity or quality of the product; this includes absenteeism, strikes, working to rule, and even voluntary unemployment as well as destruction.

As these definitions indicate, the flurry of interest in sabotage has created terminological confusion. It is doubtful whether applying the same label to all the phenomena listed by Dubois is helpful. Such a listing reproduces all the difficulties with the definition of industrial conflict noted in Chapter 1: what do the various phenomena have in common, what means are given for deciding whether an action is a case of sabotage, and how far does a specific action such as going absent reflect sabotage? Since Dubois is explicitly concerned with intentional acts, these problems are severe. Brown's definition is more restricted but, as he recognizes and indeed stresses, much of his subject-matter comes under the conventional rubric of restriction of output. While there may be advantages in evading the negative overtones of the word 'restriction', we doubt whether it is helpful to employ the new term to refer to a very wide range of practices. This point was made by Brissenden (1920: 279) in his early study of the Industrial

Workers of the World (the 'Wobblies'), an organization which was of course closely associated with a strategy of 'sabotage': in its mildest form sabotage is simply the traditional union practice of restricting output, and direct action at the point of production can assume a variety of forms.

A more serious problem concerns the nature of the evidence used in these studies. Taylor and Walton (1971: 220) admit that their data may not be wholly reliable, for they came from the popular press as well as sociological studies and 'notes on hundreds of casual conversations with workers about sabotage'. We have two reservations about this. First, and most obviously, although press reports can give a few colourful anecdotes about the phenomenon, they cannot be relied upon to give an accurate appraisal of its extent or significance. Second, Taylor and Walton give no indication of the nature of their 'casual conversations' or of how much reliance can be placed on them. Now we are not saying that they should have conducted 'rigorous' surveys of random samples of workers, for an elusive activity such as sabotage needs to be tracked down by informal methods. But Taylor and Walton are merely able to sketch three main types of motivation for sabotage, a classification which is itself open to some question as we argue below. They cannot explain the significance of the behaviour in specific settings or why some groups of workers engage in it when other do not. Similarly, Brown provides a historical survey of behaviour which comes within his wider definition of sabotage but gives little analysis of patterns of the behaviour or the reasons for its use in particular settings. One of his few specific hypotheses is that the extent of destructive sabotage in the car industry reflects the payment system in operation: in Ford plants workers on measured day work had no control over the speed of the track, and direct action was the only way of exerting control; whereas the piecework system in British Leyland factories served to institutionalize conflict in bargaining about piece prices and the like, with the result that sabotage was not necessary (G. Brown, 1977: 366–9). The first difficulty here is to show that the extent of sabotage does indeed differ: press reports and the study by Beynon (1973) indicate that sabotage occurred in Ford plants, but they do not indicate the extent or significance of the phenomenon.[1] Still less does the absence of such reports from Leyland factories indicate that there was no sabotage there. Moreover, a day rate payment system is neither necessary nor sufficient for sabotage to occur. For example, destructive sabotage was, as far as we could establish, unknown among the time-rate workers in the Process Factory. And Company B workers had developed

1. Beynon (1973: 139–41) in fact relates the occurrence of destruction to the characteristics of the work force (young men who were not interested in the job) and the technology (sabotage on the 'wet deck' of the paint shop was easy to carry out and hard for management to check). And he stresses the difficulties of sustaining such action elsewhere. Such detailed consideration of specific practices is what we are proposing here, although one may still doubt the typicality and importance of some of the incidents which Beynon cites.

sufficient controls over manning to make destruction largely unnecessary. The Ford case probably rests on the company's well-known insistence on keeping line speeds and manning levels under its own control and not on the measured day work system as such.

Despite these problems the concept of sabotage remains important in directing attention to action at the point of production and in indicating that such action is not the prerogative of the Wobblies or other groups using the term sabotage explicitly. Thus we saw in the previous chapter that withdrawal of co-operation was, in the Large Metals Factory, a crucial shopfloor response to what was seen as a managerial attack on custom and practice. In the eyes of Brown and Dubois this action would qualify as sabotage but, as we have said, such an all-embracing use of the concept is unhelpful. Following Taylor and Walton we will use the term to refer to deliberate behaviour leading to the destruction of, or damage to, the company's property; this includes deliberate poor work as well as the destruction of existing work. We use the term restriction of effort to refer to the withdrawal of co-operation and other non-destructive actions although, as we will see in Chapter 7, 'restriction' takes a variety of forms. The distinction is necessarily somewhat arbitrary. Thus some of the means of 'controlling the track' discussed in the following chapter, notably in the Large Factory pushing the emergency stop button without 'good reason', border on sabotage. But they were not directly destructive and were part of a wider set of controls over effort.

We concentrate in this chapter, then, on sabotage in the limited sense of destruction. There remains the possibility, however, that this ignores the deliberate 'withdrawal of co-operation' by workers as a means of clogging the machinery of capitalism. We therefore consider some broad aspects of strategies on non-cooperation in so far as these relate to the debate about sabotage; other aspects of these strategies are examined at more length in subsequent chapters.

Utilitarian Sabotage

Taylor and Walton distinguish between sabotage to facilitate the work process, which they call utilitarian sabotage, and sabotage aimed at asserting a wider control over that process. Although the distinction is far from clear-cut, since easing the work process by altering the wage-effort bargain necessarily involves some assertion of control, the broad difference between the two forms of sabotage is clear enough. Most forms of sabotage in our factories were utilitarian in that they concerned specific aspects of work and not a self-conscious attempt to undermine or challenge managerial control more generally.

The Components Factory

Perhaps the most important example of utilitarian sabotage occurred among pieceworkers in the Components Factory. As noted in Chapter 2, one section of the plastics shop consisted of moulding machines whose operation depended on correct temperatures and cycle times, with workers being paid on individual piecework. If workers could cut cycle times they could increase their earnings, although this involved the risk that scrap would be produced. Operators had some discretion over cycle times to allow for variations in the raw material. As operators pointed out, the raw material could vary within an individual batch, which made it very difficult to turn out components of a consistent quality. But cutting cycle times was undoubtedly a widespread practice, and many workers made no bones about it: as long as they produced acceptable components management did not mind what they did, and the piecework system was meant to encourage them to maximize earnings. If they took the opportunity of using the system and occasionally went too far it was not their fault. Production supervision took an essentially similar view. Foremen knew that the practice went on, and felt that there was little they could do to stop it. Their concern was production, and cutting cycle times helped to ensure that targets were met. They would certainly act if the situation got out of hand, but they stressed that most men were experienced operators who had brought the whole matter down to a fine art. If a new man started cutting times before he had learned the necessary skills they would have taken a less sanguine view.

This view that cutting cycle times was an accepted, though formally illicit, part of custom and practice was challenged by quality supervisors. In this company production and quality departments were distinct, with foremen in the latter owing no allegiance to local production management. Instead, their line of command went up to their own manager, who had the formal right to ignore even the factory manager on a quality question, being able to refer the matter to divisional level. This split may have encouraged complaints from quality supervisors, who felt that there was little they could do to control cycle times. They could refer the matter to production supervisors but this, they felt, was only a temporary measure, for these supervisors would crack down for a while and then acquiesce in a return to old practices. The feeling that poor quality was the result of deliberate sabotage was widespread throughout the quality department. For example one foreman when asked what was his greatest quality problem, unhesitatingly said that it was the cutting of cycle times, going on to explain the difficulties which the practice created for him. This was not simply a general moan: foremen elsewhere in the factory and in the Electrical Factory mentioned technical difficulties and not worker performance as their main problems.

Cutting cycle times reflected the opportunity for the behaviour provided by the technology and the incentive to engage in it provided by the payment system. In the metals shop, where individual piecework had been in operation until recently and where the current system of group incentives was equally favourable to sabotage, the technology offered little opportunity for altering times and the action was virtually unknown. On the automated plastics machines it was possible to alter cycle times but the system of guaranteed bonus payments provided no incentive to do so. Cutting times was a utilitarian attempt to improve earnings which was possible only under certain specific conditions. The behaviour was one aspect of 'making out', or the achievement of piecework bonus and has a great deal in common with the practices described by Roy (1954) and Burawoy (1979: 51–62). For example, Burawoy describes how, once a job had been priced and the first piece passed, a worker would look for the 'angles' on the job which would enable him to earn bonus. These angles often involved the risk of turning out scrap or damaging the tool.

The behaviour of men in the Components Factory was thus similar to that in other piecework environments: sabotage was a formally illicit act which threatened quality standards and thus the value of the product to the firm, but which was not a strategy of destruction for its own sake. This raises the question of the role of sabotage as a form of struggle or resistance. Burawoy (1979: 162) defines struggle as an attempt to shift the curve relating rewards to effort in the workers' favour. Competition, on the other hand, involves moving up or down an existing effort curve. Since sabotage enabled workers to earn a given amount of money more quickly than if they followed planned times, it appears that the behaviour qualifies as a type of struggle. Similarly, the forms of making out discussed by Burawoy may be seen as aspects of struggle whereas Burawoy himself stresses that making out is really a form of competition. This ambiguity in Burawoy's usage of the two terms seems to stem from uncertainty about the term 'struggle'. On his formal definition, sabotage is a form of struggle, but he also wants to use the term in its wider sense to denote resistance and attempts to exert control. The confusion can be eliminated by arguing that, while there is a distinction between acceptance of the existing rules of the game and attempts to change those rules, different attempts to change the rules have different implications. In other words there are degrees of struggle. Thus, sabotage altered the rules, but it did so covertly and at the margin. Moreover, in meeting the managerial aim of increased output it was not directly contrary to management's interests. And bending the rules by cutting cycle times may deflect workers' attention from wider questions about the rules; we show in the following chapter, for example, that there was little collective pressure on piece rates. As a form of struggle in the sense of collective resistance, sabotage had crucial limitations.

The Clothing Industry
This discussion, together with the detailed accounts of piecework shops given

by Roy, Burawoy, and many other writers, may suggest that systems of individual piecework necessarily give workers the incentive to increase earnings through producing poor quality work. This incentive may be reduced, however, if management are able to exert strong control over quality standards. The clearest example of powerful managerial control was in the Hosiery Factory. In the preparation department garments had to be properly laid out and packaged if subsequent operations in the firm's other factory were to be carried out correctly. Since workers were on straight piecework there was an incentive to rush the work, but few attempted to do so. As they pointed out, each box of work was tagged with the worker's number and any unsatisfactory work could be traced back to its source. Consistent bad work would lead to a formal disciplinary warning, but there were also more immediate financial penalties: all bad work had to be rectified in the worker's own time. Anyone turning out bad work knew that she would probably lose out, since the probability of its being discovered was high and since it would take longer to rectify the work than to do it correctly in the first place.

Management's ability to operate a system of financial penalties and to discipline individuals without arousing accusations of victimization reflects the extent of managerial control and the absence of collective organization on the shopfloor. In a more organized factory one would expect claims that the bad work was not the workers' fault and that some allowance should be paid for rectification. The absence of such arguments was particularly revealing since at the time of the research management were introducing new quality standards. There were various production difficulties which management felt could be resolved if garments were prepared to higher standards. The imposition of these standards was announced, and workers were expected to work to them. There was no suggestion that the extra work which would undoubtedly be entailed should merit a higher piece rate. Workers thus found it harder to 'make their money', but there was no organized protest. The amount of poor quality work recorded and the number of disciplinary warnings certainly increased, but this can be attributed to management's concern to establish the new standards and not to any resistance through sabotage. Management were thus able to keep a very tight rein on the quality of work. As a study of a similarly weakly-organized plant found, managers can affect workers' earnings by altering quality standards and yet have this unilateral action accepted as legitimate because management are 'responsible' for quality (P. Armstrong et al., 1981: 68).

A similar control system, based on records of who had done a particular job and unpaid rectification of faults, was in operation in the Underwear Factory. The work was more complex than that in the Hosiery Factory and quality standards were even more critical since the firm relied on its reputation for high quality work to retain good links with its customers. The pressure to maintain standards was thus considerable. Every piece of work was inspected and any worker turning out more than a set number of unacceptable pieces was given a warning. In cases which we witnessed the shop representative was called in to acknowledge the warning but was not expected to challenge it or even to ask for clarification of the reasons for it. Workers took a fatalistic view: 'going in the book' was something which happened to everyone and was not a source of particular resentment. As one worker who had just been disciplined put it, she did not specifically resent the warning or feel that it was unjustified, but neither did she worry about it let alone feel guilty. She felt it was one of the ways in which work was conducted and that it was necessary to live with it and not 'let it get you down'. But warnings for bad work, and in particular a feeling that they were distributed somewhat arbitrarily, contributed to the general feeling which we have discussed in previous chapters that managerial authority was too strict. This feeling may also have led to the expression of discontent through quitting, since it was apparently quite common for a worker who had accumulated a couple of formal warnings to leave rather than risk a final warning and the sack. But the discontent was not expressed directly through poor quality work, or through collective action over disputes concerned with it.

Management certainly did not see poor quality in conflictual terms. For them it was the result of 'carelessness', not deliberate action. They denied, moreover, that sub-standard work could be blamed on variations in the raw material. Workers claimed that it was often difficult to sew up particular garments properly because the size and shape of the material varied. Management's attitude is summed up by the response of one shop manager who was asked whether workers should not receive an allowance for these variations: 'these girls are skilled [operators]', she said, and they were paid precisely to handle variations in the raw material. She felt that management had to keep a constant check on quality, an endeavour in which they achieved a substantial degree of success.

The incidents discussed so far illustrate the general situation in the clothing factories, namely an absence of collective resistance. A final example shows that this was not always so, and also reveals the use of sabotage as part of a deliberate strategy. In a case with many similarities to the alteration of quality standards in the Hosiery Factory, management in the Underwear Factory asked workers in the packing department to carry out a final inspection of the work in addition to packing it. A casual examination for obviously faulty work had always been part of the job, but management were now asking for a more rigorous inspection. They argued that inspection had always been part of the job, and offered no extra payment. After complaining about this for a time, workers took the further step of failing to do any systematic inspection; management were forced to introduce subsequent spot checks on work which was ready for despatch, and these revealed substantial amounts of sub-standard work. Written warnings were issued, and the dispute continued to simmer until the workers refused to do any inspection at all. The managing director was immediately called in. He demanded that workers work 'properly' and invited anybody who did not wish to comply with the factory's working methods to hand in her resignation. Resistance then crumbled. There was no one who was willing to represent the shop, the previous union representative having been sacked some time previously for allegedly swearing at a supervisor. Although they had engaged in a form of collective sabotage for a time, workers lacked the organization to maintain a determined campaign against management. The incident also illustrates managerial expectations: the factory should be run on management's terms and negotiation over new working practices was not necessary. Anyone who did not like the arrangements could leave or, like the previous shop representative, be sacked. It is not surprising that the turnover figures analysed in Chapter 3 were so high.

The limited amounts of utilitarian sabotage in the clothing factories did not attain the degree of acceptance of similar practices in the Components Factory because of management's ability to control such action. Although the technology and payments system were conducive to sabotage, it was the context in which these two influences operated which was crucial. Management were able to define the situation in such a way that sabotage did not become widespread and that individual workers did not stand to gain from it.

The Large Metals Factory

In contrast to these small firms with weak shopfloor organizations the Large Metals Factory apparently provides an atmosphere which was highly conducive to sabotage. A common theory about sabotage is, as we saw in Chapter 1 (p. 20), that it is a response to the frustrations of working in large factories doing boring tasks in a noisy and unpleasant atmosphere. Certain sections of the factory fitted this image: in the advanced assembly shop, Shop X, in particular workers were tied to the track. In addition workers had, in their decline in the wages league, a ready source of discontent, and they also possessed the collective traditions to engage in sabotage. Yet the assembly shops saw very little sabotage. There was, indeed, considerable pride in the quality of work in the factory. Stewards in both main assembly shops frequently made the point that, all the managerially-induced frustrations notwithstanding, they still managed to turn out a good product; one steward in particular was fond of arguing that, in terms of standard criteria such as clearances between moving parts, the plant's products were as good as those of the acknowledged leader of the industry. The plant had always had a good reputation for quality; this was, indeed, one of the few elements of pride left among a work force which was otherwise demoralized.

The answer to this apparent paradox lies in the existence of a whole range of sophisticated means of exerting control over the effort bargain. These means, discussed in detail in the following chapter, made sabotage as we have defined it largely unnecessary. As we saw in Chapter 5, a general strategy of non-cooperation and the withdrawal of effort could prove highly effective. Such a strategy could well involve an increased attention to quality standards and not the reverse. Hence on one occasion workers in Shop X refused to allow products to leave their stations until they met quality standards in all respects. The result was chaos as the line soon became clogged up with sub-standard units which could not be moved.

There was, however, one area of the factory where sabotage was felt, by management at least, to be a problem. Managers in the machine shop mentioned, on their own initiative, deliberate destruction as a significant problem and even applied the term 'sabotage' to it. Consideration of this case can reveal the particular circumstances which encourage sabotage.

Several managers mentioned, on several different occasions, cases of cut air lines and mysteriously broken conveyor belts which they attributed to deliberate action by workers. Managers were not disinterested observers, however, and we need to put the matter in perspective. Hence stewards denied that there was a significant amount of sabotage, and accused managers of assuming that any case of sub-standard work was the result of workers' negligence or deliberate action. These differences of interpretation raise the question of whether there was, indeed, any amount of sabotage or whether claims of its existence were merely managerial attempts to blame workers for quality problems. There were certainly some well-documented instances of deliberate sabotage, notably one where a worker was seen by a manager damaging a tool, and our problem therefore becomes two-fold. Why did this type of action occur only in this one shop? And why did feelings about it run so high?

The answer to both questions lies in a dramatic breakdown of trust between management and the shopfloor. Workers' feelings about management were intensely antagonistic and highly personalized, whereas in the rest of the factory there was more of a generalized and less focused complaint about management. Stewards in the machine shop were very forceful in their criticisms of the shop manager, arguing that there was a constant threat of discipline if workers failed to attain targets and that, in relation to one particular case, management had sought the sternest penalty possible. Managers were seen as stern and unbending. This view was echoed by workers; one group, for example, said that managers were 'corrupt', that they did not care about workers' problems, and that they would not trust 'them up there if they'd been dead 25 years'. Managers and foremen, for their part, bemoaned the loss of their own authority, growing absence rates, and a general collapse of responsibility on the shopfloor. The depth of these feelings, at least on the workers' side, can be attributed to several factors peculiar to the machine shop, as well as to general frustrations about wage levels which were shared with other workers. It was felt that workers in the assembly shops were being treated too leniently by management; as two stewards complained, for example, they knew that discipline was enforced in a lax fashion in the assembly shops and that workers 'got away with too much', although they admitted that they could not prove this. A particular complaint in the machine shop was that assembly shop workers had virtually guaranteed overtime whereas they themselves were often on short time. There was thus a feeling that they were being treated unfairly, a feeling which had some degree of truth: we saw in the previous chapter that disciplinary rates in the machine shop were very high, and short time was common. The low trust syndrome in the factory as a whole was given a further downward push by these developments. Workers resented management and had no interest or pride in their work, and an occasional episode of sabotage was one response.

We must not forget, however, the technical conditions which made sabotage a worthwhile strategy for workers. As in the rest of the factory there was an incentive to finish work quotas early to gain leisure at the end of the shift. This apparently made sabotage pointless. But the complexity of the machinery, together with the need to check it very thoroughly for safety reasons in the event of any malfunction, meant that breakdowns could last several hours or all day. Persuading the machine to malfunction could thus create a substantial period of leisure. The more common tactic, however, did not involve sabotage as we have defined it. Part of the agreed safety procedure was that a machine which had malfunctioned had to be checked by being turned over 500 times by the maintenance department.[2] This gave production workers a substantial break. There was, moreover, no way of checking on the genuineness of a reported malfunction, so that workers could make false reports with little risk of being found out. Again, perceptions of the prevalence of this practice varied, but the very fact that it was discussed so much was a further indication of the collapse of trust between managers and workers. Spurious reports of malfunctions involved the withdrawl of normal amounts of co-operation, a topic which we now examine in more detail.

Withdrawal of Co-operation

We have so far considered sabotage in the restricted sense of actions which lead to the destruction of the product or a decline in quality and which stem from a broadly utilitarian motivation. As we have said, this is in some respects too narrow a definition. Consider for example the case cited by Taylor and Walton (1971: 221) in which steel workers know that a slab of steel is too cold to be rolled but still allow it to go through the rolling process. The destruction here

2. Interestingly, in the technically similar machine shop in the Small Metals Factory there was no such procedure, and our questioning about it and about 'sabotage' was treated with amazement. For stewards and foremen alike deliberate sabotage was unthinkable. It was the particular traditions of the Large Metals Factory's machine shop which were crucial.

is the result of deliberate inattention and seems to lack any immediate rationale. From Taylor and Walton's source (Eldridge, 1968: 252–3) the action seems to be the result of resentment against the removal of control over the process from the shopfloor to a distant planning office: workers felt that they were no longer being trusted to take decisions and responded by doing exactly what the new decision-makers told them to do, even though they knew that this was incorrect. They were turning the system of rules against itself by following the rules exactly and refusing to exercise their own discretion.

We do not deny that what we call withdrawal of co-operation can be a highly effective form of pressure. Indeed, we can provide an impressive-sounding list of instances which we came across: toolmakers were said to drill three holes in a piece of metal because the blueprint required this even though they knew that there should be only two holes; or workers might refuse to notify management when they ran out of raw materials, simply waiting until someone noticed that they were doing nothing. In other cases workers exploited the rules in other ways, for example by insisting on the strict application of safety and other rules when in 'normal times' a blind eye was turned to such rules. Specific examples, which we discuss more fully in other chapters, include insisting that welding guns be 'properly' clean before they were operated, that a section be fully manned before any work was done, and a demand that the least drop of oil be cleaned from the floor before any more work was done. But it is obvious that very different influences are at work in these various cases. Most obviously, there is a difference between 'deliberate carelessness' and over-conformity to organizational rules. The withdrawal of co-operation takes many forms, the use of specific forms reflecting the nature of shopfloor organization and a variety of strategic considerations. In the following chapters, notably in the discussion of the processes of conflict in Chapter 9, we analyse particular cases of non-cooperation. The present consideration, apart from its bearing on the concept of sabotage, is intended simply to provide the context for the more detailed analysis of later chapters.

The use of tactics of non-cooperation reflected, at the broadest level, the nature of factories' collective organization: as would be expected, where organization was weak, most notably in the clothing factories, workers lacked the ability to deploy collective sanctions. This point requires some elaboration, however. It was not that workers here knew that there was, in principle, a large range of sanctions open to them and that they did not employ them because of the threat of managerial counter-action. We term such a view the tool-box theory of sanctions: the theory that, just as the mechanic has a set of tools ready to perform specific tasks, workers have a pre-existing set of sanctions to be drawn on according to strategic and tactical needs. But the nature of organization of a factory cannot be separated from the sanctions available. Most obviously, the frontier of control in the clothing factories, and to some extent in the Company A and Process Factories, was such that certain sanctions simply could not exist. For example, stewards in the Small Metals Factory had long had a considerable degree of control over the allocation of workers to particular tasks. In 'normal times' a degree of flexibility was allowed to management on the question of the mobility of labour, but an obvious sanction was to withdraw this co-operation. Such a ban on the mobility of labour was literally unthinkable in the clothing factories: workers could not think of it because control over the allocation of labour did not come within the bargaining arena. More generally, the tool-box theory assumes that even in organized workplaces sanctions exist in a pre-formed state. But a sanction is possible only because it is sustained by organization, and its usefulness may alter if the situation changes. For example, insisting that a welding gun is properly clean is a useful tactic because it delays production without imposing any costs on workers. If management decide that such exploitation of the rules is unacceptable they may discipline workers and thus alter the value of the sanction. And, as Hicks recognized in the case of strikes, 'weapons grow rusty if unused, and a Union which never strikes may lose the ability to organise a formidable strike, so that its threats become less effective' (Hicks, 1932: 146). This is even more true of the withdrawal of co-operation than of strikes: there are several famous instances in which apparently quiescent workers organized long and effective strikes, whereas more limited sanctions may more easily decay if they are not, as Hicks puts it, kept 'burnished for future use'. In short, sanctions are constituted by organization and by the process of their use.

What, then, are the advantages of a strategy of withdrawal of co-operation? Batstone et al. (1978: 41) provide a useful summary of the main points: the relevant sanctions impose few costs on workers; the action can be defined as conformity to the rules and not as a sanction at all; since many aspects of day-to-day co-operation are negotiated on a continuing basis the sanction is readily available; and stewards can often impose the sanction without needing the active compliance of the work force. Batstone et al. also note that, in their factory, the assembly shop was the area where management relied most on day-to-day co-operation from the stewards. A similar situation existed in the assembly shops in the Large and Small Metals Factories. For stewards, co-operation was something to be given to management at their own discretion; it could be withdrawn at any time. If management were felt to be acting unreasonably then the normal degree of co-operation would not be forthcoming. We have seen in Chapter 5 how this worked in the Large Metals Factory when management at factory level attempted to alter clocking out requirements. But co-operation could also be withdrawn on much smaller-scale matters. As mentioned above, one tactic, if there was a dispute on manning levels on a particular job for instance, was to leave the job unfinished with the result that the assembly line became clogged with uncompleted units.

The possibility of using sanctions depended, however, on management's willingness to accept certain aspects of the structure of the situation. Some of the advantages listed by Batstone et al. could become disadvantages if management refused to accept the current definition of the situation. It may be tactically useful to define a sanction as conformity to the rules but it is always open to managers to insist that the normal way of doing things is not being followed and that, as a result, workers will be penalized. For example, on one occasion workers in a subsidiary machine shop in the Large Metals Factory refused to move into the main shop and management, insisting that such mobility was normal practice, suspended any worker who refused to move. This resulted in a strike by all the workers in question which soon collapsed, with the workers being required to move. Using a strategy of withdrawing co-operation depended on management's not escalating the dispute. For most of the time in the Large and Small Metals Factories workers could be sure, from past experience, that managers would choose to live with the sanctions. But such certainty could never be absolute.

In general we may suggest that the use of a strategy of non-cooperation was largely restricted to the craft areas in Company A and to the two Company B plants, where shopfloor organization was capable of sustaining the behaviour. It is only in this kind of situation, or in the kind of plant studied by Batstone and his colleagues, that the advantages of the withdrawal of co-operation are likely to be perceived. Moreover, even where workers had a fairly well-equipped tool-box of sanctions, the tools were not in continuous use. Most of the cases which we have mentioned involved a managerial action which was viewed as illegitimate, with the sanction being imposed in an attempt to alter that action or at least to protest about it. They were used for highly specific purposes. As Batstone et al. (1977: 262) note, stewards in their plant rarely tried to make anything more than marginal adjustments to the frontier of control, although they certainly defended the existing frontier vigorously. Similarly, withdrawal of co-operation cannot be seen as an attack on managerial prerogative in any radical sense, a point on which we enlarge in following chapters.

Conclusion: The Significance of Sabotage

At the end of their essay Taylor and Walton (1971: 243) argue that previous accounts of sabotage have been too abstract and 'too removed from the actual industrial setting in which the critical behaviour occurs'. Much of this chapter can be taken as an argument that Taylor and Walton, and other recent writers, have tended to fall into the same error by treating under one heading very disparate phenomena from a variety of settings and by advancing very partial explanations of why it occurs in one setting and not in another. Thus Brown expects sabotage to be most common under day work, whereas Taylor and Walton (1971: 242) expect utilitarian sabotage to be greatest 'where the worker has to "take on the machine" in order to push up his earnings', presumably meaning individual piecework. Neither of these competing hypotheses is sufficient to account for the patterns which we observed. In the piecework shops 'destructive sabotage' occurred only in one shop in the Components Factory where the opportunities and incentives for the behaviour were particularly great. As we have stressed, it was a consequence of attempts to 'make out' and was tolerated by foremen who needed to meet production targets. Although plainly a utilitarian action it did not fit the picture normally associated with the word sabotage for it was in many respects a way of playing the game and not of trying to change the rules of the game. Still less was it the response of 'alienated' workers. Sabotage was rare throughout the day work factories, occurring only in the machine shop of the Large Metals Factory and then only for very special reasons: it was neither a means of easing the work process nor an attempt to assert control against management but a negative response to a situation of intense frustration.

More generally, as Nichols and Armstrong (1976: 74–9) note, sabotage at 'ChemCo' was directed against fellow workers as well as against management, and much rule-breaking had the tacit consent of management. Similarly, in our factories there was not always a direct clash of interests over sabotage. Foremen in the Components Factory had a direct interest in the cutting of cycle times since the practice enabled them to meet production targets. And a certain amount of rule-bending was necessary in the Company B plants if anything was to be done; it was precisely this ambiguity which enabled workers to put on pressure by insisting that the rules be followed. Yet managerial interests were far from uniform. While production foremen may be concerned to 'shove it through' to meet targets, quality managers and managers who have to deal with complaints from customer plants are likely to take a different view. Intra-managerial bargaining is central here. A good example of this occurred in the Large Metals Factory when a customer plant began to raise unusual objections about quality standards; according to managers in the Large Metals Factory this was because there was a battle over the siting of a new production facility, and management in the customer plant were exploiting quality problems so as to strengthen their own hand in this battle. For our purposes the importance of this is that some degree of rule-breaking may be in the interests of workers and their immediate managers, although possibly against the interests of other groups of management and almost certainly against the interests of consumers. Hence to analyse the behaviour as an unambiguous indicator of conflict is unhelpful.

We have argued that the significance of sabotage has to be assessed in terms of very particular aspects of the labour process, in two senses. First, regarding the occurrence of sabotage, aspects of technology and payment systems encourage its use in some settings and not in others. Second, in terms of the implications of the behaviour, much utilitarian sabotage involves minor alterations in the effort bargain and not substantial struggle. In the following chapter we examine the effort bargain itself, considering how particular levels of effort are negotiated under different types of labour process.

7
Effort Bargaining

Lists of the forms of industrial conflict often include 'restriction of output' (C. Kerr, 1954: 232) or 'limiting production' (Goodman and Whittingham, 1973: 190). The concern of this chapter, namely the daily bargain over the amount of effort that shall be expended, thus has obvious implications for our wider interest of studying patterns of conflict. Yet to examine the effort bargain in terms of 'restriction of output' imposes too narrow a focus. First, it ignores wider aspects of the frontier of control which help to determine the terms on which an individual bargain is set. If managers are free, for example, to transfer workers between jobs they can, in effect, switch workers between bargains at will. The effort bargain cannot be divorced from other aspects of the frontier of control, in this case the extent of shopfloor controls over management's ability to allocate labour between tasks. Controls over the supply and allocation of labour are considered in Chapter 8, and their discussion constitutes part of any proper understanding of controls over effort in our factories. Second, output restriction has generally been studied in terms of workers' motivations, notably their responses to conditions of uncertainty (Roethlisberger and Dickson, 1939; Hickson, 1961). While important in revealing the rational basis of apparently irrational behaviour, the tradition gives insufficient attention to managerial attempts to control the labour process. We found that collective restriction of effort was far from common in our factories, and we need to consider the means whereby informal output norms are prevented from developing.

A 'radicalization' of the study of effort restriction, whereby 'restrictive practices' are analysed in terms of worker resistance, may seem to be the answer. Yet this is unsufficient if it merely follows the terms of the existing debate. As we saw with absenteeism, radicals may stress the rational bases of behaviour which other accounts see as irrational or as a managerial problem, but may fail to alter the type of questions asked. In the same way, Burawoy (1979: x) notes that 'radicals point to restriction of output as an expression of class consciousness, of the structural and inevitable conflict between capital and labor, or of the alienating nature of work'. For Burawoy, this merely alters the assumptions of 'conservatives' and fails to address the central question of why workers work as hard as they do. An example of the approach which Burawoy finds unhelpful may be found in the work of Lamphere (1979) and Shapiro-Perl (1979). These studies, of the American clothing and jewelry industries respectively, are of more than passing interest here, for they examine the work of women in weakly-organized workplaces and thus overlap with our interest in the British clothing industry. Their central problem is that, while a few examples of workplace activity are discussed, neither writer is able to explain the significance of such activity in the context of relationships as a whole. Behaviour is labelled unproblematically as 'resistance' without dealing with its impact on the structure of the situation. Lamphere (1979: 271–3) for example, in a section on 'fighting the piece-rate system', mentions workers' insistence on a fair allocation of work and their practice of keeping a record of output to ensure payment of the correct wages. Yet such practices reflect attempts to make the existing piece-rate system operate 'properly' and not a desire to 'fight' that system. Indeed, we argue below that one way in which managers in our clothing plants prevented 'resistance' to their own control was by being seen to be scrupulously fair in the allocation of work. The significance of workers' actions in effort bargaining needs to be investigated instead of being assumed to be part of a strategy of 'resistance'.

We assess, then, the effort bargain in the context of the frontier of control as a whole. As will be obvious from previous chapters, there were very great differences between our factories. We are concerned less with explaining these differences (for the broad outline of an explanation in terms of the weakness of collective organization in the clothing industry and powerful shopfloor control in Company B has already been sketched) than with exploring exactly how the effort bargain operated. How, for example, did management in the clothing industry keep the effort bargain strictly within its own control, and what types of shopfloor control operated in Company B? Yet we can do more than describe the consequences of the structure of the situation. As argued in Chapter 1, events at the overt level can reinforce or alter that structure. Hence we show how various attempts at 'resistance' in the clothing plants collapsed, and how this strengthened the system of managerial domination. Similarly, by looking for example at negotiations over manning levels in Company B, we can show how stewards manipulated the firm's known need for output to obtain manning standards in excess of those proposed by management. This company also provides an example of how changed structural conditions can affect the effort bargain: specifically, a threat of closure led stewards to accept manning cuts which would have been unthinkable earlier. The Process Factory provides a revealing example of a similar series of events.

The existing literature on effort restriction, including the work of Burawoy, focuses entirely on production workers. It will be convenient to follow this tradition, since the involvement of such workers in a daily effort bargain is particularly obvious: the effort of these workers is intimately connected with the level of output achieved by management. Craft workers are also, of course, involved in a bargain over the terms on which their effort shall be expended. But, since the link between their own efforts and levels of production is more remote, craft workers will not be discussed until Chapter 8. We begin the present discussion with the clothing plants, going on to compare them with our other plants where piecework was in operation. As we have seen, piecework had been ended in Company B, while it had never been employed in the Process Factory. Since one reason for ending piecework is often seen as the removal from the shopfloor of day-to-day bargaining, the comparison between our piecework and day work environments will be particularly instructive.

Control of Piecework

The Clothing Factories
Both clothing factories employed one of the simplest possible forms of piece-work: workers were paid so much per dozen items, with only a low basic time rate.[1] There were no formal attempts by management to limit the amount an operator could earn as long as she maintained quality standards. Work study techniques were not employed, with rates being set by rule of thumb methods. On the face of it, this system gives plenty of opportunity for shopfloor bargaining: piecework systems have been described as creating 'hot-house conditions' (William Brown, 1973: 1) for the development of informal bargaining, and a system where wages depend directly on output might be expected to be particularly prone to attempts to negotiate loose rates. Yet challenges to managerial control, either at this explicit level or more implicitly in terms of attempts to 'fiddle' the system in various ways, were very rare. The factories displayed remarkable similarities with the poorly-organized plants described by Armstrong and his colleagues: managerial demands that workers move to new jobs or quit, unilateral changes in work content by management, and the extreme individualism of the work force (P. Armstrong et al., 1981: 61, 68, 143) all had very close parallels in our factories.

We may begin with the individualism of the work force. It has become something of a truism that even unorganized work groups can exert some form of collective control over effort (Mathewson, 1969), but no such control was apparent here. We asked workers about collective controls and about personal output targets whereby a worker has a set figure for how much she will produce

1. Men in these factories were paid on time rates and they are not, therefore, discussed here.

and does not go above it. Neither form of control was evident. No worker said that there was any kind of group norm and, while some workers said that they had a rough idea of how many dozen they needed to do per day, they all said that they would go above the target if they could.

We tested for the presence of norms which were either more implicit or which were being concealed from us by examining data on earnings. Yetton (1979: 255) shows that informal effort norms may be assessed by examining the distribution of piecework bonus: assuming that 'natural ability' follows a normal distribution, bonus should, in the absence of norms, also be normally distributed. Any deviation from a normal distribution is not in itself, of course, proof of the presence of norms, but the absence of such deviation is certainly strong evidence for the lack of norms. The present case provides a particularly strong test since earnings varied directly with output and since all earnings can thus be seen as 'bonus'. We looked at the pattern of earnings in the Hosiery Factory over a period of a year, using average hourly earnings to allow for differences in hours worked. There was a very marked spread of earnings, with the highest earner having an hourly rate more than 50 per cent above that of the lowest earner; and the distribution approximated to a normal distribution.[2] Together with the interview evidence this points to the total absence of collective output norms.

How can this be explained? Studies of output restriction have established that a major influence on the behaviour is uncertainty: there may be a general fear of working oneself out of a job or a more specific concern that high earnings will lead management to cut rates. In neither of our firms was rate-cutting at all common whereas it appeared to be a standard practice in many other firms in the area. This can be attributed to our firms' relatively secure product market position: their well-established ties with major customers gave them a degree of predictability denied to most other firms in the industry. Some of the immediate fears associated with output restriction were therefore absent.

This can be no more than a background influence, however, for managers in our firms were explicit about the need to maintain competitiveness, in terms of quality and delivery dates as well as price. They could not afford to allow their costs to move far out of line with those of other firms in the area; and, in addition, they were worried about cheap imports of clothing. While our firms' tradition of secure employment without rate-cutting was important in making some forms of output restriction unnecessary, we still have to consider how piecework drift was prevented.

Part of the answer lies in the characteristics of the work force. We showed

2. A chi-square test for the difference between the observed distribution (N=60) and that which would be expected from a normal distribution was carried out. The test is explained by Yeomans (1968: 281–3).

in Chapter 3 that job experience outside the clothing industry was rare and that quit rates were high. The former influence tended to make workers' standards of comparisons low: they took for granted wage rates and employment practices in the industry because they had little direct experience elsewhere. We also saw that managers were clear about the advantages which they gained from this: workers did not bring with them 'bad habits' from outside the industry. In addition, for young workers straight from school, factory wages were undoubtedly attractive. A typical comment by workers about piece rates was that 'the money's all right, but you have to work for it'. While it was not easy to earn a satisfactory wage, workers accepted that they were there to work and felt that a reasonable amount of effort would bring an acceptable return. The high quit rate meant that workers did not necessarily plan to stay for long with one firm and that it was easier to move firms in search of more money than to fight an unequal battle over rates within one firm; an example of this is given below. All this contributed to a strong individualistic orientation among the work force. We have seen that no output norms were enforced, but perhaps a more dramatic illustration of individualism was workers' extreme secrecy about earnings. Some of the longer-serving workers, for example, reported that they might have worked alongside someone for years without knowing how much she earned and without expecting to know. By contrast women in the Electrical Factory discussed their pay slips in detail every pay day. Workers' individualism in the clothing plants plainly made the enforcement of collective norms impossible.

Although we can identify important strands of individualism, and although we can locate them in specific aspects of the composition of the work force, it remains to be shown how managerial domination was maintained. Part of management's control lay in the establishment of piece rates on new jobs. As we shall see, it was taken for granted in our engineering factories that a rate would be set according to the ability of an 'average' operator under 'average' conditions. This was sometimes taken further, as in the Components Factory where stewards argued that every worker should be able to attain a fair level of piecework earnings: the basis of a rate should be the slowest worker. In the clothing factories the opposite principle applied. As a manager in the Underwear Factory put it, a job would be given to the 'best girl' to try out, and a rate was fixed according to her output. This system would not necessarily lead to a 'tight' rate, for the operator under trial could employ a variety of tactics to slow down her output while appearing to work at full efficiency. The means by which workers can try to fool the rate-fixer are now well-known (Klein, 1964: 16—26). We do not need to consider them here, for, as far as we could discover, they were unknown in the clothing plants. Workers said that they worked as normal during a trial and that there was no point in doing otherwise. An immediate influence on their behaviour was the absence of a fall-back day rate. In our other factories workers under work study were paid an agreed day rate, which in Company A was not very different from average piecework earnings, whereas in the clothing plants they were 'on their own time'. Anyone holding back on a job would simply lose money for herself and, given the strength of workers' individualism, a refusal to act in the common good becomes more understandable. But perhaps most remarkable is workers' unthinking acceptance of this means of setting rates. There is a danger of assuming that all workers will treat as axiomatic the need to fight for a loose rate. In our more organized plants workers did indeed take this view; as a steward in the Small Metals Factory put it, it was 'the working man's birth right' to play the game of holding back effort during work study, with the result depending on a battle of wits with the rate-fixer. Yet workers in our clothing plants simply accepted a trial at face value.

A neat illustration of this occurred in the Underwear Factory. Management announced that students from a nearby technical college would be visiting the plant as part of their training as work study engineers. About a dozen trainees arrived one morning and began to conduct detailed studies of workers in one section of the factory. In our engineering plants, this would have been unthinkable, but all the workers on the section accepted that they should be studied, and they continued to work as usual. This was despite considerable uncertainty about the purpose of the exercise; some workers accepted the official management explanation that the study was purely for training purposes and had no implications for rates, while others did not know even this. There was no questioning of management's right to bring the trainees onto the shopfloor and no suspicion of any underlying motives. Managers were in private quite open about what they hoped to gain from the exercise. They had no intention of engaging in simple rate-cutting, but they planned to introduce work study techniques on a permanent basis and saw the use of the trainees as a way of breaking down shopfloor suspicions of such 'modern' methods. The absence of any questioning about the exercise suggests that they would be able to introduce full-scale work study with the minimum of resistance.

This is not to suggest that acquiescence in managerial control was total, although such resistance as did emerge was certainly very muted. Another case in the Underwear Factory illustrates the possibilities and limitations of resistance. As a result of changes in the style of garments being produced management wanted to transfer a group of workers from one section to another. The operations performed were very different, and management therefore offered to protect workers from a fall in earnings by paying them their previous average earnings over a period of 13 weeks. The workers involved, however, felt that they could not master the new operations in this time and feared a substantial drop in earnings after the 13-week period. Unusually, they expressed their unwillingness to accept management's request and, equally unusually, senior managers offered to extend the period of average earnings to 26 weeks. This probably reflects the fact that these workers were among the longest-serving group in the factory; managers said that they did not want to upset a group whose skills and general co-operativeness were highly valued. With management's new offer, and in particular with what they took to be a firm promise that they could return to their old machines if they could not manage their new work, six women agreed to move. Their old machines were, however, soon removed from the plant, which made such a return impossible. The workers felt that management had gone back on its part of the bargain, but, despite this, there was no organized response.

One of the six decided to quit, a decision which sharply illustrates several general points. In the absence of collective resistance, quitting was the only way for someone to pursue a better effort bargain. And, significantly, she was the only one of the six who was the main breadwinner of her family: she could not afford to risk a cut in her earnings whereas other women could make do with reduced earnings. This point is particularly important here, for many of the women who were threatened with a move worked part-time hours suited to their own needs, and they recognized the impossibility of finding such convenient working hours elsewhere. They accepted, albeit unwillingly, the managerial view that the move was necessary and that anyone who was dissatisfied would have to quit; since they did not want to leave they had no real alternative. Workers' individualism was also important: the women remaining on the old section felt that, while management had acted wrongly, the decision did not directly affect them and that no action on their part was required. This was despite the obvious fact that their turn would come. The main concern was to be the last to move so that the reduction in earnings would be delayed as long as possible.

This example, together with those in the previous chapter, indicates how managerial domination could be maintained: managerial actions worsened the terms of the effort bargain for workers and there was some discontent about it, but workers were too individualistic and the system of managerial control was too all-embracing for an effective challenge to be mounted. Resistance collapsed, workers who were particularly discontented left, and managerial domination was reinforced.

Even these limited challenges were, however, unusual. We have argued that many aspects of managerial control were taken for granted and have indicated various forces which brought this result about. One additional factor was managers' self-conscious concern with being fair to their workers. This is no more than a secondary factor, for it operated within the context of tight managerial control over all aspects of the labour process and we doubt whether managers would be over-concerned with fairness if they were faced with a serious challenge to their authority. But it helped to moderate challenges, since, if managers were felt to be generally fair, workers lacked a focus for complaints. We saw in earlier chapters that managers had a general paternalistic concern for their work force and that in individual cases of need they were prepared to go out of their way to be helpful. Our concern here is with fairness in the allocation of work. With a highly individualistic work force paid on straight piecework it was plainly important for management to be seen to be fair in the allocation of 'good' and 'bad' jobs. In both our factories managers, and particularly first-line supervisors, were keenly aware of this. In the Underwear Factory the introduction of supervisors who were responsible for their own sections had reduced management's problems, and complaints about unfairness were rare. In the Hosiery Factory, where there were few supervisors, there was an interesting way of dealing with the problem. Male workers, who were graded as labourers, were given the task of allocating work and checking on its progress. Any complaints were therefore deflected away from supervisors and onto other workers. As one man said, it was more than his life was worth to be seen to be unfair in distributing work.

The main elements of the piecework system were thus firmly under managerial control. But this still leaves the possibility that there were more covert ways whereby workers could bend the system in their own favour. One way, which does not directly alter the terms of the effort bargain, is to reduce fluctuations in earnings by booking in only part of the work done on good jobs, saving up the remainder to balance subsequent bad jobs. Other ways, which do alter the bargain, include various 'fiddles' such as booking the same work in twice or altering work dockets.[3] Altering the timing of bookings may have been possible to some extent, but the workers whom we questioned about it could not see any point in the practice: again, there was simple acceptance of the managerial rules of the system. There were a few possibilities of engaging in more illicit practices but, as we saw in the case of sabotage, the control system was too thorough to permit any but the most minor fiddles. As far as booking clerks were aware such fiddles were very rare. And given the very narrow limits in which any fiddle could operate, it was, as one worker said, not work the risk, for anyone caught would be sacked at once.

Even minor attempts to bend the rules were rare. Although piecework provides the opportunity for the growth of customary rules which may supplant formal rules, there is no certainty that such informal rules will emerge. Armstrong and his colleagues found that many customary practices lack the stability normally associated with rules, for management could confidently clamp down on them: custom as such has very little legitimacy (P. Armstrong

---

3. Burawoy (1979: 58, 228) equates the English term fiddling with what his American workers called chiseling: building up a kitty of work to balance earnings. This is unhelpful. Fiddling means any act of cheating, and we use the term to describe any means of beating the system which involves alterations in the amount of work booked or in the number of hours booked on particular jobs (cross-booking).

et al., 1981: 87). Similarly, we found some customary practices which moderated managerial control over the effort bargain; the Underwear Factory for example had an informal five-minute smoking break in addition to the agreed tea break. But this was treated as a concession by management and not a customary right. More generally, there was none of the bargaining which is often associated with piecework systems. There were no attempts, for example, to argue that the time rate which applied when no work was available should be increased on the ground that workers were in the plant and willing to work. The firms' product markets played some role in reducing the need for some forms of workers' response over piecework, but more important was the pattern of workplace control. Product market conditions might be expected to encourage workers to exploit the firms' relatively secure position. But low standards of comparison, strong traditions of individualism, and the loss of potential leaders through quitting, combined with tight managerial control of all aspects of the payment system, meant that no effective challenge could be mounted.

Company A

The contrast with Company A is revealing, for here was a firm with a relatively well-organized work force and a piecework system which reflected a range of bargaining pressures. While this case illustrates several aspects of effort-bargaining under piecework, its implications for notions of conflict or resistance are far from obvious. We saw in the previous chapter, in relation to sabotage in the Components Factory, that actions which shift the curve relating effort to rewards need not necessarily imply the presence of widespread struggle. Many aspects of the effort bargain in this factory and the Electrical Factory had become institutionalized: the overall framework of the piecework system was accepted by both sides, and the amount of active struggle was limited. While this institutionalization certainly meant that managerial control was far more restrained by the shopfloor than was the case in the clothing plants, the rarity of attempts to shift the terms of the effort bargain also meant that active struggle was contained.

Despite very great differences from the clothing plants there was one crucial similarity: the absence of rate-cutting. Work study personnel were genuinely surprised when we asked them whether they had tried to reduce a rate: the company never tried, they said, to go back on an agreed price. As William Brown (1973: 169) suggests in his study of piecework in engineering factories, the product market and the production technology may be important influences on this. Company A sold the great bulk of its output to other firms making goods for the consumer market, and pressures on labour costs were far from direct. And most of its products were standardized items produced in long production runs, which meant that there was a stable set of conditions on the shopfloor. There was no sudden shifting between one item and another, and hence workers did not feel the need to defend loose rates in case of a sudden move to a bad job.

This is far from being an adequate summary of the nature of product market and technological influences, and a proper understanding would require detailed consideration of the firm's relationship with its customers, for the situation seems to have been far more complex than that in the clothing industry. Our main concern, however, is with how these broad influences affected shopfloor bargaining. Such conditions plainly do not have determinate effects, as is most obvious from wide differences in the extent of piecework drift between different factories in Company A despite an identical payment system and despite similarities in market conditions. Whatever the precise nature of external factors, their effect was certainly to make rate-cutting, and hence responses to it such as output restriction, largely irrelevant. We examined the distribution of bonus earnings in one of the shops in the Components Factory which was on individual piecework and found, as in the clothing factories, that there was no significant difference from a normal distribution. This evidence was supported by interview material which indicated the absence of collective norms. But the sharpest illustration of the lack of norms was the presence in the shop of several workers who, in other contexts, would be known as rate-busters: workers who regularly produced far more than the average. In this shop they were not subject to any sanctions by their work mates, being called 'high flyers' and not rate-busters and being treated with awe rather than contempt.

The overall significance of this result differs from that in the clothing plants because earnings were not directly related to output. On the contrary, variations in bonus did not have a large effect on total earnings: in both Company A factories the day work rate for jobs without piecework times was over 90 per cent of average earnings, while the fall-back rate for waiting time was equivalent to 85 per cent of average earnings. In the clothing plants the lack of output norms left earnings free to vary by very large amounts, whereas in Company A the day rate and the rate for waiting time meant that earnings, as distinct from piecework bonus, did not display anything like the same degree of variation.

The growth of fall-back guarantees was one of the results of collective pressure on the piecework system. This was an historical phenomenon of the company as a whole, with waiting payments coming closer to average earnings over many years; as a result we are not able to say anything in detail about the nature of the pressure which was exercised. But it obviously reflected a feeling that, if workers were at the factory and prepared to work, they should be reasonably compensated if the lack of work was no fault of their own. We can analyse other aspects of the payments system in more detail.

As noted earlier negotiating the rate when a new job is introduced is crucial to the subsequent wage-effort bargain. In Company A the work study engineer would time a job and produce a standard time. The operator was free to argue about this and to call in the shop steward if there was no agreement. Unlike Company B, however, where the steward was involved in all aspects of timing and negotiation, stewards had no formal right to be present when a job was being timed or to negotiate a price if operators were satisfied with it. Bargaining took place around what was known as the off-standard allowance (OSA); this was formally a means of making allowances for aspects of a job which could not be incorporated in the standard time based on work study, but was in practice a means of bargaining about the rate for the job. The company clung to the idea that work study times were the correct ones, being based on 'objective' factors, and treated OSA as a separate feature of the job. It is possible, therefore, to consider OSA as a measure of 'piecework drift', that is of the extent to which rates diverged from those negotiated at national or company level (see William Brown, 1973: 25–7). In the Electrical Factory OSA had consistently run at low levels over the previous years, and the plant was well towards the bottom of the company earnings league. The Components Factory was higher up the table, although management felt that the amount of pressure was not unreasonable. By contrast it was claimed that strong pressure from stewards in another factory had led to exceptional levels of OSA and that the system was more out of control. Under identical formal systems, the outcome seems to have varied according to the willingness and ability of stewards to bargain about work study times.

At the time of the research, no new jobs had been introduced into either of our plants for some time, and we were not able to examine the processes of bargaining. But we were told by people in the Components Factory that workers were in a strong position. A new job would be wanted urgently, and there was powerful pressure on management to pay OSA in order to have the job on a piecework price. The costs to the shopfloor were slight, since workers on such a job were guaranteed day rate. One foreman cited a case where he had tried to resist giving OSA and thus creating a loose time, but he had been overruled by higher management who were desperate for output. This case seems to have been far from common, however; indeed, the opportunity for exerting pressure on new rates came only rarely, given that most jobs ran for several years.

The obvious test of the result of pressure is the average level of bonus earnings. Bonus was calculated on the basis of the time taken to perform a job compared to the time set by work study (including OSA). This produced a bonus index (BI) which was multiplied by a 'bonus calculator' of so many pence to produce a monetary figure. We will consider the negotiation of the calculator element shortly; for present purposes the level of the BI provides the clearest measure of drift in that it reflects workers' ability to earn high timings through loose standards. In the Electrical Factory, the average level of BI was about 55 arbitrarily-defined units. For workers on individual piecework in the Components Factory it was about 75, with the highest earner achieving a figure of 140. This last figure was considered exceptional, however, and was attributed by management as well as by workers to the man's extra-ordinary dexterity and effort. By contrast, it was claimed that, in the factory with the highest rates of OSA, a bonus index of 150 or more was regularly achieved. The piecework system in our two factories was comparatively 'under control'.

In view of the self-confidence of stewards in the Components Factory and the symbolic role of their wage strike of several years previously,[4] one might have expected a more 'militant' approach to piecework bargaining. When questioned about this and about the existence of the factory (which was only a mile or so away) with much higher bonus levels, stewards turned to the second element of earnings, the bonus calculator. They argued that they had been able to achieve levels of the calculator which largely outweighed their disadvantage on BI levels. This argument is hard to assess in detail since the calculator was supposedly based on the skill of the job, and many production jobs in the factory were more skilled than those performed in other plants. But the calculator for semi-skilled jobs was somewhat higher than that for similar jobs in the Electrical Factory. In concrete terms the difference was worth about £1.25 a week at Electrical Factory bonus levels, with the remaining difference in pay rates between the plants of about £2.75 being attributable to the higher level of BI in the Components Factory.

The crucial feature of the stewards' position, however, was that they felt that the battle on calculator levels had been largely won. They had established a fair balance of effort and reward, they felt, and did not see themselves as being involved in a day-to-day struggle with management. Management were able to claim with considerable justification that they had good working relationships with their stewards and that the stewards generally took a 'responsible' approach. Piecework struggle in the Components Factory was to a considerable extent institutionalized: the framework had been set and hence there was little day-to-day collective struggle on the shopfloor. The same picture applies even more strongly in the Electrical Factory, where even management were becoming concerned at the low level of OSA. As a work study officer said, his department was carrying out a thorough review of rates to see whether allowances could be made more generous. In his view the reason for this was higher management's fear that, if the plant were too far out of line, the conveners might be seen to be too much in the pockets of management and might then be replaced by more militant stewards. This is unlikely to be the whole story. Thus one reason for seeking to increase rates was probably a desire to reward workers who were seen as the most co-operative and productive in the company. In particular, a productivity scheme had previously worked well in the factory, and had enabled

4. See above, p. 33.

workers to increase their earnings considerably. The end of this scheme and the consolidation of the productivity bonus into basic earnings may have encouraged management to find new ways of rewarding the workers. But, whatever management's motivations, it is notable that the main source of initiative here came from management itself and not from the shopfloor.

Although bargaining about piecework was heavily institutionalized there remained opportunities for workers to come to terms with the system in other ways. As we saw in the previous chapter, cutting the margins of quality standards was a widespread means of increasing bonus in one part of the Components Factory. More direct fiddles were also employed. The problems which most directly concerned management were payments for time when machines were idle ('down time') and the incorrect booking of output. There was an incentive for workers to book more down time than actually occurred, because their total production would then be attributed to a lower number of hours on piecework, and bonus earnings would be correspondingly increased. This was a standard example cited by managers in both factories when asked about fiddles, and it even featured in training material produced by the work study department. It was in many ways a symbol of the problems of the system and did not necessarily represent widespread practice. Operators could certainly alter bookings of down time by a few minutes, but this depended on foremen's ignorance as to the correct time or connivance in mis-booking. On the assembly lines in the Electrical Factory neither condition was likely to be fulfilled. Elsewhere, there were some opportunities for the practice, but it is unlikely to have been widespread.

Incorrect booking of output was similarly constrained by technical factors. The output of the assembly lines was readily checked against quantities in the warehouse, and booking clerks in the Electrical Factory reported few cases of discrepancies. It was said that at one time workers had tried to fiddle the system by putting components past the recording station twice, but this had been rendered pointless by an independent counter with which it was impossible to tamper, and in any event provided only limited scope for increasing earnings. In the Components Factory, with more workers operating their own machines, there were more opportunities for fiddles of this kind. Some managers claimed that the problem was rife and blamed a change in booking arrangements: in the past operators had been responsible for booking their own work and any inconsistencies rendered them liable to instant dismissal, whereas the new system of leaving the task to booking clerks encouraged fiddling since errors could be blamed on the clerks. Other managers claimed that fiddling was of decreasing importance, because increasing wage levels and a high rate of payment for down time made it less attractive. As with sabotage, we cannot estimate the true extent of the phenomenon, but it certainly existed, particularly in the form of booking the same box of work twice. It was controlled by a range of managerial practices. One work study man, for example, said that he regularly checked the wage booking sheets: from his knowledge of the performance of individual workers he could pick out any deviations from the normal pattern and prevent at least the more blatant fiddles. More generally foremen retained a considerable degree of authority. Each foreman, together with one or two assistants, covered a geographically small area and was intimately involved in the operation of his shop. The claim of many that they knew their workers and could treat them as individuals was not an idle boast. Thus they knew that 'sabotage' occurred but tolerated it because it met ends which they saw as legitimate. They did not turn a blind eye to booking fiddles and were probably justified in claiming that fiddling was limited to minor matters.

There were, then, powerful limits to fiddling: although it could not be prevented, management sought to contain it within acceptable bounds. In many ways fiddling can be seen not as an expression of conflict with the employer but as one aspect of work satisfaction under piecework. Roy (1953) has pointed to the social rewards of 'making out' under piecework; more generally, Baldamus (1961) has shown that monotonous work can create its own 'traction' or feeling that work is pulling the worker along with the result that boredom is dissipated. Fiddling the system can be seen as an additional means whereby workers gain satisfaction: they have won a game against the system. As Burawoy (1979: 72, 81—94) suggests in his analysis of making out as a game, various formally illicit practices help workers to increase production and thus contribute to the maintenance of the system of which they are part. Fiddling as we have defined it goes one stage further than this, since it involves an increase in wages for the same effort and thus a shift in the effort bargain. Its extent was limited, however, by the managerial control system: giving workers a relatively cheap source of satisfaction may have assisted managerial interests by deflecting their concerns from other questions.

Conclusions

We have considered the various forms of 'resistance', in terms of bargaining about times and rates and in terms of more covert fiddles, which occurred in our piecework factories. In none of the factories was struggle, defined as active attempts to shift the effort-reward bargain, actively pursued. This indicates the success of different forms of managerial control over payment systems. In the clothing factories direct control over the effort bargain, together with the total absence of bargaining awareness on the shopfloor, meant that managerial domination went unquestioned. In Company A bargaining awareness was substantially greater but the company was able to moderate challenges to its own control by careful operation of the payment system. Indeed, perhaps the most remarkable feature of this system is its ability to survive growing shopfloor pressure during the 1960s and 1970s while retaining its main features from a period when such pressure was largely absent. If our clothing plants show very strong parallels with other weakly organized factories, the Company A plants also have strong similarities with the engineering factory described by Burawoy. Workers aimed to 'make out' within the existing rules of the game; in our terms conflict was institutionalized. Burawoy (1979: 167–70) notes the progressive withdrawal of work study men from the shopfloor, and a similar lack of rate-fixing and work study on a regular basis was apparent in our factories: direct conflict between operators and management was thus very limited. Management could achieve its aim of producing at an acceptable cost without having to impose the same sort of direct control that was practised in the clothing plants. As long as workers played by the rules the careful planning of work and the use where appropriate of assembly lines did the rest. Control did not need to be exercised more directly.

This is not to deny that piecework could create problems for management. As at least some work study managers said, any payment system can decay and lead to the re-emergence of the problems it was designed to remedy. Managers in Company A were concerned not about the usual problems of piecework such as a drift away from standards and the growth of leap-frogging claims by militant stewards but about the problems of motivation. With the gradual rise in day work rates as a proportion of average earnings it was felt that the incentive element of the system had been lost. Or, more precisely, relatively senior managers were worried about these things while foremen and shop managers were reasonably content with piecework. This again parallels one of Burawoy's observations: while the payment system did not lead to conflict on the shopfloor, it did create problems for senior managers, who were more concerned than were shop managers with labour costs and profitability. Senior managers may then act to alter the system, which may well set off a cycle of renewed shopfloor-level conflict. Specifically, the pay system in one shop in the Components Factory had been altered to create what was felt to be a more rational system. We may begin our consideration of effort bargaining under measured day work and similar systems by looking at it.

Control of Effort Under Measured Day Work

The Components Factory

Individual piecework had become something of a rarity in the Components Factory. One section of the plastics shop was paid a fixed bonus, while the whole of the metals shop had been moved onto a group bonus scheme. We concentrate here on the latter. In addition to worries about incentives it was felt that piecework was unduly time-consuming in that it generated endless arguments about the rate for a particular job and the amount of down time to be paid. The metals shop was therefore chosen for an experiment in group incentive schemes because of the interest of the plant's work study manager in the idea, not because the old system was felt to be particularly out of control here. The scheme which was introduced had two main elements. First, workers were grouped into teams, with members of each team being paid the same bonus, which was calculated according to how far production exceeded a base figure. Second, the system of paying for down time was eliminated. Each job was studied for six months and an average capacity utilization figure was derived; this figure was used to set the base output level. Production at or below the base level was paid for at a standard rate, with bonus being applied to any extra production.

The simplicity of the system had many advantages for management and for the stewards; indeed, the shop's senior steward had been actively involved in the creation of the scheme. There was, however, a widespread feeling that the scheme was not working properly. For several foremen the reason for this was obvious: workers no longer had an incentive to work hard, with high flyers in particular being unwilling to exert themselves for the good of the group as a whole. This perspective was shared by some stewards, although the blame was allocated differently: it was not a problem of irresponsible workers but of a failure by management to provide a situation in which workers wanted to work hard. Other stewards questioned management's assertion that workers were putting in less effort than they had done under individual piecework: the workers were willing to work, but management's failure to maintain the machinery properly meant that they had no opportunity of earning bonus. This was disputed by management, who cited the machine utilization study as evidence that the amount of down time allowed was realistic.

The scheme was felt to be a complete success in only one area, the finishing department where women trimmed excess metal from the components. Earnings figures which we examined showed that the women earned bonus more often than the male machine operators. Management's explanation of this was that the trimmers worked closely as a group: they were in sight of each other and anyone not pulling her weight could be brought into line by the others. Men, by contrast, were relatively isolated at individual machines and were less open to group pressures. The trimmers themselves shared this view to some extent, stressing that they were the 'best' group and that they liked the system. A second factor, however, was simply that trimming, as hand work, was not subject to the exigencies of machine breakdowns and offered a fertile environment for a group payment scheme.

In general, while there was certainly not the universal condemnation of the new payment system which we found in Company B, there were doubts about the effect of the system on effort levels. Some foremen felt that the retained control: one in particular stressed the disciplinary procedure for warning workers for lack of effort and shop stewards' acceptance of its use when a genuine case of shirking was involved. But the very need to use the procedure suggested that the system had created shopfloor problems which were largely absent under piecework. And other foremen roundly condemned what they saw as the encouragement of workers to be lazy. Piecework had institutionalized the effort bargain at shopfloor level, but this had produced undesirable consequences for higher management. The response of changing the payment system had re-created problems on the shopfloor. In all of this, though, management continued to retain some control. All problems are relative, and managers were right to stress that, by and large, things were not too bad. Foremen, even the critical ones, agreed that reasonable levels of effort were maintained. Management's problem in Company B was far more severe, as we go on to demonstrate.

Company B

As we saw in Chapter 2, measured day work was universally condemned in our Company B plants by workers, stewards, and foremen alike. And in subsequent chapters we have seen some of the consequences of the shift from piecework such as declining effort levels as stewards concentrated their bargaining pressure on the effort side of the wage-effort bargain. But, as we have also seen, much of the condemnation of MDW was couched in very general terms. Foremen, for example, looked back fondly to the time when gangs would want to cut down on manning wherever possible and would insist that anyone who was incapable of pulling his weight be removed. Since we cannot compare shopfloor practices directly with those common under piecework in order to see whether hindsight was an accurate reflection of what went on, we concentrate here on specific aspects of effort bargaining under day work. Three issues are particularly salient: manning levels, control of effort in an automated environment, and withdrawal of effort by craft workers.

Manning levels. In neither plant was measured day work introduced as a complete package. Instead, old piecework times were converted into equivalents for an eight-hour day. In areas where the product had remained unchanged these times were still in operation. It might seem that it would be easy to measure pressure on manning in these areas by comparing trends in manning levels with trends in output. However, apart from substantial difficulties with securing suitable data, there are several reasons to doubt the value of such a comparison. First, general economic problems had led to cuts in planned levels of output; since economies of scale were substantial at the margin, a decrease in output would lead to an increase in the number of man-hours per unit which was not due to pressure on manning levels. Second, it was the practice under piecework to negotiate rates so that workers could expect to increase their earnings from year to year. In other words, a certain amount of 'drift' was built into the system.

It is necessary to rely on less direct measures of manning pressure. Here, a marked difference emerged between the two factories. In the Small Metals Factory management at all levels argued that efficiency levels were quite good. The work study manager, for example, cited figures for 'off-standard' work of about 10 per cent, compared with figures for other plants of between 30 and 200 per cent. These figures are similar in principle to those used to calculate OSA in Company A: they reflect the extent to which actual manning levels deviated from work study standards. On the assumption that work study standards were similar across the company, figures on off-standard items can be used to compare pressure on manning levels, although differences in the basis of calculation mean that they cannot be used to make direct comparisons with other companies. In the Large Metals Factory, off-standard work was running at a rate of 30 per cent or more.

The relatively low levels of off-standard in the Small Metals Factory can be attributed to two influences. First, MDW was not seen as a threat. The plant's strong union organization had already brought piecework under centralized control, as we noted in Chapter 2. As the work study manager put it, the earnings ceiling imposed by the stewards was already a form of MDW. The introduction of MDW is often opposed by stewards who have built up control on a particular section and who fear that centralized control will undermine their power. This type of reaction was absent in the Small Factory. Moreover, the new pay system carried distinct advantages. As a supplier plant, the factory was prone to frequent lay-offs and short-time working,[5] and lay-off guarantee which was introduced as part of the change-over helped to protect earnings.

The second factor was the availability of other forms of pressure. As we show in the following chapter, control over the mobility of labour was a powerful means with which stewards could exert pressure on management. The plant also differed from others in the strategic use of health and safety issues to slow down production. In the Components Factory, for example, these issues were used specifically to obtain such things as safety shoes and spectacles, but they were not used as sanctions in a wider campaign. In the Small Metals Factory, however, safety questions which had lain dormant were frequently raised when stewards wished to exert pressure on management. For example, during the course of the long-running dispute which we analyse in Chapter 9 the safety of a fork-lift truck was made an issue so that production would be slowed down. The safety issue ran for some time and raised management's uncertainty as to whether planned levels of output could be secured.

This is not to suggest that management found manning and effort levels

5. It was a standing joke in the factory that lay-offs were so frequent at one time that the staff of the local employment exchange knew all the workers by name. The effects of this are discussed in more detail in Chapter 8; see below, pp. 202–6.

acceptable. As some senior managers pointed out, the targets used to calculate off-standard items were themselves inflated by years of shopfloor pressure, particularly in relation to demarcations; again, these are discussed in the following chapter. But the fact that MDW did not threaten the steward organization, together with the availability of other sanctions, meant that there was little need for stewards to attempt to increase manning levels on existing jobs. On new jobs, of course, they did bargain strongly about planned manning levels, and this was itself an important sanction: management could not introduce new work quickly because the stewards, as a matter of conscious strategy, sought to delay work study trials in order to obtain concessions. We came across several instances of this, with workers being able effectively to frustrate attempts to study them by working in such a way that even experienced work study men could not obtain useful measures on which to base standard times. New jobs, however, provided only a small proportion of total employment and off-standards were therefore low.

The pattern of control in the Large Metals Factory was much less conducive to the introduction of MDW: stewards operated in a less centralized way, which in turn had two effects. First, the individual steward and, even more, the leader of each gang feared the loss of his own autonomy. Second, different trades watched each other to see what they were gaining. For example, skilled production stewards refused to agree their own manning levels until they saw what the semi-skilled grades had obtained. There was fierce resistance to the end of piecework; as noted in Chapter 2, at the time of the research, several years after MDW was brought in, the plant had still not reached an agreement on the 'buy-out' of piecework practices and was operating an interim system. This meant, most notably, that the shopfloor refused to recognize work study men, on whose role there was no formal agreement. This is itself an interesting example of resistance, and it also had implications for the way in which manning levels were negotiated.

As an example of manning level pressure we may consider negotiations that took place over the introduction of some modifications to the product made in Assembly Shop Y, one of the shops operating on translated piecework prices. According to management's figures, manning levels on the old design already had a considerable amount of slack built into them, with the number of man-hours per unit running at about 30 per cent above the planned level. Changes in design were generally minor, and managers saw no need to go beyond existing manning levels. When the new design was introduced on a trial basis, however, there was a clear shopfloor campaign to restrict effort in order to justify claims for extra manning when the work formally came up for negotiation. In one key area, for example, workers restricted output to well under half the amount managers were demanding.

With this background foremen entered the manning negotiations in a mood of pessimism. Before serious bargaining started several commented that the result was a foregone conclusion: the stewards knew that management were desperate for output and could not afford, given the highly effective go-slow operated by several gangs, to delay agreement indefinitely. Foremen felt that, while they could dispute particular parts of the stewards' case, there was little point in doing so since they would eventually be bound to give way. The conduct of the negotiations reflected these expectations: bargaining was carried out ritualistically, with stewards taking the lead and with very little articulated response from managers. In the end virtually all the stewards' claims were met, involving manning levels about 10 per cent higher than those proposed by management.

We have here, then, a very clear example of the way in which the structure of the situation affected the process of negotiation. Both sides knew that higher management needed output urgently. Considerable weight was placed on obtaining a speedy resolution of the negotiations, as was illustrated by the drafting in of extra managers from other shops to deal with day-to-day matters while the regular managers gave all their attention to the manning discussions. Local managers had few resources at their disposal since they could not afford to prolong the negotiations or to escalate the dispute: the last thing senior management wanted was a strike sparked off, say, by a decision to discipline workers who were engaged in restricting effort. The stewards effectively used this situation. Moreover, as one foreman said, their victory strengthened their hand for the next time: the structure of the situation was reinforced.

It would be wrong, however, to read this case as a precise reversal of the situation in the clothing factories, with shopfloor domination in Company B playing the part of managerial domination in the clothing plants. First, the basis of shopfloor power needs to be considered carefully. This has two aspects: the size of the demands stewards felt they could make, and the relationship between stewards and members. If the stewards were so powerful, why did they not demand manning levels even higher than the ones they suggested? A difference from management of about 10 per cent was far from dramatic and seems to have reflected an idea of what could reasonably be obtained. There was always the danger that management would take the stewards on if it was felt that their demands were totally unacceptable. The power of the stewards rested, moreover, on their ability to take the membership with them. The go-slow gave the stewards a bargaining lever which was useful not least because they could deny that sanctions were being imposed. As we saw in Chapter 5, in relation to the dispute about early leaving, the withdrawal of co-operation was a shopfloor tactic which did not require formal organization by the stewards. It reflected a long history of bargaining awareness on the shopfloor and could not simply be called on at will by the stewards. The stewards' bargaining successes, in other words, did not result directly from management's needs for output: they also rested on the willingness and ability of the shopfloor to operate sanctions. In this case the willingness of workers to restrict their effort was not in question. Indeed, after the agreement the stewards' problem was to sell the settlement to a membership which was, in some areas, keen to continue its sanctions. The stewards succeeded only with difficulty and only after arousing fears that the introduction of extra managers, several of whom had a reputation as hard-liners, signalled management's willingness to escalate the dispute if agreement was not reached.

The second point about 'shopfloor domination' leads on from this: external constraints are not absolute, and management can always re-define the situation. Whereas management in the clothing factories had enormous resources with which to buttress their legitimations of their actions the shopfloor in Company B had no such resources. Their power rested on managerial acquiescence in certain practices such as withdrawal of co-operation. This is, moreover, more than a ritual recognition of the frailties of workplace power. It had practical consequences. Some time after these manning negotiations the whole future of the Large Metals Factory was put into question by higher management, and there were threats that the plant would be shut if productivity did not improve. As part of a 'viability plan' plant management persuaded stewards in several important areas to accept considerable cuts in manning levels. A matter of a few weeks previously foremen in these areas had been complaining that stewards held the whip hand and that efficient operation was impossible. Yet now they reported that acceptable manning standards had been achieved and that morale had improved dramatically. This change in relationships may have reflected, however, merely the first flush of enthusiasm. It is impossible to say whether it would have continued since higher company management rejected plant management's proposals and proceeded with the closure of most of the factory. Management's ability to close the whole operation plainly reflects a power to redefine the situation which was absent on the shopfloor. We take up this point further below.

Control of effort in an automated environment. Since large parts of both Company B plants operated on translated piecework times and retained many working practices from piecework days they do not exemplify a full measured day work system. Assembly Shop X in the Large Metals Factory, however, was commissioned after the move to day work and was designed to operate under the new system. Workers' means of controlling effort here are thus of central interest, not least because large areas of the shop involved machine-paced work on a moving conveyor and thus came close to the standard picture of assembly lines with workers tied to the track doing a series of fragmented tasks.

As would be expected from the previous discussion, a key aspect of controls over effort depended on the manning levels established when the shop was built. According to management's figures, negotiated off-standards led to manning levels about 40 per cent above the work study department's estimates. But it was argued by some managers that, because the cycle time had never been reduced to the planned level, over-manning was effectively about 60 per cent. Work study men estimated that about three-quarters of the excess manning was due to concessions when the shop opened, with the remainder growing up as extra men were brought in to cover particular operations, the size of the absentee pool was increased, and so on. The most obvious result of this was, as we saw in Chapter 4, the ability of workers to take turns of 'unauthorized absence', with their work being covered by others. We consider now means of 'controlling the track' when at work.

The most obvious tactic is simply to try to stop the track. There were one or two directly destructive attempts in this direction, but such sabotage was unusual. Far more effective was tactical use of the emergency stop button on the conveyor. 'Pushing the button' had become something of a way of life in the shop, as the very existence of a label marking it off as a distinct form of social activity suggests. It was something which greatly exercised foremen, as was shown not only in their comments to us but also in communications between themselves. For example, a report book was kept in which day shift and night shift foremen noted such things as technical information and levels of output of various components. In a three-month period there were, in addition, six specific references to the men being 'button-happy', as well as other comments indicating a lack of co-operation from the work force. As one foreman wrote after noting a high level of button-pushing, 'I think they call it working without enthusiasm'.

An obvious explanation for the behaviour is a desire to escape the boredom of machine-paced work. Many investigators report workers' joy when the line breaks down and they have the chance to relax. Some workers in Shop X said that they found the work 'mind bending' in its boredom and that they engaged in button-pushing as a result. However, the simple equation of button-pushing with boredom must be qualified. First, a major reason for it, according to the workers, was the fact that the track did not move quickly enough for them to build up a good working rhythm; the relevance of Baldamus's concept of 'traction' is again apparent. Second, monetary discontents were again in evidence: as some workers put it, the low level of wages contributed to a feeling of 'sod the job', which might be absent in other circumstances. Third, button-pushing was not a random, spontaneous, response to boredom but a tactic which was employed when the benefits from it were greatest.

The third point may be considered in relation to the patterning of track stoppages through the day. Thus one foreman produced the interesting theory that breakdowns were concentrated in periods before break times, so that workers could lengthen their leisure periods. It was possible to test this view since part of the shop's high technology was a sophisticated recording system which noted the time and duration of every stoppage of the track. Included in the information was the reason for the stoppage, which was given to the control room by foremen using walkie-talkies.

As the classification of breakdowns by time of day in Table 7.1 shows, stoppages were far from randomly distributed throughout the day as one would expect if they were purely the product of machine failures. Even those stoppages, comprising just over half the total, for which technical reasons could be found did not occur randomly throughout the day: they peaked just before the morning break when the value of stopping the track for a few minutes was obviously greater than it was at other times. Such stoppages may well have had a control element in that workers would on occasion push the button over some trivial 'technical' problem which they would normally tolerate. But perhaps a stronger indication of the deliberate use of stoppages is the presence of a large number

TABLE 7.1

PER CENT DISTRIBUTION OF TRACK STOPPAGES
BY TIME OF DAY IN ASSEMBLY SHOP X,
LARGE METALS FACTORY

Successive Half-hour Periods of Day[a]	Technical Reasons (N=628)	Manning Shortages (N=117)	No Reason (N=456)	Expected Frequency[b]
1	3.8	47.9	10.5	6.7
2	7.3	17.9	3.9	6.7
3	7.2	3.4	3.9	6.7
4	11.0	2.6	6.6	6.7
5[c]	4.3	1.7	3.7	3.3
6	7.2	0.9	5.5	6.7
7	9.2	0.9	5.7	6.7
8	8.4	0.9	4.2	6.7
9	5.9	0.9	10.3	6.7
10	6.1		6.6	6.7
11	7.5		5.9	6.7
12	7.8		4.4	6.7
13	5.1		11.4	6.7
14[c]	2.4		3.1	3.3
15	5.3		5.0	6.7
16	1.4	23.1	9.2	6.7

SOURCE:
Company records. Figures relate to stoppages on 15 days, randomly selected over a three-month period.
NOTES:
a. Periods 1–9 were in the morning, and periods 10–16 in the afternoon.
b. On the assumption that stoppages were randomly distributed over the whole day.
c. Fifteen-minute tea break included in period.

of incidents, almost 40 per cent of the total, for which no reason could be found. Stoppages in this category tended, moreover, to peak before break times and at the start and finish of the day. This pattern is clearly consistent with a systematic strategy of stopping the track when the benefits were greatest.[6]

The third category of reasons for stoppages, namely manning shortages, is also revealing for the light it throws on the nature of control. It was necessary for all jobs to be fully manned before the track could run properly, and absenteeism and shortages of labour delayed the start-up in the morning. Stoppages due to manning problems were thus heavily concentrated at the start of the day, with delays often lasting half an hour or so. This was more than simply a technical problem. As we have seen in previous chapters stewards had built up an impressive array of controls not only over total manning levels but also over all aspects of the allocation of work. Foremen could not assign workers to specific tasks as they chose but were required to negotiate on the details of this and to seek the stewards' agreement on transferring labour between sections. The impact on effort controls was obvious.

An indication of the effectiveness of these controls may be obtained by looking at the pattern of output over the day. Under a fully-functioning mechanized system output should be spread more or less evenly over the day. As Table 7.2, which gives the rate of output each hour as a percentage of the average daily rate, shows, this was far from being the case. Even in the most rigidly machine-paced department, labelled (3) in the table, there were substantial output fluctuations. Workers were able to exert considerable control over the amount and timing of their efforts, and this control had demonstrable effects on the pattern of output.[7]

Withdrawal of effort in the toolroom. For our third example of effort bargaining we turn to the totally different environment of the Large Metals Factory's toolroom, where craft workers operated with a considerable degree of autonomy. We have already seen that toolmakers were the group which was perhaps the most discontented over their fall in the earnings league and that one expression of this discontent was to quit. But other expressions of 'withdrawal' such as absenteeism or breaches of discipline seemed to be rare. We may now consider action at the point of production in this context.

6. As a check on this argument we analysed the pattern of machinery stoppages in the totally different environment of the Hosiery Factory. Apart from a peak at the start of the day, which managers attributed to failures of machines to start up from cold, the distribution was remarkably similar to a random distribution. Our conclusions from the statistical pattern in the Large Metals Factory are correspondingly strengthened.
7. Again, as a check on this we looked at output patterns on the assembly lines of the Electrical Factory. Production was maintained at a remarkably steady rate throughout the day. In view of our earlier discussion this might imply some sort of output restriction, but, while there was a target figure, this was defined by management which workers strove to achieve and not a ceiling which they would not exceed.

TABLE 7.2

HOURLY OUTPUT AS PER CENT OF AVERAGE DAILY RATE IN SHOP X, LARGE METALS FACTORY

Successive Hourly Periods	Department			
	(1)	*(2)*	*(3)*	*(4)*
1	55	59	70	79
2	101	101	95	111
3	156	171	87	110
4	143	142	108	111
5	95	106	151	98
6	104	103	113	120
7	129	138	90	120
8[a]	62	49	45	117
9[b]	67	30	73	50
Average rate	100	100	100	100

SOURCE: As for Table 7.1.
NOTES:
a. Half-hour period, adjusted to hourly rate.
b. Period of overtime, worked for 12 of the 15 days considered.

The most common action seemed to be the simple one of working less hard. There are no ways of measuring this precisely since the essence of toolmakers' work is that it is not subject to machine control or even to detailed supervision. But withdrawal of effort was obvious and widespread. It was reflected, for example, in increasing turn-round times of maintenance tooling and in times for the manufacture of new tools which were longer than the planning department estimated. It was a deliberate action by toolmakers who openly stated that they stretched out work and spent long periods doing nothing other than talk to their mates. Even the most casual observation would confirm this picture. And toolmakers were equally clear about the reasons for the behaviour: as one of their standard phrases put it, part-time wages deserved only part-time work. Some explained that they felt so disgruntled that it was impossible to motivate themselves properly: toolmaking required close involvement in the job and could not be carried out in the routine fashion in which semi-skilled tasks could be performed, and frustration with the company had reached such a degree that the necessary enthusiasm could not be generated. It is difficult to capture the extent of workers' sense of grievance. Suffice it to say that a group which prided itself on its craft skills had reached the point where no one had the interest to exercise those skills. There was no joy in frustrating management by restricting effort but, rather, a deep sense of apathy and disillusionment.

This behaviour can be described as individual in that it was not part of an organized campaign articulated by the shop stewards. But it was also collective since the whole shop was involved and since it reflected a strong shared grievance. Moreover, the shop's strong tradition of solidarity made it difficult for management to break down this passive resistance: it was not a matter of an individual worker going slow and of thus rendering himself liable to disciplinary action, but of joint action in which the disciplining of one man would be seen as a collective issue. We saw earlier how this joint attitude to discipline worked in the case of managerial action against early leaving,[8] and a similar response would certainly be forthcoming over discipline for lack of effort. Apart from this collective resistance, two factors explain toolroom management's inaction in the face of a withdrawal of effort of which they were well aware. First, they had considerable sympathy with the workers' claims and aspirations, which is not surprising since they had generally started their careers on the shopfloor and identified strongly with the craft. There was, indeed, an unofficial foremen's organization aiming to represent craft supervisors and to obtain a differential over foremen supervising production workers. The discontents underlying this body were identical to those motivating toolmakers. Second, of course, management's increasing worries about the high quit rate meant that managers were unwilling to risk losing more workers by imposing a strong policy on effort levels.

Conclusion. We have considered a variety of ways in which pressure was applied on the effort side of the wage effort bargain in different parts of our Company B plants. We have also tried to indicate how the structure of the situation permitted such pressures to emerge and how that structure can change. In particular, external changes can lead management to alter a structure which seems to be well-established.

The practices which we have described can plainly be discussed in terms of resistance since they involved methods, often sophisticated ones, for challenging managerial determination of the amount and timing of workers' efforts. Yet they occurred in a context in which the importance of production was taken for granted and in which stewards were proud of their role in the planning of production. Resistance was plainly limited by this, a point which we pursue in the final section of the chapter.

The Process Factory

Finally in this section we consider the case of the Process Factory, which has similarities with and differences from Company B. The obvious difference was the weakness of shopfloor involvement in the details of the effort bargain, but there was an important similarity in that changing market conditions were

8. See above, p. 145.

leading management to question existing practices and to try to increase effort levels.

This must be seen in the context of the plant's history, for part of the co-operative spirit fostered by management involved a continuous awareness of the need for change. Some relatively minor changes in working practices reflected this. In one shop, for instance, it had been the practice for the workers to take turns at operating the truck which moved finished goods to the warehouse. Management suggested that each worker should now move each batch as he completed it, with the result that one man's work was effectively saved. This met no resistance from workers, who thought it was a good idea. Similarly, in the same shop, men used to stop their machines at break times, but a new arrangement meant that break times would be staggered so that a worker would cover his neighbour's machine, which was left running while he was at break. This had created some resentment, but had been achieved through two means which the shopfloor saw as typical of managerial strategy. First, the new arrangement was presented direct to the workers by the foreman, thus preventing stewards from putting their own interpretation on it. Second, one shift was persuaded to accept the change, with this then being used as an argument for its introduction on other shifts. In both instances, more effort was attained for no extra reward.

The change with which we are chiefly concerned involved a cut in the standard times for jobs in one of the main shops in the factory. These times had been established on the basis of conventional work study techniques, and each team of workers was required to achieve a rating of 100 points per day. How they did this was largely their own responsibility: they could do a few time-consuming jobs with a high rating or more lower-rated jobs. And the allocation of jobs over the shift was also their own responsibility, with most teams choosing to work hard early in the shift to earn leisure at the end, much as Company B workers did. The difference from the engineering industry, however, was that workers did not cling to this leisure as a right. In a period of eighteen months there were two cuts in standards, each of between 5 and 10 per cent, but workers continued to turn in an effort rating of 100 which, after the second of the cuts, would have been equivalent to a rating of between 110 and 121 on the old standards.

Moreover, at the time of the research, management were proposing further cuts. There was a widespread feeling among managers that standards set by work study were increasingly unrealistic: workers developed new and quicker ways of working which were not reflected in studies based on formal job specifications. To measure these new working practices management proposed a form of work study known as activity sampling. This involved a large number of random samples of what workers were actually doing, instead of studies of particular tasks under normal work study conditions. The stewards originally resisted this but, with the threat of a further 10 per cent cut in standards as the alternative, they acquiesced in the sampling, while reserving the right to negotiate the outcome. During the sampling exercise there was, as far as we could discover, very little resistance to the work study men. There were complaints that management was trying to claim as its own improvements in working which stemmed from the abilities and initiative of the shopfloor. But there were no attempts to make these complaints effective by refusing to accept the sampling exercise: no go-slows, no insistence on working to the letter of job descriptions, and no attempt to spin the work out until the end of the shift. Most workers said that they worked normally, thus leaving their leisure at the end of the shift as evidence for management that they could work harder. Not surprisingly, foremen estimated that standards would be cut again by substantial amounts, and some further cuts were accepted as inevitable on the shopfloor.

It is obviously difficult to explain why there was so little resistance to management, but certain suggestions may be put forward. First, and most obviously, there was no tradition of collective organization on the shopfloor. This may appear to be so general an influence that citing it is merely to re-state the problem, but it had certain specific consequences. There were few shop stewards to cover a physically large shop and organize the details of a go-slow.[9] All section stewards in any event worked at their jobs and had less time to spare for organizing a campaign than did their counterparts in engineering. And the notion that the work force should act as an entity was lacking. We have mentioned the divisions which existed between shifts; there was certainly a feeling on the shopfloor that management were exploiting these divisions in the present case. In addition, each team tended to operate without reference to others. Some workers mentioned that they had thought that there should be some resistance but that they found this difficult when teams working at the other end of the shop were working as normal. One reason for the absence of a collective identity was mentioned in Chapter 3: workers came from a wide range of jobs, many of them outside manufacturing industry, and there was no tradition of questioning all managerial statements as a matter of course such as that which we found in Company B.

More specifically, management were able to make their own definition of the situation stick. In Company B, managerial statements about the problems facing the company tended to be treated with contempt: workers felt that they had heard it all before, that most of the problems were of management's own

---

9. This does not contradict the point made in relation to Company B that go-slows can emerge without explicit steward leadership (see above, p. 142). This is possible only where shopfloor controls allow workers considerable influence over their own efforts. Elsewhere explicit leadership would be required if a go-slow were to be made an effective collective campaign.

making, and that they did not care very much whether their factory closed. In the Process Factory trust in management had not broken down to this extent: managerial assertions were taken seriously, and there was a feeling that the company's problems were genuinely outside its own control. At one point the plant's manager told the workers that their jobs could be at risk if improvements were not made. Workers were genuinely concerned about this, and felt that their jobs were worth saving. Many said that they were capable of extra effort, and that it was reasonable to give it. Management's ability to communicate directly with the workers may have been important here. The financial problems caused by foreign competition, falling market demand, and a high exchange rate were explained in detail, as were the precise changes which management wanted. Managers were proud of their ability to 'get the message across' without distortion and to obtain a direct response from the shopfloor over their proposed changes.

Given management's well-organized campaign and the known weakness of the shopfloor, the stewards felt that there was little they could do. They recognized the structure of the situation, but did not attempt to change it. Their perspective is most dramatically illustrated by an event before our research, namely a strike in another factory against the introduction of cuts on the lines of those being introduced in the Process Factory. The strike was defeated, which the stewards took as evidence of the futility of attempting to resist cuts. But, despite the presence for a short time of pickets from the other plant, they did not attempt to rally the Process Factory workers behind the strike, feeling, with justification, that such an attempt would have been a failure. This did not mean that stewards accepted the situation. Indeed, a widespread complaint was management's new stance: in the past consultation had meant proper negotiation but now management were treating the consultation machinery as a means of informing workers of actions which they were going to take regardless of what the stewards said. For some years management had indeed followed a policy of not introducing changes unless they had the active agreement of the shopfloor. But the changing economic climate forced them out of this inactive policy that change was desirable only if everyone wanted it. As managers themselves put it, they had to make decisions for the good of the plant as a whole. They would consult fully with the shopfloor but ultimately they had to act if the plant was to survive. Their re-definition of the situation was imposed with a large measure of success.

The Limits of Control Over Effort

In this chapter we have described and tried to account for the very different patterns of control over the day-to-day effort bargain which existed in our factories. In this final section we enlarge on a theme which has developed in the

course of the discussion and which will assume considerable importance in subsequent chapters, namely the limitations and frailties of shopfloor controls.
But the discussion of these limitations must be seen in context, for we have also
demonstrated in this chapter the absence of any form of shopfloor control over
effort in our clothing factories. We must consider the significance of this before
going on to look at the limits of the undoubtedly stronger forms of control
which existed in our other factories.

The absence of collective output norms in the clothing plants has the clearest
implications for traditional plant sociology and what we may call naive radicalism. As noted at the outset, both perspectives take for granted the existence of
the same sort of practices although what for the former view is a group norm
based on social needs is for the latter view a type of resistance against capitalism.
Yet we have seen that these practices did not exist in our clothing factories and
we have been able to produce specific reasons why this was so. Our argument is
strengthened by the close parallels which we observed with other workplaces
where shopfloor organization was rudimentary. There are also implications,
however, for what we take to be the conventional wisdom about piecework
bargaining: piecework systems are prone to disorder and to the development of
informal rules which cut across formal rules, with the result that earnings drift
out of control. The environment of our clothing plants, however, prevented
the development of all but the most limited forms of custom, and management
were always in a position to deny the legitimacy of customary understandings.
Moreover, product market influences did not operate in the way which might
be expected from studies of the engineering industry (William Brown, 1973). We
have argued that our firms did not face the intense forms of product market
competition which other firms in the industry faced. This did not mean, however, that they were able or willing to take a lenient view of workplace practices.
They remained very concerned about labour costs and about retaining strict
control of their operations. Product market conditions contributed to stability,
and hence to the absence of rate-cutting and the lack of group output norms.
But they did not imply any weakening of managerial control.

Finally in this connection we may note an intriguing possibility for change
which was creeping into the system of managerial domination. We have argued
that Burawoy's observations in an American factory had a close parallel in
Company A. Rate-fixers, who used to have an active role in the shopfloor,
had been replaced by work study men who were generally concerned with
overall planning, and this reflected a shift in the terms of conflict, with direct
conflict between management and workers becoming progressively hidden. The
plans of management in the Underwear Factory to introduce work study reflect,
however, a different process: simple and direct control which was based on
the absolute rights of management to manage, was felt by a self-consciously
modernizing management to give insufficiently precise control over piece-rates

on particular jobs and was being replaced by a more 'rational' system. This system might be expected to bring conflict more into the open as the process of rate-fixing becomes more open to negotiation. We cannot, of course, predict the precise effects of this change on the overall system of managerial domination. But the case exemplifies the point made earlier that any system of control tends to create problems for those managers most directly concerned with costs, efficiency, and the consistency of application of the payment system. Reforms may well give a new impetus to immediate conflict at shopfloor level.

In our engineering factories it was generally recognized that the effort bargain contained elements of conflict: piecework prices and manning levels had to be negotiated, and the interests of management and the shopfloor plainly diverged. Yet, as we stressed in Chapter 1, conflict cannot be the sole organizing principle of any labour process.

This comes out particularly strongly in Company B, where production workers' controls over effort were much stronger than those of similar workers elsewhere and where such controls had been preserved despite the introduction of measured day work. One obvious conclusion from this case is that changing the payment system does not guarantee the restoration of managerial control. Day work is often seen as a way of attacking shopfloor controls, but in this case the new system did not disturb the pattern of these controls although it did, as we have shown, affect the uses to which they were put. More important for present purposes, however, is the question of the broad aims of shopfloor controls. Stewards had achieved considerable involvement in all aspects of the planning of work, and, as we shall see in more detail in Chapter 8, they also exerted control over the supply of labour. Yet the purpose of this control was not to challenge management's aims but to assist in the achievement of the broad aim of production. It was accepted that the need was to produce in quantity, with the dispute being about the terms on which work was organized to this end. This point was illustrated most sharply by the attitudes of stewards in Assembly Shop X in the Large Metals Factory. This shop had the unenviable reputation in the rest of the factory as being a hot-bed of unrest, with stewards doing everything in their power to resist management. Yet inside the shop we found stewards who were perhaps more fully committed to making a success of the operation than were their counterparts in other shops. The shop's target was 2500 units a week. Shop managers held daily production meetings with all the stewards to discuss progress towards this and the causes of problems. In the meetings which we observed stewards were eager that the target be achieved and were as concerned as managers that the great hopes which they had all had when the shop was established were not being realized.

Stewards did not, of course, simply accept everything that management told them. Their main theme was that managers were incapable of managing the plant properly and that, if they would only leave things to the good sense of the stewards and the work force, far greater success would be achieved. Commitment to the ideology of production was, then, considerable. Stewards' actions in bargaining over effort must be understood in this context. There was no straightforward resistance to management, if this implies principled opposition to management's aims as well as the means of achieving those aims. Yet the outcome of their actions can be described in terms of resistance, for the effect of strenuous bargaining over manning levels and the like was undoubtedly to prevent managerial conceptions of efficient production from being attained. There was, as it were, an unconscious form of resistance whereby stewards' everyday practices challenged managerial rights in many ways even though their articulated ideology involved commitment to the same aim of producing large numbers of high-quality products.[10]

There is a danger here of implying that stewards were simply short-sighted or unrealistic; surely they could understand that their actions were undermining their own aims of successful production on which, as they themselves stressed, the livelihood of their members depended. Yet to look at things in this way is, at the practical level, to take an unduly managerialist stance and, at the theoretical level, to ignore the conflictual elements of labour processes. Stewards were using the only weapons available to them to influence the terms on which effort was expended. While in some ideal world they would no doubt have preferred a co-operative approach to production, in the real world they faced a management which was making unacceptable demands. From their viewpoint it was management who were being irrational in that managers were unwilling to trust the work force or to take workers' concerns seriously. To take one minor but revealing example, managers in Shop X regularly complained that workers were stopping work before the official tea breaks in order to queue at the refreshment kiosks. The stewards saw this as a typical case of incompetence, in that management had failed to introduce the agreed number of kiosks, and also of disregard for workers' welfare, in that men could not be expected to go without refreshment. As one steward put it, there might well be a strike about the matter, and this would be described by managers and the local press as an irresponsible stoppage by workers seeking any excuse to stop work. Yet the need for a tea break was a real one, and the whole situation was in any event of management's own making. Stewards' resistance to management, in this case a refusal to accept that tea breaks should be cut to the formally-agreed length, thus had a perfectly rational basis.

The resistance was limited, however, by the foundations on which it rested. Stewards in both Company B plants had developed an impressive range of controls over effort, and the growth of these controls can be related to management's willingness to give up various aspects of managerial rights in exchange for

10. Compare the quotation from Gramsci on p. 12.

continuous production. Yet this was a temporary accommodation, and changing external conditions, notably a falling market share, problems of profitability and a need to 'rationalize' operations, led management to challenge the pattern of control which had been built up. We have seen that plant management in the Large Metals Factory were able to persuade stewards of the need for considerable cuts in manning standards when the future of the factory was put in jeopardy and that even this was insufficient to meet the needs of higher management, who proceeded with the run-down of the plant. Management's power simply to sweep aside a whole structure of shopfloor controls could not be more clearly illustrated. When we returned to the plant some two years after our research we found that the machine shop and all but one of the assembly shops had been closed, with the remaining assembly shop being attached to a different division of the company. Only the toolroom remained as a distinct entity, and it was claimed by management that it was now the most efficient toolroom in the firm and that the problem of a lack of morale which had been so apparent during our research had been removed. We could not assess the truth of this nor the basis on which the claimed changes rested, but the destruction of shopfloor controls was plainly apparent.

While we have pointed to the very important contrasts between shopfloor control in Company B and the system of sophisticated managerial control in the Process Factory, we have also seen that there was one crucial similarity between these two situations: faced with changing external circumstances management tried to alter manning standards. Indeed, the similarity goes beyond this. For some years before our research shopfloor relations in the Process Factory had displayed a strange calm in which changes were not introduced without the explicit agreement of the stewards. This created an illusion of shopfloor power and accounted for the depth of stewards' dismay when management came to re-assert its prerogatives. The similarity, in other words, lies in managerial acceptance of various forms of shopfloor control as structural conditions which were not to be questioned. The main difference was simply that this acceptance had not gone very far in the Process Factory, with the re-assertion of control being accomplished without overt resistance. The frailty of shopfloor controls in the factory was easily exposed.

As noted at the start of this chapter, controls over particular effort bargains are only part of the picture of shopfloor controls over the expenditure of effort. Another part concerns the supply of labour to these bargains. If workers can control, for example, the allocation of labour between tasks, or even the total supply of labour available to the firm, their overall control will be strengthened. Our interest in the present chapter has, moreover, been solely with production workers. Looking at the supply and allocation of labour in Chapter 8 balances this interest, for it was among craft workers that the widest controls over this aspect of the frontier of control had developed.

8

The Supply and Allocation of Labour

The previous chapter dealt with activities that were fairly directly linked to the wage-effort bargain. The concern now goes wider to consider other forms of control over the labour process, namely the institutional means that workers and unions use to challenge managerial planning of the supply and allocation of labour. One practice, of well-known historical significance, is the control of entry to a trade through rules on apprenticeship and the like. But 'a union which is unable directly to control entry into its trades may yet develop other, and formal, controls which have an analogous, if less direct, effect on the supply of labour' (Turner, 1962: 255). In addition to recruitment, therefore, we examine overtime, for the amount of overtime that is worked is plainly a crucial influence on the total supply of labour. This is not to suggest, of course, that workers simply attempt to limit the amount of overtime that is worked. As the Donovan Commission (1968: 79–80) pointed out, the heavy use of overtime may mean that decisions about the amount and allocation of it do not reflect production requirements: it is the employer's freedom to take these decisions that may be curtailed by shopfloor controls over overtime. As well as the total supply of labour the allocation of workers to specific tasks is important in the employer's control of work; limitations on the freedom to move workers between jobs are a crucial aspect of workers' attempts to assert their own control.

Controls over the mobility of labour obviously merge with the final topic of this chapter, namely demarcations: a rule as to who can do a particular job restricts management's freedom to shift labour freely. But demarcations do not have unambiguous implications for control. They were dismissed by Goodrich (1975: 100): 'disputes over demarcation are not an extension of workers' control but a division of it'. This theme, of the tendency of demarcations and other divisions to introduce conflict between workers and hence to reduce solidarity as against the employer, has been followed in more recent work. The well-known study by Stone (1973) of the American steel industry, for example, stresses the interests of employers in creating divisions among the work force so as to prevent a solidaristic challenge to their own authority from emerging. Yet, as Rubery (1980: 248) points out, such 'radical' theories share with earlier 'dual labour market' theories a tendency to look at the segmentation of the work force from the side of the employer, ignoring the active role of worker organization. Rubery goes on to discuss the way in which craft unions in particular have protected themselves by developing demarcation lines around their own trades. It is, then, unsatisfactory to write off demarcations as forms of division within the work force without also giving attention to their role in advancing the frontier of control for groups of workers and thus in challenging managerial authority. It is this latter aspect of demarcations to which we give greatest attention, partly as an attempt to correct existing emphases; but we return to the question of fragmentation and cohesion in the final section of the chapter.

Restrictions on entry and demarcations tend, as in Turner's study, to be analysed historically. Part of our aim is to reveal their present-day role. But to do this we have to give more attention to historical matters than we have needed to do in earlier chapters. It is relatively easy to describe the extent of demarcations in our various factories, but the important question concerning their relationship to the frontier of control is: how did they originate, and why did management acquiesce in them? Without an answer to this question it would be hard to understand the significance of the various practices that we describe. We therefore try to explore the sources of particularly important examples of shopfloor controls. We cannot investigate every matter in detail, for to do so would require a great deal of historical investigation, the material for which might well not be available. Hence, for example, we found that toolmakers in the Large Metals Factory were more willing than their counterparts in the Components Factory to permit mobility between different sections of the toolroom; there were no obvious reasons for this. We were able, however, to give considerable attention to the origins of controls in the Small Metals Factory. This reflects, in the presence of detailed minute books of the shop stewards' committee of the ex-craft union, a valuable source of information on past practices; it also reflects the exceptional degree of co-operation that we were given in this plant. The plant is, moreover, particularly relevant for a study of shopfloor controls over the supply of labour. As noted above, studies of such controls tend to be historically-based, and they also generally relate to whole trades or industries. A contemporary study of factory-level controls in a plant with a powerful craft tradition can make a significant contribution to analysis of the origins and role of controls over labour supply.[1]

---

1. We hope to present the full results of this study elsewhere. In this chapter we confine our attention to matters of immediate relevance.

The Supply of Labour

Recruitment
Outside Company B there were no formal union controls over recruitment. In the clothing plants, and in Company A and the Process Factory in relation to production workers, management had sole control over how many, and which, workers to employ. In the craft areas of these last three plants stewards limited managerial control to the extent of ensuring that recruits held the appropriate union card before they were allowed to work. In the Large Metals Factory there was rather more union control: all recruitment was carried out through union offices, with the company informing the relevant union of how many workers were needed and the union supplying a list of names. This system did not affect managerial freedom to decide how many workers to employ, and management also remained free to reject applicants who were deemed unsuitable. It probably grew out of the practice of hiring through union offices that was set up during the second world war, while its continuation reflected, among other things, a trade union desire to protect the closed shop. At the time of our research it was taken for granted by management, and seemed to create few problems.

The situation was very different in the Small Metals Factory, where a remarkable, and probably highly unusual, degree of control over recruitment had been obtained by the stewards. This had two main elements. First, when management wanted to recruit they approached the stewards, and not the union office, for a list of names. It had become established over the years, moreover, that anyone put forward by the stewards would, other than in exceptional cases, be employed: the stewards, and not managers, had the decisive say as to who would have a job in the plant. Second, and more importantly, the stewards reserved the right to refuse to submit any names if they felt that the plant's position did not warrant an increase in the size of the labour force. They thus effectively controlled the supply of new labour.

At the time of our research management certainly experienced this control as a severe constraint. Together with demarcations it was mentioned spontaneously by several managers as one of the main problems that they faced in 'modernizing' the plant's industrial relations. It was also a matter exercising industrial relations staff at the firm's head office. On two occasions in the past all plants had been asked for details of restrictions on recruitment together with possible strategies for overcoming them. The list of replies showed that the Small Metals Factory was unique in the company in the extent of steward control and that plant management felt that there was little that they could do to change the position. On one occasion, for example, the plant's personnel manager had indicated that he was being prevented from recruiting skilled production workers but that the system was so well-established that there was nothing he could do about it.

The extent of this challenge to managerial control can hardly be over-emphasized: the 'right to hire' is generally seen as a central part of managerial prerogative and yet this right was severely constrained. Managers were, moreover, actively concerned about this constraint. How, then, did the system come to be established? Part of the answer lies in the nature of the steward organization in the plant. The union that we have described as having an ex-craft character had, in the past, much more of a craft-like structure: by the time of our research it had gone through a series of mergers and had opened its doors to semi-skilled grades, whereas in the past it had had a very limited concern with a specific craft. In particular, it had displayed many of the characteristics of Turner's 'closed' unions, one of which is, of course, a concern to control the supply of labour to the trade. We need to go further, however, for the same union operated in the Large Metals Factory without insisting on craft-like practices. The difference between the union organizations in the two plants reflects three main influences. First, the ex-craft union in the Small Metals Factory organized all the direct production operations of the plant, so that it did not have to bring its practices into line with unions such as the TGWU which orga-nized among such grades in the Large Metals Factory. Second, and relatedly, the smallness of the plant enabled the stewards to develop a strong central organization which was capable of dealing with questions such as recruitment on a plant-wide basis. Third, the peculiarities of the plant made control over recruit-ment more important than it was elsewhere. As we will see in more detail later, the plant, as a supplier of a few major customers, had been subject to wildly fluctuating demand for its products. These fluctuations could lead to substantial lay-offs, and the stewards had long been concerned to control them. One means of doing this was to resist such things as night shift working, which increased the plant's capacity and which therefore worsened the problems of bringing capacity into line with demand. And another was to restrict recruitment so as to increase the possibility of a steady flow of work for workers already in the plant.

None of this explains, however, why managers were prepared to tolerate the system. Their acquiescence in it was, indeed, far from total. Thus during the late 1950s and early 1960s, as our study of the stewards' minute books reveals, the general union had been able to assert a degree of control similar to that enjoyed by the ex-craft union. But a determined managerial attack in 1967 restored the previous position, namely recruitment through the union office (and not the stewards), together with the full right of management to reject unsuitable applicants. The success of this challenge reflects, however, the relative youth of the general union's organization, for this had begun at the end of the 1950s, labourers and other indirect workers having been unorganized until then.[2] The rapid development of control over recruitment on a basis similar to that operated by the ex-craft union seems to have stemmed from the absence at the time of any clear managerial policy on such matters: the ex-craft union had a particular form of control and this was, for a time, taken for granted and hence permitted in new areas.

How, then, had this form of control been attained? Stewards in the ex-craft union had controlled the recruitment of skilled workers since at least the early 1950s; and when, in the late 1950s, the union widened its ranks to embrace semi-skilled workers control over the recruitment of these workers was successfully established. The minute books of the union reveal, moreover, that, unlike their counterparts in the general union, the stewards were able to resist several attempts by management during the 1960s to challenge their control of recruitment. The system was, then, firmly established by the 1960s. This reflects managerial acceptance of shopfloor controls over the labour process at an earlier period. After the second world war the factory was largely an independent contracting shop. 'Management' involved not controlling labour but attempting to meet customers' demands for production. As a manager who had worked in the plant for many years put it, 'the company simply had to produce the goods and the profits looked after themselves'. As long as there was a sufficient supply of labour to meet the demands of an expanding market managers were probably unconcerned about how the supply was controlled or, indeed, about the control of other aspects of the labour process. They were prepared to cede to the stewards the detailed control of the piecework system, for example, as long as the outcome was a high level of production; unit costs were of secondary importance.

As argued in Chapter 7, stewards were as committed as any manager to achieving production targets. There had been cases during the piecework period, for example, of the stewards refusing a job to a man if they felt that he was incapable of doing the work.[3] This commitment to a high level of production was plainly consistent with management's interests at a time when labour costs were a minor consideration. Hence, if stewards felt that they could not permit management to recruit workers, they did not necessarily insist that production

2. This reflects, of course, the 'closed' character of the ex-craft union at the time: including semi-skilled workers was bad enough, but organizing labourers was unthinkable. Remnants of this craft contempt for unskilled workers were still present at the time of our research; for example a foreman who had been a steward for the skilled grades and who had worked in the plant for many years argued that the ex-craft union should not try to obtain a job that was also claimed by the general union because it was demeaning for the union to seek such unskilled work.

3. Although stewards denied management the right to test the abilities of a proposed recruit, they themselves would conduct a test if necessary and were prepared to reject workers deemed to lack the required qualities. Evidence from the minute books also points to covert collaboration between stewards and foremen to reject 'unsuitable' workers despite their possession of an introductory card from the union office.

should not be increased. They could meet a temporary increase in demand by overtime working or by raising the 'earnings ceiling', that is the maximum amount that workers could earn under the centralized piecework system (see above, p. 184). Stewards also worked very closely with their union office. They might be prepared, for example, to allow recruitment if there was a large number of unemployed workers 'on the book' at the office. But it was not unknown for them to reject the advice of their officials if restricting recruitment was felt to be in the best interests of the existing work force.

We have argued, then, that the system did not contradict immediate managerial interests when it was introduced and that, by the time it came to be experienced as a constraint, it was too firmly established to be challenged. One further influence on its persistence must also be mentioned. As we have seen, the factory went through a series of mergers from the early 1960s but successive company managements did not try to alter shopfloor controls over recruitment or other matters. This probably reflects the smallness of the plant and its peripheral role in the company as a whole. Managements faced a series of more general problems concerning the integration of plants with very different traditions into a coherent whole. The Small Metals Factory's prime attribute was its ability to meet production schedules and, as long as it did not create any particular problems for company managers, higher management were probably prepared to leave its arrangements undisturbed. It is also relevant here that all foremen and shop managers, and often more senior plant managers, came from within the plant and were thus in many respects as strongly committed to traditional ways of doing things as were the stewards.

Overtime
In view of all this it will come as no surprise that overtime was under considerable steward control in the Small Metals Factory; it will be convenient to continue our discussion of this plant before turning to the situation in our other factories. Two aspects of overtime are central: the amount, and the allocation among workers. The latter is the less important in so far as controls over the supply of labour are concerned, although it is obviously crucial in other ways, notably in challenging management's freedom to exercise discretion in the distribution of overtime. Here, and also in the Large Metals Factory, stewards had gained complete control over the allocation of overtime: stewards in each shop kept lists of workers who wanted to do overtime and of whose turn it was, allocating the work strictly in accord with a worker's position on the list. As with other aspects of stewards' control, this system was largely taken for granted and was thus an institutionalized form of control.

In the Small Metals Factory the amount of overtime had also been brought within the bargaining arena. For 25 years or so it had been the practice for management to hold a weekly meeting at which overtime requirements for the whole factory were announced. This system denied management the right to allocate overtime on a shop-by-shop or day-to-day basis. And in cases when managers wanted to alter their plans stewards could refuse to co-operate; for example, on one occasion a foreman wanted two labourers to work overtime for two days, but the steward refused this, saying that it was not worth the men's while to upset their domestic arrangements for such a short time. But, while this certainly kept management's use of overtime within tight bounds, it did not in itself mean that the stewards could insist that a particular amount of overtime be regularly available.

Control here was achieved through what was known as an 'overtime buffer': an agreement that production schedules and manning levels would be planned to include a built-in element of overtime. While many aspects of shopfloor control in the factory go back many years, the establishment of a buffer was a relatively recent achievement. Analysis of its origins can deepen our understanding of worker and management interests in controlling the supply of labour. After a campaign by the stewards during the early 1970s management eventually agreed, in 1973, to the introduction on a temporary basis of a scheme whereby the plant's production schedules would be planned for 48 hours' work a week. This reflected increasing concern among the stewards at the frequency of short-time working: the plant had always been vulnerable to fluctuations in demand, and this vulnerability was further exposed by a series of disputes affecting its main customer plants.[4] The overtime buffer met the stewards' concerns by building in a protection of the basic 40 hours, although it certainly did not guarantee any specific level of overtime.

Managers also saw advantages in this arrangement. As one senior manager put it, 'if we had not introduced the overtime buffer the plant would have been in an almost continual lay-off situation through the failure of customers to take the full product. In this situation nobody knows whether they are coming or going and nobody benefits.' Other managers cited more specific advantages: it was argued for example that management would have been unable to obtain any co-operation with various changes that they were seeking to introduce had employment remained as volatile as it had been during the early 1970s. By the late 1970s, however, there was a growing feeling among management that the plant now relied too heavily on overtime. The stewards were able to prevent managers from acting on this feeling through their control over recruitment: controls of overtime and recruitment were closely linked, for the ability to

---

4. One interesting feature of the stewards' campaign was that in addition to sanctions such as refusing co-operation, several work-ins were staged. On several occasions when it was decided to resist managerial announcements of lay-off workers reported for work as normal. These work-ins sometimes lasted for several days, with management eventually agreeing to pay for the production that had been achieved. This was our only plant where work-ins occurred. The action is an interesting variant on other uses of sit-ins and work-ins.

prevent increases in the size of the work force ensured that a certain amount of overtime would normally be needed.

This is not to suggest that stewards could afford to be complacent. Managerial acquiescence in their controls was contingent on their ability to deliver required levels of production. This was revealed very clearly in one of several attempts by management to introduce night shift working, a practice which was, as we have seen, generally disliked by the stewards. On this occasion a section had been failing to attain production targets, and the introduction of a night shift was suggested; stewards were able to resist this only by persuading their members to maintain targets. In cases where management could present a watertight case for an alteration in overtime levels the stewards were extremely reluctant to oppose this for fear of provoking a serious managerial counter-offensive. There would certainly be resistance if it was felt that managers were cutting back on overtime for tactical reasons; we give an example of just such a reaction in Chapter 9. But in general stewards recognized that their control could not be absolute. They had been able to persuade management to tolerate certain practices, but this toleration operated only within certain limits.[5]

In the Large Metals Factory too regular overtime was an established feature of operations, although this was not formalized in any arrangement such as the overtime buffer. Workers had come to see a 48-hour week as a necessary evil if they were to attain anything approaching a satisfactory level of earnings; and we saw in Chapter 5 that there could be a considerable response if management tried to attack this expectation. While we cannot go into the details of management's acceptance of the arrangement the broad picture that we have described for the Small Metals Factory probably applied here, with managers seeing overtime as a means of obtaining shopfloor co-operation. In particular, the shopfloor controls over effort levels that we described in Chapter 7 meant that production targets could not readily be achieved in 40 hours and that overtime would generally have to be worked. Again, the interaction between different aspects of shopfloor controls is evident.

Despite these considerable controls, management in both Company B plants retained the formal right to limit overtime to workers who were needed for production. Craft workers in Company A had been able to go further than this: overtime had to be offered to the whole of a shop if management required any

---

5. One further aspect of shopfloor control of overtime is worth noting. Under an arrangement affectionately known as 'take and bake' workers operated a job and finish system whereby they would do their overtime quotas during the regular working day, being paid for this at overtime rates. The arrangement was always formally illicit and it had been banned by plant management some years before our research, although we came across cases of foremen offering overtime on a 'take and bake' basis to encourage workers to do it. Stewards complained that ending the arrangement served no useful purpose, but there was little that they could do to counter management's demand that workers be present for hours that they were paid for.

work outside the normal 40 hours.[6] As the toolroom manager in the Components Factory explained, control of overtime had shifted to the shopfloor in a series of stages. At one time management had been able to select individuals for overtime; this had been replaced by a system of rotas to prevent favouritism; stewards had then begun to insist that overtime be offered on a 'one in, all in' basis, which meant that if management wanted one job done in the toolroom they had to offer overtime to the whole shop. This arrangement also operated in the maintenance areas. The toolroom had now gone one stage further, however, by demanding that overtime be available for specific periods: before any overtime working would be contemplated, management had to offer not just, say, one Saturday morning's work but a programme of work throughout a twelve-week period. Stewards had, therefore, established a considerable degree of control not only over the distribution of overtime but also over the amount available.

Not surprisingly management pointed to the increase in their costs which resulted from workers doing unnecessary overtime. There were also some attempts to control the situation. In the maintenance areas of the Components Factory for example a new manager had been introduced and he had become alarmed at the way that regular Sunday overtime was accepted regardless of whether it was needed. He therefore set about reducing overtime levels, and achieved this in the face of complaints from workers but without any organized resistance. While it would be dangerous to speculate on the reasons for management's success, as compared with the way in which cuts in overtime were resisted in the Company B plants, two factors may have been important. First, regular weekend overtime had not become so well-established as it was in Company B. In particular, it was not a product of a whole battery of controls over effort, and workers did not, therefore, see managerial actions as an attack on custom and practice. Second, workers did not depend to anything like the same extent on overtime as a means of supplementing inadequate basic wages. They were thus less committed to defending it.

In general, however, there were few managerial attacks on the system of regular overtime as a whole. This reflects several factors. First, toolroom and maintenance workers were recognized as the most 'troublesome' groups, with those in the Components Factory being seen as particularly difficult. Since these workers were a relatively small part of the work force as a whole it was reasonably cheap for management to mollify them by permitting large amounts of overtime. Second, and relatedly, the dangers of a spread of these arrangements to production areas were slight. And, third, there were few immediate

---

6. Production workers simply did overtime as and when management asked for it, on a shop-by-shop basis. There was no problem of allocation since if managers wanted to increase output they simply offered overtime to the whole shop.

problems for local management: work was done and the needs of production were met. In any event, it would be wrong to lay too great an emphasis on the reasons for management's acquiescence. Toolmakers in particular were a self-consciously militant group, and they were capable of forcing management into positions it did not want to adopt. The situation was, in other words, not simply one of managerial weakness or of the ability of management to use overtime arrangements to buy co-operation. Workers here, as in the Small Metals Factory, were active participants in the system and not mere exploiters of loopholes in the managerial control system.

We have argued then, that controls over the supply of labour owed a great deal to craft and craft-based traditions. The craft ethic (Hinton, 1973: 56–7) is obviously a very powerful factor in British industrial relations, and it has been used, for example, by Batstone et al. (1977: 143) to explain the wide differences in patterns of control that still exist between craft and production workers. The remainder of this chapter will point to various other differences that existed in our factories. But we have also tried to identify specific aspects of the broad craft tradition and to point to features of the managerial control system and the market environment which led to the emergence of particular forms of control over recruitment and overtime. Hence the very powerful controls operated by stewards in the Small Metals Factory depended on product market uncertainties and managerial acquiescence as well as the strong traditions of a 'closed' or partially closed ex-craft union. A similar argument can be developed in relation to controls over the mobility of labour.

The Mobility and Allocation of Labour

Shopfloor control over management's right to allocate workers to jobs constitutes a crucial, and neglected, means of resisting managerial domination: it means, most obviously, that foremen cannot reserve the best jobs for their favourites, but it also means that managerial authority is challenged much more generally. Instead of being free to move workers to meet their own needs or whims managers find that they have to justify their requests for movement. By the same token, workers can feel secure that they will not be moved around the factory without warning. Whether the issue concerns the allocation of workers to jobs or jobs to workers depends on the technology employed. In assembly shops, for example, there are distinct work stations that have to be manned up, whereas in machine shops workers may remain at their own machines with batches of work being allocated to them. But the principle is the same in both cases. As with controls over the supply of labour, shopfloor control of mobility was most developed among craft workers in Company A and both craft and production workers in Company B. Before looking at these cases in detail it will be useful to outline the position in our other factories.

In the clothing plants, as we saw in Chapter 7, the distribution of batches of work between workers and the right to move workers from one section to another lay within managerial control. Such control was not, however, exercised in an arbitrary fashion. Thus we saw that managers were conscious of the need to be fair in the allocation of work. For example, it was the practice in one shop in the Hosiery Factory where three different sizes of garment were handled for workers to receive batches of each size in turn. Similarly, managers would try to be reasonable when asking workers to move to other sections to deal with temporary fluctuations in the demand for particular products. But such practices had not reached the stage of being informal rules that workers could insist on being followed: anyone 'declining' a managerial 'request' that she do a different job from her usual one would not get very far. And the system did not challenge any immediate managerial interests: a 'fair' allocation of work reduced the danger of complaints about favouritism without upsetting the way that work was carried out.

In the Electrical and Components Factories custom and practice had developed further. For example, in the Electrical Factory there was an informal rule that, if a worker was moved from her regular job, no one would be put on that job until she had had the chance of returning to it. The rule was enforced on one occasion when a foreman failed to observe the practice: the steward registered a formal 'failure to agree' to 'bring him into line' as she put it, withdrawing the failure to agree once the point had been made. In general, however, foremen in the production areas faced few problems with labour mobility as long as they observed customary understandings as to how particular moves should be handled. In particular, and in contrast with Company B, stewards had no established role: if a move could be amicably agreed between management and the workers involved, that was the end of the matter. A broadly similar situation existed in the Process Factory: as long as managers were reasonable in their requests there was little perceived conflict of interest over mobility.

Among craft workers in Company A, however, more formal shopfloor controls had been established. In the maintenance areas it had long been the practice that the foreman would prepare lists of repair jobs, with workers taking jobs off the list in turn: foremen had no right to select individual workers to do particular jobs. In the toolroom of the Components Factory shopfloor control was even more firmly established. The shop was divided into sections comprising lathes, drilling machines, and so on. It was an absolute rule that there was no movement between sections, so that a lathe operator could not move onto drilling, even if he was eager to do so. Moreover, mobility within each section depended on the steward's agreement: a foreman could not move a worker between one lathe and another without such agreement.

The effectiveness of these controls may be illustrated by a dispute which arose when management, faced with falling demand, announced a total ban on recruitment throughout the company. Toolmakers responded by banning the limited amount of mobility that was normally permitted within sections, which meant, for example, that when a man retired from the Components Factory toolroom his machine was left vacant. It happened that this action occurred during the annual pay negotiations with the toolmakers at company level, and the company attempted to exploit this by tying the pay settlement to a demand that all restrictions on mobility and the 'one in, all in' policy on overtime should be ended. The effectiveness of the toolmakers' sanctions, which took place, of course, across the whole company and which included action against the sending of work to outside contract toolrooms as well as the mobility ban, was, however, considerable. The outcome was that, in addition to resisting management's new demands, toolmakers were able to obtain some limited recruitment to the toolroom. More general questions about such company-wide sanctions are considered in the following chapter, but for present purposes it is notable that the Components Factory toolmakers were particularly firm in their sanctions and that they saw themselves as leading the fight against the company: in action as well as in rhetoric they were proud of their militant reputation.

We cannot establish with certainty why mobility was controlled so strictly here. Not only was the control much firmer than it was in the Electrical Factory's toolroom, but it was also stricter than that exercised by toolmakers in the Large Metals Factory where there was a feeling of craft solidarity that was as well-developed as that in the Components Factory. Hence it was possible for management in the Large Metals Factory to obtain mobility between different sections and it was also accepted that, as a man grew older, he would be free to move to the less demanding jobs. Management thus had some freedom to respond to changes in production schedules by moving workers between jobs. This difference from the broadly similar environment of the Components Factory toolroom probably reflects very specific historical, organizational, and even accidental factors. Detailed aspects of the frontier of control cannot be reduced to a few neat patterns.

At a more general level, however, controls on mobility were obviously related to other aspects of shopfloor control. Hence it was only in the Company **B** plants, where controls on manning and effort levels were considerable, that production workers had established substantial controls over the movement of labour. The involvement of stewards in every aspect of the planning of work was taken for granted: in addition to handling overtime rotas, stewards were involved in allocating workers to particular jobs and in dealing with any problems that arose. To cite one minor but revealing incident, a worker who was to do overtime in a section where he did not usually work approached the steward, and not the foreman, to ask what he should do. Stewards had obtained such a degree of involvement in the system and such detailed knowledge of jobs that they could handle man assignments as capably as any foreman.

What did this mean, though, for patterns of control? The involvement of stewards in the detailed allocation of labour does not in itself prevent management from achieving an 'efficient' use of labour; as the stewards' frequent claim that 'we run the factory' implies, stewards could simply be performing for managers a task that they were unable or unwilling to carry out. The implications for control were two-fold. First, management could never be sure that they would be able to man up particular operations. Although stewards were proud of their involvement in the planning of production they were able and willing to restrict this involvement. Hence, as we saw in Chapter 7, the start of the track in assembly shops could be delayed until man assignments were agreed. Similarly, if stewards wanted to put a little pressure on management over, say, manning levels on a particular job they could raise objections about how workers were assigned to it. Co-operation was, as stewards constantly stressed, something that they gave to management and that they could withdraw if they saw fit. Second, labour mobility occurred in the context of various demarcation lines. As we show in more detail in the following section, the Large Metals Factory had a number of divisions between grades of production worker. There were two grades whose members, organized by two different unions, claimed to be skilled, and there were also some semi-skilled operations that were the preserves of one union or another. All these boundaries were absolutely rigid, so that when mobility was discussed it was in relation to a fairly narrow range of jobs. Management's freedom of manoeuvre was correspondingly restricted.

In the Small Metals Factory, by contrast, stewards generally permitted mobility between all grades of labour organized by each union. This was unique among our engineering factories, and may seem surprising in view of our argument about the extent of shopfloor control over manning levels, recruitment, overtime, and many other aspects of the organization of work. As with the overtime buffer and such things as resistance to night shift working, however, stewards recognized the demands of production and modified their approach accordingly. This may be seen by considering how the system of mobility between grades, which was, as the stewards stressed, a form of co-operation with management that was unknown in the rest of the company, had come about.

Our study of the ex-craft union's minute books reveals that until 1965 no movement had been allowed by skilled men onto semi-skilled jobs, although some temporary mobility was permitted between the various trades within the semi-skilled grades. In this year an acute economic crisis struck the plant: it had been taken over some years earlier, and was now under intense pressure from its new parent to halt the slide into loss-making that had occurred during the previous two years. Top management pointed to a lack of competitiveness and argued that this was preventing the plant from attracting new work, which meant in turn that its whole future was in jeopardy. A particular problem for local managers was the large amount of 'waiting time' being booked by skilled workers: shortages of labour among the semi-skilled grades meant that the flow of work was often halted, with skilled men having to be paid for the time that they spent waiting for work. Managers believed that a great deal of this waiting time could be eliminated if skilled workers were moved onto semi-skilled jobs to cover temporary shortages of labour. The stewards had strongly resisted this in the past, but now agreed, in the face of the new crisis, to permit a greater degree of flexibility.[7]

This did not, however, weaken the stewards' role in the allocation of labour. Indeed, in certain respects this role was strengthened. Thus it was agreed that it was the prerogative of the stewards and not management to decide how to deal with any shortage of semi-skilled workers. And any transfer of labour, within as well as between grades, was to be on a purely voluntary basis; this effectively denied managers the right, which they had had when mobility was between semi-skilled grades only, to select individuals to move when there was a shortage in a particular area.

Over the next decade the stewards permitted further developments in the trend to a more flexible use of labour in order to counter threats of short-time working or redundancy. Hence in 1969 they agreed to 'semi-permanent' mobility within semi-skilled grades, which meant that movement between these grades would normally be granted without management having to justify every request for mobility. In 1975 full mobility between all grades of labour was granted in exchange for a package of benefits of which the introduction of guaranteed lay-off pay was, given the plant's history of short-time working, the most significant.

The significance of this must not, however, be exaggerated. As one experienced foreman said of the 1975 agreement, 'this was only a paper agreement which did not prevent the stewards withdrawing their co-operation [over mobility] when they saw fit to do so'. The stewards were prepared to allow management a greater degree of mobility, but they still reserved the right to withdraw it. Hence at the time of our research at the end of the 1970s management were still trying to tie the unions down to a formal, written, agreement whereby mobility between certain jobs would normally be available. For the stewards, however, such an agreement was either meaningless or a severe threat to their own position. If it simply stated the existing position, whereby stewards were prepared to grant a substantial degree of mobility, then it was pointless. But if it meant that stewards did not have the right to withdraw mobility if they saw fit then it was a serious attack on their traditional patterns of control. The

7. They also agreed to cuts in piecework prices, which again points to their acceptance of the 'need to be competitive'.

history of controls over mobility helps us to understand the stewards' position: stewards felt that they had gone out of their way to help the company by removing some of the divisions between skilled and semi-skilled grades that had existed in the past and that were still present in plants such as the Large Metals Factory. They felt that they could not do more without handing over to management the right to decide how labour should be allocated, a right which had successfully been denied for many years.

In this plant, then, controls over mobility were exercised flexibly but, as in the Large Metals Factory, stewards insisted that they had the ultimate right to refuse mobility, either between particular grades or across all grades. As we will see in the following two chapters, this gave them a powerful set of sanctions in disputes with management. These controls merged, however, with more formal boundaries between grades, and to complete our study of controls over the supply and allocation of labour we must now turn to these demarcations.

Demarcations

The notion of a demarcation is, at first sight straightforward: a demarcation is a division along craft lines such that, for example, a pipefitter does one strictly defined set of tasks, an electrician performs a different set, and so on. But the principle can be applied to other lines of division. Hence in the clothing industry men's and women's jobs were rigidly demarcated, with women being restricted to the cutting of fabric and the sewing of garments and men carrying out the unskilled labouring jobs as well as the skilled tasks in the knitting rooms. Such divisions are obviously important for considerations of the characteristics of the labour market or of the position of women workers. And their role in contributing to the fragmentation of the work force into sectional groupings must not be forgotten. But, as noted earlier, a proper assessment of them would involve a detailed examination of their operation and of whose interest they appeared to serve. Our present concern is with the more specific issue of the role of demarcations in influencing the allocation of labour. We begin with craft demarcations before looking at divisions between groups of production workers.

Craft Demarcations
The most firmly established demarcations were those in our engineering companies which rested on some craft or craft-based justification for their existence. In all four plants the distinction between production operators and workers who had a craft qualification, earned through apprenticeship or a recognized time 'using the tools of the trade', was so widely accepted that it was largely unquestioned. But there remained interesting differences in the degree to which it was enforced. Thus in the Electrical Factory some groups of maintenance

workers were prepared to turn a blind eye if a foreman or production worker occasionally tinkered with a machine, whereas in the Large Metals Factory demarcations were rigidly enforced.

There was, however, one area where the division between craftsmen and other workers was coming under challenge by management. As we saw in Chapter 7, management in the Process Factory was coming under increasing pressure to control labour costs. In addition to trying to increase effort levels among production workers, managers were proposing that certain routine jobs normally done by fitters should in future be carried out by fitters' mates. A part of the craftsman's job, in other words, was to be handed over to semi-skilled workers. At the time of our research the fitters' stewards were resisting these proposals, but their resistance was far from total, for their main concern was an adequate 'buy out' of the demarcation and not to defend it as such. Management's proposals were, moreover, only part of a more general attack on craft controls. Some years before our research management had succeeded in increasing the mobility of labour by removing the old practice that workers were assigned to the workshops or to maintenance work in production areas; there was now a rota system for movements between the two types of work. And the fitters' stewards were worried about another threat, namely that management would try to reduce manning levels in the workshops and use outside contractors for large-scale overhauls. Interviews with management suggested that these fears were realistic: in general terms managers saw the craft areas as the most 'difficult', and there was concern that it was inefficient to employ a permanent staff of fitters when demand for their services fluctuated. Although fitters' ability to prevent the use of outside contractors had not yet been put to the test, management's past successes, together with the difficulties which any plant-based organization faces when work is to be removed from the factory, suggested that the fitters would find it hard to organize effective resistance. The fitters appeared to lack, moreover, the intense commitment to the craft ethic which characterized craftsmen in our engineering factories. Although an assessment of the general character of craftsmen's orientations must necessarily be rather impressionistic, fitters in the Process Factory seemed to be more willing to tolerate change than those elsewhere. This, together with management's articulated policy of seeking continuous 'improvements' in working practices, makes it far from surprising that the Process Factory was the only one in which craft demarcations, and other forms of control, were coming under active challenge.

In addition to divisions between craft and production workers, distinctions between different types of craft worker must also be considered. These were, again, largely taken for granted: although some managers in our engineering companies expressed a desire to see an all-round technician instead of several separate trades (this often being accompanied by references to the alleged absence of distinct trades in countries such as Germany), this was not seen as an immediate aim. The distinction between pipefitters and machine tool fitters, for example, went unchallenged.

There was, however, one important exception to this. In the Large Metals Factory two types of fitter, called machine tool fitters (MTFs) and mechanical maintenance fitters (MMFs), were recognized. Management made several attempts to obtain agreements whereby specified parts of one group's work could be handled by the other group, for management felt that the skills of the two trades were very similar. All these attempts foundered, however, on the refusal of the MTFs to have anything to do with the MMFs, whom they saw as a lower grade even though their earnings were virtually identical. The MTFs were perhaps the most 'closed' and exclusive of any craft group in our factories. They claimed that their craft skills were peculiar to themselves; hence, for example, while they claimed that they were equal in status to toolmakers they would not accept even a toolmaker as a foreman over them, for the skills of the two trades were seen as equivalent but not identical. This exclusiveness was illustrated in a dispute over the appointment of a foreman. An MTF had been made foreman of a section of MMFs, and management now wished to bring him back as a supervisor of his old trade. The MTFs insisted, however, that anyone who left the trade could not return to it, and refused to accept the man as a foreman. A strike lasting three days occurred over the issue, a dispute which we analyse in more detail in the following chapter (p. 244). Its present significance is that workers were prepared to strike to defend the integrity of the trade. They were largely successful, for it was agreed that any foreman coming from outside the trade would offer no supervision on technical matters; the separate skills of the MTFs were thus re-affirmed.

There were, then, cases in which craft demarcations were brought by management into the bargaining arena. But such overt challenges were rare, with the controls over the use of labour that the demarcations implied being firmly institutionalized. This was also broadly true of divisions between groups of production workers.

Divisions Between Production Workers

As noted earlier, a discussion of demarcations cannot be separated from consideration of the mobility of labour. Hence we have seen how formal demarcations between grades can, as in the Small Metals Factory, be modified so as to allow mobility between them and how, conversely, informal rules governing mobility can develop that owe nothing to formal demarcations. Our aim here is simply to explore further the use that workers made of demarcations to develop their own control. Since, as we have already seen, formal demarcations between groups of production workers were absent in Company A, the clothing plants, and the Process Factory, discussions can be limited to the Company B plants.

The situation was the more straightforward in the Small Metals Factory.

The major line of division was between the two main unions, the ex-craft union and the general union. Although the division was associated with the concern of the former union to retain craft-like controls, it was not a strictly craft demarcation: this union now organized semi-skilled grades, and the general union had also succeeded in obtaining a foot-hold among such grades, so that it was an inter-union and not an inter-craft division. Its operation may be illustrated by two cases.

First, a classic demarcation dispute arose shortly before our research period, with both unions claiming that their members should carry out work that was to be introduced into the factory. The details of the dispute are again of secondary importance here: after management made an initial allocation of work that neither union found acceptable, there was a three-day strike by the general union which ended when the matter was sent for arbitration, with the result of the arbitration being the re-affirmation of management's earlier ruling. The strike, then, seems to have been particularly 'irrational', for the general union gained nothing by it. But stewards did not see the matter in this light. While admitting that they had made tactical mistakes in being manoeuvred into a position in which they struck while the ex-craft union did not, they felt that the strike had been essential. It was part of the union's historical struggle in the plant to gain control of production work, and without a determined stand management would, they felt, always stick to tradition by giving all such work to the ex-craft union. As with the MTFs' strike discussed earlier, workers were prepared to protest if they felt that their interests in particular work were being endangered. In this case the dispute reflected the long-standing hostility between the established ex-craft union and the relative newcomer of the general union. The direct challenge to managerial interests was limited, for, as managers pointed out, they did not mind who did the work as long as someone did it. There was, however, a less immediate challenge, for uncertainties over whether new jobs could be introduced quickly and without arguments made it more difficult, managers claimed, to attract work to the plant. As we will see in later chapters, the dispute was a frequent source of reference when this problem came to the fore.

The second case was the operation of the demarcation in the machine shop, where workers who were known as machine operators belonged to the ex-craft union, with 'machine assistants' being members of the general union. The differences between operators' and assistants' jobs were slight, and the pay of the two groups of workers was now identical.[8] But the distinction between the jobs was strongly defended, and there was a history of disputes around it.

8. In the technologically identical machine shop in the Large Metals Factory there was no such demarcation. Specific historical and organizational factors again have to be considered in accounting for such differences.

According to managers the demarcation seriously inflated labour costs. In addition to any costs due to general over-manning, the demarcation limited flexibility of operations. Some jobs required one operator and two assistants, others three operators and two assistants, and so on. It was thus difficult to allocate labour without waste. Management made various attempts to break down the demarcation. For example, during our research period they proposed that, in the event of absenteeism among one group of workers, members of the other group could cover their jobs on a temporary basis. Although this proposal was far more limited than previous managerial attempts to end the demarcation almost entirely, it was resisted by the stewards. Thus they demanded that either union should be able to end the agreement if it were being 'abused' by management. This was part of their general suspicion of formal agreements with management and neatly illustrates their whole approach of making agreements on mobility conditional on management's behaviour. Hence the unions could end the agreement whenever they wished to put pressure on management. The main stumbling block, however, was the question of payment. For many years it had been agreed that workers who were transferred to the machine shop from other shops under the existing rules on mobility would receive one hour's pay to compensate them for the fact that they could not be expected to work as quickly as regular machine shop workers. The stewards requested a similar scheme for transfers within the shop, a 'buy out' that was favoured by many managers in the plant. But because of the implications of any buy out for other plants, managers stressed that they could not reach any agreement on payment. Given the operators' lingering suspicions of recognizing assistants as equals, it would have been hard for the ex-craft stewards to sell any agreement to their members, but without hard cash as an inducement it was impossible.

What lessons can be learned from these examples? First, and most generally, a preparedness to sell demarcations is not necessarily against workers' interests. Unions are often criticized for giving up practices which defend workers' interests in controlling production in return for mere monetary compensation. But in this case any sale was contemplated on a purely conditional basis: management would benefit by gaining extra work from men who would otherwise be idle, and the stewards naturally wanted a share of the benefits, but management would not be granted any permanent rights over the movement of labour. This approach reflects, of course, the unions' traditional policy of treating mobility of labour as conditional. Although in plants without such traditions the sale of 'restrictive practices' may have unforeseen consequences in terms of the loss of control that the sale implies, in this plant stewards were in a position to negotiate a sale that did not harm their other interests. Second, the demarcation dispute is a clear example of 'the division of control' since it was a dispute between unions and not against management. But to leave the matter here is too simple. To understand why the dispute arose we need to relate it to the type of controls that the ex-craft union had built up. Controls over the supply and allocation of labour were based, as we have seen, on a policy of exclusiveness. The clash with the general union was not the product of an irrational tendency of unions to squabble with each other but the result of the structure of the situation: a union that tries to deal with managerial challenges to its members' interests through 'closed' policies is likely to have disputes on the boundaries it has drawn around itself. This reflects not irrationality but the nature of strategies that try to challenge managerial control of the supply and allocation of labour. Third, the demarcation had identifiable consequences for management's freedom of action, and was thus not simply a division of control.

In the Large Metals Factory demarcations were more pervasive but their impact on managerial freedom was, perhaps surprisingly, less clear. Whereas in the Small Metals Factory workers could, in principle, move between any of the direct production jobs organized by the ex-craft union, in the Large Metals Factory such mobility was impossible. Workers were allocated to distinct trades and could not move between them. Within the general trade of welding, for example, workers were employed as gas welders or arc welders and did not move between jobs. Similarly, a distinct semi-skilled job known as 'polishing' was separated from other jobs and was carried out by a group of workers with their own stewards and bargaining arrangements; in the Small Metals Factory, for example, the identical tasks were carried out as part of the general duties of semi-skilled workers and were not seen as part of a distinct 'job'. The Large Metals Factory's work force was, then, extremely fragmented: in addition to groups such as electricians, toolsetters, and toolmakers, production workers formed a large number of groups which had deep-seated suspicions of each other. Semi-skilled workers, for example, were openly critical of what they saw as the pretensions of the more skilled trades: the jobs they carried out were not 'really' skilled, and workers were being recruited to them with very little experience, the only qualification being to obtain the relevant union card.

The direct implications of all this for the conduct of production were, however, limited. Although managers could not move workers between grades, it was possible to transfer them between different shops. Hence, given the size of the plant, there were few of the shortages of particular grades of labour that rapidly affected the Small Metals Factory whenever the stewards chose to restrict mobility. Moreover, while managers claimed that demarcations sometimes meant that two men had to be employed where only one was needed, the main managerial complaint related to over-manning and inadequate effort levels. These problems owed little to divisions between trades. And, unlike the Small Metals Factory, there were few disputes as to which grades of production worker would do a particular job, although there were a few arguments about this in the indirect areas. Union organizations were firmly established, and there was no active hostility between an established organization and a new challenger.

Demarcations were, then, probably less important means of control in the Large Metals Factory than were the other ways in which stewards could control effort and the mobility of labour. Their main implication was for the solidarity or otherwise of the work force: a crucial feature of the factory's union organization, on which we commented in Chapter 2 and some of whose consequences we discuss in the following chapter, was its fragmentation into separate, if not actively competing, groups. How, then, had this situation come about? While we cannot give the sort of detailed account that was possible in relation to mobility controls in the Small Metals Factory, we may suggest that the same sort of influences that affected those controls operated in relation to demarcations in the Large Metals Factory. A large number of unions had been recognized for many years, and no one could remember exactly when the pre-entry closed shop had been established. Demarcations probably grew up without any particular direction and without anyone worrying unduly about them. As Zweig (1951: 20) noted, market conditions are important: 'in a contracting industry, like the cotton industry, any practices are more likely to take on a restrictive shape and direction than in an expanding industry like engineering.' At the time Zweig was writing the Company B plants were expanding and their shop steward organizations were developing. Management were probably not too worried about who organized particular trades or about divisions between trades so long as production could be maintained. The differences in the types of control that were exerted in the two plants can be explained in terms of the particular problems that product market conditions created in the Small Metals Factory and by the dominant position of the one ex-craft union in this plant.

It is notable in this connection that complaints about demarcations in the Large Metals Factory surfaced only when the plant's future became uncertain. For example, after the plant's partial closure was announced, a foreman, reflecting on his many years' experience in the plant as a steward as well as a supervisor, argued that strong demarcations had always been one of the plant's main problems. Such arguments were absent only a few months earlier. And a convener explicitly used the product market argument in defending demarcations: when output was rising management had not cared about demarcations but now that there was a fall in demand, which could itself be explained, the convener argued, by managerial failures in the design and marketing of the product, managers were beginning to blame shopfloor practices. There is a great deal of truth in this. Demarcations and other controls were allowed to be established when they seemed to pose few threats, and by the time of our research they had become firmly institutionalized.

This is not to suggest that demarcations unambiguously affected management's costs. It is easy for managers to argue that they lead to inefficiency, but if they simply provide rules for allocating labour to jobs they need have no such effect. If they give workers a feeling of security, in the sense that they have a right to a particular type of work, they may discourage other 'restrictive practices'. And, as noted at the outset, managers may have an interest in having a fragmented work force. Estimating the balance between these and other effects would be a fruitless task. We have, instead, tried to explain how particular controls operated and what effect they had on the frontier of control as a whole. This leads us back to the wider question of the fragmentation of the work force implied by various 'restrictions'.

Cohesion and Fragmentation

As noted at the start of this chapter, demarcations are widely seen as sources of division within the working class. The evidence that we have considered, in relation to restrictions on entry to a factory as well as demarcations, plainly indicates that there is a great deal of truth in this assertion. Stewards' control in the Small Metals Factory, for example, was explicitly designed to protect workers in the plant against competition from those outside it. To the outsider the most notable consequence of this was that, in a plant located in an area of considerable West Indian and Pakistani immigration, there were very few black or brown faces to be seen on the shopfloor. Similarly, craftsmen's demarcation lines were set up to mark off craftsmen from production workers, towards whom there was sometimes a feeling bordering on contempt.

Yet to write off demarcations and other sources of fragmentation is unsatisfactory. There may be good reasons why unions limit the basis of solidarity and try to restrict membership. As Offe and Wiesenthal (1979: 80–81) suggest, for a union movement located in a market that is already organized on capitalist lines, maximization of membership may not serve the unions' interests. They give two reasons for this. First, a large membership may lead to bureaucratization and thus create difficulties of mobilization. Second, as size increases so membership becomes more diverse and it becomes harder to generate agreed demands. This argument can be applied to the present case. Toolroom stewards in Company A, for example, certainly felt that they would get nowhere if they had to take the mass of production workers with them; and we have suggested that one reason for management's toleration of controls by craft workers was their knowledge that these controls could be restricted to these limited groups. But an even clearer example is provided by the Small Metals Factory. Stewards' controls over recruitment and overtime reflected, among other things, a need to come to terms with one of the peculiarities of the plant's market position, namely rapidly fluctuating demand. Given their situation in such a market their most logical course was to try to reduce the effects of these fluctuations by achieving a buffer of overtime and by restricting recruitment. Hence we have seen that the introduction of the overtime buffer stemmed directly from a period of short-time working. But demand fluctuations also had other effects, most notably the way that they brought into question the whole future of the plant. When stewards were convinced of the reality of this threat they were prepared to moderate other aspects of their control and in particular to permit increased mobility between grades.

All this points to a certain duality in the system of shopfloor control. First, demarcations and other restrictions challenged managerial control but also created and sustained divisions within the work force. Second, stewards' controls over mobility limited managerial rights to allocate labour but were themselves limited by being dependent on turning the rules of the market system against that system. As argued at the end of Chapter 7, stewards in both Company B plants were committed to the needs of production, although they also challenged managerial means of attaining those needs. We have now seen that the needs of production also influenced other aspects of stewards' behaviour: stewards did not wish simply to obstruct management through demarcation rules or restrictions on mobility but insisted that co-operation was something that managers could never take for granted. The success of stewards' controls depended on operating within the rules of the market economy. This meant that any wider challenge was not mounted.

This argument is consistent with the view of Beynon (1973: 98) that British trade unionism has always been based on a factory class consciousness which 'understands class relationships in terms of their direct manifestation in conflict between the bosses and the workers within the factory'. Yet two further points must be made. First, the term factory consciousness is inappropriate since the whole effect of demarcations was to fragment the work force of a plant into competing groupings. Divisions between craft and non-craft groups, and indeed between grades of non-craft workers, meant that there was no more than a sectional consciousness. Second, even the degree of sectional consciousness implied by controls over the supply and allocation of labour was absent in several factories. We have argued that a tradition of craft organization, together with features of managerial organization and the product market, helps to explain the particular form of control in the Small Metals Factory. We have been able to give a less detailed account of the origins of controls over mobility in other areas, but again the presence of craft forms of organization and of a management that was willing to cede some aspects of control seems to have been significant. Large parts of the working class lack the means to make even a sectional challenge to management, and such a challenge must not be dismissed simply because it does not develop into anything broader.

This and the preceding two chapters have been centrally concerned with institutional forms of control over the labour process. We have considered examples of overt actions where relevant, but we have not looked at forms of overt conflict in their own right. In the following chapter we try to relate cases of overt action to the patterns of control that we have analysed here.

9
Strikes and Sanctions

In this chapter we move to our most detailed level of analysis: the examination of specific cases of strikes and disputes. Since strikes are the most obvious, and perhaps also the most studied, type of conflict their relevance to a study of the various expressions of industrial conflict requires no explanation. Yet their relationship to the general argument which we have been developing is far from obvious. We have examined the position and shape of the frontier of control in our factories, looking at comparative patterns of workplace behaviour. Analysis of the detailed processes of strike action does not necessarily fit into this theme: such analysis, at least in its most sophisticated form (Batstone et al., 1978), concentrates on social organization in the sense of systems of argument and modes of mobilization as distinct from organization in the sense of relating specific practices to structural conditions. There are, however, several continuities between our present concerns and those of previous chapters.

First, the nature of strike action is one index of the frontier of control. Most obviously, collective organization in the clothing plants was too weak to sustain strikes, let alone more sophisticated sanctions such as overtime bans. More interestingly, the deployment of sanctions on a very sophisticated basis was one of the means whereby craft workers in Company A had built up their distinctive type of control, and analysis of these sanctions thus helps to develop our earlier argument. In particular, the use of sanctions at a company level was one of the few ways in which Company A craft workers had extended their collective organization beyond that of workers in Company B. This reflects a second link with our earlier arguments: we pointed in Chapter 7 to the limitations of plant-level controls over effort bargaining in Company B and in Chapter 8 to the substantial divisions which existed among the work force. We develop these themes by considering the absence of company-wide sanctions and by indicating the sectional character of strike action in the company. Third, we can follow up some more specific points from earlier chapters, most importantly the effects of the shift from piecework to measured day work in Company B. Day work is often felt to be associated with a different type of dispute from that common under piecework, with a shift away from sectional wage issues and a reduction in the number of strikes as sectional disputes are replaced by plant-wide ones. Our material on strike trends allows us to throw some light on this issue. Fourth, we have pointed to various managerial attempts to regain control over the labour process. One aspect of this, in which Company B again featured most strongly, involved a particular strategy in strikes. Management was adopting an articulated policy of taking a determined line in disputes: instead of letting an argument last for a long period a decision was taken to implement the changes desired by management, with managers being willing to 'take a strike' if necessary. This approach is worth following in detail since, as argued in Chapter 1, trying to unravel managerial strategies is a crucial but neglected aspect of the study of industrial conflict.

We begin by outlining the broad pattern of strikes in our factories. As we will see, the definition of a strike is much less clear-cut than might appear: at what point, for example, does the extension of a lunch break become a strike? We may take as a starting point, however, one of the standard definitions of strikes as collective stoppages of work 'to express a grievance or enforce a demand' (Peterson, 1938: 3). But we restrict the term 'strike' to stoppages in which the workers lost pay. A 'stoppage' is then defined as a collective cessation of work to express a grievance or enforce a demand in which pay was not stopped. This excludes, for example, any lengthening of break times or finishing work early which did not have a specific grievance or demand behind it. We then consider particular strikes in more detail with special reference to the managerial strategy which was involved in them. This is followed by a consideration of sanctions short of strikes; the general nature of such sanctions and of strategies of the withdrawal of co-operation has been considered in previous chapters, and the particular concern here is with the deployment of sanctions at company level as part of a sophisticated bargaining policy of craft groups in Company A. Finally, we consider the relationship between strikes and the patterns of control and conflict in our factories.

Patterns of Strikes

If strikes 'are appallingly difficult subjects to study' (William Brown, 1973: 148) then studying patterns of strikes at plant level is particularly dangerous. It is certainly possible to investigate broad patterns of strike activity using official statistics and to say, for example, that there appear to be more strikes at one time than another. But it is well-known that the official statistics do not include every strike that occurs (William Brown, 1981: 97–101). The analysis thus depends on the assumption that such under-recording is insufficient to affect the overall picture. This is a reasonable assumption for aggregate analyses, but it breaks down when the plant is the level of analysis. The idiosyncracies of individual factories become of prime importance. The concern of the official statistics, moreover, is with stoppages which meet certain minimum criteria of size and length; this reduces definitional difficulties of what is to count as a strike. But for workplace relations stoppages which do not fall within the official definition may be crucial and this raises the question of what is to be included as a strike. As Clack (1967: 88) discovered in his study of a car factory, it was impossible to give a precise estimate of the number of strikes to occur during his research period because some stoppages were so small as to escape even detailed search and since the boundary of what was to count as a strike was vague. The latter point does not refer simply to the fact that different plants will have different criteria of what to include or even to the possibility of deliberate attempts to hide stoppages from senior managers. These and other points reflect practical difficulties of recording phenomena which the investigator may wish to include under the rubric of strikes, but there is also a more fundamental difficulty of principle involved: how do certain workplace activities come to be defined as strikes? We must tackle this question first.

Strike Definitions
The most systematic approach to this issue is provided by Batstone et al. (1978: 19) who point out that

> strikes are defined as such primarily by the managerial act of taking the Men involved off the clock; this is virtually automatic if the men leave the plant .... Management often have the power to define a situation as a strike or not ... they do not define stoppages as strikes if the workers do not leave the plant and if, at the time or afterwards, the men's case is seen as legitimate by management.

There are, then, two key elements in the managerial decision of whether to define a situation as a strike: whether workers leave the plant and whether their demands are seen as legitimate. The former is the more powerful, however, for if workers leave the plant their action is almost bound to be called a strike.

Both elements of this argument are open to question. On the former we give an example below of a case where stewards in the Small Metals Factory left the plant to protest against certain managerial actions but were not taken off the clock. This is probably unusual, however, and it is the second element of the argument which is more important. The legitimacy of workers' demands is less important to management than practical consideration about the consequences of defining an action as a strike. In the example we have just given management were eager not to escalate the dispute with the stewards and hence declined the stewards' clear invitation to define it as a strike. The same dispute illustrates the converse of this: workers were taken off pay by management, ostensibly for refusing instructions, but the stewards did not choose to take this as the signal to call a strike.

In giving so much weight to the legitimacy of workers' demands as the key influence, Batstone et al. follow their more general claim that systems of argument and the 'mobilization of bias' are crucial elements in the negotiation of order on the shopfloor. As we argued in Chapter 6, in relation to the strategy of withdrawal of co-operation, the key question, however, is why some sets of definitions are used and not others. Such a strategy depends on management's willingness to play the game according to accepted practice, so that a sanction can be defined as the careful following of formal rules. This willingness is more likely, we suggest, to reflect an appreciation of the balance of power than an acceptance that workers have right on their side. To take another example, a group of workers in the Electrical Factory stopped work over a bonus payment, an action which all the managers involved saw as totally unreasonable since the action was in breach of procedure and since the demands themselves were unacceptable. Yet the workers were not taken off the clock because it was well understood by the personnel manager that the strike was a political device of one of the conveners: the convener did not want to pursue the bonus claim and, by persuading the workers to stop work, he could let them blow off steam and at the same time convince them of the futility of their claim. Managers could only have upset this arrangement had they stopped the workers' pay.

Legitimacy may, it is true, be relevant in some circumstances. But even then there are degrees to which managers are willing to accept a grievance as legitimate. To take another example from the Electrical Factory, there was one section where it often became very cold and where it had become virtually a part of custom and practice for workers to stop work from time to time. They would retire in ritual fashion to the canteen, which gave the foreman the necessary bargaining leverage to persuade the maintenance department to install some temporary heaters. Stopping work was seen in this case as legitimate, and workers were not usually taken off the clock. But in the space of a month there were two stoppages, and in the second one the foreman involved originally refused all payment. A compromise was eventually worked out, but it was made clear that, in future, complaints must go through the proper procedure and that any stoppage of work would be defined as a strike. Although the complaints behind workers' actions were still felt to be legitimate, managers did not want to encourage stoppages and the by-passing of procedure, and hence re-defined what they considered to be legitimate.

This point about managerial pragmatism raises a more general issue. Only in some circumstances is it possible for the niceties of the legitimacy of demands or the balance of advantage to come into consideration. In our clothing plants, as several instances cited in previous chapters have shown, processes of definition were quite straightforward. Any refusal to work 'properly' was met with a firm line by management, the usual argument being that anyone who did not like the factory's way of working was free to quit. Strikes could certainly occur, but there was none of the process of negotiation which characterized our engineering factories and the plant studied by Batstone and his colleagues. As Batstone et al. (1978: 218) put it 'strike action is a continuous possibility in our system of industrial relations' but they immediately qualify this by adding that it 'merges into other forms of collective action' and that 'the normality of strikes lies in the common practices whereby workers attempt to improve the wage-effort, or reward-deprivation, bargain by negotiation with management, and by individual and collective "making out" strategies'. Since workers in our clothing factories had no coherent making out strategy and since, in particular, other forms of collective action were rare, strikes were not a normal part of industrial relations. That is, they were not normal if 'normal' is taken to mean an understood part of everyday workplace relationships. It was only where the notion of a collective making out strategy had any meaning that strikes could be said to be part of the understood pattern of relationships.[1] In our clothing factories they were more likely to reflect a breakdown of relationships, a point we may consider further by examining the pattern of strikes in our factories.

Strike Rates

The only strike which anyone in our clothing plants could recall occurred in the Underwear Factory some years before our research. We are confident that such recollections were accurate, given the rarity of collective action of any sort. In our other factories, of course, the presence of some sort of collective organization makes it impossible to take such statements at face value. We were told by management in the Process Factory, for example, that the plant's only strike had been in 1964 and, more surprisingly, by workers in the Large Metals Factory that their last 'real' strike had been in 1956. Yet, at least in the latter plant, actions which we would want to count as strikes appeared to be quite common. We tried to gain some indication of the frequency of such actions by using

---

1. It is precisely this embeddedness of strikes in normal relationships which makes the comments of Batstone et al. (1978: 206–7) about strikes and class consciousness hard to understand. They rightly point out that workers in their factory did not demonstrate class consciousness in the sense of identification with one's own class or the recognition of a structural conflict with other classes. (On these and other elements of class consciousness, see Giddens, 1973: 112–13). Strikes here did not, therefore, involve an 'explosion' of consciousness (compare Mann, 1973: 45–54). But this is hardly surprising given the nature of strikes in the plant. If the interest is in the explosion of consciousness, the factory studied by Batstone et al., or for that matter our own engineering plants, is not the place to look. The absence of an articulated class consciousness does not, moreover, preclude analysis of collective shopfloor action in class terms. We have indicated in previous chapters the way that such action can in practice challenge management even if it is not the result of an articulated class strategy, a point to which we return in Chapter 10.

organizational records where possible, but only in the Large Metals Factory were there any records which gave a picture of strikes in the plant as whole. More importantly, we searched for incidents which might qualify as strikes and tried to jog people's memories about past events. We probably did not miss much in the smaller factories, but we spent varying periods of time in our plants and no doubt our diligence in looking for strikes also varied. In any event a short period may be far from 'typical'. We do not, therefore, claim to have accurate estimates of the number of strikes in our factories, although we can given a rough indication of the position. More importantly, we can consider the significance of our findings for patterns of workplace activity.

Thus the strike in the Underwear Factory is of interest precisely because it stood out for participants far more than a similar event at some distance in time would have done for people in our other plants. Even then, however, management were able to interpret it as an event which did not contradict the plant's harmonious industrial relations. Rumours had developed that substantial rate-cutting was planned, and there was a spontaneous walk-out which developed into a two-day strike. In view of our earlier argument about the stabilizing effect that the general lack of rate-cutting had in our two plants, it is notable that the fear of rate cuts provoked such a response. More important here, however, is management's argument that the rumours had been incorrect and that the strike was the result of a simple misunderstanding together with poor communication with the shopfloor. One senior manager used the strike as an example of the dangers of the firm's old managerial style: for him it was significant as an impetus to improve communications and not as an indication of lasting conflicts with the shopfloor. The strike was seen as a mistake which would not happen again, a view with which the senior union representative at the time (who was now, interestingly enough, a departmental manager) concurred.

If the rarity of strikes, together with the limited significance placed on them, is unsurprising here, it is perhaps more surprising that two of our other plants, the Process and Components Factories, had experienced very few strikes. This is particularly so since both plants had working conditions that are often felt to be conducive to spontaneous stoppages: both could become extremely hot during the summer, and workers doing often strenuous tasks in such very unpleasant conditions might be expected to stop work now and again. Yet not even brief protest stoppages came to our attention, and neither were there any more general complaints from shop managers or foremen about the problems of operating under difficult working conditions. In the case of the Components Factory this is particularly surprising since, as we saw in Chapter 2, production workers had engaged in a long and successful strike some years previously and since, during our research period, the plant was solidly behind the 1979 national engineering strike.[2] The absence of brief strikes, or 'downers' as they are often known (Clack, 1967: 55), cannot be attributed to the absence of organization. The answer probably lies in the way that shopfloor relations were conducted. The position in the Process Factory is the more straightforward, for we have seen in previous chapters that management had succeeded in creating an atmosphere of trust: management would try to moderate the effects of doing mundane jobs on a continuous shift basis by providing generous fringe benefits and the like, and workers were expected to work to the best of their abilities within this framework. Workers accepted that, while conditions were unpleasant, management could do little to alter them and they thus saw little purpose in striking. There was a similar perspective, although in a somewhat different context, in the Components Factory. As workers in the metals shop, where conditions became particularly unpleasant, said, the general working environment was not as bad as in other similar plants: the comparison was with the foundry and metal-working industry where, as one manager in the shop put it, even a concrete floor was a luxury. Most workers had long periods of service and were used to the conditions and took them for granted. This is not to suggest that they remained tied to their machines regardless of conditions, for in very hot weather managers would turn a blind eye to rather longer rest breaks than were normally accepted. But workers saw no purpose in a strike in the sense of a stoppage with some articulated protest as its basis. And stewards felt that they could gain what they wanted without needing to strike. As one said, conditions were quite good for a foundry and he rarely needed to threaten to impose sanctions: even if sanctions were imposed the chance of a strike was, he felt, remote.

There was in both these plants, then, a feeling of trust and mutual understanding on the shopfloor. The contrast between the Components and the Electrical Factories is revealing here, for the latter plant seemed to be considerably more prone to downers despite the absence of a tradition of collective action and despite a union organization which was comparatively weak. As a rough indication of the difference between the two plants, in research periods of similar length we were able to study four downers in the Electrical Factory in some detail whereas there were none in the Components Factory.[3] All these downers were very short, and they were similar to such stoppages in the factory studied by Clack (1967: 61) '"attention getters" rather than actions to obtain general economic concessions'. Hence the stoppage over the bonus issue, mentioned above, lasted about 40 minutes, while the others were even shorter. In

2. We analyse the details of the organization of this strike within the factory elsewhere: Edwards and Scullion, 1982b.
3. Both factories were affected by the foremen's strike mentioned in Chapter 4 (p. 121). This dispute is not relevant to the discussion of shopfloor downers.

this dispute the protest element was clearly apparent, as it was in the other three downers: there were two protests over cold working conditions and one stoppage over improper managerial action towards a shop steward. While we cannot give a decisive answer to the question of the 'causes' of these downers we may tentatively suggest that they reflect the particular character of shopfloor organization in the factory. When managers were asked about the reasons for their good industrial relations they often turned to the characteristics of the two conveners and particularly of the AUEW convener: they were responsible people who were prepared to negotiate realistically on reasonable demands. There was responsibility at the top but an absence of bargaining awareness on the shopfloor: one index of both these factors was the plant's low level of piecework drift discussed in Chapter 7. Although there was a considerable amount of interpersonal trust between foremen and stewards, relationships were less firmly-established than they were in the Components Factory. Workers felt the need to protest occasionally even though they did not stand to gain directly from a strike. Downers were a minor means of letting off steam.

In the Large and Small Metals Factories strike action was undoubtedly more common than it was in the Electrical Factory. Management records in the Large Metals Factory, which we analyse in more detail below, showed that strikes lasting an hour or more occurred on average 14 or 15 times a year. This understates the plant's comparative strike position, for none of the four downers we encountered in the Electrical Factory would have entered the records and in at least one shop of the factory there was a customary understanding that no dispute would be counted as a stoppage so long as production was 'pulled back'. The position in the Small Metals Factory is less clear but managerial records in the assembly shop, which we examine shortly, suggested that there was an average of two plant-wide stoppages a year together with a larger number of shop-level disputes. While the status of these shop disputes is unclear, since many were very short and did not involve the loss of pay, their presence indicates a 'stoppage-proneness' which was probably higher than that in any of our other plants apart from the Large Metals Factory.

The place of strikes within collective making out strategies was most apparent in the Small Metals Factory. We consider this point in relation to an extremely detailed diary of events which was kept by the manager of the assembly shop; this recorded production figures on a daily basis together with the causes of any reasons why production schedules were not met and details of other notable happenings. From this we have built up a picture of the use of various shopfloor actions over a six-year period, as shown in Table 9.1. We give figures separately for the piecework and day work parts of the period since, as mentioned above, changes in payment systems are often held to be associated with changes in dispute patterns. However, given the centralized control over piecework which had long existed in the factory, we would not necessarily expect the

TABLE 9.1

**SANCTIONS IN THE ASSEMBLY SHOP OF THE SMALL METALS
FACTORY IN TWO THREE—YEAR PERIODS**

	Piecework Period	*Daywork Period*
Number of sanctions[a]	46	36
Number of occasions of loss of output attributed to labour problems	6	31
Number of sanctions by type[b]	53	49
stoppages: health and safety	5	9
wage payment	4	0
wage payout	1	7
canteen facilities	0	7
movement of labour	3	1
plant-wide	7	4
other/D.K.	12	2
all stoppages	32	30
overtime or mobility ban	4	5
output restriction	5	1
shop meeting	6	6
general non-cooperation	0	2
work in	2	1
other/D.K.	4	4
Production as per cent of:		
target	97	97
theoretical maximum[c]	94	91

NOTES
a. Includes all cases of an organized stoppage or refusal to work normally.
b. All types counted once, i.e. an incident involving a strike and an overtime ban is counted twice, hence the difference from the number of separate sanctions.
c. i.e. maximum if all days of lay-off due to external factors had been worked normally..

plant to reveal a change in the nature of strikes, let alone of small workplace actions short of strikes. The table confirms that the picture was similar in the piecework and day work periods, and we return to the question of changing payment systems later.

For the purpose of this analysis we have counted as a sanction any refusal to work 'normally', although, as Table 9.1 shows, the majority involved a stoppage in the sense of a collective refusal to work during a normal working period 'to express a grievance or enforce a demand'. Few of these stoppages would have involved the loss of pay, and many were very short. For example, the stoppages classified as over 'wage payout' revolved around persistent complaints that wages were not being paid out at the proper time. One means of protesting about this was for workers to leave their work stations to queue up in front of the wages office until they received their pay. Rather longer stoppages occurred on other issues. A typical diary entry for a stoppage classified as a health and safety matter, for example, is 'stopped half hour in a.m. due to exhaust fumes from lorries outside'. This involved the loss of about 7 per cent of the day's output but, as the table shows, substantial output losses were rare. If the frequent problems caused by difficulties in supplier and customer plants are excluded the plant achieved 97 per cent of its production target, and the 'missing 3 per cent' was largely the result of relatively large-scale strikes at plant level and not shop-level disputes. Sanctions imposed at shop level were part of the daily negotiation of consent. Stewards had a range of ways in which they could put pressure on management, and stoppages for a few minutes were part of this wider process. They were certainly not designed to inhibit production, for stewards were extremely proud of the plant's record of high production levels. They served to remind management that this production relied on the co-operation of the shopfloor.

This pattern of sanctions can probably be generalized to the assembly shops of the Large Metals Factory: sophisticated controls over the labour process and a strong bargaining awareness gave the shopfloor the ability to hold brief stoppages which maintained pressure on management without developing into full-scale strikes. In other parts of the Large Metals Factory, however, strikes appeared to be less directly related to strategies of control, reflecting instead more general attempts of various groups to assert their autonomy from managerial demands. Consideration of some of these strikes helps to reveal the extreme sectionalism of workplace action here.

One clear example came during the factory's long-running saga concerning early leaving. Two toolroom labourers were caught leaving early and were disciplined, which they felt to be unfair since they had been selected from among a large number of workers who were moving towards the factory exits. They agreed to accept the discipline, however, until they discovered that the toolmakers' stewards had succeeded in challenging the application of discipline against their members by placing the matter in the disputes procedure. The labourers struck for half a day against these 'double standards' of management, but this was a pure protest action with no attempt to have the disciplinary action rescinded. Interestingly in view of our previous discussion, management stopped the men's pay only for the period after they left the plant: a stoppage for 3½ hours was recorded as a strike lasting 2 hours.

Two other examples of the limited nature of downers are worth mentioning. In the first case management wanted to transfer women from a small machine shop into the main shop. The women involved refused to move, claiming that management had in the past accepted that their own small shop was an entity

234 Strikes and Sanctions

on its own and that the means of selecting workers to move was unfair. There was eventually a strike lasting two days. The extremely limited nature of this action was reflected not only in the open hostility of women in the main machine shop to their colleagues' demands but also in the fact that only the members of one of the two unions representing the machine shop joined the strike, with the members of the other union working as normal. The second case occurred in one of the plant's outlying assembly shops when management announced that the whole plant was to be put on what was known as two hours' stand-by: two hours' notice of lay-off in connection with an external dispute. Stewards in the shop argued that they had always operated independently from the rest of the factory because all their work went to another plant. They called a strike, which resulted in the loss of six hours' production and which successfully defended the customary understanding that the shop would not be made part of factory-wide procedures.

It is not a coincidence that all these disputes involved workers outside the main areas of the factory, namely the big assembly shops and the main machine shop. Other examples could readily be cited from the building and transport departments and similar service areas. While strikes certainly took place in the main shops, stoppages here were far less common, when the number of workers employed is taken into account, than they were in the peripheral areas. It was here that workers were most acutely aware of the need to assert their own sectional interests, whereas in the main shops a *modus vivendi* had been worked out with management. The divisions among the work force could not be more apparent: several shops operated as virtually independent units with their own customs and with no more than formal contact with other shops. This sectionalism was, moreover, encouraged by the presence of several different unions, as the case in the machine shop indicates. But more was involved than simply multi-unionism, for unions such as the TGWU represented workers throughout the factory. The key influence was the division of the work force into separate shops which had very little in common.

All this refers, however, to the character of strikes under day work. Since the move away from piecework was felt, in both Company B plants, to have had a profound effect on the conduct of shopfloor relations we must consider whether the pattern of strikes reflected this.

Strike Patterns under Piecework and Measured Day Work
The question of the effect on strikes of changing the payment system is also of more general interest, for it is widely held that such change can be one part of the reform of industrial relations. Early assessments of the move to day work certainly suggested that the climate of industrial relations should improve and that the number of strikes should fall (Office of Manpower Economics, 1973). But subsequent experience has suggested that this judgement was premature:

in the coal and car industries, where day work had been widely employed, there has been no reduction in strike frequency (Clegg, 1979: 147). The expected effects of a change in payment systems are far from obvious. To the extent that MDW reduced the 'disorder' and fragmentation of bargaining which is said to characterize piecework, the number of separate disputes should decline. And, on the theory that fluctuations in earnings contribute to a high strike rate, any tendency for day work to reduce the variability of earnings should have a similar effect. But this may be off-set by the presence of unresolved disputes about grading and about differentials generally when MDW involves an overhaul of the whole payment system (Clegg, 1979: 279–80). A standard view is certainly that strike frequency should decline; but the size and and length of strikes would be expected to increase because the scope of disputes would be wider and because the issues in dispute would be less readily solvable: a strike about a piece price in one shop will be small and easily settled whereas a claim for regrading might raise important issues of principle throughout a factory.

As we have seen, the Small Metals Factory's centralized piecework system does not provide a direct test of the argument about moving to MDW. The Large Metals Factory is a more relevant case, and strike figures for two comparable four-year periods under piecework and day work are given in Table 9.2. There was no tendency for strikes to become any less frequent: the number of strikes in the two periods was virtually the same. There was a slight tendency for stoppages to become longer: for example the number of strikes lasting less than two hours fell from 18 per cent to 9 per cent.[4] Nor did strikes become substantially larger, as the figures for the number of strikers per strike show. There was, however, a shift in the issues in strikes with a switch away from pure wage matters to issues of manning and working conditions. These figures reflect a tendency which we have discussed elsewhere, namely a shift of attention by stewards from the wage to the effort side of the wage-effort bargain. This shift was probably greater than the strike figures imply, for part of our argument in earlier chapters concerned the growing importance of controls over effort. This means that strikes were less relevant as a picture of sanctions as a whole, a view which was shared by at least some stewards: one in particular argued that his union organization in the plant had learned to do without strikes whereas in the past they had often had disputes which had served little purpose.

Two disputes illustrate the pattern under daywork. The first was about

---

4. Since strikes lasting less than an hour are excluded from the figures it is possible that this underestimates the shift to longer strikes: proportionately more strikes under the piecework period would not enter the statistics. But the kind of dispute which is not counted is likely to be the very short protest, of which we have cited examples during the day work period. The underestimation is thus unlikely to be very great.

TABLE 9.2

LARGE METALS FACTORY: STRIKES IN TWO FOUR-YEAR PERIODS

	Piecework Period	Daywork Period
Number of strikes	59	55
Per cent of strikes lasting[a]		
1—2 hours	18	9
2—4 hours	20	20
4—6 hours	13	11
6—10 hours	11	20
10—20 hours	25	11
over 20 hours	14	27
Per cent of strikes over		
wages	39	13
manning and conditions	22	47
management rights	9	13
other	31	27
Number of workers per strike[b]	252[c]	189

SOURCE: Management files.
NOTES:
a. Stoppages lasting less than an hour were not, formally speaking, recorded as strikes. One strike of less than an hour was in the records of the daywork period which is why the figures for that period do not sum to 100 per cent. The number of stoppages of less than an hour which escaped inclusion in the figures cannot be estimated.
b. Number directly involved only (i.e. excludes those laid off as a result of strikes).
c. Excluding two protest strikes against the 1971 Industrial Relations Act.

grading and involved a group of skilled production workers who had been told, through a carefully-contrived leak of information from supposedly confidential negotiations at company level, that they were placed in the same grade as semi-skilled workers. A protest stoppage of a day plainly helped the stewards to convince management of the depth of shopfloor feeling on the issue. The second strike was by toolsetters. It was ostensibly over training new recruits, but it also involved grading questions. The setters were worried that their job description would place them in a low grade and they banned training not because they objected to it but because, as they put it, they wanted to know where they were in the grading structure before taking on more training. Management lived with the situation for a while but, with increasing shortages of setters, they insisted on bringing in trainees, at which the setters struck for two days. As managers had been aware, this was little more than a protest gesture since the men lacked the backing of their conveners, who insisted that an existing agreement concerning training be adhered to, and since company managers were unlikely to risk establishing a precedent in the grading negotiations by granting the workers' claims.

This kind of dispute seems to have replaced sectional disputes on piecework prices. Despite this shift in the issues in dispute and despite a general change in the character of shopfloor bargaining, the move to MDW had no dramatic effect on the frequency of strikes. Since the factory was operating under a converted piecework system and since it retained strong elements of a 'piecework mentality', this is far from surprising. But it demonstrates, if demonstration be needed, that moving to day work has no automatic consequences for strikes. For any effect to have been noticeable, a far more thorough 'reform' of industrial relations would have been required. Simply changing the payment system is unlikely to make management's 'strike problem' disappear.

Conclusions

The two Company B plants appeared to be more 'strike-prone', or, to be more exact, more 'stoppage-prone' than our other factories.[5] The Electrical Factory experienced a number of small downers, while our other plants appeared to be remarkably strike-free. Parts of this pattern, most obviously the lack of strikes in the clothing plants and the use of stoppages as an aspect of collective effort controls in the Small Metals Factory and parts of the Large Metals Factory, reflect differences in patterns of control. But to explain other features of strikes, notably the difference between the Electrical and Components Factories and the use of protest actions in parts of the Large Metals Factory, requires attention to more specific aspects of workplace relations. This is far from surprising. Individual strikes occur for an enormous range of reasons and it is unlikely that the pattern which emerges from them will be explicable in terms of broad background influences. As explained elsewhere (P. Edwards, 1981), even when survey data from large numbers of plants are employed the amount of variation in strike frequency which can be explained in terms of structural conditions is small. This limitation applies even more strongly when features of strikes other than their number are the focus. We have been able, nonetheless, to provide some explanation of why downers were more prominent in some settings than others. Their protest role was a particularly important common feature, although the precise nature of the protest varied according to workplace conditions. Since the protest was often directed at managerial decisions the question arises of whether managements followed a particular strategy in disputes.

5. Comparisons with other plants are difficult given differences in strike figures and definitions. Only the Large Metals Factory can be compared with other plants, and that no more than approximately. Its average of 14 strikes a year would certainly have placed it in the top 2 per cent or so of plants in the whole country, if survey data are any guide (William Brown, 1981: 82). But it was less strike-prone than the similarly-sized plant studied by Batstone et al. (1978: 34) which had an average of 24 strikes a year in the early 1970s.

Management Strategy in Strikes

Most of our managements did not have a strategy in the sense of an articulated policy of, for example, fomenting strikes to deal with problems of over-production or taking a hard line in negotiations in order to regain control of the labour process. Apart from our engineering companies the possibility of strikes was too remote for any specific strategy to be required. In Company A there was certainly a stock of broad strategic considerations which could be used if a strike seemed likely. During the annual wage negotiations, for example, it was always possible that the stewards would reject an offer and call for strike action, and the company plainly took account of this. There were also, for example, attempts by managers in the Electrical Factory to discourage strikes which occurred outside the disputes procedure. But there is little in this which is relevant to our wider concerns.

This is certainly not to deny the importance of strategic decisions by Company A management. In the following section and in the final chapter we try to take account of some of those decisions in discussing the changing nature of shopfloor relationships. But we cannot say anything systematic about this strategy in so far as it related to strikes in particular. In Company B, however, there was a clearer general policy on strikes, and this could be related in turn to the company's wider strategic aims of challenging shopfloor controls. In this section we try to explain the broad features of this policy.

The Small Metals Factory

In both plants senior personnel managers had been introduced with the explicit task of placing industrial relations on a more 'rational' basis. The Small Metals Factory provides an interesting illustration, in a lengthy and often acrimonious dispute between management and the unions, of the nature and weaknesses of managerial strategy. We therefore begin by looking at this dispute in some detail.

It is easy to assume that managements have a clearly-articulated strategy in which aims, and the means for attaining them, are explicit. Such an assumption is encouraged by the recent upsurge of studies stressing that such things as productivity bargaining and the formalization of procedures are means for management to maintain or regain control. While we do not deny the general importance of these studies, we argue that strategy is often more complex than they allow and, in particular, that a distinct policy for the prosecution of a dispute with the shopfloor cannot be read off from a wider aim of regaining control. In the Small Metals Factory there was certainly a coherent managerial aim; to distinguish this from more specific strategic concerns we call it management's change philosophy. The senior management team, comprising the plant manager, the production manager, and the personnel manager, shared a common view that it was essential to shake the plant out of its old ways. They argued that, with the run-down of some of the plant's main jobs, it was essential to attract new work, and that the only way to do this was to be seen to be operating efficiently. Unions must not be allowed to play their old game of dragging their feet whenever a change in working practices was proposed and of withdrawing co-operation whenever it suited them. They must, managers claimed, be tied to formal written agreements that specified managerial rights. Managers stressed that they were not trying to undermine the legitimate negotiating role of the shop stewards, arguing that they were merely trying to secure the future of the plant, which was in everyone's interests, and to commit the unions to specific agreements that would prevent delay and prevarication.

The broad change philosophy dominated management's handling of the dispute but it did not carry with it a distinct dispute strategy, that is a set of considerations which determine whether a dispute will be created over a specific issue. Managers clung to their aim of 'rationalizing' industrial relations and responded to each event in the dispute in a consistent way. But they did not foment the dispute or try to exploit it by pushing the unions into a strike. The stewards, however, placed a different interpretation on events. As we have seen in previous chapters, the plant was dominated by the tradition that stewards had a right to close involvement in the planning of production and that co-operation with management could be given or withdrawn at will. The stewards had an intense antipathy to written agreements and a strong commitment to customary ways of doing things. They saw managerial actions throughout the dispute as part of an organized campaign to push them into a fight or even into a strike. The dispute was dominated by this clash of logics, with managers responding to each event in terms of the change philosophy and with stewards interpreting such responses as part of a machiavellian scheme to create a confrontation.

The dispute itself was long and confused and we will not discuss all its twists and turns. The main outline can be given from three aspects. First, the issue which began the dispute was not deliberately engineered by management, although the view that it had been so engineered dominated the stewards' thinking. A worker was 'taken off the clock' for refusing a managerial instruction to move to another job. For the stewards, this was a highly provocative action for, as we saw in Chapter 8, all mobility was normally subject to agreement. The stewards also felt that there must have been some purpose behind the action, and the only rationale that they could place on it was that managers were trying to undermine established practice. There was, however, no considered managerial policy, as was illustrated most clearly by the sharp criticism that the personnel manager made of the decision: the proper procedure for taking workers off the clock had not been followed, and the action made more difficult the task of persuading stewards to stick to the procedure. Rather than back down, however, senior managers decided to take a firm line, arguing that the original instruction to move jobs had been entirely proper and that if stewards wanted to complain about the subsequent stopping of the worker's pay there was a procedure for doing so. Managers, in other words, stuck to their broad aim of rationalizing relationships. Hence throughout the dispute they continued to take workers off the clock for refusing 'reasonable' managerial instructions. Stewards naturally saw such actions as part of an attempt to escalate the dispute, particularly since they sometimes occurred when a settlement seemed in sight. Managers, however, distinguished between the particular matters in dispute and their general need to have instructions followed, thus justifying taking workers off the clock in terms of the need to remove barriers to efficiency: the stewards were refusing to negotiate, and management could not afford to let matters drift.

The second aspect concerned shop steward rights more directly. The increasingly frequent meetings of the various stewards' committees were taking stewards away from their shops for longer than was usual. Management became worried about the effect on production, particularly in the inspection department, where the original 'off the clock' incident had occurred, for here workers had imposed a ban on mobility as a protest. This meant that the absence of the steward, which was normally covered by flexibility among the rest of the section, was causing bottle-necks in production. Managers therefore decided to stop the pay of the inspectors' steward for any time that he was absent from his section without his foreman's permission. The stewards saw this as straightforward victimization. As the convener of the ex-craft union said at the next stewards' meeting, regular meetings had been held for as long as he could remember, and management was attacking the rights of the whole union organization in the plant. To express their concern, the whole union committee left the plant and invited management to stop their pay. The walk-out lasted half an hour but, as noted in the discussion of the definition of strikes, management did not stop the stewards' pay. Although managers were presented with a perfect opportunity to foment a strike they were not engaged in a campaign to push the unions into a confrontation. Pragmatic considerations were more important, and managers made no response to the stewards' walk-out. The relevance of their change philosophy was, however, again apparent. The action of stopping the steward's pay reflected two aspects of the philosophy. First, the existing custom, that stewards could leave their sections without their foreman's approval, was challenged, with managers demanding that a proper procedure be agreed and followed. Second, the needs of production had to be made paramount, and stewards could not, managers argued, ignore these needs. The stewards had been warned of the consequences if their own actions created problems, and they must bear the responsibility.

The third feature of the dispute was the way in which each side imposed sanctions on the other. Although the dispute became very bitter both sides tried to avoid escalating it into a strike or lock-out. The stewards had always been cautious of 'going up the road' in a dispute with management, preferring instead to deploy a range of weapons based on their impressive control over the labour process; the weapons which they chose in this particular dispute will be discussed shortly. And in this particular case the stewards' reading of management's intentions was that managers were trying to create a strike, and the stewards were careful to avoid falling into this trap. On one occasion, for example, the absence of the inspectors' steward led to the exhaustion of the supply of components to the assembly shop, and the whole shop was stopped pay for an hour and a half. The chief steward of the shop argued persuasively against staging an immediate walk-out, for this would simply be to play into management's hands. For their part, managers were concerned about the effect that a strike would have on the plant's reputation with company management. They were thoroughly concerned about the difficulty of attracting new work and therefore preferred to try to settle matters without involving higher management.

The dispute was thus delicately-balanced, with each side suspecting the motives of the other but being unwilling to risk an escalation of the conflict. However, the determination of management to impose its own definition of rationality, and the equal determination of the stewards to defend custom and practice, made a solution difficult and the escalation of sanctions more likely, even though this was a course desired by neither side. The push was provided by an announcement by management that overtime levels were to be sharply reduced. As we saw in Chapter 8, the 'overtime buffer' was an established part of the plant's operations, and even in 'normal times' a cut-back would have met considerable opposition. In the current climate of distrust the stewards saw it as another attempt to put pressure on them. Managers, however, explained their action, to us as well as to the stewards, as an entirely rational response to external pressures: the company as a whole was going through an exercise in which production levels and labour inputs were being closely monitored, and it was essential to operate within targets if the future of the plant was to be safeguarded.

In rejecting this argument the stewards made two responses. First, arguing that they could play the same game as management, they banned all overtime. Second, they decided that their previous policy, of avoiding sanctions that directly threatened production and that thus might give management an excuse to escalate the dispute, was no longer sufficient. A total ban on mobility was considered, but rejected because of the danger of its back-firing in the form of widespread lay-offs. The most effective way of disrupting production while minimizing costs for the shopfloor was to 'work to the hour'. This meant a rigid adherence to the production targets established under the measured day work system, with the briefest hold-up in the flow of work leading workers to drop the appropriate amount of product. The policy was thus a form of work to rule, but it gained its real significance from the overall structure of control. Working to the hour meant the withdrawal of all the normal co-operation that workers gave to management; just as workers in the Large Metals Factory withdrew co-operation when they were in dispute over early leaving (see Chapter 5), so workers here began to look for ways to disrupt production. And, again like the Large Metals Factory, stewards could be confident that their policy would be pursued by the rank and file without their having actively to organize an overt campaign. Once the policy was announced workers knew what to do. Hence we found that working to the hour was the rule throughout the factory, even though it required workers to spin their work out throughout the day and thus removed the benefits of finishing early. While the overall effect is hard to measure, production records in the assembly shop indicated that the impact was substantial, with output being as much as 20 per cent below target levels.

How did management respond? One possibility was to threaten a lock-out if the sanctions were not lifted. Managers were still worried, however, about the effect of a lengthy confrontation on the plant's reputation, not least because several other factories relied on components that it produced. They therefore took a cautious approach. Their first counter to the stewards' sanctions was to argue that overtime was a 'semi-contractual' obligation and not voluntary; they consequently began to stop pay whenever there was a loss of production which could be attributed to the effects of the overtime ban. The second, and more important, development was the result of events elsewhere in the company. The factory's main customer plant became involved in a large and potentially very serious strike. Plant managers warned the stewards of the danger that their own factory's prospects looked bleak if the strike was prolonged, a warning which the stewards hardly needed, for they had feared for some time that management would use the strike as an excuse to institute a lock-out. The stewards therefore decided to relax their sanctions. By this time the domestic dispute had dragged on for over two months with little prospect of resolution and with the issues involved becoming increasingly confused; the series of off the clock incidents, the stopping of pay in the assembly shop, the alleged victimization of the inspectors' steward, and the stopping of pay over the overtime ban, together with several secondary issues, had become hopelessly tangled and the original issues had become lost. Both sides seem to have become tired of the argument and, after a series of largely symbolic meetings, the dispute fizzled out, with a few minor concessions being made but with the major issues unresolved.

What general lessons may be drawn from this complex series of events? First, we have seen how the stewards could draw on their battery of controls over the labour process to impose sanctions on management, but also how the use of the sanctions was varied to meet tactical considerations. Related to this was the high level of cohesion of the shopfloor organization, which meant that the stewards did not have to worry about mobilizing support or the danger of being undermined by a lack of rank and file support. Second, management also had a wide range of sanctions at their disposal. Strikes and sanctions are often discussed as though it is only unions which upset relationships by refusing to work normally, but here managers deployed a range of devices including stopping the pay of workers who refused instructions (even though such instructions were contrary to accepted practice and thus went against the notion of the *status quo*), cutting overtime requirements, reacting to an overtime ban by stopping pay, and making several explicit threats about what would happen to the future of the plant in the absence of co-operation from the shopfloor. Third, we have been able to identify different levels of management strategy. The general aim of rationalizing industrial relations dominated management's reactions to the various events of the dispute. For example, if a worker refused a 'reasonable' request and if the stewards refused to negotiate on the matter management's only course was to take him off the clock; otherwise, it was felt, managers would be acquiescing in old and out-worn traditions which enabled the stewards to tie them hand and foot. But the change philosophy did not lead to a dispute strategy in the sense of a plan to create a confrontation. It encouraged management to read the stewards' actions in a particular way: managers literally could not understand that the stewards had any real worries, feeling that the stewards were exploiting the dispute to create delay on matters such as the introduction of new working arrangements and that such tactics were against the best interests of the plant as a whole. But the course of the dispute was determined by the clash of logics between the two sides and by tactical concerns to avoid a strike, not by a deliberate managerial policy.

Finally, the dispute has one more general implication. Management's change philosophy failed, in that the stewards were able to resist its introduction. Part of this was the result of the considerable resistance power of the stewards, based on substantial and long-established controls over the labour process. But part was the direct result of the weakness of management's approach. Managers had a clear aim, but in trying to move towards it all at once they set off a chain of events which moved them further away from their goal. Had they been able to concentrate on, say, a procedure for stewards to attend meetings they might have had some success. But, in responding to every event with the firm line that change was essential and that any compromise would endanger the whole enterprise, managers created a situation in which their goal could not be attained. This is not to say, however, that management's defeat was inevitable. The key weakness in management's position was that an attempt was made to introduce change without there being a dispute strategy to back up the attempt, which meant that managers were caught between the stewards' power within the plant and their desire not to upset their own relationships with higher management. In other circumstances different outcomes are possible. Thus, soon after our main research period a whole package of measures was introduced by the company; this included such long-cherished goals of Small Metals Factory management as mobility between grades and the general assertion of managerial rights over the planning of production and the allocation of labour. We are not in a position to assess the success of the package, but even at the time of our research stewards were aware of the company-wide nature of the attack and of their limited ability to resist with plant-based weapons. We consider this issue in detail in the final chapter, but its present significance is to place the dispute in context: managers are not always unable to introduce change, and the ability of the stewards to fend off an attack which was limited to the one plant and which was not prosecuted as vigorously as it might have been should not be read as a universal rule.

The Large Metals Factory
In the Large Metals Factory, too, there was managerial concern about the stewards' power, although the emphasis was rather different. The concern here was less with challenging existing working practices directly than with formulating a policy on strikes in particular. As the personnel manager put it, in the past management had allowed disputes to 'fester' indefinitely as, say, a failure to agree at the final domestic stage of the disputes procedure. He was now taking a more active policy in order to resolve issues one way or the other. This would show stewards that they could not lightly take up any matter and register a failure to agree, for they faced the danger of being taken on by management. In the past stewards could protest against any change, knowing that they were risking little, but now they could find themselves in a strike or face the alternative of retreating and thus losing credibility. This new managerial policy was meeting with considerable success, as several examples show.

In one case, which the personnel manager saw as potentially one of the most important ever to occur in the company, the plant's machine tool fitters refused to accept as a foreman an MTF who was supervising maintenance fitters because they did not recognize his craft qualifications. While this argument was a reflection of the extreme exclusiveness of the MTFs which we discussed in Chapter 8, it also raised other problems for management. The most severe of these was whether management had the absolute right of appointment of supervisors. It was therefore decided to proceed with the appointment of the foreman. Management were aware, however, of the danger of a long and costly strike: attitudes had hardened, and the union's district committee had agreed to make the dispute official. They therefore proceeded cautiously by trying to contain the issue within the plant and, in particular, by agreeing to take the unusual step of calling in an independent mediator. The strike was limited to a stoppage of three days, and the result of the mediation was broadly satisfactory to management.

The stewards who were involved in the dispute had an interesting view of management's strategy. First, they felt that there was a direct attempt to force a strike, for could not management have agreed to mediation before the strike began? As management pointed out, however, agreeing to mediation after the strike had started was very different from doing so in advance. By taking the strike management had forced stewards to follow through the consequences of their position; it was only by making stewards aware that they could not win the strike easily that they accepted mediation as a way of 'getting off the hook'. Second, stewards felt that there was a deliberate managerial strategy in another respect, namely a policy of attacking craft rights. They drew this conclusion from the occurrence at virtually the same time of a very similar dispute about the appointment of a non-craftsman over a craft area. That there was no such simple managerial strategy was confirmed by several factors. Not only did managers deny that a deliberate policy was being followed, but their actions revealed the lack of premeditation. Thus the MTF stewards were allowed to enter their grievance in the disputes procedure even though the core of management's argument became that management had the absolute right to select supervisors, in which case the matter could not properly be processed through the procedure. That the two cases entered the bargaining arena at the same time was a matter of chance. They represented separate decision-making processes of which the personnel department would not have been aware. Once they had become issues in dispute, however, a conscious strategy was applied. This was to deal with the matter firmly, while being aware of the risks of a severe strike and acting to minimize these risks.

In another case the plant's electricians claimed that the complex production control equipment which they had been installing in Assembly Shop X should, because of its complexity, be operated by them and not by the semi-skilled progress chasers who controlled similar equipment in the rest of the factory. Management had no particular interest in who did the work, but, since neither side had shown any inclination for compromise, 'we had to have a dispute with someone', as the personnel manager put it. Managers were again willing to act to resolve the problem, although a strike by the group which had not been given the work, the electricians, was the inevitable result. In this case, again, such managerial action was successful, since after a brief strike the electricians reluctantly accepted management's ruling. The strike also illustrates, however, the possible dangers of management's strategy: the electricians' stewards admitted that they had followed a faulty strategy in committing themselves to a strike that they could not win. In a similar dispute in the future, they said, they would seek ways of frustrating management short of a strike. Management's policy of bringing disputes to a head might not be so successful in future.

Other examples of managerial action illustrate the careful planning of strike policy. As the plant manager explained management could be as 'opportunist' as the unions, and there was nothing wrong in this since both sides were playing the same game. In the toolsetters' strike in the machine shop mentioned above, for instance, the personnel department was closely involved with shop management in planning when to insist that training be carried out and in monitoring the opinions of the setters' conveners. When the conveners' opposition to the setters' claims had been established and when shop managers had ensured that a strike would not lead to an immediate shortage of a key component, the decision was taken to trigger the strike.

Yet this case also points to certain weaknesses in the managerial strategy. Machine shop managers complained here, and also in relation to the dispute over mobility between machine shops, that the personnel department was out of touch with shopfloor realities and that it clung too rigidly to procedure: both matters could have been sorted out more quickly and with less bitterness had the shop been left to itself. Such resentment is interesting in itself in revealing yet again divisions within management in the factory: shop managers wanted to stick to traditional ways of doing things and saw the wider strategic concerns of higher management as obstacles in their pursuit of production. In similar vein the personnel officers, who had been introduced to assist the personnel manager by dealing with day-to-day industrial relations matters, complained that it had taken them a long time to break down the suspicions of shop managers that they were attempting to usurp shop management's functions. More importantly, however, the managerial strategy was limited by being directed specifically at significant disputes which had entered procedure. It was not a consciously articulated aspect of a wider strategy of regaining control over effort levels and the like but was a narrowly 'industrial relations' policy. It may have worked in challenging the power of conveners to put into dispute virtually any disagreement with management but it did not directly contribute to the managerial aim of efficient production.

While it is dangerous to speculate on the reasons for the difference from the Small Metals Factory in this respect, two possible influences can be suggested. First, the sheer size of the Large Metals Factory made it difficult for a thorough-going managerial strategy of regaining control to be imposed on shop managements which were sceptical of such a policy. In the Small Metals Factory the aims of the plant manager and the personnel manager could be impressed on the rest of management relatively speedily. Second, several of the Large Metals Factories' products were in urgent demand in the rest of the company. As we saw in Chapter 7 this had a profound effect on the conduct of manning negotiations and it was plainly a constraint on a policy of straightforward confrontation with the shopfloor. In the Small Metals Factory these pressures were much less intense and, as we have seen, managers felt that the plant's only realistic hope of survival lay in being able to compete effectively for new orders, and this involved shifting the plant out of its traditionalist ways.

Conclusions

In both plants, then, there was explicit managerial concern with the problems of shopfloor power, and this concern lay behind the strategy that was adopted in disputes. It did not, however, directly determine the strategy. Managers did not have a simple policy of attacking shopfloor controls at every opportunity but had the more general aim of creating order and of having procedures followed. It is easy to see how stewards saw management's policy as an unveiled attack on their own position and on custom and practice, and in an important sense they were right. Just as shopfloor actions which challenge managerial control need not be part of an articulated policy of shifting the frontier of control, so we should not expect management's actions to be based on a fully-developed ideology. Managers trying to bring order and rationality to industrial relations were effectively challenging shopfloor controls even though these managers were not straightforwardly 'anti-union' and even though their actions were not defined in terms of the struggle for control. In the terms introduced in Chapter 1, management's handling of overt conflict cannot be read off from a general interest in control; in particular, dispute strategies may be vague, rudimentary, or contradictory. But, by examining the logic of management's situation and relating it to the context of the particular struggle for control (most importantly the shopfloor constraints on managerial action), managerial strategy can be located in the broader pattern of control.

The problem of 'shopfloor power' which faced Company B management was, as we have seen, limited in that it was restricted to the level of the individual plant. In Company A, by contrast, the challenge had been broadened to cover several plants; the difficulties which this created for management are considered in the following section.

Sanctions and Company-Level Organization

If counting the number of strikes in a factory is difficult, trying to establish how many cases there were of the application of sanctions is impossible. As argued in previous chapters a central characteristic of the Company B plants was the conditional nature of shopfloor co-operation with management, and to try to count the number of times this co-operation was withdrawn or modified would plainly be fruitless. It is possible, however, to give a rough idea of the use of more formal sanctions such as an overtime ban in the pursuit of a particular claim or a ban on mobility on jobs throughout a shop or grade.

This kind of action was, of course, unknown in the clothing factories, and it was also rare among production workers in the Process Factory and the Company A plants. As we have already seen a ban on mobility could be a powerful sanction in the Company B plants. But perhaps the most important feature of the pattern of sanctions was their sophisticated use by craft workers in Company A. As noted in Chapter 2, the various bargaining groups of craft workers operated at company level. The electricians' group, for example, was more important to electricians in our plants than was the body of stewards from various unions within the plant. Policy was made at group level, and the factory organization of each group were expected to follow group decisions. A refusal could lead to expulsion from the group, a fate which befell toolmakers in the Electrical Factory during our research period and which had also occurred within other groups elsewhere in the company. Apart from losing any influence over the group's pay bargaining with the company, an expelled organization could also be subject to sanctions such as the blacking of its work by other parts of the group. The trade groups were well-organized and were firmly disciplined, and as a result they could deploy a range of sanctions at company level. Their ability to do this was much greater than the ability of steward organizations elsewhere in our factories to operate above plant level.

An example of the power of trade group sanctions occurred when we were in the Components Factory. The case reveals the ability of a group to pursue a local plant-level matter through company-level action. In view of general economic difficulties it was management policy not to replace anyone who left, and the non-replacement of an electrician who had been sacked meant that electricians felt that they were undermanned. They therefore banned the work which they customarily did outside their own shops, which was mainly for the toolroom and the transport department. Factory managers said that there was nothing they could do on their own initiative to resolve the problem. The decision not to recruit was a company matter, so they could not agree to the workers' demands. Neither could they try to force a resolution of the issue by, for example, instructing an electrician to work in the blacked areas. As the electricians' steward pointed out, the company had learned through experience that the group would stick by its policy of 'one out, all out': if management took anyone off the clock for refusing to do the blacked work electricians throughout the company would cease work. This was well understood by local management who could do nothing but await a solution at company level, which eventually came as part of a package deal in the annual wage negotiations.

The company's electricians also illustrate a second use of group sanctions, namely their role in support of a campaign for 'general economic concessions'. Like many craftsmen they were worried about their differential over production workers, and the group began to press for extra pay for the exercise of additional skills on the new and complex electronics equipment which the company was introducing in several plants. This was backed up at one point with a ban on all work which was defined as electronics. The outcome was a bonus, worth £5 a week in 1979, for any electrician deemed capable of handling electronics. This reflected and reinforced group solidarity, not least because the agreement incorporated a procedure for assessing qualifications for the bonus in which the electricians' group played an important role.

This example reveals what company industrial relations managers saw as an important problem with group bargaining: the development of leap-frogging claims by the various groups. In this case the toolmakers' group demanded that all its members should be paid an equivalent bonus. And the electricians' claim had itself been stimulated by the recent success of the toolsetters' group in obtaining an increase of £2 a week in recognition of the task of training new toolsetters. This increase had been won in a campaign which had involved a highly effective overtime ban.

We will return to the significance of such actions within the company. But it will be useful first to compare the position with that in Company B, for the Company A toolsetters had achieved a successful outcome in a dispute about training new setters while, as we saw earlier, their counterparts in the Large Metals Factory had staged an unsuccessful strike on the same issue. This raises two questions: how had company-level bargaining in trade groups been achieved, and why was it successful? The answer to the first question is that it had developed without conscious design. It was based on the organization of the toolmakers' group, which occurred over twenty years before our research and on which we cannot comment in detail. Once the company had agreed to recognize the toolmakers' group it was apparently willing to follow this precedent by recognizing a succession of other groups. Present company managers were clear, however, that they would have preferred a unified set of negotiations instead of an apparently unending succession of claims from one group or another. The groups' success in organizing at company level probably owes a great deal to the geographical concentration of the plants which they covered and to the absence of any well-developed plant bargaining prior to their establishment. It was relatively easy to bring group members together, and there were no strong plant traditions to defend. Craft workers in Company B had, by contrast, a heavy burden of plant loyalties and, indeed, sectional loyalties within plants. The company, moreover, had its own views on bargaining structure and was plainly unwilling to recognize separate trade groups.

The problems of company-level organization in Company B were dramatically illustrated by an attempt by craft workers to establish such an organization, which we have called the Combine Craft Committee (CCC). By considering the particular case of toolmakers we have seen in previous chapters that there was deep and widespread discontent among craftsmen about their decline in the wages league and the company's lack of concern with their interests. This broad feeling was common among all craftsmen, and the CCC was an attempt to bring together at company level the previously fragmented organizations of tool-makers, electricians, pattern-makers, and other trades. In view of the company's clear attitude on bargaining arrangements it was decided at a meeting of the CCC to call a strike on negotiating rights and other demands. The obstacles facing stewards in the Large Metals Factory[6] in mobilizing support for the strike were considerable. They themselves had opposed the strike call, feeling that it was premature. There was a long tradition of the autonomy of individual trades to be broken down. And management and union officials were strongly opposed to the CCC, the former on the grounds that it challenged existing bargaining relationships and that a strike was bound to damage the company, and the latter because the CCC was an unofficial body. Despite all this, craftsmen were so embittered at what they saw as a series of broken promises, for which they held their unions as well as the company to blame, that they felt that some action on their own behalf was their only hope. All the craftsmen in the plant were brought together and they voted to support the strike. Such joint action for the first time in the plant's history was a considerable achievement in itself.

Even at this stage there was, however, pessimism among the stewards, since management was plainly willing to take a long strike and since support from other plants was patchy. These doubts were reinforced on the first day of the strike when a group of electricians reported for work. By the third day about a dozen electricians, out of a total of just over 200, were at work. This may not have been of any great significance in itself, but it symbolized the split in the ranks which had always been feared. In addition, management were able to keep the plant running: although foremen in the toolroom refused to 'blackleg', managers in other areas carried out essential maintenance work with at least the tacit agreement of production workers' stewards. The contrast with Company A is remarkable, for here management was very careful not to antagonize the trade groups: managers would not have allowed a small group to work, and they would not have tried to carry out the strikers' work for fear of having the work blacked when the strike was over. Given the trade groups' established position it was possible to play on these fears. But the CCC was not recognized and management were prepared to take it on in a way that would have been unthinkable for Company A management.

In view of management's reaction and of existing doubts about the strike, pressure grew among electricians in the plant for a separate meeting to decide whether to continue with the strike. A decision to return to work was eventually taken without reference to the rest of the CCC. This marked the effective end of the strike, and the remaining craftsmen returned soon afterwards.

6. There were very few craftsmen in the Small Metals Factory. They were members of the ex-craft union in the plant and had no contact with the CCC.

The action of the electricians had plainly destroyed the unity which had been built up before the dispute. This problem of forging solidarity was the main 'internal' reason for the weakness of the CCC. In addition the 'external' factor of opposition from management prevented the organization from making any progress. Two lessons may be drawn from this. First, of course, there is the difficulty of changing bargaining arrangements in the face of determined managerial opposition. Second, the strike was unusual because it attempted to alter the generally-accepted pattern of sectional bargaining. Plants had no tradition of working together, and even within plants there were considerable suspicions between different groups, as the action of the electricians shows and as the presence of carefully-defended demarcation lines illustrates more generally.

One more specific result of the strike must be indicated: there was a dramatic effect on 'morale'. As we have already seen, discontent and apathy were widespread in the toolroom before the strike, and the collapse of an attempt to right a whole series of wrongs reinforced this feeling. For example, several toolmakers quit during or immediately after the strike. But at least in the past toolmakers had maintained their traditions as a collective and well-disciplined body. Collective organization now began to fall apart. Thus on a domestic issue the stewards failed to obtain support from the shopfloor, which was itself very unusual given the shop's traditions. The stewards resigned, and no one was prepared to replace them. To take another example, part of the shop's craft tradition demanded that anyone recruited as a toolmaker must have a 'grade 1' union card. This had been a firm tradition for many years, and it had obvious links with wider traditions of resisting the employment of 'dilutees' on craft jobs. But there was very little response when management, in an attempt to deal with growing labour shortages, introduced workers without the grade 1 card. Management were able to push the frontier of control in their own favour with surprisingly little resistance, an action which would have been unthinkable even a year earlier. A once proud and well-disciplined shop had altered beyond recognition.

We have so far contrasted the weaknesses of company-level organizations in Company B with their strength in Company A. But even in the latter company they were not as powerful as might appear. At the most general level, of course, the trade groups were an expression of the fragmentation of the work force. Mutual jealousies, and often overt hostility, were undisguised. Now it might be argued that this did not matter since, as noted at the end of the previous chapter, a limited solidarity is better than none at all and since concrete gains were being made. But there were specific disadvantages. For example, a campaign was being organized to found a joint stewards' body to bargain with management over pensions, holidays, sick pay, and lay-off pay. The coolness of the trade groups towards this new body greatly reduced its chances of negotiating improved conditions in these areas. And the existence of separate trade groups reduced the possibility of a united front on joint issues. Toolmakers and electricians may have been able to resist the company's attempt to reduce manning levels through a policy of natural wastage (see above, p. 211), but such successful resistance was not generalized to the work force as a whole. Management certainly disliked the competitive claims of the various groups, but it was possible to grant some concessions to one group without this becoming a precedent.

Two other aspects of fragmentation further reduced the groups' power. First, while expulsions from a group could be a useful means of maintaining solidarity the penalties of expulsion were not always large. Toolmakers in the Electrical factory, for example, continued to have the same terms and conditions as other toolmakers even after expulsion, and, although any tooling work for the factory should have been blacked by other toolmakers, workers in the company's main toolroom did not bother to carry out this policy. This failure was strongly criticized by toolroom stewards in the Components Factory, but there was little that they could do about it. Second, the trade groups were restricted to the plants of the one operating company which we have called Company A. But this was part of a conglomerate whose interests spread far wider than the small industrial and geographical base of Company A. Expansion into new markets together with a series of take-overs meant that Company A was far less central to the firm as a whole than it had been when the trade groups were established. Their power in relation to company policy in general, be it expansion of a subsidiary in South Africa, the run-down of a factory in the north-east of England, or the channelling of investment into new products and away from the older technologies employed in Company A itself, was very slight.

Thus, while the trade groups had considerable power within Company A even this power was not so great as might at first appear. And, in the context of the firm as a whole, Company A was of declining importance, which may be one reason why management was willing to live with the system of separate groups. Despite all this, however, the ability to organize sanctions successfully on a multi-plant basis marked the trade groups off from all our other steward organizations. As the contrast with Company B shows, historical factors and managerial recognition of the groups were key influences: the powerful forces inhibiting the creation of multi-plant unity in Company B proved insurmountable.

The Significance of Strikes

That the 'problem of strikes' has long been a central aspect of discussions of British industrial relations requires no detailed justification here (see Hyman, 1972). The simplest way of putting our findings in context is to point out that we have devoted only part of one chapter to strikes. And we have pointed out, in similar vein to many other writers, that many stoppages are extremely short, that their effects on production are often minimal, and that they involve a brief protest against managerial actions and not an attempt to make 'unreasonable' gains through the use of force. This leads us to consider the general role of strikes in our factories.

A central but neglected point is that workers and managers do not spend their time contemplating the details of strike action. We have seen that workers in the Large Metals Factory felt that their last strike had been in the distant past even though the plant had been the scene of some significant disputes in recent years, such as the strike of the CCC and the disputes over the appointment of foremen in craft areas. This can be explained by the fact that the great majority of workers had no interest in the matter in dispute and no say in what happened. A strike by toolsetters or building department workers could well go completely unnoticed in the assembly shops. Even when workers are laid off as a result of a strike they are by no means certain to see themselves as 'involved' in it or to take a close interest in its conduct. The clearest example of this occurred in the Electrical Factory, where our research took place some six months after a long strike by toolmakers which had resulted in a lay-off lasting several weeks for all the production workers. Many women workers were not even sure who had been on strike or what the issue had been. 'Real' strikes are events in which workers themselves 'go up the road' for some time: as we were often told by foremen and workers, a section might have the occasional brief stoppage but no real strikes.

This is not to deny that workers held general opinions about strikes. We spent some time observing and speaking to women in one section of the Electrical Factory, and they complained frequently and at length about the irresponsibility of craft groups who were 'always striking' and who failed to appreciate the need to work for a living. But this was no more than a generalized view that strikes are a 'bad thing' which may be attributed, at least in part, to the presentation of strikes and industrial relations issues in the mass media (Glasgow University Media Group, 1976). The perspective had no necessary implications for workplace action. The section was one of those where downers over working conditions were quite common, and workers saw no connection between the condemnation of strikes in the abstract and their own willingness to stop work in certain circumstances. Now this may not be surprising, for there is a vast difference between a downer which may cost no production at all and a strike involving large numbers and lasting several weeks. But it indicates again the gap between broad perceptions and workplace practice: the women who stopped work over cold conditions did not see themselves as being 'on strike'.

Given that an obsessive concern with strikes is relatively easily brought into question, what do strikes reveal about the pattern of control in our factories? We have suggested that it is necessary to go beyond the point that strikes are part of a collective strategy of control to investigate the circumstances under which they do, indeed, merge with other forms of action. This was the case only in our Company B plants, where the degree of shopfloor control was highest. And this role for strikes did not seem to be universal in those plants, for a straightforward protest function was also apparent. Even in these plants strikes were not means of advancing the frontier of control. They defended the frontier in two main ways. First, brief stoppages served to reinforce the frontier by making it apparent to management that shopfloor co-operation could be withdrawn at will. Second, they were defensive in a more negative way: most of the substantial strikes in both plants involved an attempt to resist a managerial initiative, and several of these were straight defeats for the workers or were protests which brought no clear gains. Even well-organized work forces found that, when they were forced to take strike action, they could not be certain of success.

In our other plants strikes were not closely connected with collective actions around the frontier of control. In most cases they were too rare for them to have any particular day-to-day role. The Components Factory provides an instructive example. The general working conditions in much of the factory made the collective use of stoppages on health and safety matters at least as relevant as it was in the Small Metals Factory. Yet the absence of any established tradition of shopfloor pressure on such issues made the use of downers appear to be a waste of time. In the Small Metals Factory stoppages on these matters did not necessarily improve conditions, although there were certainly cases where continuous bargaining pressure and the threat of sanctions had brought concrete gains. But they prevented management from taking shopfloor co-operation for granted. Although the Components Factory was well-organized in the sense of having an effective shop steward body which could certainly apply sanctions if it chose, bargaining awareness had not reached the point where shopfloor involvement in every aspect of production was taken for granted. Hence the continuous use of downers was felt to be unnecessary. Only in the Electrical Factory were downers at all common, and here they involved protests and not attempts to pursue wider collective strategies.

In discussing the purposes of strikes it is too easy to concentrate on workers' motivations. Yet managers play a central role. Thus we have pointed to management's role in the definition of an action as a strike, suggesting that various pragmatic and political considerations will influence the decision as to whether to take workers off the clock. At the level of sectional downers the types of consideration involved are likely to be very broad: the decision will depend on an assessment of the individual situation. But two general influences seem to have been important: the extent to which an action threatened production; and the consequences for the agreed disputes procedure if management appeared to condone actions outside that procedure. Other influences could readily be suggested. We have also examined managerial strategy at a higher level by looking at broad policies on strikes. In Company B a distinct policy of bringing matters to a head and of trying to prevent stewards from using delaying tactics could be discerned.

We have attempted in this chapter, then, to relate collective actions at the overt level to the broader frontier of control in our factories. We have suggested, in particular, that the significance of strikes has to be understood in the context of the struggle for control as a whole, and that approaches to the 'strike problem' which treat strikes in isolation are, at best, very limited.

10

Conclusions and Implications

At the start of this study we set ourselves the ambitious aim of analysing the common assertion that conflict can be expressed in many ways by considering, through an examination of seven very different factories, how in fact it is expressed in various circumstances. In this chapter we review our argument before going on to assess the implications of our findings for a number of theories of industrial conflict.

Review of the Argument

Despite the prevalence of lists of the forms of industrial conflict, it is immediately apparent, as we argued in Chapter 1, that industrial conflict is less easily defined than such lists might imply. It is one thing to say that absenteeism, for example, may express conflict and another to show how and why it does so. Our approach to this problem can be summarized in a series of propositions. First, it is not helpful to assume that the occurrence of a particular form of behaviour has any necessary implications for the motivations of those engaged in it; participants' perceptions must be examined to assess how far they see the behaviour in terms of conflict. Second, this investigation cannot be restricted to workers: managerial perceptions of, and reactions to, various actions help to shape the significance of those actions. Third, and closely related to this, it must not be assumed that conflict is something that only workers engage in; managerial behaviour, be it a strategy in strikes, an attempt to increase effort levels, or the enforcement of discipline on the shopfloor, requires careful attention. Fourth, an empiricist concern with concrete behaviour is insufficient; conflict may be institutionalized so that it receives no concrete manifestation, or it may remain implicit in the structure of the situation if the resources which would shift it to the behavioural or institutional level are absent. Fifth, having identified different levels of conflict, we must investigate the link between them: in addition to showing how behaviour depends on structural conditions we must consider how it reinforces or alters those conditions and how structural conditions themselves can shift.

All this implies a view of what it is that is said to be reflected or expressed in various forms of behaviour or institutional arrangements. We suggested that it was not sufficient for our purposes to argue that conflict is inevitable in industrial relations without trying to specify the basis of that conflict. If the concern is purely with, say, patterns of strikes or the influences on piecework drift then explicit consideration of the structural bases of conflict may not be necessary. Hence in discussing piecework bargaining William Brown (1973: 144) uses the concept of bargaining power, defining the bargaining power of workers as 'the capability of influencing the actions of management in a deliberate and predictable way' through collective action. Our concern also embraces, however, the conditions which may prevent workers from being aware of their bargaining power and which prevent conflict from emerging in such things as disputes about piecework prices. We require an explicit statement of the bases of conflict for two reasons. First, if we are to take seriously the point that conflict may exist without any behavioural or institutional expression we need a means of analysing such conflict. Second, and closely related to this, relating behaviour to structural conditions requires consideration of the nature of those conditions.

We argued in Chapter 1 that the most fruitful approach to these two problems lay in Marxist theories of the labour process. These theories locate conflict in a struggle between workers and employers for control over the terms on which labour power is translated into effort. We have developed our concept of implicit conflict, that is conflict that remains within the structure of the situation, from these theories; and we have also found them useful in assessing the frontier of control and the limitations of various types of shopfloor control over the labour process. But we have not tried to argue that empirical matters can be reduced to the struggle for control or that this struggle should be the sole focus of attention. Any labour process contains elements of co-operation as well as conflict, and we have tried to consider how these strands come together to give various forms of workplace behaviour their significance in various settings. Hence in Chapter 1 we criticized attempts to explain specific behaviour in terms of resistance or struggle without exploring the relationship between the behaviour and its context.

This concern to locate behaviour in its context has underlain our whole approach. Hence in Chapter 6 we argued that sabotage was neither a spontaneous or irrational protest nor a self-conscious attempt to resist the employer's control over the labour process. It was a response to particular circumstances. Hence in one plant, the Components Factory, it was closely bound up with attempts to 'make out' under piecework and its significance as a form of struggle was very limited. Similarly, in Chapter 7, we criticized the naive radicalism which sees all attempts to influence the payment system as aspects of an undifferentiated resistance. Resistance implies some attempt to alter the terms on which effort is expended, whereas some actions, such as ensuring the correct payment of wages, merely provide a check on the existing way in which effort is extracted while others, notably concerns over the 'fair' allocation of work, may even assist management by deflecting attention away from management itself and onto the relationships between workers.

What, then, was the relationship between various forms of behaviour and notions of conflict or resistance? We will not, with one exception, consider separately each form of workplace activity that we have examined, for the concluding section of each substantive chapter already contains an assessment of the relevant behaviour in each factory. Instead, we take each plant or group of plants in turn to provide less of a summary of our findings than a brief outline of the salient points.

The exception to this approach is our analysis of industrial accidents. As noted in Chapter 1, our material on accidents does not directly advance our argument about control, and it is considered in detail elsewhere (P. Edwards and Scullion, 1982a). But one of our aims has been to look at each of the activities that appear in typical lists of the form of conflict, and it will be useful to outline our main conclusions about accidents. Accident rates have been used by several writers as indices of industrial conflict (for example Hill and Trist, 1953 and 1955; Paterson, 1960). Yet the theoretical rationale underlying this procedure is weak. It has to be argued either that workers deliberately hurt themselves to express discontent or, more plausibly, that workers who are in a state of conflict with their work reduce their level of attention and thus render themselves liable to accidents. Two problems are immediately apparent. First, as Scott et al. (1963: 45) point out in arguing against the use of accident figures as indices of conflict, the figures are influenced by so many factors other than psychological withdrawal that they are extraordinarily difficult to use. Accident researchers have used data that are unsuitable for testing the view that accidents are an index of conflict or morale. Second, even if suitable data could be constructed, there remains the question of whether accidents do indeed reflect a state of conflict. A worker may be strongly committed to the goals of the firm but still have accidents; indeed, given that the prime aim of the firm is production, workers who are most firmly wedded to this goal are likely to strive to increase output and thus to engage in unsafe working practices. We argue that there is little evidence that accidents are an expression of conflict and that including them unproblematically in lists of the forms of conflict is unhelpful. We suggest instead that patterns of accidents can be explained in terms of the distribution of effort across the working day. Hence, for example, there were very few accidents in the Small Metals Factory in the afternoon because workers' collective controls meant that very little work was done at that time of day. This illustrates a more general point that we have made repeatedly: forms of conflict do not simply exist but have to be actively sustained through organization. Accidents may in some circumstances reflect individual withdrawal from work but this is not a universal phenomenon, for it depends on the structure of control within the workplace. Only in very special circumstances when other expressions of conflict are unavailable, as perhaps in armies or prison camps, are accidents likely to be significant expressions of protest. Even in our clothing plants, where shopfloor organization was rudimentary, other forms of action, notably absenteeism, were used.

The Clothing Factories

In both clothing plants the majority of workers, namely the female operatives, were subject to 'simple control' (R. Edwards, 1979: 19): effort was extracted in a very direct fashion through tight discipline over all aspects of the labour process.[1] Starting and finishing times were strictly enforced, workers' freedom to move around on the shopfloor was limited, and the levels of effort that were required were made very clear. The control systems in the two factories were, moreover, virtually identical despite the differences, which we outlined in Chapter 2, between the 'styles' of the two managements. Despite the attempt by one of the firms to introduce a more consultative style, the pattern of control over the labour process was unaffected, and workers responded to control in the same way as they did in the other firm. We saw in Chapters 6 and 7 how the system of shopfloor control was sustained. Managers controlled all aspects of the payment system so that collective challenges did not emerge: the 'bargaining power' of workers was conspicuous by its absence. Hence there was no bargaining over piecework prices, and there were very few attempts to alter the effort bargain in more covert ways. As we showed in Chapter 6, for example, reducing the level of effort was prevented by strict quality standards and by management's ability to insist that workers rectify faulty work without extra payment. One reason for management's success lay in the characteristics of the work force: as we showed in Chapter 3, most workers had worked for only the one firm or for other very similar firms. And the substantial numbers of workers who had come straight from school found factory wages relatively attractive.

But while labour force characteristics were important sources of the weakness of collective awareness, the central feature of the factories was the way in which compliance was created within the workplace. Management's success lay in the fact that workers treated the control system as natural and inevitable. While there was certainly resentment at the way in which control was exercised this resentment was, as we saw in Chapters 3 and 5, neither universal nor focused on the control system itself. Some workers found that as long as they worked

---

1. We consider below (p. 273) the extent to which typologies of managerial control can be applied to our data.

within the rules management did not act against them, and hence they had few immediate sources of complaint. And even those who experienced discipline as harsh or arbitrary tended to focus on the personal characteristics of managers and not on the intensity of managerial control as a whole. Collective forms of protest were thus rare, with those that occurred tending to be sporadic. We have given several examples of the collapse of incipient collective organizations, a notable feature of them being the tendency for leaders to be sacked or to leave 'voluntarily'.

The more common situation, however, was for workers simply to drift away when they became dissatisfied with the situation: turnover rates were very high and the stability of the work force was low. Yet this quitting, while certainly reflecting the pattern of control and thus being open to interpretation as a form of conflict, did not stem from shared discontents on the shopfloor and it posed few problems for management. Indeed, to the extent that it removed potential 'trouble-makers', it was directly in management's interests. Hence it had important elements of implicit conflict. Similarly, absenteeism, while even more clearly a form of escape, did not challenge managerial control within the workplace. Workers themselves saw it as a means of escaping from the pressures of work and as an entirely natural action. On one level this points to the importance of the behaviour, and hence also to the inadequacy of studies of weakly-organized plants that fail to give it any systematic attention. Workers' deliberate use of absenteeism, together with their hostility to management more generally, points to the lack of any normative commitment to managerial interests despite the expectation from (some of) the existing literature that the firms' explicitly anti-bureaucratic and paternalistic approach would foster such commitment. Workers' close relations with management did not lead to feelings of loyalty. On the contrary, exposure to arbitrary authority led to resentment and a felt need to escape. But, despite all this, absenteeism remained a limited form of protest. Some writers expect work groups to enforce norms on absenteeism but here, and indeeed in most of our other factories, there were no such collective controls of absence; the individualism of the work force made such control impossible. Workers did not directly relate taking a day off to managerial control. And the impact of the behaviour on management was slight.

All this shows very clearly how activities at the behavioural level reflected but also reinforced structural factors. Patterns of quitting and absenteeism plainly reflected the intensity of managerial control. This was apparent not only through comparison with our other factories but also through analysis of the position of men in the clothing industry. Men were subject to much less detailed and direct control than women, and their patterns of quitting and absence, and also their much less hostile attitudes towards management, reflected this. In other words, the details of control over labour processes, and not influences such as firms' overall managerial styles or their level of bureaucracy, explain patterns of workplace attitudes and behaviour. Yet, although women were more 'conflict-prone' than men, the nature of women's protest served to reinforce managerial domination. Protests remained individualized. This is not simply to say that activity was restricted to 'individual' types of conflict such as quitting, for in some of our other factories such actions had strong collective elements. By saying that the behaviour was individualized we mean that workers did not experience any shared sense of grievance and that they saw their actions as a response to their individual needs to escape from work and not as an expression of discontent with the system of control as a whole. Such individualization acted as a powerful brake on the growth of collective organization, and hence we can say in a very precise way that the system of domination was being reinforced.

We have argued that this system had its roots in the process of production: management had an interest in maintaining control of the labour process so as to secure a high level of effort, and employees' interests in challenging this failed to be articulated. This argument is, we claim, a crucial corrective to existing accounts of the origins of 'industrial peace' such as those to be found in the work of Goodman and his colleagues in their work on the footwear industry (Goodman et al., 1977; E. Armstrong et al., 1978). Goodman's main point is that the system of rule-making at national level served to institutionalize bargaining and that the absence of technical or organizational change enabled this institutionalized structure to remain intact. But, while there may have been industrial peace in the sense that there were very few strikes, it does not follow that there was peace if this means a state of friendliness or the absence of strife. The studies of the footwear industry contain no consideration of absenteeism, quitting or managerial discipline. By looking at the rule-making system on its own terms, they ignore the actions of workers, who were subject to the system worked out between managements and national and local union officials but who had no control over it. Moreover, the argument implies that the sole purpose of employers was to stabilize the industry in order to reduce the amount of competition in the product market. While this is certainly important, it pays insufficient attention to the interest of management in retaining control within the workplace. Two aspects of this are crucial here. First, control within the factory is necessary if the institutionalized bargaining system is to produce results that are acceptable to management. While that system may have contributed to stability, its actual operation depended on employers' ability to prevent wage drift and so forth; analysis cannot proceed as though the rule-making system were a self-contained entity. Second, control in the workplace is of considerable importance in itself: it contributes to the creation of profit by securing a high level of effort in return for a given wage.[2]

2. As argued in Chapter 7, a further study of footwear and other weakly-organized plants (P. Armstrong et al., 1981) effectively analyses the nature of employer domination in the

Direct control is not, however, the only means of obtaining compliance. The Process Factory exemplifies a very different system.

The Process Factory

Management's control system in the Process Factory was in many ways the reverse of that in the clothing plants. Instead of being subject to the exigencies of piecework, workers received a guaranteed annual salary, which also protected them from the uncertainties of lay-off that characterize much of manual employment. They were not required to clock in or out, and their work was organized on the basis of participation and work group independence and not direct managerial control of operations. Yet in some ways patterns of workplace relations were similar. Workers' labour market experiences contributed to the absence of collective orientations, and managers were successful in individualizing potential expressions of conflict. Hence the shift working system and the powerful constraints which it placed on workers' social lives were obvious sources of discontent. But what we have called a policy of sophisticated managerialism prevented the emergence of collective protests and even of any substantial feeling of shared grievances. There certainly were grievances, notably over the rigidity with which the shift system was operated, but these had only a limited significance. They were far from universal: in replies to questions about absenteeism, for example, substantial numbers of workers mentioned loyalty to the firm as a reason for not going absent. And discontents were expressed in ways such as workers taking the occasional day off. Not only was such action rare but it was also kept firmly under control by management's policy of monitoring casual absences and stepping in quickly to prevent 'abuse'. Such control was exercised by speaking discreetly to individual workers; given most workers' acceptance of the 'needs' of the shift system, it is doubtful whether an offender would receive any support or even sympathy from most of his work mates.

Here again, then, we can see how managerial control and the absence of collective orientations on the shopfloor reinforced each other and contributed to the stability of the system. Managers were able to present the needs of the shift system as inevitable and unchangeable. Workers by and large accepted this. Those who tried to escape the rigours of the system by taking days off were soon noticed and brought into line. If they were unable to correct their behaviour they were readily eased out by having it made clear to them that they were not suited to shift work. Similarly, those whose health gave way after working shifts for several years were encouraged to leave, albeit in a way which reflected management's genuine concern with their welfare as individuals.

---

workplace in a way that parallels several of our own observations. Our reading of this study is that, its own protestations notwithstanding, it reveals the importance of the creation of control on the shopfloor and the limited value of concepts of the 'industrial relations system'.

In other words, our analysis of the Process Factory, like that of the clothing plants, points to the two-fold significance of 'conflict' in situations which are generally agreed to be marked by industrial peace and good industrial relations. First, we have shown that peace was less total than might at first appear. There were identifiable sources of discontent; such things as complaints about the way in which the shift system forced workers to be dishonest by taking time off to attend to outside commitments while claiming to be ill plainly reflected an absence of harmony. This is particularly remarkable given the Process Factory's sophisticated system of participation and management's consultative style. We found few positive expressions of satisfaction with these arrangements: workers were no more likely to approve of management or to feel that they were involved in a participative enterprise than were workers in other plants which lacked this self-conscious managerial approach.[3] There was more of a feeling of resigned acceptance than of positive commitment. Duty to the firm meant a generalized obligation to work in return for benefits which were admittedly considerable, and not a broader commitment to management's philosophy. Second, however, while all this points to the lack of harmony and consensus, the implications of workers' responses for the system of managerial control were slight. Any potential expression of conflict was limited in extent and was individualized, and the structure of the situation was reinforced.

The limits of workers' collective orientations were dramatically revealed when management, faced with increasing foreign competition, began to seek increased levels of effort. Workers accepted the reality of the external situation and also admitted the legitimacy of management's demand that manning levels be cut. This is not to suggest, however, that changes in the economic environment led directly to changes in the labour process. Hence we have seen in relation to our Company B plants that it is by no means certain that workers will accept management's interpretation of 'inexorable' market forces or that they will trust management sufficiently to accept the means suggested for coping with those forces. And we have pointed to the general weakness of shopfloor organization in the Process Factory. Management's success depended, in part, on the existing form of control within the plant: in the past management had been able to operate on the basis of consent, but the ability to achieve change had never been given up and shopfloor control had thus been more apparent than real. Success depended, too, on the firm's more general strategy

---

3. See above, p. 93. The implications of our findings for naive theories of job enlargement, to the effect that giving workers more responsibility will lead to lasting commitment to the goals of management, are obvious. We studied the factory some ten years after a package of new working practices had been introduced and found that workers and managers alike felt that the initial wave of enthusiasm had subsided. As managers openly admitted, work tasks remained boring and repetitive, and the limits of the existing division of labour had generally been reached.

of control. As we suggest later, other firms did not respond either so rapidly or so effectively to competitive pressures, or they responded through means other than a direct attack on working practices. In the Process Factory management control was not so much re-asserted as moved from the structural to overt level when managers decided to respond to a particular set of 'market forces' in a particular way.

The Process Factory shows, then, how 'industrial peace' was created and sustained in a firm operating in several advanced sectors of the economy. Sophisticated managerialism was, of course, very different from the direct control exercised in the clothing plants, but in both cases managers were able to create a system of control that served to reinforce their own domination.[4] One important reason for this was the absence of strong, autonomous shop steward organizations. Since such organizations are widespread in the engineering industry, particularly in large firms such as the two companies that we studied, the contrast with our engineering plants should be particularly revealing.

Company A

In fact, however, the major feature of our two plants in Company A was the limited extent of shopfloor bargaining pressure among production workers and a frontier of control that allowed management considerable freedom in matters such as the allocation of labour and manning levels. We consider the reasons for this before going on to examine the very different situation among craft workers.

The similarities with factories with weak steward organizations must not, of course, be exaggerated. Stewards in Company A were given a substantial degree of recognition by the company, and workplace relations were conducted on the basis of negotiation and not unilateral management rights. And the atmosphere on the shopfloor was very different from that in the clothing factories: there was a relaxed spirit, with foremen and workers feeling that they could settle their differences amicably and with none of the arbitrary authority which characterized the clothing plants. This atmosphere had, we argue, an identifiable effect on workplace relations. As noted in Chapter 5 there was a relatively high trust relationship (Fox, 1974) between foremen and stewards and workers. Both sides felt that they understood the other and that there was no need to engage in disputes to settle differences. This situation was one reason why, for example, problems of early leaving did not attain anything like the level in the Large Metals Factory.

---

4. This similarity points to the weaknesses of studies that try to prescribe one set of recipes for industrial peace. See for example the 'causes of industrial peace' studies (Golden and Parker, 1955) and the criticisms thereof by Northrup and Young (1968). It is moreover easier to describe a pattern of peace than to explain its causes; we have tried to correct this by stressing ways in which systems of control were created and sustained.

Trust relationships were not free-floating but were located in the traditions of the company. While we were not in a position to go into these traditions in the sort of historical detail which might be desirable, we can indicate their main elements. The company had developed a distinct 'welfarist' image, providing stable employment (together with such things as long-service pay awards) and taking a concern for the well-being of its employees. There was a distinct company 'way of doing things'. Hence, when the Electrical Factory was established it was staffed with experienced managers and foremen from other plants so that workers would be integrated into the firm's traditions. Foremen in both plants were concerned to build up good working relationships on their sections and to establish what they described as good human relations. In the past the company's traditions had contained important elements of paternalism, but there was now more of an openly negotiatory stance. This reflected the development of steward organization during the late 1960s, but the company was still able, for example, to retain the piecework system that had been instituted much earlier. Stewards were prepared to work within the system and to be, as managers often stressed, 'responsible'.

Conflict was, in important respects, institutionalized. Hence we noted in Chapter 7 the absence of overt conflict over the operation of the piecework system; and in Chapter 6 we showed that 'sabotage' formed an understood part of 'making out' under the system and that its implications as a form of struggle were very slight. Similarly, while 'individual' actions such as quitting and absenteeism occurred at a higher rate than they did in, say, the Process Factory the link between such actions and conflict was far from direct. Quitting seemed to reflect the immediate needs of workers and not an expression of dissatisfaction with the control system. And absenteeism similarly lacked a specific focus. The company provides a good example of the point that it is unhelpful to assume that particular actions are 'forms of conflict'. Applying the label of conflict does not help us to understand the patterns of these activities here. This is not, of course, to suggest that conflicts of interest had been removed from the system. It is simply to point out that production processes can operate without such conflicts of interest being manifest in action and without the exercise of managerial power being such as to enable the observer to locate conflict at the implicit level. Behaviour such as quitting in the clothing plants could be analysed in terms of implicit conflict because, among other things, it could be objectively related to the pattern of control over the labour process. But, as argued in Chapter 1, to be helpful this category has to have some boundaries or else everything to do with the employment relationship could be deposited in it. We find it more useful to exclude various activities from the category, with individual actions in Company A being the best example, than to use it indiscriminately. As in any capitalist organization conflicts of interest were present, but workplace activities were not so constituted as to express or reflect this conflict in any clear fashion.

The situation was very different in the craft areas. Particularly in the tool-room in the Components Factory, but also in the maintenance areas of both factories, workers had developed a strong collective organization which had succeeded in pushing the frontier of control well in its own favour. Hence we saw in Chapter 8 that considerable controls had been built up over the alloca-tion of labour and the amount and distribution of overtime, while we showed in Chapter 9 that the organization of craft workers on a company-wide basis enabled workers to deploy a very sophisticated range of sanctions against the company. Again, while we cannot consider in detail the origins of this control, the relevance of a self-conscious craft tradition, which was explicitly contrasted with what was seen as the weakness of production workers, was unmistakable. Also important was the gaining of recognition from the company before the company had developed a distinct policy on bargaining levels: personnel managers were unhappy about the need to bargain continuously with several competing groups but felt that they had to live with the situation.

Despite all this, we have also pointed to certain limitations of the craft workers' position. They were perhaps as well-organized and powerful as any group in the engineering industry; they certainly felt that they had surpassed the achievements of workers in Company B in terms of wages and conditions, and they were proud of their successes whereas in Company B there was a more defensive and gloomy atmosphere. Yet their power was strictly limited to traditional collective bargaining aims. They made no attempt to control such things as investment policies or production plans. Now this point about the 'factory consciousness' (Beynon, 1973: 98) of British unionism has become something of a commonplace. We do not make it to develop such a general critique but to indicate some particular consequences that stemmed from it. As noted in Chapter 9, the multi-national firm that owned Company A was diversifying into new products and establishing manufacturing capabilities, through take-overs and new investment, in several countries. Company A was a marginal part of its operations and was diminishing in size: the work force of the Components Factory declined by about one-third between 1971 and 1979, and after our research period the company announced considerable redundan-cies and plant closures. While this had no immediate impact on craft workers, for redundancies were concentrated among production workers, the long-term threat to jobs and to craftsmen's bargaining power was very clear. While crafts-men's pride in their own importance had been a significant factor in the development of their organization, their division from the rest of the work force was also a source of weakness. We have noted at various points the mutual antagonisms that existed between toolmakers in particular and production workers. One example at the time of our research was toolmakers' refusal to co-operate with an attempt, led by one of the conveners in the Electrical Factory, to establish an organization to bargain for all the company's workers over such things as pensions, holidays, and lay-off guarantees.

The strength of the craft workers lay in turning certain aspects of the market economy against itself. As Hyman and Brough (1975: 20–23) point out, workers who are taught the logic of maximizing returns may use this principle in relation to their own labour power. And, as we argued in Chapter 8, there may be distinct benefits in limiting organization to a particular part of the work force. Yet all this does not challenge the rationality of the market economy. Workers, even those in advanced and successful organizations, can only respond to decisions by management over which they have no control. Their power is consequently severely restricted, a point to which we return later.

Company B

In Company B there was a similar situation, with the additional factor that organizations were largely limited to the individual plant so that even the level of multi-plant bargaining achieved by craft workers in Company A was lacking. This is not to deny, however, that considerable controls over the labour process had been built up within each plant. Stewards of production as well as craft areas exerted a powerful influence on manning levels, the allocation of labour, overtime, and (in the Small Metals Factory) recruitment. Their controls over all aspects of production were far greater than those in our other factories. While our main aim has been to analyse the nature of these controls and their implications for forms of conflict, the question of their origins naturally arises. We cannot give a decisive answer to this question, for the growth of the controls in Company B and not elsewhere reflects, in part, the very particular historical circumstances of each firm. But certain influences seem to have been important. First, the existence of craft and craft-based forms of union organization, and their early recognition by the firms that were later to become part of Company B, encouraged the growth of various controls, particularly those concerning the supply and allocation of labour. Second, in the years during which these practices were established managements were prepared to cede some aspects of control to the shopfloor in return for continuous production. This obviously reflected a third influence, namely the nature of the product market: firms were operating in a sellers' market and unit labour costs were of little immediate consequence.

We have seen in Chapter 8 how these three influences operated in the Small Metals Factory in relation to controls over recruitment. If they were a central part of our argument, or if they were part of a novel explanation of shopfloor controls, they would need considerable elaboration. But they contribute to our argument without being central to it, and they are among the factors which are commonly employed in discussions of the growth of steward organizations (see for example Zeitlin, 1980). One point of clarification is, however, called for. We do not see product market factors as determinate, with easy product market conditions permitting managerial leniency towards shopfloor controls. Hence shopfloor organizations do not lie dormant, ready to spring up whenever managements are weak enough to permit this. They have to be developed, and craft traditions seem to have been important in this process. Similarly, managerial leniency reflects the character of firms themselves, and in particular their control strategies, as well as product market circumstances.

Whatever the origins of shopfloor controls, we have argued that certain forms of workplace action were impossible without them. We suggested in Chapter 9, for example, that strikes and organized sanctions in Company B were merely part of a whole range of controls over the labour process. Co-operation with management could be withdrawn at any time. Hence withdrawing mobility and imposing the form of work to rule known as working to the hour were very effective sanctions in the Small Metals Factory, and we saw in Chapter 5 how, in response to managerial attempts to control early leaving, workers in the Large Metals Factory could hit back by withdrawing their normal co-operation. Yet the ability to deploy a wide range of sanctions rested on the structure of the situation: management can, in principle, declare that the withdrawal of co-operation is a breach of contract and that counter-measures will be taken. There was nothing natural or inevitable in workers' ability to work without enthusiasm or to define sanctions as merely the careful application of the firm's own rules. The niceties of such definitions and legitimations were less important than the structure of control that had been built up. Hence we argued in Chapter 6 that workers do not have a 'tool box' of sanctions out of which to select the most appropriate form of pressure. Sanctions are constituted through organization, and a very developed form of organization is required before such things as restricting the mobility of labour or withdrawing co-operation more generally can become an effective collective strategy. This is not to say, of course, that workers in unorganized workplaces have no collective means of influencing effort levels; as noted in Chapter 7 there is an extensive literature on effort restriction among such workers (see especially Mathewson, 1969). But such means are limited to the details of the effort bargain, and they do not challenge very large parts of management's control over the labour process. Substantial organization is required before controls over effort at the level of the work group can become part of a collective strategy that challenges managerial control more widely and that enables workers to impose sanctions at will.[5] Hence we

5. Montgomery (1979: 116) makes this point well. Referring to Mathewson's work, he notes that restriction of effort may occur among unorganized groups, but adds that the 'customary craftsman's stint had been an overt and deliberate act of collective regulation by workers who directed their own productive operations. The group regulation which replaced it was a covert act of disruption of management's direction of production'. We have seen, moreover, that such regulation is far from universal.

showed in Chapter 9 how strikes in the Company B plants stemmed from more general collective 'making out' strategies. But we also argued that this picture of strikes could not be generalized to our other plants, for strikes here were not embedded in a wider set of shopfloor controls.

Similarly, we showed in Chapter 4 how in the Large Metals Factory, and only here, absenteeism was part of custom and practice: shopfloor controls gave workers a considerable amount of leisure and this, together with the traditions of the gang system and the weakness of managerial controls, enabled workers to develop informal rotas for time off. Recorded absence rates were very low, but the practice of leaving the plant during the working day was one of management's main problems. The practice reflected very particular aspects of the control of work in this factory, as was most clearly shown by its absence in the similar environment of the Small Metals Factory. It was not, therefore, a product of universal 'social norms' about absence but a reflection of the ability of workers to develop custom and practice in many areas of the labour process.

Perhaps the most striking feature of the Company B plants, however, was the change in workplace relations that was being brought about by the plant's rapid decline in the local earnings league. Even powerful shopfloor controls were insufficient to guarantee a satisfactory outcome on one of the dimensions of control listed by Goodrich (1975), namely wages. One result was an increase in quitting which, we argued in Chapter 3, had strong elements of overt conflict since it was plainly the product of shared discontents and since it was a conscious expression of dissatisfaction with management. Another result was a more generalized feeling of demoralization on the shopfloor; this was reflected most dramatically in a marked withdrawal of effort in the toolroom (see Chapter 7).

This situation was the product of management's attempts to cope with a crisis of profitability that was affecting the whole company. But shopfloor controls were also coming under more direct challenge. Managements in both plants were adopting a consciously firm approach to industrial relations, although, as we saw in Chapter 9, the details of this were significantly different. And the threat of closure which had hung over both plants for some time finally materialized with the decision to close a substantial part of the Large Metals Factory. The immediate danger of closure had been enough to persuade stewards to accept cuts in manning levels, but this was insufficient for company managers who, significantly, cited industrial relations problems as one reason for selecting this particular factory for closure; and this was despite substantial recent investment in the new assembly shop, Shop X, and several other modern and expensive facilities. The limitations of factory-level controls, based on the details of the labour process itself, could not have been more powerfully illustrated.

Some Overall Conclusions

Finally in this section it will be convenient to bring together some more general points which have run through the preceding chapters. First, we have tried to bring out the importance of shopfloor controls as well as their limitations. A central feature of our argument has followed the quotation from Gramsci which we gave in Chapter 1 (p. 12): although workers may adopt the ideologies of dominant groups their practices may reveal at least a partial rejection of these ideologies. Hence we have stressed the need to examine concrete behaviour and not simply attitudes. A good example of this is the attitude of stewards towards production in the Company B plants. As argued at the end of Chapter 7, stewards were firmly committed to the general ideology of production even though in their practices they challenged managerial definitions of how production was best achieved. Such a situation is often described as being ambiguous or, less emotively, as part of the dual nature of British trade unionism. But for the stewards themselves, of course, there was no duality; a high level of production, of a commodity whose broad design was taken for granted, was a desirable aim that could best be achieved if management would only use the expertise and good sense of the worker instead of trying to impose their own procedures. Whether or not stewards' (and workers') attitudes can be analysed in terms of their ambiguity, duality, or lack of coherence is not our concern here, although it is worth noting the dangers of academic condescension: while it is important to show that attitudes are not as coherent or all-embracing as analysis in terms of 'orientations to work' may imply, it is not really all that surprising that shopfloor workers do not have an articulated philosophy. Our concern has been to examine concrete practices and to reveal how they relate to different forms of organization of the labour process.

This leads into our second point. By considering the nature of control we have been able to explain why certain forms of attitude and behaviour which are often associated with factory work were not in fact present in our plants. Most importantly, workers in the Large Metals Factory, although working in a huge and impersonal factory and although performing mundane tasks often on an assembly line, displayed few of the characteristics of 'alienated' workers. They did not, for example, engage in spontaneous sabotage or report that they found their jobs boring. The reason for this is the form of social control that had been achieved over jobs that certainly were monotonous and repetitive and that were often carried out in unpleasant working conditions. To take one revealing example of a different situation, we may consider the recent description of work in a French car factory given by Linhart (1981). Linhart describes from his own experiences the intensity of work, the fragmentation of tasks, and the soul-destroying monotony of jobs in the plant. Yet he also describes the enormous power of management to demand high levels of effort, to move workers between jobs at will, and to repress any collective protest. His analysis, in other words, can be read as an account of the effects of intense managerial control and not as a description of the alienating effects of a particular technology. He relates, for example, how he was moved between jobs ranging from labouring to welding. In our Company B plants such arbitrary authority was out of the question: not only were distinct grades of labour recognized which made it generally impossible for management to move workers between grades, but allocation of work within a grade depended on negotiations with stewards. This is not to deny that work may be extremely unpleasant, and dangerous, in large factories. It is simply to point out that some of the more extreme of these aspects of work can be counteracted by the form of social control that is achieved over mass-production technologies. Or, to take a case where there was little shopfloor control, we have argued that, in our clothing plants, the 'boredom' that some workers reported was not the result of the technology that was employed, for other workers said that work was not boring. 'Boredom' was the result of intense managerial control which meant that workers had none of the freedom to escape from their tasks or to control their own efforts that workers in other factories enjoyed.

Third, as mentioned above, we have shown that various forms of workplace activity, notably custom and practice, were not so widespread as some accounts of them might suggest. In other words, while it is true, as noted in Chapter 1, that the terms of the effort bargain are necessarily indeterminant, it does not follow that workers will be able to exploit this indeterminacy. Substantial control over the labour process is required before certain means of restricting effort become feasible or even thinkable. By taking account of patterns of control we can, then, explain why certain activities are possible only in certain circumstances. This in turn enables us to locate existing studies of workplace relations in a broader framework than they themselves employ; we return to this point below.

Fourth, one key implication of these last two points is that various conventional measures of trade union strength, such as union density or, at plant level, the presence of full-time stewards or of formal shop stewards' committees, are at best imperfect indicators of what they attempt to measure. The underlying premise of attempts to measure union power, either for its own sake or for use as an independent variable in models predicting wage inflation, strike activity, or many other things, is that the analyst needs a measure of the ability of workers to resist management and to attain their own ends. A high level of union organization may be necessary for this, but it is far from sufficient. All our plants had high levels of union density, and all of them apart from the clothing factories had full-time stewards and other characteristics that are often associated with union strength, but patterns of shopfloor relations were very different. This helps to explain the limited success of attempts to show why some plants are more strike-prone than others (P. Edwards, 1981), a point which applies to similar exercises with other dependent variables.

Fifth, we have argued that managerial control in all our plants had a variety of bases. As noted in Chapter 4, Etzioni (1961) has distinguished between coercive, remunerative, and normative means of achieving compliance. A firm that relied exclusively on any one form would, however, be very unstable: pure coercion plainly has very great limitations so far as keeping workers with the firm and motivating them to give a high level of effort is concerned; to rely on remuneration, or the pure cash nexus, is, as Westergaard (1970) points out, to depend on a single and fragile bond between the worker and the firm; and normative commitment is similarly inadequate on its own, particularly in profit-oriented organizations. Thus we have noted that our clothing firms used aspects of paternalism in an attempt to create some form of normative commitment; although such commitment was certainly not widespread it may have had an effect in some cases for, as noted earlier, critical views of management were far from universal. These traditions seem to have been particularly important for long-serving male employees, who were often treated by management with a good deal of consideration. More generally, we suggested in Chapters 4 and 5 that the 'abuse' of such things as sick pay schemes or managerial laxity in the enforcement of discipline was limited by the unquestioning acceptance by workers of the values of regular attendance at work. In many respects the interesting question is why workers take as little time off as they do, particularly when time off is covered by sick pay. While we cannot go into the origins of workers' acceptance of the need to work regularly, our argument is consistent with the view that forces which operated inside and outside the workplace acted in such a way that certain features of work were simply taken for granted. Whether or not these forces are best analysed in terms of normative consensus or ideological hegemony or the economic dependency of workers on employers is not of central importance here.[6] We have argued that workers attend work not out of a deep sense of loyalty to the firm but because of a more general acceptance of the need to work. By the same token absenteeism was justified not in terms of attempts to 'get back at' management but as a response to a more general need for a break from the routines of work. Having said all this, however, we must also stress the variations within this broad unquestioning

6. We noted in Chapter 4 (note 15) that Abercrombie et al. (1980) have criticized notions of hegemony and dominant ideology. They stress, instead, the political and economic control that is exercised over subordinate classes, and in particular they make great play of a phrase that they take from Marx: 'the dull compulsion of economic relations'. Our argument is certainly consistent with the view that workers take certain things for granted because existing relationships are presented to them as inevitable. And the idea that some forms of compulsion reside in the economic sphere is plainly very important. But it may still be possible for certain forms of compliance to reflect an ideological element: economic relations do not simply 'affect' workers, and the way that they are presented by dominant groups can properly be described as ideological.

acceptance of industrial discipline (in its widest sense). As we have seen, workers' practices varied markedly within this acceptance, with those with a substantial degree of control over the labour process being able to challenge management's interpretations of discipline.

Finally, it will be useful to make explicit the implications of our argument for recent accounts of managerial control strategies such as those of Richard Edwards (1979) and Friedman (1977). Edwards identifies three forms of control: simple, technical, and bureaucratic. Simple control is the most straightforward, but even here there are difficulties since Edwards implies that there is only one type based on direct repression. We have stressed, however, that our clothing plants, which came closest to Edwards's ideal-type, were not sweatshops and that they differed in important ways from factories where savage repression is practised. Patterns of managerial control, moreover, differed markedly within the clothing firms, a complication which is not allowed for in broad-brush characterizations of control strategies. Now we are not simply pointing to empirical complexities that prevent ideal-types from having exact parallels in the real world. Managements pursue a mixture of control strategies in which, in the case of the clothing industry, paternalism, welfarism, repression, and other elements were all involved. To describe such complex strategies as simple control is to ignore the multi-faceted nature of workers' relations with management in even the 'simplest' situations. Similarly, to turn to Edwards's other two categories, both our engineering firms would come under the label of technical control in that both were modern mass-production enterprises (R. Edwards, 1979: 20). Yet patterns of workplace relations were very different: the struggle for control may be conducted very differently under the same general type of management structure.

This leads to a more general point. While writers such as Edwards and Friedman stress their concern with worker resistance, and thus criticize Braverman (1974) for his alleged neglect of workers' ability to resist managerial control, their analysis of resistance is undeveloped. Resistance tends to be seen as a residual category, with workers necessarily reacting against different forms of managerial control in different ways but with the implications of workers' own strategies being left unexplored. It is as though management acts and workers simply react. We have stressed, by contrast, how the frontier of control is shaped by the interaction between employer strategies and the particular strategies followed by workers. The centrality of the struggle to control the supply and allocation of labour in the Small Metals Factory, for example, cannot be understood without reference to the craft-like forms of control developed by workers in that plant and to the strategic concerns which developed from them. Edwards and Friedman both seem at times to take a decidedly non-Marxist approach in that, instead of concentrating on the dialectics of the struggle for control, they give central attention to the behaviour of management.

While not denying the importance of management, we have tried to correct this emphasis by examining the precise form of different struggles for control and the way that employer and worker strategies affect each other to produce a particular pattern of control. It is the struggle for control, and its changing nature, that must be given central attention.

Our general argument, then, is that workplace activities have to be related to the frontier of control before their significance as forms of 'conflict' can be understood. What does this imply for the common view that there are 'alternative forms' of conflict, with some actions being the functional equivalent of others?

Alternative Forms of Conflict

As noted in Chapter 1, the obvious point that conflict may be expressed in many forms has been developed into the argument that one form of conflict will be an alternative to another. For example, groups with a high strike rate will have a low rate of absenteeism, and *vice versa*. This is an appealing argument, and it underlies the common practice of correlating rates of various sorts of behaviour to see whether there is a relationship between them (Knowles, 1952: 225–6; McCormick, 1979: 165–70; O'Muircheartaigh, 1975: 38; Williams et al., 1979). Yet it needs to be made more precise. We may, first, distinguish between strong and weak forms of the argument. The strong form asserts, for example, that a factory with a high strike rate will have a low rate of other forms of behaviour such as absenteeism or labour turnover. The *locus classicus* for this argument is the work of Scott et al. (1963), who found that work groups in the coal industry who engaged in 'organized' actions had a low rate of 'unorganized' forms of behaviour such as absenteeism. The weak form of the argument is that, if the number of strikes falls, a rise in the rate of 'unorganized' or 'individual' actions can be expected. Turner et al. (1967: 190) for example note that in the car industry there was no general link between collective demonstrations and other forms of 'withdrawal', and thus argue against the strong hypothesis; but they suggest that, if collective action is inhibited in some 'forceful way', discontent may find its expression in more individual forms.

Second, the forms of behaviour to be compared must be specified. It tends to be assumed that some actions, most obviously absenteeism and quitting, are 'individual' forms of conflict while others such as strikes are 'collective'. And perhaps the dominant tradition has been to compare the group of individual actions with the group of collective actions. But it is also possible to make comparisons within these groups; as we saw in Chapter 4, for example, the theory of the induction crisis developed by Hill and Trist suggests that new recruits to a firm will be marked by a high quit rate but that this will decline and be replaced by absenteeism as the main form of 'withdrawal'. More importantly, it is no more than an assertion that some activities are distinctively unorganized or individual. It is certainly unhelpful to analyse absenteeism as though it is simply unorganized; activities that occur at the individual level may well be carefully organized, as the evidence of Handy (1968) on the strategic use of absenteeism by workers shows.[7]

This leads us to our first main point of criticism of the alternative forms hypothesis. It has to be shown why particular actions do, indeed, tend to occur together or apart. To show that absence and strike rates are inversely correlated is not to demonstrate why such a relationship holds. The evidence that they are inversely, and not directly, related is in any event far from overwhelming (Bean, 1975: P. Edwards, 1979a). The positivist assertion that there is a necessary relationship between rates of different forms of activity is, then, relatively easily dismissed. The more sophisticated argument is to point to a factor which explains an observed association. For Scott et al. for example this factor is morale: groups with a high level of morale tend to engage in collective actions while those with low morale use individual forms of protest.

This argument is useful as far as it goes, but several additional points must be made. First, for Scott et al., and for many other writers in a similar tradition (for example, Sayles, 1958), the use of collective sanctions reflects the skill of work groups and their strategic position in the division of labour.[8] Yet we have found that sanctions could be deployed skilfully by groups with little or no formally-recognized skill and without a strategic position. One of the most 'bargaining aware' stewards that we came across represented labourers in the Small Metals Factory; by contrast the skilled knitters in the clothing industry held a key position and yet their use of collective (or for that matter 'individual') forms of action was very limited.

Second, while Company B workers could certainly be described as demoralized, in that there was a spirit of apathy and disillusionment on the shopfloor, it did not follow that they employed simply 'individual' forms of protest. The extent of collective controls was considerable. We have also described, however, the diminishing effectiveness of these controls and the consequent growth of the 'individual' action of quitting. It might be argued that collective controls were simply a residue of a period of high morale and that they were now decaying. While this is consistent with the weak alternative forms hypothesis, it is certainly contrary to the expectations of the strong form. But even the weak form is shaky if it is taken as implying that a decline in collective action implies

7. This evidence comes, interestingly enough, from the coal industry. The need to replace the label 'unorganized' with the term 'individual' is now well-established (Hyman, 1975: 187; McCormick, 1979: 167).
8. In so far as this argument implies a position of technological determinism it would also now be rejected for the reasons adumbrated by Goldthorpe et al. (1968) and many other writers.

an increase in all types of individual action. Turnover may have been increasing in the Large Metals Factory but other types of action showed no marked increase. It would be wrong, in any event, to imply that collective controls had simply collapsed. Their effectiveness in bringing satisfactory wage levels was certainly declining, but the controls themselves remained in position and were used very successfully to deal with a range of non-wage issues.

Third, this discussion has already gone beyond the strict confines of the alternative forms hypothesis in that it has considered collective controls over the labour process and not simply the incidence of collective actions such as strikes. The link between work group power and strike rates is far from obvious: it is never clear whether workers with a great deal of bargaining power will engage in strikes because they use their power or will have relatively few strikes because their ends can be attained by other means.[9] This may explain why the results of different studies seem to be contradictory, with some finding inverse associations between forms of action, others finding direct relationships, and yet others being unable to indicate any pattern of association. If collective controls mean that overt action is unnecessary no prediction as to the direction of association between rates of behaviour will be possible. More generally, the debate about alternative forms of conflict ignores the crucial prior variable, namely the pattern of control. Correlations of absence rates and strike rates are merely contingent on the pattern of control, and to explain why particular correlations are observed requires explicit attention to this 'missing variable'.

Despite all these criticisms, however, the fact remains that our clothing plants had high rates of 'individual' action and very low levels of collective organization, while organization in Company B was considerable and rates of individual action were low. Our argument is that the alternative forms hypothesis, while adequately describing this situation, does not explain it. The explanation is to be found in different forms of control over the labour process, which made some forms of action impossible in the clothing plants and which also made certain forms of escape the only option available. Consideration in terms of control also explains features of the situation which lie quite outside the terms of the debate about alternative forms of action. Hence the role of unrecorded absenteeism in the Large Metals Factory can be explained in terms of collective custom and practice, and it was, indeed very much a collective action that had few similarities with the model of individual protests as spontaneous and unplanned outbursts.

In general, then, the notion of alternative forms of conflict is not robust enough to stand up to detailed scrutiny. If it is used to point out, for example,

9. The origins of this problem can be traced back at least as far as the economist Alfred Marshall. For a recent example, which has spawned a considerable literature, see Ashenfelter and Johnson (1969) For criticisms, which include the point that the likely effects of measures of bargaining power are ambiguous, see P. Edwards (1978) and Mayhew (1979).

that conflict cannot be equated with strikes then it is unobjectionable but correspondingly unilluminating. When it is rendered in a precise form it faces severe difficulties, of which perhaps the most basic is the assumption that behaviour which is labelled as, say, absenteeism has the same meaning in different settings. A related difficulty is that it is assumed that individual actions can usefully be described as forms of conflict. We have stressed, by contrast, the way in which activities are constituted as aspects of conflict by different forms of organization of the labour process. Attention to the labour process provides a grounded explanation of why particular actions occur in some settings and of how they relate to a notion of conflict.

The Theory and Practice of Workplace Relations

Finally we turn to the implications of our argument for theories of workplace relations and for various practical matters concerning those relations. We begin with 'theory' before considering one key aspect of 'practice', namely how workplace relations were and are changing.

Theories of Workplace Behaviour

This is not the place to review in detail the various theories of workplace activity that have developed since the early 'human relations' studies. Our aim is simply to explain how our argument improves on some existing approaches. We have attempted throughout to take seriously the point, developed at the most general level by Giddens (1979), that 'action' and 'structure' are intimately related, with each continuously affecting the other. Now the distinction between structure and process, or at the epistemological level between voluntarism and determinism, is, of course, fundamental to a great deal of social theory. We do not claim to have solved any of the problems that this raises, but we do claim to have been able to use, in an empirical context, Giddens's broad argument. Hence we have suggested that arguments about the effects of assembly-line work ('under capitalism') are unsatisfactory in so far as they imply that such aspects of 'structure' as the technology and the basic capitalist organization of work have particular effects at the level of action: forms of social control over these structural constraints are crucial in understanding how the constraints worked in practice. Similarly, we have pointed to the inadequacy of approaches to behaviour that pay insufficient attention to 'structure'.

These general points have specific consequences. They can be most conveniently developed in relation to the study by Batstone and his colleagues of a vehicle assembly plant to which we have often referred in previous chapters (Batstone et al., 1977 and 1978). We use this study in particular as a foil for our own arguments not because it is uniquely vulnerable to criticism but because it represents the most clearly articulated and crystallized expression of arguments that can be found in less developed forms elsewhere. Many studies, for example, discuss the ways in which shop stewards put arguments over to their members or the processes of mobilization in strike action. But they do so in an unsystematic way as compared with the detailed concern with 'systems of argument' and 'vocabularies of motive' that characterizes the work of Batstone et al.

Despite its sophistication, and despite its thorough exploration of steward behaviour, *Shop Stewards in Action* (Batstone et al., 1977) has been criticized for having an 'idealistic problematic' (Hyman, 1979: 64). While the term idealism is open to several constructions, some of them pejorative, we take it to mean a mode of explanation which treats actors as free agents and which does not relate behaviour to its structural conditions. *Shop Stewards in Action* can reasonably be described as idealist or voluntarist in so far as it treats workplace activities purely in their own terms. It analyses in detail various vocabularies of motive that are deployed by stewards and managers and yet arguably does not show why some arguments are developed and others are not. Now in describing this work as idealist we do not wish to deny its importance. It would require a detailed discussion of the study to sustain the claim that it is idealist and to explore the consequences of this. In any event, it is presented in terms which suggest that it deliberately set out to answer certain questions, which can best be tackled using an idealist approach, and not other questions. The central concern of the authors is the 'debate over union government and goals' (p. 2): what is the nature of union democracy at workplace level, how do shop stewards influence their members, and how are patterns of behaviour created and sustained? Similarly, in their work on strikes, the same authors are interested in processes of mobilization and in how, given a set of conditions in which strikes are likely, stoppages of work actually occur (Batstone et al., 1978: 1). It is, in other words, unsatisfactory to take the idealism of the study as a criticism, since it set itself an idealist problem. As Plummer (1979: 114, 115—16) says in his defence of interactionist approaches in the sociology of deviance, 'every social science theory brings with it its own distinctive problematic and set of concerns, and to accuse theories of failing to deal with what they do not intend to deal is unfair'. Interactionists 'do not neglect the concept of structure out of ignorance' but they deny its 'relevance for the interactionist task. The notion of structure, they argue, is a reification which does not do justice to the central interactionist concerns of emergence, process, and negotiation'.

Our reference to interactionism is not a chance one, for we mentioned in Chapter 1 the argument that such an approach to the study of conflict needs to be balanced by a concern with structure. By taking account of structural influences it is possible to locate idealist approaches, of which the work of Batstone et al. is simply the best example because it follows through the implications of an idealist programme. We deliberately use the term 'locate', as distinct from some phrase like 'go beyond'. It is common to find studies arguing that they have 'gone beyond' the existing state of knowledge in an area, but what this means is often far from clear: an idealist account is not necessarily to be criticized because it tackles only a certain range of questions, and to say that an alternative account has gone beyond it is to imply that it has simply been superseded. By introducing a concern with structure we have not gone beyond idealism, since idealism can operate perfectly well on its own territory. Indeed, we have not asked questions about 'emergence, process, and negotiation' in any detail, and hence idealism 'goes beyond' our own concerns. By 'locate' we mean that we can place idealist approaches in a wider setting: we can draw on their concern with the processes of mobilization and so forth to develop a fuller understanding of workplace relationships.[10]

Thus we argued in Chapter 6 that forms of non-cooperation with management have to be seen in structural as well as idealist terms. Batstone et al. (1978: 41) rightly point to various advantages to workers and stewards of a strategy of withdrawing co-operation, but the success of such a strategy depends ultimately on management's willingness to treat as structural those aspects of the situation on which they depend. Hence, such facets as the low cost of the strategy, and the ability to define a sanction as no more than the close following of managerial rules, depend on management's explicit or implicit decision to let the sanctions persist; as argued earlier, managers can, in principle, increase the cost of the sanctions by escalating the dispute. This has two consequences. First, as we argued in Chapter 6 and also, in relation to strikes, in Chapter 9, certain forms of workplace action can be sustained only under specific structural arrangements. The shopfloor has to develop a .very particular form of control

10. We may also locate the theoretical approach of idealist writings. It is no accident that Batstone et al. draw heavily on the work of Lukes (1974) in their conceptualization of power. In discussing the broadest form of power, which corresponds to Lukes's 'third dimension' and which is an important corrective to the view that power stops with bargaining power, they say that 'a convener, say, will have far less "trouble" and hence will achieve greater power if, instead of having to argue about issues or having to squash or amend the issue initiative of others, he is able to develop a situation in which members see it as his right to decide what are the problems and how they are to be handled' (Batstone et al., 1977: 9). Given the concern with union democracy, it is not surprising that this relates to the power of a convener over his members and not to the power of employers over workers, but even in these terms it takes on a voluntarist slant: conveners 'develop' situations and members 'see' them in a certain way, whereas it is the unconscious and unseen forms of power that concern Lukes. This is not to suggest that the authors could or should have followed Lukes more closely, for, as indicated in Chapter 1 (note 4, p. 8), we have found Lukes's approach to interests unhelpful. It does not explain how different sets of interests are reconciled or, as Batstone et al. (1977: 271) recognize at the very end of their first book, how attempts to change the structures which, from the observer's view point, seem to prevent workers from realizing their real interests may be against workers' other, short-term, interests. In the majority of their work Batstone et al. use a voluntarist reading of Lukes to avoid these problems, while in their more general comments they recognize, but do not resolve, them. We return to this point later.

before certain forms of action, and the systems of argument that go with them, become possible. The significance of these sanctions cannot be understood simply in terms of the processes of mobilization within the workplaces in which they take place; we also need to know what factors permit them to occur here and only here. Second, if management re-define what is treated as structural then the relevance of systems of argument, or, rather, the bases on which they rest, is challenged.

In talking in terms of the re-definition of structure it may seem that we are not so much re-locating the idealist argument as extending it slightly: are not the parties free to define what they treat as structural, and is our argument not, therefore, a voluntarist one? There are three answers to this. First, we have suggested that action and structure interact, and it is no part of our argument to suggest that actors have no freedom of choice. Second, however, choice occurs in the context of constraints. Some actors have more resources than others in ensuring that their definitions of the situation stick; hence we have seen that the arguments of women workers in the clothing industry concerning management's arbitrary use of discipline had little or no force and that managerial domination was buttressed by a whole range of legitimations and taken-for-granted assumptions about what was normal and acceptable. Similarly, even where managements tolerate shopfloor controls they can always challenge that control; we have discussed several instances of this. Third, and closely related to this, there are various levels of structure. Managers may be free to tolerate certain practices if they are broadly consistent with their own interests, or are at least not too far out of line with those interests. But changes in market or other conditions may change the nature of the constraints under which management may operate. And, more generally, shopfloor controls are constrained by the market system of which they are part. Stewards are not free to define the situation as they please but have to come to terms with the limitations of their own controls. Hence we saw in Chapter 8 that stewards in the Small Metals Factory operated controls on recruitment and mobility in an explicit response to changes in the market environment. This is not to suggest that the environment has determinate effects but simply that controls based on limiting management's freedom to hire labour power were necessarily constrained by the nature of the market in which they operated. At the broadest level, the structure of market relationships permitted some forms of workplace control to develop and inhibit others.

This returns us to issues of resistance and class consciousness. As but one example of an unduly strong emphasis on structure consider the following:

> there is a class struggle under way even when people are working 'normally'.
> As already admitted, the situation may not ordinarily be seen in these
> terms....Nevertheless, from a wider perspective it is possible to discern a

pattern of conflict recurring right across the industrial system and to call it a class struggle is no flight of fancy but just realism (Roberts et al., 1977: 90).

As we have argued throughout, there may be a broad conflict of interest that covers the whole industrial system, but to describe this as struggle, and to imply that it is ubiquitous and continuous, is unhelpful. We have shown how active struggle was contained under some forms of the labour process and institutionalized under others. While it is important to be aware that even 'normal' practices can contain elements of conflict, to treat them unproblematically as a form of struggle, and class struggle at that, is to conflate several matters that must be kept separate. Workplace activities need have little direct implication for active struggle, in the sense of attempts to shift the frontier of control, and even when there is such struggle its implications for class-wide action need to be demonstrated and not assumed.

We have also, however, had cause to criticise the view of consciousness developed by Batstone et al. (in Chapter 9, p. 228). We cited their argument that consciousness was factory-based and not class-based and suggested that, while this is a reasonable summary of the situation and one that would be shared by other writers, this was insufficient to deal with the question of class relations. The problem with their account is most clearly apparent in their argument that as part of the conflict over the frontier of control 'strikes may constitute an aspect of class relations. In other words, strikes may have a class significance in that they constitute one means whereby class relations are modified. We would argue that the strikes typical of the plant we studied and, indeed, of British industry more generally can be seen to play only a marginal role in terms of developing class consciousness' (Batstone et al., 1978: 218). This slips from a consideration of strikes as an objective element of class relations to their role in fostering class consciousness. Yet the former is very different from the latter: strikes need have no tendency to promote class consciousness but can still be seen as an aspect of class relations, that is, in terms of the relationship between workers as sellers of labour power and employers as users of that power in the labour process. This distinction is one which a strictly idealist account cannot properly handle, and it is significant that in their discussion at the end of *The Social Organization of Strikes* Batstone et al. move away from such an account. They stress, for example, the involvement of the worker in the wage-effort bargain, and say that an understanding of strikes 'may start from an awareness of the subordination of the worker, but it has to go further and recognize the complex historical interplay between structure and consciousness as mediated by organizational processes' (p. 223). The latter point is, of course, one that we have stressed throughout. But we have also stressed that 'structure' must be given detailed attention and that different levels of structure can be distinguished. In other words, while the substance of our argument about consciousness and action has similarities with that of Batstone et al., we claim that this argument is intimately connected with our broader approach, whereas in the case of Batstone et al. it is necessary to bring in, at the end of the discussion and in a passing reference, notions of structure and the effort bargain in order to tackle the objective significance of strikes.

As suggested in note 10 above, when they come to discuss the general implications of their analysis Batstone et al. confront problems such as imputing real interests to workers. We do not claim to have solved such problems, or the problem of the link between consciousness and action; and we have not tackled the specific question of how class and class relations should be analysed.[11] But we have been able to analyse these matters within a clear framework. Hence we have argued that shifting the frontier of control is a form of class action because it affects the relationship between workers and employers; and it has objective, identifiable, consequences for managers in terms of their own control of the labour process. Yet class action contains contradictory elements: by being based on turning the rules of the existing market economy against itself, such action limits the challenge posed by those workers who can exert some control over the labour process, encourages fragmentation within and between factory organizations, and so on. These points are well-known and require no detailed repetition here. They stem, however, directly from our argument as a whole so that, we claim, they can be comprehended more satisfactorily than is the case with other accounts. We return to some of their implications in discussing changes in workplace relations. But we must first deal with one other outstanding matter, namely the question of policy.

The 'problem of industrial conflict' has a central place in popular discussions of industrial relations, and it might be expected that a study of workplace conflict would produce a set of answers to the problem. It will be obvious, however, that the logic of our whole approach goes against the view that policy prescriptions can be appended to the analysis. One obvious, but still important, point is that identifying something as a problem immediately raises the question: a problem for whom? As is now widely recognized, giving advice on how to deal with apparent problems such as strikes or restrictive practices cannot be disinterested, for the nature of the problem depends on where one is standing. But even those who do not pretend to be disinterested will face difficulties. Our central argument is that patterns of behaviour reflect patterns of control, and that actions gain their significance as forms of conflict within particular structures of control. To identify one aspect of behaviour as a problem is to imply that it does indeed have problem status and that some resolution is possible. We argued in Chapter 4, however, that the prevailing managerialist tradition in studies of absenteeism

11. For a useful development of Marxist theories of class see Wright (1978).

is unable to come to terms with the significance of absenteeism because it pays little or no attention to the structure of control over the labour process. Hence, managers in the clothing plants did not find that absence was a problem, and attempts to help them cope with absenteeism were largely irrelevant. Such attempts may, indeed, have unintended consequences. It is often noted, for example, that managements may be ill-advised to try to control absence levels, for absenteeism may be a relatively harmless form of worker protest and suppressing it may create other forms of action that are more costly and difficult to control. We can go further than this, however. Suppose that managements in the clothing plants attempted to deal with absence and quitting not by direct control but by altering their whole style of management to permit workers more freedom on the shopfloor, to reduce the number of arbitrary acts of discipline, and so on. This might well produce two related effects. First, if the changes were genuine, effort levels would fall and unit labour costs would rise, which would in turn endanger the firms' competitive position. Second, workers might come to expect further changes and an entirely different type of treatment from management: introducing changes would threaten the existing basis of compliance with managerial wishes and would de-stabilize the pattern of order and control on the shopfloor. Not for nothing were moves in the direction of participation and consultation in the Underwear Factory more cosmetic than real. Certain 'problems' may, then, be insoluble if they are treated simply in their own terms. A further example is the problem of quitting in the Large Metals Factory: quitting reflected the plant's fall in the earnings league, and a 'solution' in terms of substantial pay increases was incompatible with the firm's need to keep down labour costs in order to compete in the product market.

Policy suggestions may, then, be biased, inoperable, or counter-productive. This is not to say that our material has no implications for policy. The central implication is that attempts to deal with the 'problem of conflict' without understanding its nature will be worthless or harmful. Conflict is not an extraneous or accidental feature of the process of production but is central to that process. It is naive to imagine that it can simply be removed. Several subordinate points follow. First, as argued above in relation to studies of industrial peace, peace cannot be equated with the absence of collective struggles. Second, and relatedly, notions of 'good industrial relations', in implying that conflict can be removed or its effects minimized, are inadequate. As soon as it is accepted that conflict is part of a continuing struggle it becomes very unclear what 'good industrial relations' mean. This is not to deny that some situations are preferable to others. Hence we suggested in Chapter 5 that formal, bureaucratic disciplinary procedures may be more in workers' interests than the arbitrary exercise of managerial authority. But, as noted above, it is not clear how the desirable situation is to be attained without fundamental changes in the control structures of the firms without formal procedures. And such procedures are still part of a control structure. The struggle for control takes a variety of forms and has a variety of consequences, and it is the outcome of the struggle, and not the implementation of this or that policy recommendation, which is crucial. Third, there are several more immediate lessons to be drawn from our analysis. For example, we saw in Chapter 9 in relation to the Small Metals Factory that managements which try to introduce all at once a whole series of changed working practices may find that their plans are frustrated by workers' resistance and that a more cautious approach may better serve their objectives. And we have suggested, in relation to the Process Factory, that shop stewards who think that they have achieved a *modus vivendi* with management and that they have attained 'industrial peace' may find that their illusions are shattered when managers re-assert their right to manage. Other examples could be given. But the central point is that 'conflict' must be understood in context. Labels such as 'sabotage' and 'indiscipline' for example imply that normal relations have broken down and that there is widespread 'disorder'. Yet, as we saw in Chapters 5 and 6, analysis of the relevant actions shows that they are often part of established custom and practice and have a much more mundane character than these labels might suggest. These and other activities should be understood and explained, and be neither stigmatized as 'problems' nor romanticized as class-conscious worker resistance.

Changes in Shopfloor Relations

One matter of obvious policy 'relevance' is the way in which shopfloor relations have been changing. Changes in the economic climate at the end of the 1970s have brought home with particular force the general point that structural conditions can alter and that patterns of accommodation can be destroyed. It is essential to try, albeit in a preliminary fashion, to come to terms with these changes.

During the 1960s and 1970s evidence accumulated that shop stewards were creating an increasingly authoritative position for themselves in industry, and the view that they were mindless agitators was frequently refuted (e.g. Turner et al., 1967: 289; R. Taylor, 1980: ch. 7). As one recent survey (William Brown, 1981: ch. 4) shows, in the decade between 1968 and 1978 shop steward organization spread throughout manufacturing industry, there was a substantial rise in the number of full-time conveners, and stewards became closely involved in formal bargaining arrangements. Yet two limitations of the position of steward organizations were highlighted. First, it is easy to assume that organization is universal, but, of plants where there was a steward body, only 12 per cent had a recognized full-time steward and 37 per cent reported 'regular' meetings of stewards 'with no other participants' (William Brown, 1981: 64). The latter figure may be taken as an indication of the extent of joint shop stewards' committees. Such committees are too easily assumed to be universal, whereas our own evidence, together with the survey material, shows that this is not so. Only one of our plants had a joint stewards' committee (JSSC), and that was largely ineffectual. And the fact of regular meetings plainly says nothing about the stewards' influence: in the Underwear Factory, for example, stewards met prior to the regular consultative meetings with management, but their general influence on the shopfloor was slight. The second limitation is that steward power may be more apparent than real:

Where shop steward organisations have sprung up in factories with little tradition of workplace bargaining, they may owe the superficial sophistication of their facilities and procedures more to the administrative needs of management than to the bargaining achievements of the workforce. It remains to be seen how they will fare in a worsening economic climate (William Brown, 1981: 120).

Our case study material bears out this argument. The Process Factory is a prime example of a plant in which there was no tradition of bargaining and in which, as stewards themselves recognized, steward organization was, despite its apparent sophistication, very weak. It also indicates very clearly the effects of a 'worsening economic climate': although stewards were able to defend some jobs, the loss of any jobs through redundancy would have been unthinkable even a few years earlier, and the continued operation of the plant depended on substantially increased effort levels. The economic crisis was not, however, limited to this plant. As we have seen, the Components Factory lost about one-third of its work force, through 'natural wastage' as well as redundancy, in eight years. And in Company A as a whole there were substantial redundancies and plant closures throughout the 1970s. In Company B, as we have also seen, a large part of the Large Metals Factory, along with several other plants, was shut. Only in the clothing industry were general employment levels holding up, but even here the drive to increase efficiency meant that the 'core' male work force was being reduced: in eight years the number of knitters and ancillary workers in the Hosiery Factory shrank from 170 to 60.

Organizations based on the workplace plainly find it difficult to respond to this general loss of jobs. But the impact of the 'economic crisis' may also be felt directly within the workplace in managerial pressure for greater efficiency, more flexibility in working practices, and so forth. This plainly challenges existing forms of shopfloor control. Our main point here is that it cannot be assumed that such a managerial challenge will necessarily emerge. It is too easy to assume that there is a universal response to the crisis, which is reflected in attempts to tighten managerial control. Two points of observation may be made on the basis of our research. First, managements will have differing perceptions of the crisis, and will face different constraints on their freedom of action. Thus the Process Factory provides a model illustration of a firm which was faced with a squeeze on profits and reacted deliberately and carefully by reducing unit labour costs. By contrast, Company B management had faced a long-running problem of low profitability and low investment; this problem had, as we saw in previous chapters, developed into a vicious spiral, with low profitability leading to low investment, which in turn led to an inability to market new products at an attractive price, with this having a further downward effect on profits. Yet systematic attempts to regain shopfloor control were not made. The reasons for such inactivity are hard to establish, but the nature of the company's problems may be a key factor. The problems were deep-seated and wide-ranging, and a series of managements battled to find solutions. There was no readily-identifiable cause of the problems, and hence no simple focus for a solution. Hence, although both our Company B plants went through a series of take-overs during the 1960s and 1970s, and although new managements are often associated with attempts to root out practices which grew up under their predecessors, it was not until the late 1970s that any serious attempt was made to alter the pattern of shopfloor accommodation. The implication is that neither economic crises nor the development of large multi-plant firms has any necessary implications for shopfloor practices.

Our second point of reservation concerns Company A's reaction to the crisis. Although operations were cut back on a large scale, there were no attempts to alter working practices in the two plants that we studied. One reason for this may be the impressive controls over the labour process, together with the company-level bargaining organizations, that toolmakers and maintenance workers had built up. The company could certainly expect strenuous opposition from these groups if it tried to attack them directly. As we saw earlier, an attempt to apply the company's general ban on recruitment to these areas met strong and successful resistance. Among production workers, by contrast, there were few obvious 'restrictive practices' that could be attacked. Hence it was probably not in the firm's interests to attempt a direct change in working practices, since in one case the costs could be considerable and since in the other the benefits were unlikely to be great.[12]

12. Since this argument, together with our wider evidence on the effects of worker resistance on managerial freedom, has some similarities with the view of Kilpatrick and Lawson (1980), that Britain's long-term industrial decline reflects worker organization and the ability to retain 'restrictive' practices which were destroyed elsewhere, it may help if we clarify our position. Although Kilpatrick and Lawson (1980: 93) say that they are not criticizing worker organization and that their argument is a comment 'on the nature of the competitive system and its uneven development', the logic of their analysis is that worker resistance is a prime cause of Britain's industrial decline. Our argument in the text relates to only one firm at one time, and cannot be generalized to other firms. In other cases, notably the clothing plants and the Process Factory, the threat of decline stemmed directly from the international competitive system and not from worker resistance. More generally, we agree that worker resistance can have real effects: it is unsatisfactory to argue, as do

This is not to say, however, that the impact of the economic crisis is slight. It is simply to point out that the crisis is likely to have differing effects and that there need be no universal attack on shopfloor practices. Company A provides an example of a challenge which was much less immediate, and hence much more difficult to resist, than a direct attack on manning levels. As noted in Chapter 9, the company was one part of a firm with interests covering Britain and several overseas countries. Many of the plants within Company A were old, and some of the firm's products, which had in the past dominated their markets, were coming under strenuous competition from other firms. For the firm that owned Company A the obvious policy was to concentrate on other, more modern, products and to run down operations in the declining sectors. There was thus little point in risking a confrontation with the powerful craft workers' organizations in plants like the Components Factory when such plants were becoming increasingly marginal. By the same token, the strength of these organizations was thrown into sharp relief: although they had overcome the limitations of purely plant-based action they had not developed their strength either into new areas of bargaining or into other parts of the company. Their bargaining power, in other words, remained limited in depth and extent. Although the long-term consequences of this situation cannot yet be assessed, what we may call a shift in the centre of gravity of the firm's operations (both geographically and industrially) seems likely to pose an increasing challenge to existing steward organizations, even though the challenge does not appear in the shape of a direct attack on working practices.

This raises the more general question of the effectiveness of stewards' combine committees.[13] It is easy to see them as the logical response to the shift in the locus of decision-making in companies. Yet the trade groups in Company A, which were well-organized and were recognized by the company, had substantial limitations. Other studies have pointed to the difficulties of establishing effective cross-plant committees and to the challenge posed by the growth of the multi-plant firm (William Brown and Terry, 1978; Beynon and Wainwright, 1979). The

some radicals, that resistance is important while at the same time claiming that unions have little impact on industrial efficiency or wage inflation. The point, however, is that one cannot simply admit the importance of worker resistance. It is essential to analyse the basis of this resistance, and its often contradictory nature, and to relate it to managerial interests, as we have tried to do in Chapters 7 and 8. Worker resistance is not simply 'restrictive', for many of the practices we have discussed were aimed at assisting production. Locating resistance in this way, and discussing its link with problems of 'efficiency', goes beyond our present concerns, but this at least indicates the basis of a more sophisticated approach than that of Kilpatrick and Lawson.

13. The term 'combine committee' is often taken to imply an organization embracing all the workers of a given firm. But there are different sorts of combine, and their implications for union organization differ. Hence the trade groups in Company A covered only specific groups of workers in specific parts of the company. And there are plainly other types of combine organization which need to be distinguished. The dangers of discussing combines as if they were identical are obvious.

problem of securing recognition from companies may prove a particularly important obstacle (Scullion, 1981). The implication is that combines may be hard to establish and that simply shifting the level of bargaining without attention to the content of bargaining may achieve little.

All this adds up to a confused picture. The general challenge of the economic crisis, in particular the impact on the number of jobs, cannot be doubted. But when aspects of the crisis are considered carefully the overall nature of its effect is far from obvious. Multi-plant firms have been in existence for many years, and the consequences of the crisis may appear in forms other than a direct attack on existing practices. Similarly, while we have stressed that plant-based organizations have important limitations, it does not follow that all such organizations will be destroyed or permanently weakened. The closure of plants in sectors where steward organizations have been strong obviously reduces the density of organization. But British workplace organizations have shown considerable resilience in the past, and those organizations that have not depended on a great degree of managerial sponsorship are likely to display this quality again. As some commentators (e.g. William Brown and Nolan, 1981) are already pointing out, if the economy enters a period of expansion workplace bargaining may well assume again an aggressive form. Its character cannot yet be predicted, but it would be as wrong to think that the crisis will destroy all vestiges of existing organizations as to suppose that it poses no challenge at all to plant-based economistic bodies.

These concluding comments have been intended to do no more than place developments in our research factories in a broader context. The immediate problems that economic changes create should not distract from our more basic argument, namely that the frontier of control is a central aspect of workplace relations and that attention to the position and shape of the frontier can help to explain a great deal about the form and significance of conflict. While the frontier may become stabilized for a time, the economic crisis shows very clearly that stability cannot be assumed in the future. The terms on which the labour process is carried out can never be settled. Hence, while we have reached some conclusions about the nature and effects of different forms of control over the labour process, these conclusions cannot be treated as a final and definitive statement. We hope that they open up, and do not close off, investigation of the labour process and changes within it.

Appendix
Data and Measurement

Labour Turnover and Stability

The most obvious measure of labour turnover, known as the crude turnover rate, simply expresses the number of leavers during a period as a percentage of employment at the start of the period. It is, however, well known that turnover tends to be higher among new employees than among longer-serving workers. As a result, an increase in the size of the work force will tend to increase the rate of turnover because of the rise in the number of short-service workers. This had led some writers (for example, Silcock, 1954: 432, 439) to argue that the crude turnover rate should be abandoned on the grounds that it says more about the past than the present. Others (Price, 1975/6: 45) feel that the rate has some value. We will use the crude rate for two main purposes. First, it shows, albeit in a gross and potentially misleading way, whether one plant has a greater movement of labour than another. The rate sets a rough standard of comparison for assessing the extent of the 'problem' of turnover. Second, and more importantly, the rate can be used to chart trends over time. As long as patterns of recruitment have not fluctuated wildly changes in the rate of turnover provide an indication of workers' willingness to remain in a plant. It may not mean very much to say that one plant has a turnover rate of 5 per cent whereas another has a rate of 50 per cent, but an increase in the rate from 5 to 50 per cent would plainly be significant. Trends can also be compared with trends in the labour market, to assess the role of external 'pull' factors in quitting, as compared with the influence of internal 'push' factors (see Pettman, 1973).

The crude turnover rate is undoubtedly inadequate on its own. An identical rate could indicate a steady depletion of long-serving workers or rapid turnover among short-service workers combined with a stable 'core' group. For many years analysts have tried to distinguish between these two very different cases by examining survival rates: taking a cohort of entrants to a firm and seeing how many are still present after, say, a year (Florence, 1924: 156). Bowey

(1969) has developed a more complex labour stability index, but it is difficult to use in practice since it requires a separate calculation every time the size of the labour force changes and since, as Bowey admits, it can be awkward where, as was the case in six of our factories, the size of the labour force is falling. The length of service distribution of current employees is sufficient for our purposes, together with two other measures of stability.

The first measure simply gives the proportion of a cohort of entrants to survive for a specific period. It has been argued that this index is not useful since people joining a plant at a particular time do not constitute a distinct social group; there are also said to be practical difficulties with creating groups which are large enough for statistical analysis over periods of time which are short enough for the groups to be treated as homogeneous (van der Merwe and Miller, 1975: 18). No one would suggest, however, that cohorts assembled in this way are distinct groups with their own identities. The purpose of the analysis is to see, for example, whether workers entering one factory tend to stay there longer than those entering another. There is no need for groups to be viewed as social entities. By the same token, it is not necessary to limit analysis to groups entering over a very short period, and hence practical objections are also of limited validity. In the present case it was a straightforward though laborious task to assemble cohorts retrospectively by using organizational records of starters and leavers. The second measure gives the length of service characteristics of leavers. This provides direct information on the question of whether workers tend to quit after very short periods with a firm and thus complements the picture of stability built up from other indices.

The starting point in assembling our data was each plant's file of current employees. This provided details of age and length of service, although in the clothing industry data on age were rarely recorded and the length of service of workers with several years' experience was not always specified. To calculate turnover rates we started with the current employees' file and worked backwards, using total numbers of starters and leavers in each period to calculate changes in the size of the labour force. Changes were then applied to the current number of employees to estimate labour force size in the past. In the Components Factory this was not possible, but record cards on all past employees were kept by the personnel office, and it was possible, by noting when each worker started and left, to build up data on labour force changes. This method is indirect, but since, as far as we could establish, we had a complete census on leavers it should provide data comparable with those for other plants.

Leavers' records also provided data on the length of service distribution of leavers, since the date of joining the firm was generally recorded in the leavers' books. There was, however, a problem of double counting since anyone leaving and re-joining a firm would be included twice. For crude turnover rates this was not a problem, since the interest was in the total rate of leaving in a given period. But it was important for the comparison of lengths of service of leavers, particularly since quitting and re-joining was more common in the clothing plants and in Company A than in the other three factories. In Company A we adopted the practice, for both stayers and leavers, of calculating the total time a worker spent in the plant; this was possible by reference to individual record cards, which contained details of each spell of employment. In the clothing factories, however, such detailed records were not available and it is possible that someone counted as having only, say, a year's service had in fact worked in the plant for several years during an earlier spell of employment. There is the danger that this vitiates contrasts between plants in terms of leavers' and stayers' length of service characteristics. However, it was apparent that one form of leaving involved a quit lasting only a few weeks: a worker might leave in a moment of discontent, only to return later. It was possible to exclude such quits. This is not to suggest that they are unimportant; indeed they reflect one aspect of the volatility of the work force in clothing. But their exclusion balances the bias introduced by double counting. We could also use replies to our questionnaire of shopfloor workers to check on the extent of more than one period of employment; we asked workers whether they had ever left the firm, when this was, and when they had returned to the plant. Replies indicated that about 20 per cent had had more than one spell of employment, compared to about 10 per cent of workers in Company A.[1] But the most common pattern was for workers to have had a substantial gap in their employment history, usually connected with bringing up a family. This has two implications. First, length of service is not usefully taken to include a spell of employment ten or even twenty years ago. Second, it does not seem to have been the case that double counting involves greatly exaggerating the proportion of workers with very short periods of service. Some stayers counted as new recruits may in fact have been starting their second terms of employment, but the bias introduced cannot have been large. More important, workers re-joining the firm are unlikely to quit a few months later: they know what it is like and return for a substantial period. Thus, the length of service distribution of leavers is unlikely to be distorted by double counting, and the comparisons used in the text can be employed with reasonable confidence.

As noted in Chapter 3, the clothing firms did not keep records on the reason workers gave for leaving, hence rates of voluntary turnover could not be calculated. Other firms kept information on this, although the amount of detail varied. It was possible to distinguish workers leaving 'of their own accord' from others, with the former being counted as voluntary leavers. There are problems,

---

1. Many of these Company A workers were Pakistanis returning to their home country and intending to return to Britain. The break in their service should not be seen as 'quitting' in the usual sense, and hence their spells of service are treated as continuous.

however. First, all plants had experienced redundancies which were carried out on a 'voluntary' basis. Workers volunteering to leave might be seen as those least 'committed' to the firm, so that their redundancy was not wholly involuntary. Second, workers who are dismissed plainly do not choose to go of their own accord, but their leaving can be seen as an indication that they are 'in conflict' with the firm and that they are unwilling to adjust their behaviour in such a way as to avoid the sack. For example, if there are plenty of jobs elsewhere a worker may be happy to be sacked rather than conform to the firm s rules. In fact, the number of dismissals was small enough not to affect rates of turnover very much. Third, many of the women leaving the Electrical Factory quit for family or domestic reasons. Some of this leaving is undoubtedly 'involuntary', and is clearly different from leaving to go to a better-paying or more pleasant job. But we have preferred to treat this kind of leaving as voluntary, in that women have some choice over staying at work or 'putting their families first'. It is true that in practice they may have little real choice: the domination of men in the household means that it is taken for granted that, for example, a woman will have to leave her job if her husband takes a job in a different part of the country. But in principle a choice is present and, so far as the relationship between the worker and the firm is concerned, this sort of leaving is best seen as a voluntary separation and not as something imposed by the firm or required by the health or age of the worker. For all these reasons, then, we do not make a rigid distinction between voluntary and involuntary quitting, simply treating the division as useful for certain purposes (for example the relationship between turnover and the state of the labour market, for which truly voluntary leaving is most relevant).

For the analysis of cohorts of entrants we used starters' books to obtain a list of names of entrants over a period. We checked these against lists of current employees to see who was still present and against leavers' records to establish who had left, and when they had done so. In a small number of cases, workers could not be traced but these numbers are not large enough to invalidate comparisons in the text.

Absenteeism

Although organizational records on absence exist in profusion, problems of measurement are considerable. Buzzard (1954: 239–44) has listed some of the more severe difficulties. For example, an index based on lost time can be misleading if voluntary overtime is widely worked: should non-attendance for a scheduled overtime shift be counted as absence? Buzzard even goes so far as to suggest that, because recording practices may vary between factories, comparisons between plants are dangerous if not impossible. More recently Latham and

Pursell (1975) have pointed to a series of practical problems and suggested that absence is best measured 'from the opposite side of the coin': by measuring the number of people at work. They argue that their attendance measure is more statistically reliable than absence measures and more useful because the analyst's concern is with behaviour and not the lack of behaviour. However, as Ilgen (1977) points out, measurement problems apply equally to both measures: the problem of how to treat leave with permission for example is a conceptual one which cannot be resolved by altering the statistical basis of measurement. The notion that absenteeism involves a lack of behaviour is simply silly.

Our aim has been to take a consistent approach precisely to minimize the dangers of inter-factory comparisons. There is no right answer to the question of which categories of absence to include, and we have necessarily tailored the approach to the task in hand. We have defined absence as non-attendance for any normal shift unless the absence was for holidays or was leave with permission. This excludes cases of workers who report for work and then have to leave because of illness since such leaving can hardly be said to be voluntary. In cases of doubt we have used the rule that only an absence for a whole shift or, where workers clock in separately for morning and afternoon shifts, the whole of a distinct session should be included in the absence figures. Absence with permission, since it has to be explicitly sought and often backed up with evidence of a hospital appointment or whatever, is generally excluded. Now it may well be that managements will differ in what they see as a legitimate reason for the granting of leave, which means that what is absence in one plant will be legitimate leave (which may even be paid for) in another. But our aim is not to refine the concept of absenteeism but to measure the extent of unauthorized absence from work. If management define a visit to the dentist as a legitimate reason for absence there would be little point in counting it as a case of absenteeism. It remains possible, however, that workers will 'abuse' the privilege of leave with permission; this would count as an instance of 'voluntary withdrawal'. While we cannot evade this problem entirely, the fact that leave has to be actively sought means that 'abuse' is unlikely to be widespread. This, together with the even greater problems with including leave with permission as absenteeism, leads us to exclude it from our figures.

This leaves the matter of sickness absence. The strategy of some investigators, of excluding absence covered by a sick note, was not open to us since most of our plants did not have data which would have enabled the exclusion of the 'certified sick' to be carried out with confidence. More importantly, as argued in Chapter 4, 'genuine' sickness is far from being a fixed category. We therefore include sickness absence in the figures. Now this may seem to go against the aim of deriving a measure of voluntary withdrawal, but we are not suggesting that all absence through sickness is voluntary. Instead our data rely on the assumption that 'genuine' sickness is randomly distributed. It is not the overall figures on absence that are important but variations within them: to the extent that variations occur between groups or over time these can be attributed to 'true' variations in the extent of voluntary withdrawal and not to genuine sickness.

Since we have followed a uniform recording procedure in all plants our estimates for absence should be reasonably comparable but, by the same token, they differ from figures produced by management. For example if a firm includes absence with permission its figures will be higher than ours. Similarly, and perhaps more importantly, we counted only workers on the 'active' payroll; inclusion of workers on a separate file of 'inactives' (known as Company A for example as the suspended register) would increase absence figures since most of these workers were off sick for long periods. In view of these and other differences our figures should not be compared directly with those reported by other researchers or by companies themselves (see for example Incomes Data Services, 1978), a *caveat* which also applies to figures which we have reported elsewhere using somewhat different recording practices (P. Edwards, 1979c).

In all cases our data come from companies' record cards or books in which the absence histories of individual workers were detailed. In Company A central records were plainly incomplete, and we used record sheets filled in by foremen each week. These sheets indicated who was absent on each day or days of the week. By transcribing the information onto records for each worker we were able to build up a picture of each individual's absence pattern. Given the nature of these data little time would have been saved by taking a sample of workers, and we therefore have a complete census. Elsewhere the task was simpler because a record was kept for each worker and it was a straightforward task to extract the relevant data. Because of the small numbers involved we took a census in the clothing factories. In Company B and in the Process Factory random samples of workers' records were taken. In this last factory the sample was of all workers, taking every fourth name in the personnel department's alphabetical list. In the Large Metals Factory particular occupations were selected and random samples taken within them. These data form the basis of the material on the current work force used in Chapter 3 as well as of the absence statistics.

To produce the absence figures we simply counted the number of one-day and other absences (taking an absence on Friday of one week and Monday of the next week as a continuous period of absence, thus making our estimates of one-day absenteeism as conservative as possible) and the total number of days lost over a period of a year. Rates were calculated by producing estimates of the number of shifts scheduled to be worked during the year, with the estimates being corrected where necessary for differences between the number of shifts worked on days and nights.

Shopfloor Questionnaire

The questionnaire was a simple document, comprising questions about length of service, the worker's last previous job, whether or not he or she had considered leaving the current job, satisfaction with wages and conditions, knowledge of wages paid by other firms in the area, attitudes to absence, attitudes on discipline, and feelings about foremen and higher management. The questioning was conducted on an informal basis during break times or when a worker had time to spare to talk to us. It was often followed by a more general discussion, and was not separated from our more unstructured interviewing.

We began by selecting names at random from personnel records and asking foremen to help us in identifying the workers we had selected. But we found this to be a time-consuming process and subsequently used a less rigorous method of approaching workers 'at random'. This was not strictly random selection in the statistical sense, and our results are not therefore fully 'representative'. But we controlled for obvious sources of bias by approaching workers of differing ages and by checking the length of service and occupational characteristics of our sample against the known characteristics of the population as a whole. We tried to approach workers literally at random, and doubt whether any serious sources of bias were introduced. Moreover, in all cases except the Small Metals Factory our sample comprised a substantial proportion of the total number of workers in a factory and problems of bias are correspondingly reduced. Because of our method of approach, non-response rates cannot be calculated with accuracy. But the rate of non-response was low where we employed strict random sampling, and we obtained few refusals to co-operate. In any event, as the main text makes clear, we take the questionnaire to be a means of supplementing more informal approaches and not as a source of 'hard' data which can be treated independently of our other investigations; its utility must be seen in this light.

References

Abercrombie, Nicholas, Stephen Hill and Bryan S. Turner. 1980. *The Dominant Ideology Thesis.* London: Allen and Unwin.

Acton Society Trust. 1953. *Size and Morale: A Preliminary Study of Attendance at Work in Large and Small Units.* London: Acton Society Trust.

Addison, John T. and John Burton. 1978. 'Wage Adjustment Processes: A Synthetic Treatment'. *British Journal of Industrial Relations*, Vol. 16, July, 208–23.

Aglietta, Michel. 1979. *A Theory of Capitalist Regulation: The U.S. Experience.* Trans. David Fernbach. London: New Left Books. (Original French edition, 1976).

Armstrong, E. G. A., J. F. B. Goodman, J. E. Davis and A. Wagner. 1978. 'Stabilising Industrial Relations in a Multi-Plant Footwear Company'. *Personnel Review*, Vol. 7, Winter, 19–30.

Armstrong, P. J., J. F. B. Goodman and J. D. Hyman. 1981. *Ideology and Shop-Floor Industrial Relations.* London: Croom Helm.

Ashenfelter, Orley and George E. Johnson. 1969. 'Bargaining Theory, Trade Unions, and Industrial Strike Activity'. *American Economic Review*, Vol. 59, March, 35–49.

Bain, George Sayers, David Coates and Valerie Ellis. 1973. *Social Stratification and Trade Unionism: A Critique.* London: Heinemann.

Baldamus, W. 1961. *Efficiency and Effort.* London: Tavistock.

Baldamus, W. 1976. *The Structure of Sociological Inference.* London: Martin Robertson.

Batstone, Eric, Ian Boraston and Stephen Frenkel. 1977. *Shop Stewards in Action: The Organization of Workplace Conflict and Accommodation.* Oxford: Blackwell.

Batstone, Eric, Ian Boraston and Stephen Frenkel. 1978. *The Social Organization of Strikes.* Oxford: Blackwell.

Bean, R. 1975. 'Research Note: The Relationship between Strikes and "Unorganised" Conflict in Manufacturing Industries'. *British Journal of Industrial Relations*, Vol. 13, March 98–101.

Behrend, Hilde. 1951. 'Absence under Full Employment'. University of Birmingham Faculty of Commerce and Social Science, Studies in Economics and Society, Monograph A3.

Behrend, Hilde. 1957. 'The Effort Bargain'. *Industrial and Labor Relations Review*, Vol. 10, July, 503–15.

Behrend, Hilde. 1959. 'Voluntary Absence from Work'. *International Labour Review*, Vol. 79, February 109–40.

Behrend, Hilde. 1961. 'A Fair Day's Work'. *Scottish Journal of Political Economy*, Vol. 8, February, 102–16.

Behrend, Hilde and Stuart Pocock. 1976. 'Absence and the Individual: A Six-Year Study in One Organisation'. *International Labour Review*, Vol. 114, November, 311–27.

Bendix, Reinhard. 1974. *Work and Authority in Industry: Ideologies of Management in the Course of Industrialization.* Berkeley: University of California Press (Original edition 1956).

Benton, Ted. 1981. '"Objective" Interests and the Sociology of Power'. *Sociology*, Vol. 15, May, 161–84.

Beynon, Huw. 1973. *Working for Ford.* Harmondsworth: Penguin.

Beynon, Huw and R. M. Blackburn. 1972. *Perceptions of Work: Variations within a Factory. Cambridge:* Cambridge University Press.

Beynon, Huw and Hilary Wainwright. 1979. *The Workers' Report on Vickers.* London: Pluto.

Blackburn, R. M. and Michael Mann. 1979. *The Working Class in the Labour Market.* London: Macmillan.

Blauner, Robert. 1967. 'Work Satisfaction and Industrial Trends in Modern Society'. *Class, Status and Power: Social Stratification in Comparative Perspective.* 2nd edn. Ed. Reinhard Bendix and Seymour Martin Lipset. London: Routledge and Kegan Paul, 473–87.

Boraston, Ian, H. A. Clegg and Malcolm Rimmer. 1975. *Workplace and Union: A Study of Local Relationships in Fourteen Unions.* London: Heinemann.

Bosquet, Michel. 1972. 'The Prison Factory'. *New Left Review*, no. 73, May–June, 23–34.

Bowey, A. M. 1969. 'Labour Stability Curves and a Labour Stability Index'. *British Journal of Industrial Relations*, Vol. 7, March 71–83.

Bowey, Angela M. 1976. *The Sociology of Organisations.* London: Hodder and Stoughton.

Bowles, Samuel and Herbert Gintis. 1976. *Schooling in Capitalist America: Educational Reform and the Contradictions of Economic Life.* London: Routledge and Kegan Paul.

Box, Steven. 1971. *Deviance, Reality and Society.* London: Holt, Rinehart and Winston.

Bradshaw, Alan. 1976. 'Critical Note: A Critique of Steven Lukes' "Power:

a Radical View"'. *Sociology*, Vol. 10, January, 121–7.

Braverman, Harry. 1974. *Labor and Monopoly Capital: The Degradation of Work in the Twentieth Century.* New York: Monthly Review Press.

Brissenden, Paul F. 1920. *The IWW: A Study of American Syndicalism.* 2nd edn. New York: Columbia University Press.

Brown, Geoff. 1977. *Sabotage: A Study in Industrial Conflict.* Nottingham: Spokesman.

Brown, Richard K. 1967. 'Research and Consultancy in Industrial Enterprises: A Review of the Contribution of the Tavistock Institute of Human Relations to the Development of Industrial Sociology'. *Sociology*, Vol. 1, January, 33–60.

Brown, Richard. 1973. 'Sources of Objectives in Work and Employment'. *Man and Organization.* Ed. John Child. London: Allen and Unwin, 17–38.

Brown, Wilfred. 1962. *Piecework Abandoned: The Effect of Wage Incentive Systems on Managerial Authority.* London: Heinemann.

Brown, William. 1972. 'A Consideration of "Custom and Practice"', *British Journal of Industrial Relations*, Vol. 10, March, 42–61.

Brown, William. 1973. *Piecework Bargaining.* London: Heinemann.

Brown, William (ed.) 1981. *The Changing Contours of British Industrial Relations: A Survey of Manufacturing Industry.* Oxford: Blackwell.

Brown, William and Peter Nolan. 1981. 'The Context of the Next Incomes Policy'. *Policy Studies*, Vol. 1, February, 138–45.

Brown, William and Michael Terry. 1978. 'The Future of Collective Bargaining'. *New Society*, 23 March, 659–60.

Burawoy, Michael. 1979. *Manufacturing Consent: Changes in the Labor Process under Monopoly Capitalism.* Chicago: University of Chicago Press.

Buzzard, R. B. 1954. 'Attendance and Absence in Industry: The Nature of the Evidence'. *British Journal of Sociology*, Vol. 5, September, 238–52.

Castells, Manuel. 1980. *The Economic Crisis and American Society.* Oxford: Blackwell.

Chadwick-Jones, J. K., C. A. Brown, N. Nicholson and C. Sheppard. 1971. 'Absence Measures: Their Reliability and Stability in an Industrial Setting'. *Personnel Psychology*, Vol. 24, Autumn, 463–70.

Child, John. 1975. 'The Industrial Supervisor'. *People and Work.* Ed. Geoff Esland, Graeme Salaman and Mary-Anne Speakman. Edinburgh: Holmes McDougall, 70–87.

Cicourel, Aaron V. 1964. *Method and Measurement in Sociology.* New York: Free Press.

Cicourel, Aaron V. 1973. *Cognitive Sociology: Language and Meaning in Social Interaction.* Harmondsworth: Penguin.

Clack, Garfield. 1967. *Industrial Relations in a British Car Factory.* University of Cambridge, Department of Applied Economics, Occasional Paper, no. 9. Cambridge: Cambridge University Press.

Clawson, Dan. 1980. *Bureaucracy and the Labor Process: The Transformation of U.S. Industry, 1860–1920.* New York: Monthly Review Press.

Clegg, Hugh Armstrong. 1976. *Trade Unionism under Collective Bargaining: A Theory Based on Comparisons of Six Countries.* Oxford: Blackwell.

Clegg, Hugh Armstrong. 1979. *The Changing System of Industrial Relations in Great Britain.* Oxford: Blackwell.

Crawford, Bob and Sam Volard. 1981. 'Work Absence in Industrialised Societies: The Australian Case'. *Industrial Relations Journal,* Vol. 12, no. 3, May–June, 50–57.

Crenson, Matthew A. 1971. *The Un-Politics of Air Pollution: A Study of Non-Decisionmaking in the Cities.* Baltimore: John Hopkins University Press.

Curran, James and John Stanworth, 1979a. 'Self-Selection and the Small Firm Worker: A Critique and Alternative View'. *Sociology*, Vol. 13, September, 427–44.

Curran, James and John Stanworth. 1979b. 'Worker Involvement and Social Relations in the Small Firm'. *Sociological Review*, n.s. Vol. 27, May, 317–42.

Curran, James and John Stanworth. 1981. 'Size of Workplace and Attitudes to Industrial Relations in the Printing and Electronics Industries'. *British Journal of Industrial Relations*, Vol. 19, March, 14–25.

Dahrendorf, Ralf. 1959. *Class and Class Conflict in Industrial Society.* London: Routledge and Kegan Paul.

Davis, Howard H. 1979. *Beyond Class Images: Explorations in the Structure of Social Consciousness.* London: Croom Helm.

Department of Employment. 1971. *Absenteeism.* Manpower Paper no. 4. London: HMSO.

Department of Employment. 1979. 'The Pattern of Pay, April 1979: Key Results of the New Earnings Survey'. *DE Gazette*, Vol. 87, October, 965–1002.

Doherty, N.A. 1979. 'National Insurance and Absence from Work'. *Economic Journal*, Vol. 89, March 50–65.

Donovan Commission. 1968. *Report* of the Royal Commission on Trade Unions and Employers' Associations. London: HMSO.

Dore, Ronald. 1973. *British Factory, Japanese Factory: The Origins of National Diversity in Industrial Relations.* London: Allen and Unwin.

Dromey, Jack and Graham Taylor. 1978. *Grunwick: The Workers' Story.* London: Lawrence and Wishart.

Dubin, Robert. 1954. 'Constructive Aspects of Industrial Conflict'. *Industrial Conflict.* Ed. Arthur Kornhauser, Robert Dubin and Arthur M. Ross. New York: McGraw-Hill, 37–47.

Dubois, Pierre. 1976. *Le sabotage dans l'industrie.* Calmann-Levy, np.

Edwards, P. K. 1978. 'Time-Series Regression Models of Strike Activity: A Reconsideration with American Data'. *British Journal of Industrial Relations*, Vol. 16, November, 320–34.

Edwards, P. K. 1979a. 'Strikes and Unorganised Conflict: Some Further Considerations'. *British Journal of Industrial Relations*, Vol. 17, March, 95–8.

Edwards, P. K. 1979b. 'The "Social" Determination of Strike Activity: An Explication and Critique'. *Journal of Industrial Relations*, Vol. 21, June, 198–216.

Edward, P. K. 1979c. 'Attachment to Work and Absence Behavior'. *Human Relations*, Vol. 32, December, 1065–80.

Edwards, P.K. 1981. 'The Strike-Proneness of British Manufacturing Establishments'. *British Journal of Industrial Relations*, Vol. 19, July, 135–48.

Edwards, P. K. and Hugh Scullion. 1979. 'Does Sick Pay Encourage Absenteeism?' *Personnel Management*, July, 32–5.

Edwards, P. K. and Hugh Scullion. 1982a. 'Industrial Accidents and Industrial Conflict'. Industrial Relations Research Unit at the University of Warwick, Discussion Paper, February.

Edwards, P. K. and Hugh Scullion. 1982b. 'The Local Organisation of a National Dispute: The British 1979 Engineering Strike'. *Industrial Relations Journal*, Vol. 13, no. 1, Spring, 57–63.

Edwards, Richard. 1979. *Contested Terrain: The Transformation of the Workplace in the Twentieth Century.* London: Heinemann.

Eldridge, J. E. T. 1968. *Industrial Disputes: Essays in the Sociology of Industrial Relations.* London: Routledge and Kegan Paul.

Eldridge, J. E. T. 1971. *Sociology and Industrial Life.* London: Nelson.

Eldridge, J. E. T. 1973. 'Industrial Conflict: Some Problems of Theory and Method'. *Man and Organization.* Ed. John Child. London: Allen and Unwin, 158–84.

Etzioni, Amitai. 1961. *A Comparative Analysis of Complex Organizations: On Power, Involvement, and Their Correlates.* New York: Free Press.

Fink, Clinton F. 1968. 'Some Conceptual Difficulties in the Theory of Social Conflict'. *Journal of Conflict Resolution*, Vol. 12, December, 412–60.

Flanders, Allan. 1970. 'Collective Bargaining: Prescription for Change'. *Management and Unions: The Theory and Reform of Industrial Relations.* London: Faber and Faber, 155–211.

Florence, P. Sargant. 1924. *Economics of Fatigue and Unrest and the Efficiency of Labour in English and American Industry.* London: Allen and Unwin.

Fox, Alan. 1974. *Beyond Contract: Work, Power and Trust Relations.* London: Faber and Faber.

Friedman, Andrew L. 1977. *Industry and Labour: Class Struggle at Work and Monopoly Capitalism.* London: Macmillan.

George, K. D., R. McNabb and John Shorey. 1977. 'The Size of the Work Unit and Labour Market Behaviour'. *British Journal of Industrial Relations*, Vol. 15, July, 265–78.

Giddens, Anthony. 1973. *The Class Structure of the Advanced Societies.* London: Hutchinson.

Giddens, Anthony. 1979. *Central Problems in Social Theory.* London: Macmillan.

Glasgow University Media Group. 1976. *Bad News.* London: Routledge.

Golden, Clinton S. and Virginia D. Parker (eds). 1955. *Causes of Industrial Peace under Collective Bargaining.* New York: Harper and Brothers.

Goldthorpe, John H., David Lockwood, Frank Bechhofer and Jennifer Platt. 1968. *The Affluent Worker: Industrial Attitudes and Behaviour.* Cambridge: Cambridge University Press.

Goodman, J. F. B., E. G. A. Armstrong, J. E. Davis and A. Wagner. 1977. *Rule-Making and Industrial Peace: Industrial Relations in the Footwear Industry.* London: Croom Helm.

Goodman, J. F. B. and T. G. Whittingham. 1973. *Shop Stewards.* London: Pan.

Goodrich, Carter L. 1975. *The Frontier of Control: A Study of British Workshop Politics.* London: Pluto (Original edition 1920).

Gramsci, Antonio. 1971. *Selections from the Prison Notebooks.* Ed. and trans. Quinton Hoare and Geoffrey Nowell Smith. London: Lawrence and Wishart.

Green, James R. 1980. *The World of the Worker: Labor in Twentieth-Century America.* New York: Hill and Wang.

Handy, L. J. 1968. 'Absenteeism and Attendance in the British Coal-Mining Industry'. *British Journal of Industrial Relations*, Vol. 6, March, 27–50.

Hart, Moira. 1979. 'Why Bosses Love the Closed Shop'. *New Society*, 15 February, 352–4.

Hicks, J. R. 1932. *The Theory of Wages.* London: Macmillan.

Hickson, D. J. 1961. 'Motives of Workpeople who Restrict their Output'. *Occupational Psychology*, Vol. 35, July, 111–21.

Hill, J. M. M. 1951. 'A Consideration of Labour Turnover as the Resultant of a Quasi-Stationary Process'. *Human Relations*, Vol. 4, August, 255–64.

Hill, J. M. M. 1972. *The Seafaring Career: A Study of the Forces Affecting Joining, Serving and Leaving the Merchant Navy.* London: Tavistock Institute of Human Relations.

Hill, J. M. M. 1975. 'The Representation of Labour Turnover as a Social Process'. *Labour Turnover and Retention.* Ed. Barrie O. Pettman. Epping: Gower, 77–98.

Hill, J. M. M. and E. L. Trist. 1953. 'A Consideration of Industrial Accidents as a Means of Withdrawal from the Work Situation'. *Human Relations*, Vol. 6, November, 357–80.

Hill, J. M. M. and E. L. Trist. 1955. 'Changes in Accidents and Other Absences with Length of Service'. *Human Relations.* Vol. 8, May, 121–52.

Hinton, James. 1973. *The First Shop Stewards' Movement.* London: Allen and Unwin.

Hirschman, Albert O. 1970. *Exit Voice and Loyalty: Response to Decline in Firms, Organizations and States.* Cambridge, Mass: Harvard University Press.

Horning, Donald N. M. 1970. 'Blue-Collar Theft: Conceptions of Property, Attitudes toward Pilfering, and Work Group Norms in a Modern Industrial Plant'. *Crimes against Bureaucracy.* Ed. Erwin O. Smigel and H. Laurence Ross. New York: Van Nostrand Reinhold, 46–64.

Hulin, Charles L. 1966. 'Job Satisfaction and Turnover in a Female Clerical Population'. *Journal of Applied Psychology*, Vol. 50, August, 280–85.

Hyman, Richard. 1970. 'Economic Motivation and Labour Stability'. *British Journal of Industrial Relations*, Vol. 8, July, 159–78.

Hyman, Richard. 1972. *Strikes.* London: Fontana-Collins.

Hyman, Richard, 1975. *Industrial Relations: A Marxist Introduction.* London: Macmillan.

Hyman, Richard. 1976. 'Strikes and Industrial Conflict: Concepts, Meanings and Purposes'. Paper presented to Psychology and Industrial Relations Conference, University of Warwick, 28 February.

Hyman, Richard. 1979. 'The Politics of Workplace Trade Unionism: Recent Tendencies and Some Problems for Theory'. *Capital and Class*, no. 8, Summer, 54–67.

Hyman, Richard and Ian Brough. 1975. *Social Values and Industrial Relations: A Study of Fairness and Equality.* Oxford: Blackwell.

Incomes Data Services. 1978. 'Absenteeism'. IDS Study no. 168, May.

Indik, Bernard P. 1963. 'Some Effects of Organization Size on Member Attitudes and Behavior'. *Human Relations*, Vol. 16, November, 369–84.

Indik, Bernard P. 1965. 'Organization Size and Member Participation: Some Empirical Tests of Alternative Explanations'. *Human Relations*, Vol. 18, November 339–50.

Ilgen, Daniel P. 1977. 'Attendance Behavior: A Reevaluation of Latham and Pursell's Conclusions'. *Journal of Applied Psychology*, Vol. 62, April, 23–33.

Ingham, Geoffrey K. 1970. *Size of Industrial Organization and Worker Behaviour.* Cambridge: Cambridge University Press.

Jarvie, I.C. 1972. *Concepts and Society.* London: Routledge and Kegan Paul.

Kerr, Clark. 1954. 'Industrial Conflict and Its Mediation'. *American Journal of Sociology.* Vol. 60, November, 230–45.

Kerr, Willard A., George J. Koppelmeier and James J. Sullivan. 1951. 'Absenteeism, Turnover and Morale in a Metals Fabrication Factory'. *Occupational Psychology*, Vol. 25, January, 50–55.

Kilpatrick, Andrew and Tony Lawson. 1980. 'On the Nature of Industrial Decline in the UK'. *Cambridge Journal of Economics*, Vol. 4, March, 85–102.

Klein, Lisl. 1964. *'Multiproducts Ltd': A Case-Study on the Social Effects of Rationalized Production.* London: HMSO.

Knowles, K. G. J. C. 1952. *Strikes: A Study in Industrial Conflict.* Oxford: Blackwell.

Lamphere, Louise. 1979. 'Fighting the Piece-Rate System: New Dimensions of an Old Struggle in the Apparel Industry'. *Case Studies on the Labor Process.* Ed. Andrew Zimbalist. New York: Monthly Review Press, 257–76.

Latham, Gary P. and Elliott D. Pursell. 1975. 'Measuring Absenteeism from the Opposite Side of the Coin'. *Journal of Applied Psychology*, Vol. 60, June, 369–71.

Lea, John. 1979. 'Discipline and Capitalist Development'. *Capitalism and the Rule of Law: From Deviancy Theory to Marxism.* Ed. Bob Fine *et al.* London: Hutchinson, 76–89.

Legge, Karen. 1970. 'The Operation of the "Regressive Spiral" in the Labour Market'. *Journal of Management Studies*, Vol. 7, February, 1–22.

Lester, Richard A. 1958. *As Unions Mature: An Analysis of the Evolution of American Unionism.* Princeton: Princeton University Press.

Ley, Ronald. 1966. 'Labor Turnover as a Function of Worker Differences, Work Environment, and Authoritarianism of Foremen'. *Journal of Applied Psychology*, Vol. 50, December, 497–500.

Linhart, Robert. 1981. *The Assembly Line.* Trans. Margaret Crosland. London: John Calder (original French edition 1978).

Lukes, Steven. 1974. *Power: A Radical View.* London: Macmillan.

Lupton, Tom. 1963. *On the Shop Floor: Two Studies of Workshop Organization and Output.* Oxford: Pergamon.

McCormick, B. J. 1979. *Industrial Relations in the Coal Industry.* London: Macmillan.

McEachern, Doug. 1980. *A Class Against Itself: Power and the Nationalisation of the British Steel Industry.* Cambridge: Cambridge University Press.

Mack, Raymond W. and Richard C. Snyder. 1971. 'The Analysis of Social Conflict: Toward an Overview and Synthesis'. *Conflict Resolution: Contributions of the Behavioral Sciences.* Ed. Clagett G. Smith. Notre Dame: University of Notre Dame Press, 3–35.

Mandel, Ernest. 1978. *Late Capitalism.* Trans. Joris de Bres. London: Verso. (original German edition 1972).

Mann, Michael. 1970. 'The Social Cohesion of Liberal Democracy'. *American Sociological Review*, Vol. 35, June, 423–40.

Mann, Michael. 1973. *Consciousness and Action among the Western Working Class.* London: Macmillan.

Marglin, Stephen A. 1976. 'What Do Bosses Do? The Origins and Functions of Hierarchy in Capitalist Production'. *The Division of Labour: The Labour Process and Class Struggle in Modern Capitalism.* Ed. Andre Gorz. Brighton: Harvester, 13–54.

Mars, Gerald. 1973. 'Chance, Punters and the Fiddle: Institutionalized Pilferage in a Hotel Dining Room'. *The Sociology of the Workplace: An Interdisciplinary Approach.* Ed. Malcolm Warner. London: Allen and Unwin, 200–10.

Mars, Gerald. 1974. 'Dock Pilferage'. *Deviance and Social Control.* Ed. Paul Rock and Mary McIntosh. London: Tavistock, 209–28.

Mathewson, Stanley B. 1969. *Restriction of Output among Unorganized Workers.* Carbondale: Southern Illinois University Press (Original edition 1931).

Mayhew, K. 1979. 'Economists and Strikes'. *Oxford Bulletin of Economics and Statistics*, Vol. 41, February, 1–19.

Mellish, Michael. 1972. *The Docks after Devlin.* London: Heinemann.

Mellish, M. and N. Collis-Squires. 1976. 'Legal and Social Norms in Discipline and Dismissal'. *Industrial Law Journal*, Vol. 5, September, 164–77.

Miliband, Ralph. 1978. 'A State of De-Subordination'. *British Journal of Sociology*, Vol. 29, December, 399–409.

Millward, Neil. 1968. 'Family Status and Behaviour at Work'. *Sociological Review*, n.s. Vol. 16, May, 149–64.

Montgomery, David. 1979. *Workers' Control in America: Studies in the History of Work, Technology and Labor Struggles.* Cambridge: Cambridge University Press.

Morrison, Denton E. and Ramon E. Henkel (eds). 1970. *The Significance Test Controversy.* London: Butterworth.

Newby, Howard. 1977a. *The Deferential Worker: A Study of Farm Workers in East Anglia.* Harmondsworth: Penguin.

Newby, Howard. 1977b. 'Paternalism and Capitalism'. *Industrial Society: Class, Cleavage and Control.* Ed. Richard Scase. London: Allen and Unwin, 59–73.

Nichols, Theo and Peter Armstrong. 1976. *Workers Divided: A Study in Shopfloor Politics.* London: Fontana-Collins.

Nichols, Theo and Huw Beynon. 1977. *Living with Capitalism: Class Relations and the Modern Factory.* London: Routledge and Kegan Paul.

Nicholson, Nigel. 1977. 'Absence Behaviour and Attendance Motivation: A Conceptual Synthesis'. *Journal of Management Studies*, Vol. 14, October, 231–52.

Nicholson, Nigel, Colin A. Brown and J. K. Chadwick-Jones. 1976. 'Absence from Work and Job Satisfaction'. *Journal of Applied Psychology*, Vol. 61, December, 728–37.

Northrup, Herbert R. and Harvey A. Young. 1968. 'The Causes of Industrial Peace Revisited'. *Industrial and Labor Relations Review*, Vol. 22, October, 31–47.

Offe, Claus and Helmut Wiesenthal. 1979. 'Two Logics of Collective Action: Theoretical Notes on Social Class and Organizational Form'. *Political Power and Social Theory*, Vol. 1, no. 1, 67–115.

Office of Manpower Economics. 1973. *Measured Daywork.* London: HMSO.

O'Muircheartaigh, Colm A. 1975. *Absenteeism in Irish Industry.* Dublin: Irish Productivity Centre.

Paterson, T. T. 1960. *Glasgow Limited: A Case Study in Industrial War and Peace.* Cambridge: Cambridge University Press.

Peterson, Florence. 1938. *Strikes in the United States, 1880–1936.* US Department of Labor, Bulletin no. 651. Washington: US Government Printing Office.

Pettman, Barrie O. 1973. 'Some Factors Influencing Labour Turnover: A Review of Research Literature'. *Industrial Relations Journal*, Vol. 4, no. 3, Autumn, 43–61.

Plummer, Ken. 1979. 'Misunderstanding Labelling Perspectives'. *Deviant Interpretations: Problems in Criminological Theory.* Ed. David Downes and Paul Rock. Oxford: Martin Robertson, 85–121.

Pollard, Sidney. 1965. *The Genesis of Modern Management: A Study of the Industrial Revolution in Great Britain.* London: Arnold.

Price, James L. 1975. 'A Theory of Turnover'. *Labour Turnover and Retention.* Ed. Barrie O. Pettman. Epping: Gower, 51–75.

Price, James L. 1975/6. 'The Measurement of Turnover'. *Industrial Relations Journal*, Vol. 6, no. 4, Winter, 33–46.

Purcell, Kate. 1979. 'Militancy and Acquiescence amongst Women Workers'. *Fit Work for Women.* Ed. Sandra Burman. London: Croom Helm, 112–33.

Revans, R. W. 1956. 'Industrial Morale and Size of Unit'. *Political Quarterly*, Vol. 27, July, 303–11.

Roberts, K. et al. 1977. *The Fragmentary Class Structure.* London: Heinemann.

Rock, Paul. 1973. *Deviant Behaviour.* London: Hutchinson.

Roethlisberger, W. J. and William J. Dickson. 1939. *Management and the Worker: An Account of the Research Program Conducted by the Western Electric Company, Hawthorne Works, Chicago.* Cambridge, Mass.: Harvard University Press.

Rogaly, Joe. 1977. *Grunwick.* Harmondsworth: Penguin.

Rootes, C. A. 1981. 'The Dominant Ideology Thesis and Its Critics'. *Sociology,* Vol. 15, August, 436–44.

Roy, Donald, 1952. 'Quota Restriction and Goldbricking in a Machine Shop'. *American Journal of Sociology,* Vol. 57, March, 427–42.

Roy, Donald. 1953. 'Work Satisfaction and Social Reward in Quota Achievement: An Analysis of Piecework Incentive'. *American Sociological Review,* Vol. 18, October, 507–14.

Roy, Donald. 1954. 'Efficiency and "The Fix": Informal Intergroup Relations in a Piecework Machine Shop'. *American Journal of Sociology,* Vol. 60, November 255–66.

Rubery, Jill. 1980. 'Structured Labour Markets, Worker Organization and Low Pay'. *The Economics of Women and Work.* Ed. Alice H. Amsden. Harmondsworth: Penguin, 242–70.

Sayles, Leonard R. 1958. *Behavior of Industrial Work Groups: Prediction and Control.* New York: Wiley.

Scott, W. H., Enid Mumford, I. C. McGivering and J. M. Kirkby. 1963. *Coal and Conflict: A Study of Industrial Relations at Collieries.* Liverpool: Liverpool University Press.

Scullion, Hugh. 1981. 'The Skilled Revolt Against General Unionism: The Case of the BL Toolroom Committee'. *Industrial Relations Journal,* Vol. 12, no. 3, May–June, 15–27.

Shapiro-Perl, Nina. 1979. 'The Piece Rate: Class Struggle on the Shop Floor. Evidence from the Costume Jewelry Industry in Providence, Rhode Island'. *Case Studies on the Labor Process.* Ed. Andrew Zimbalist. New York: Monthly Review Press, 277–98.

Silcock. H. 1954. 'The Phenomenon of Labour Turnover'. *Journal of the Royal Statistical Society,* Series A, Vol. 117, Part 4, 429–40.

Special Task Force. 1973. *Work in America.* Report to the Secretary of Health, Education and Welfare. Cambridge, Mass.: MIT Press.

Stone, Katherine. 1973. 'The Origins of Job Structures in the Steel Industry'. *Radical America,* Vol. 7, no. 6, November, 19–64.

Strauss, A. et al. 1971. 'The Hospital and Its Negotiated Order'. *Decisions, Organizations and Society.* Ed. F. G. Castles, D. J. Murray and D. C. Potter. Harmondsworth: Penguin, 103–23.

Talacchi, Sergio. 1960. 'Organization Size, Individual Attitudes and Behavior'. *Administrative Science Quarterly,* Vol. 5, December, 398–420.

Taylor, Laurie and Paul Walton. 1971. 'Industrial Sabotage: Motives and Meanings'. *Images of Deviance.* Ed. Stanley Cohen. Harmondsworth: Penguin, 219–45.

Taylor, Robert. 1980. *The Fifth Estate: Britain's Unions in the Modern World.* Revised edn. London: Pan.

Terry, Michael. 1977. 'The Inevitable Growth of Informality'. *British Journal of Industrial Relations*, Vol. 15, March, 76–90.

Thompson, E. P. 1967. 'Time, Work-Discipline, and Industrial Capitalism'. *Past and Present*, no. 38, December, 56–97.

Turner, H. A. 1962. *Trade Union Growth, Structure and Policy: A Comparative Study of the Cotton Unions.* London: Allen and Unwin.

Turner, H. A., Garfield Clack and Geoffrey Roberts. 1967. *Labour Relations in the Motor Industry: A Study of Industrial Unrest and an International Comparison.* London: Allen and Unwin.

Van der Merwe, Roux and Sylvia Miller. 1975. 'The Measurement of Labour Turnover'. *Labour Turnover and Retention.* Ed. Barrie O. Pettman. Epping: Gower, 1–30.

Van Houten, Donald R. 1980. Review of *Contested Terrain* by Richard Edwards. *Economic and Industrial Democracy*, Vol. 1, November, 583–7.

Waters, L. K. and Darrell Roach. 1971. 'Relationship between Job Attitudes and Two Forms of Withdrawal from the Work Situation'. *Journal of Applied Psychology*, Vol. 55, February, 92–4.

Waters, L. K. and Darrell Roach. 1979. 'Job Satisfaction, Behavioral Intention and Absenteeism as Predictors of Turnover'. *Personnel Psychology*, Vol. 32, Summer, 393–7.

Westergaard, J. H. 1970. 'The Rediscovery of the Cash Nexus: Some Recent Interpretations of Trends in British Class Structure'. *Socialist Register*, 111–36.

Williams, Allan et al. 1979. 'Factors Associated with Labour Turnover among Ancillary Staff in Two London Hospitals'. *Journal of Occupational Psychology*, Vol. 52, March, 1–16.

Wilson, David F. 1972. *Dockers: The Impact of Industrial Change.* London: Fontana-Collins.

Wright, Erik Olin. 1978. *Class, Crisis and the State.* London: New Left Books.

Yeomans, K. A. 1968. *Applied Statistics.* Vol. 2 of *Statistics for the Social Scientist.* Harmondsworth: Penguin.

Yetton, Philip. 1979. 'The Efficiency of a Piecework Incentive Payment System'. *Journal of Management Studies*, Vol. 16, October, 253–69.

Zeitlin, Jonathan. 1980. 'The Emergence of Shop Steward Organization and Job Control in the British Car Industry: A Review Essay'. *History Workshop Journal*, no. 10, Autumn, 119–37.

Zweig, F. 1951. *Productivity and Trade Unions.* Oxford: Blackwell.

Index